A History of the Low Countries

PALGRAVE ESSENTIAL HISTORIES
General Editor: Jeremy Black

This series of compact, readable and informative national histories is designed to appeal to anyone wishing to gain a broad understanding of a country's history.

Published

A History of the Low Countries   Paul Arblaster
A History of Russia   Roger Bartlett
A History of Spain   Simon Barton
A History of the British Isles (2nd edn)   Jeremy Black
A History of Israel   Ahron Bregman
A History of Ireland   Mike Cronin
A History of the Pacific Islands   Steven Roger Fischer
A History of the United States (2nd edn)   Philip Jenkins
A History of Denmark   Knud J. V. Jespersen
A History of Poland   Anita J. Prażmowska
A History of India   Peter Robb
A History of China   J.A.G. Roberts
A History of Germany   Peter Wende

Further titles are in preparation

Series Standing Order
ISBN 1–4039–3811–3 HB
ISBN 1–4039–3812–1 PB

If you would like to receive future titles in this series as they are published, you can make use of our standing order facility. To place a standing order please contact your bookseller or, in case of difficulty, write to us at the address below with your name and address and the name of the series. Please state with which title you wish to begin your standing order. (If you live outside the United Kingdom we may not have the rights for your area, in which case we will forward your order to the publisher concerned.)

Customer Services Department, Macmillan Distribution Ltd
Houndmills, Basingstoke, Hampshire RG21 6XS, England

A History of the Low Countries

Paul Arblaster

First published 2006 by
PALGRAVE MACMILLAN
Houndmills, Basingstoke, Hampshire RG21 6XS and
175 Fifth Avenue, New York, N.Y. 10010
Companies and representatives throughout the world

PALGRAVE MACMILLAN is the global academic imprint of the Palgrave Macmillan division of St. Martin's Press, LLC and of Palgrave Macmillan Ltd. Macmillan® is a registered trademark in the United States, United Kingdom and other countries. Palgrave is a registered trademark in the European Union and other countries.

ISBN-13: 978–1–4039–4827–4 hardback
ISBN-10: 1–4039–4827–5   hardback
ISBN-13: 978–1–4039–4828–1 paperback
ISBN-10: 1–4039–4828–3   paperback

This book is printed on paper suitable for recycling and made from fully managed and sustained forest sources.

A catalogue record for this book is available from the British Library.

Library of Congress Cataloging-in-Publication Data
Arblaster, Paul.
    A history of the Low Countries / Paul Arblaster.
        p. cm.—(Palgrave essential histories)
    Includes bibliographical references and index.
    ISBN-13: 978-1-4039-4827-4 (alk. paper)
    ISBN-10: 1-4039-4827-5 (alk. paper)
    ISBN-13: 978-1-4039-4828-1 (pbk.: alk. paper)
    ISBN-10: 1-4039-4828-3 (pbk.: alk. paper)
    1. Netherlands—History. 2. Belgium—History. 3. Belgium—Civilization. 4. Netherlands—Civilization. I. Title. II. Series.
DH131.A73 2005
949.9—dc22

                                                        2005051169

10   9   8   7   6   5   4   3   2   1
15   14   13   12   11   10   09   08   07   06

Printed in China

To Dad, with love

The degree of a country's civilization does not depend upon the extent of its land; the intelligence of its people does not depend upon the extent of its territory.

Sofu Kōhei, *Berugīkoku-shi*, 1877

Contents

Preface	ix
Maps	xi

Introduction — 1
Diversity — 1
Water and windmills — 4
Convergence — 7

1   From Pagans to Crusaders, 57 BC to AD 1100 — 10
The Belgians are the bravest of the them all, 57–13 BC — 10
Beyond the Rhine, 13 BC to AD 80 — 14
Romanization, AD 80–396 — 19
The End of Roman Rule, 396–500 — 25
The Age of Saints, 500–800 — 27
The Empire of the West Renewed, 800–1018 — 34
Feudalism — 41
The Eleventh-Century Reform, 1018–1122 — 43
The First Crusade, 1095–1099 — 46

2   Patterns of Power and Piety, 1100–1384 — 49
The County of Flanders, 1037–1157 — 49
East of the Scheldt — 52
Town and Country — 56
The New Monasticism, 1098–1147 — 63
The Renaissance of the Twelfth Century — 65
The Empire and the Low Countries, 1155–1256 — 67
Religious Life in the Thirteenth Century — 72
War, Marriage and Murder, 1246–1305 — 79
Civic Culture and Governance around 1300 — 86
The Dismal Century, 1305–1384 — 90
The Beginnings of Burgundian Rule — 95

3 The Low Countries United and Divided, 1384–1609   **96**
The Burgundian Century, 1384–1477   96
The Arts of Peace   101
From Burgundy to Habsburg, 1477–1515   108
The Renaissance   109
World Market – World Empire   111
The Reformation, 1517–1566   113
Iconoclasm to Abjuration, 1566–1581   120
The Netherlands Divided, 1581–1609   127

4 From Delftware to Porcelain, 1609–1780   **132**
The Republic as a World Power   132
The Multi-Faith North   137
The Catholic South   141
The Golden Age   143
The Eighty Years War Continued, 1621–1648   151
The First 'Stadholderless' Period, 1650–1672   155
A Happy Few   158
The Return of the Stadholder, 1672–1702   160
The Second 'Stadholderless' Period, 1702–1747   162
The Age of Enlightenment, 1747–1787   163

5 The Rise and Fall of the Liberal Order, 1776–1914   **167**
Patriots and Revolutionaries, 1782–1799   167
Napoleon the Lawgiver, 1800–1815   173
The United Kingdom of the Netherlands, 1815–1830   175
The Belgian Revolution, 1830–1839   178
The Confessional Divide, 1840–1878   181
Emancipatory Movements, 1878–1914   187
The Second Golden Age   199
Around the World   204
The Peace Movement   208

6 World Wars and World Peace, 1914–2002   **210**
The Great War, 1914–1918   210
The Crises of Peace, 1919–1939   215
The Second World War, 1940–1945   221
After the War, 1945–2002   231

Chronology of Major Events   242
Select List of Dynasties and Rulers   250
Selected Further Reading in English   261
Index   267

Preface

The historical traditions of the English-speaking world have something of a blindspot when it comes to the three small states of Belgium, the Netherlands and Luxembourg. My purpose here is to introduce the history of these countries to a general readership, and to do so required consulting works which I would never have glanced at for my specialized academic research. The rewards of discovery have convinced me more than ever that the usual neglect is altogether unwarranted. Whether considered as a frontier zone of the Roman Empire, as the medieval and Early Modern commercial crossroads of Northern Europe, as the cockpit of modern warfare, as the heart of the European Union, or as a region of quite remarkable spiritual, intellectual and artistic fertility, the Low Countries have never ceased to fascinate. I hope that the reader feels something of the excitement and joy of discovery that fell to the author. In composing such a general work I have had to fight my professional urge to provide detailed footnotes at every point. If I have erred the other way and done an injustice to any of the many authors on whom I have relied, I beg their pardon.

To write a broad, brief overview of the history of three countries is necessarily an exercise in excision. Most such works seem to concentrate on the political history of the postwar decades, relegating earlier centuries to the status of introduction. I have always found this puzzling, but in the case of the Low Countries it is simply impossible. Their ages of European greatness stretch from the thirteenth to the seventeenth centuries, and their contributions to the arts and sciences, commerce, industry and the life of the spirit far outweigh any recent political achievement. Writing this book while attached to the Literature Department of the University of Leuven furthermore made it difficult to see the course of events mainly through the prism of political history. The broadest outlines of modern party politics are provided, with advice on further reading for those who desire more detail.

A number of friends and/or colleagues have provided considerable aid in correcting and encouraging my efforts. I express my thanks to them with a mournful awareness that any book with which their names are associated ought to be far better than this can be. Geert Claassens (by appropriate coincidence the first alphabetically), Simon Dell, Kyril Drezov, Luc Duerloo, Christel Germonpré, Jan Goossens, Gergely and István Juhász, Guido Latré, Hilde Meijns, Naomi Morgan, Patrick Nefors, David Petts, Lee Preedy, Susan Reed, Joël Schuyer, Margit Thøfner and Edward Vickers all gave invaluable support. Between them they ferreted out many factual errors, over-bold interpretations, inexplicable gaps, and infelicities and obscurities of style. The many that no doubt remain are no fault of theirs but entirely my own. Diederik Derhaeg, Zana Etambala and André Wessels provided leads on overseas history. Terka Acton and Victoria Huxley gave the all-important encouragement of having confidence that there would be readers for such a work.

In delving into unfamiliar periods of history I have been thrown back on the basic skills and methods learnt as a schoolboy and undergraduate, and my gratitude to my teachers has grown accordingly. Without them I would not have been able to begin such a work. I leave it to their judgements whether I have satisfactorily ended it.

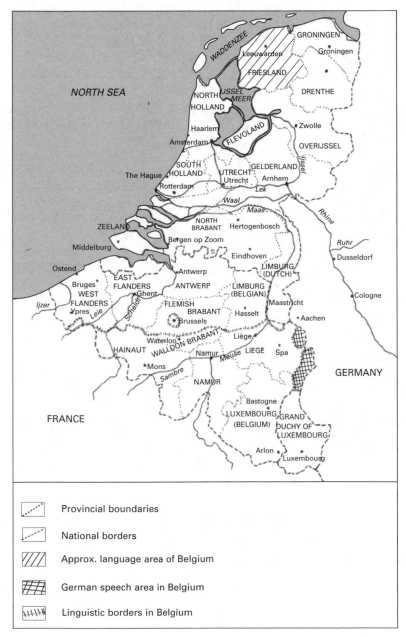

Map 1 The Benelux

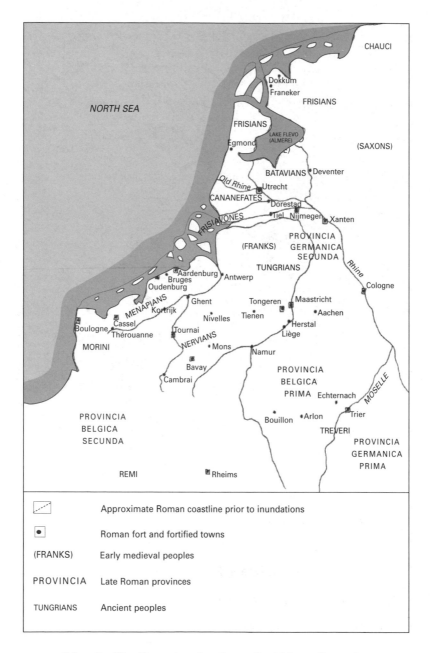

Map 2 The Roman and early medieval Low Countries

Map 3   The late medieval Low Countries

Map 4   The Burgundian complex of territories

Introduction

Belgium, the Netherlands and Luxembourg are notoriously 'artificial' countries. Their borders correspond with little but the outcomes of bygone diplomatic and military campaigns. The Benelux countries are what is left when France and Germany have taken all they can on either side, and nobody has managed to establish rule over the whole of the remainder. In the view of some, such as Charles de Gaulle, this made them an aberration, a left-over; in the eyes of their own nineteenth-century historians, it made them (pre)determined survivors. The area might best be described as a frontier region, as long as 'frontier' is taken not to mean a sharp border, but an area of interaction and overlap. It is not that the pulls of Paris and Berlin, or of Rome and Geneva, failed to reach the Low Countries, but rather that this is the zone where all such forces were felt but none completely overcame.

DIVERSITY

Borders of all sorts cut through the Netherlands, Belgium and Luxembourg. The Rhine, which the French once declared their 'natural frontier', runs through the heart of the Netherlands. Other boundaries include three linguistic borders, between Dutch and French in Belgium, between French and German in Belgium and Luxembourg, and between Dutch and Frisian in the Netherlands. One of the boundaries between areas where Catholic and Protestant churches traditionally predominate is also found within a single Benelux country, again the Netherlands. The Belgian village of Baarle-Hertog, bordering the Dutch province of North Brabant on every side (and physically contiguous with the Dutch village of Baarle-Nassau), is one of the last remaining examples of a landlocked territorial exclave of one European state lying entirely within a neighbouring country. With its mixture of linguistic and religious

1

communities in a geographical frontier zone the Low Countries are a flatter counterpart to Switzerland, at the far end of the French-German border – except that where Switzerland has largely remained aloof from the power politics of Western Europe, the Low Countries have for centuries been at their centre, and have taken a leading role in the recent movements towards the greater economic and political unification of Europe.

Another difference is that Switzerland has long been a loose but fairly stable confederation of cantons, whereas the Low Countries have tended to fragmentation. The one attempt to rule them as a single centralized state, in 1815–30, ended in revolution and war. Within each Benelux country there are surprisingly provincial and parochial variations in language and outlook. Even the tiniest, bilingual Luxembourg, has those whose mother tongue is French rather than Letzebürgesch (Luxembourgish), and is divided between a forested north-west, an agrarian east, an industrial south-west and a centre dominated by the service sectors of the city of Luxembourg.

Cultural differences are apparent in day-to-day encounters. Dutch bluntness can unintentionally offend, while Belgian indirection can seem mere hypocrisy. The Belgians tell miser ('Scottish') jokes about the Dutch and the Dutch tell idiot ('Irish') jokes about the Belgians. Such jokes seem funny to those who tell them because of frustrated expectations of similarity. Even cultural differences are not defined entirely by national borders. Within the national borders Flemings tell yokel ('Welsh') jokes about Belgian Limburgers, as do Hollanders about Frisians. In the Netherlands the exuberant carnival festivities of the traditionally Catholic cities south of the Rhine delta until recently called up a sense of foreignness in the more puritanical north.

Besides the untidiness of the boundaries of customs, language, laws and religion, and the local variations of provincialism and parochialism, the institutions of civil society in the Benelux countries have also shown a strange sort of fragmentation. The social organization of Belgium and the Netherlands in the nineteenth and twentieth centuries was marked by a phenomenon known to English-speaking historians by the terms 'pillarization' or 'columnization' (literal renderings of *verzuiling*, from *zuil*, a pillar or column). The image of the pillar was meant to suggest that all segments of society together held up the roof, but none of them touched at any point. Protestant, Catholic, liberal-secularist, socialist and to some extent communist groups organized bodies to support their members in every aspect of life from the cradle to the grave: churches and lodges, political parties, trade unions, insurance unions, savings banks, hospitals, schools, universities, newspapers – in some cases even radio and television companies – and cultural, musical and sporting associations. At the late nineteenth- and early twentieth-century high-point of pillarization even big businesses might be identified with a confessional or 'life-philosophical' bloc, and there were those who would avoid a department store or grocery chain if the profits were known to go to a particular pillar.

Luxembourg had the same sort of debates about Church and State, but there the liberal political elite was more willing to give state sanction to Catholic educational and charitable organizations, and the clerical elite was comfortable with much greater oversight by the state than was tolerated elsewhere. The result was a more homogeneous social and political whole, but a compromise of principle that would have satisfied none of the parties in Belgium or the Netherlands. In Belgium, and to a lesser extent in the Netherlands, pillarization leaked from party-political patronage into all aspects of public life (the supposed common roof), so that positions of responsibility in such bodies as the police forces, the post office, the railways, even the judiciary and ceremonial appointments at court, could be divided up or alternate between the different pillars. The phenomenon is now residual but still strong, especially in Belgium.

Belgium shows further tendencies to fragment not apparent in the Netherlands or Luxembourg. The country has been federalized, with many political and economic competences devolved to three territorial 'regions': Dutch-speaking Flanders, French-speaking Wallonia, and the officially bilingual Brussels Capital Region. Cultural and educational policy has been shared out between three distinct linguistic 'communities', the Dutch-, French- and German-speaking. There is a close match between the Flemish region and the Dutch-speaking community, and the Walloon region and the French-speaking community, but the German-speaking community is within the Walloon region, and both French- and Dutch-speaking communities have powers in the bilingual Brussels region. This communitarian divide means that all the pillars in national life came to be duplicated in separate linguistic organizations, whether political, social, cultural or economic. Even today, nonsense about 'Germanic' and 'Romance' racial types can sometimes be heard, although plausible sounding but equally fictitious 'cultural differences' are more frequently invoked. Time and again surveys of European attitudes and values have shown that Flemings and Walloons are much closer to one another (and in some cases to German Rhinelanders) than either are to the Dutch or the French. They are seldom distinguishable by build, looks, dress or manner, and the only way of telling Dutch speakers and French speakers apart is by ear. The maxim that proximity accentuates difference should always be borne in mind when Belgians start speaking of their divisions.

Besides the linguistic divide, Belgium is also sundered by a more profound confessional divide between Christians and Secularists. The anticlericalism of the nineteenth century has had a vigorous afterlife. Masonic lodges of various disciplines play an acknowledged role in public life, especially in the liberal parties, that seems bizarre from a British perspective but would be familiar to a Mexican. The secular/confessional divide has also been prominent in the Netherlands, but lacks the bitterness of Belgian anticlericalism. And where Belgium has a Protestant minority so tiny as to be negligible, the Netherlands has, besides a plethora of active Protestant confessions, a substantial, well-integrated Catholic minority, most numerous south of the Rhine delta but by no means confined to that area.

As in all Western European countries, longer standing cultural, confessional and social distinctions are now paling in the broader spectrum of an ageing society largely indifferent to every religion except Islam, and seeking in various ways to accommodate substantial concentrations of immigrants from outside Europe. Despite the parochial, provincial, national, linguistic and confessional divisions of the Low Countries, the Benelux countries have for a hundred years been models of democratic multi-party consensus politics. Barring foreign invasion they have constituted free, well-ordered, dynamic and prosperous societies for even longer. Now the most disruptive element in this picture, not to be overestimated but certainly not to be ignored, is a growing and vocal minority opposed to prudent openness to foreigners.

WATER AND WINDMILLS

Apart from the artificiality of national borders, the Netherlands is famously artificial in another fashion. Large parts of the provinces of North and South Holland, Friesland, Groningen and Flevoland lie below sea level. Outside the cities the dominant colours are the green of the land and the grey of the air and water. In jottings for a poem never written, Coleridge recorded his own impressions of a trip through the Netherlands:

> Water and windmills, greenness, Islets green; –
> Willows whose Trunks beside the shadows stood
> Of their own higher half, and willowy swamp; –
> Farmhouses that at anchor seem'd – in the inland sky
> The fog-transfixing Spires –
> Water, wide water, greenness and green banks,
> And water seen –

Descartes supposedly once remarked that God made the world but the Dutch made Holland, a statement much repeated either in enthusiasm for the achievement or as an explanation for the shortcomings of the country. Even here, nature lent a hand: Holland and Zeeland would not be dryish land at all were it not for the constant deposit of soil by the rivers and the tides, and a natural but highly unreliable sea-wall formed by the dunes of the North Sea coast. The low-lying juncture of rivers and sea that brought trade and wealth also brought constant dangers of flooding. Nature provided the first foothold, but the work of making these lands more than saltmarsh has been human.

As long ago as the late Iron Age, rising water levels led to the building of artificial mounds, *terpen* or *wierden*, on which those who clung tenaciously to their ancestral peat bog could live with dry feet. Among the curiosities of the world noted by Roman geographers were the inhabitants of Frisia, who dwelt on tiny islands accessible only at low tide, lived off fish and wildfowl rather than the fruits and beasts of the earth, and burned dried mud for their fires. Thousands of terps were constructed from the late Iron Age to the high Middle Ages, some for individual farmsteads, others for whole villages, and some forming the basis of later cities, including Amsterdam.

Land reclamation projects have characterized the coastal region for centuries. Methods of diking and draining to turn land below sea level into fertile polders were pioneered in medieval Flanders. In Dante's *Divine Comedy* the river of boiling blood in the seventh circle of Hell is diked by a wall which calls to mind that (in the translation of Dorothy L. Sayers):

> . . . the men of Flanders anxiously
> 'Twixt Bruges and Wissant build their bulwarks wide
> Fearing the thrust and onset of the sea.

The techniques were widespread in the Netherlands by the twelfth century. They were perfected in seventeenth-century Holland with the use of dikes, sluices and wind-powered ('windmill') pumps to drain polders. When diking became widespread most ancient terps not inaccessible under houses and gardens were dug up as fertilizer for lower-lying fields.

The twentieth century saw the most decisive human interventions in the waterscape. Between 1927 and 1932 the Zuider Zee was separated from the North Sea by a 20-mile dike. Between then and 1968 over 160,000 hectares of land were drained from the resulting lake, more than half of this becoming the entirely new province of Flevoland. The 'Deltaworks' of Zeeland, begun after the devastating spring floods of 1953, turned much of the Rhine delta into freshwater lakes. This was a fearsomely complex operation, involving not only damming the delta itself but also regulating the flow of the rivers upstream, to prevent river flooding replacing the threat of tidal flooding. During the 1960s the desirability of the original project was called into question, and modifications were made to the plan. In response to the protests of fishing communities and environmental activists, the maritime fauna and flora of the Eastern Scheldt estuary, including oyster and mussel beds, were retained behind a two-mile long flood barrier which can be closed in emergencies. The flood barrier in Rotterdam, finished in 1996, was the crowning achievement of the works. The one part of Zeeland still separated from the main body of the Netherlands by water, the strip of land south of the Western Scheldt estuary and contiguous with Belgian Flanders, was linked to the rest of the country by a road tunnel in 2003: a comparatively modest postscript to what must be reckoned one of the most impressive engineering projects of the twentieth century.

Human ingenuity and endeavour have made the Low Countries not only habitable but comfortable and wealthy. The cast of mind of the people of the Netherlands, Belgium and Luxembourg is particularly taken with solving problems, finding a way round obstacles, and in a word, achieving comfort. Politics is marked by compromise and co-operation to a degree unusual even in other stable democracies. The cosiness of public spaces in the Low Countries (whether marketplaces, 'stoops', parks or courtyards) stands in marked contrast to their grandeur in France and tattiness in England. The assumption that getting along comfortably together is a basic human drive sometimes leads to hopelessly over-optimistic estimations of what human effort can bring about elsewhere in the way of peace, prosperity and social concord.

Throughout the modern age, what are now the Netherlands and Belgium have served as a model for foreign reformers of one sort and another – social, educational, political and agricultural. The Dutch and Belgian achievements in channelling social, confessional and communitarian conflict into peaceful courses have inspired efforts elsewhere without being successfully replicated.

CONVERGENCE

Despite the divisions and variety within and between Belgium, the Netherlands and Luxembourg, it is still possible to treat the three countries together. Most obviously, the area has twice been briefly unified politically (1543–81 and 1815–30) and in 1948–58 the three countries formed themselves into a zone of economic co-operation, the Benelux, which was an inspiring model for further European integration (thanks in part to a dose of wilful blindness to its problems). More broadly, the political boundaries of earlier times nowhere quite fit the borders of the three states as they now exist.

It is impossible to treat the histories of the Netherlands and Belgium as distinct from one another at any time prior to 1650 when the political separation begun in 1581 was finalized, or Luxembourg as distinct from either Belgium or the Netherlands before 1839. Pieter Geyl, who for years lectured on Dutch history at University College London, is one of the best-known Dutch historians in the English-speaking world. In the early 1930s he forcefully pointed out the folly of the then common practice of studying the medieval and Early Modern history of the Netherlands without taking detailed notice of the Dutch-speaking parts of Belgium. At the time his argument was controversial. Now it is generally accepted, at least for the period before 1581. Several historians have since shown that it is impossible to do justice to the facts without taking equally detailed notice of those parts of Belgium where Dutch is not spoken. In the Middle Ages the county of Flanders, the duchy of Brabant and the prince-bishopric of Liège all straddled the linguistic frontier between Dutch and French, while the subjects of the dukes of Luxembourg spoke both French and German. Dynastic fortunes meant that two of the most important monolingual counties, Holland and Hainaut, shared a ruler from 1299 until 1581.

A more fundamental way in which the Low Countries form a unity of sorts is in their geography. They are the western, coastal edge of the

North European Plain along with the fringe of hills which divides it from the Paris Basin and the Plateau of Lorraine. The area is defined by the low-lying North Sea coast, and especially by the delta area where Scheldt, Maas and Rhine meet the sea. (The Maas will be referred to by its French name, the Meuse, when speaking of Wallonia.) To either side of this North Sea Basin, at some remove, lie the rivers which gave definition to other European states and cultures: the Seine of northern France, and the Weser and Elbe of Saxony. It was the importance of water-borne traffic, and its tolls, that led the medieval principalities of the Low Countries to extend along the rivers without regard to linguistic differences.

Within the Benelux, the central delta area and its immediate low-lying environs contain some of Europe's most built-up conurbations, busiest road, railway and canal networks, and the continent's two largest container ports, Rotterdam and Antwerp (see Map 1). This area largely accounts for the Netherlands and Belgium being the two most densely populated countries in Europe, with (respectively) 372 and 333 inhabitants per square kilometre – as against 239 in Britain or 29 in the United States. Inland from the delta area and its immediate surroundings are a number of isolated patches of low hills: the Drenthe plateau in the northeastern Netherlands, the Veluwe just south of the IJsselmeer, the Kempen in Brabant and Limburg, and the 'Flemish Ardennes' south of Ypres. These slightly hilly areas tend to be on sandy soils, as is most of northern Belgium. In the Netherlands the broad river valleys and low-lying plain are clay and peat.

Beginning in the southern part of Dutch-speaking Belgium and particularly characterizing the landscape of the French-speaking part of the country are three ranges of higher plateaus, divided by depressions and river valleys. The first of these are the plateaus of Hainaut, Brabant and Hesbaye, with rich loamy agricultural land. They lie to the north of the Sambre-Meuse valley, which cuts them off with a dramatic fall from the Condroz plateau to the south. As Wordsworth wrote of the Meuse valley, in 'Between Namur and Liège':

What lovelier home could gentle Fancy choose?
. . .
How sweet the prospect of yon watery glade,
With its grey rocks clustering in pensive shade –
That, shaped like old monastic turrets, rise
From the smooth meadow-ground, serene and still!

The Condroz itself is split into two parts by the upper Meuse, flowing south to north before veering eastwards at Namur. South of the Condroz is the Fagne-Famenne depression, and south of that the forested hills of the Ardennes, which dominate southernmost Belgium and the Grand Duchy of Luxembourg. The very southernmost tips of Luxembourg and Belgium lie over iron-bearing Jurassic limestone and are geologically part of the Lorraine plateau. Natural caves in the plateaus of southern Belgium have provided some of the oldest signs of human habitation in the Low Countries, including Neanderthal remains. Another area of prehistoric habitation was the Drenthe plateau, where many late Stone Age dolmens survive. The graves of the Drenthe dolmen-builders (a branch of the Beaker People) are similar to those found elsewhere in Western Europe, but contain earthenware of a North European type, and copperware imported from Central Europe. As early as the Neolithic period, the Low Countries were something of a cultural crossroads.

The importance of the Low Countries as a place of mercantile and cultural exchange is closely related to its position on the North Sea and on the Scheldt-Maas-Rhine delta, the point of intersection of maritime and continental zones. Some historians have spoken of this as a 'golden delta', which has for centuries put the towns of the region at the forefront of Northern European trade. For most of its history the Low Countries, conceived as such a geographical, economic and cultural zone of interchange, has been rather wider than the modern Benelux area. For much of the time it should be taken to include France north of the Somme and parts of the German Rhineland and North Sea coast. The three small states of the Benelux are sandwiched between France and Germany and in close proximity to England, all medium-sized states of greater power. The Benelux countries have historically shared many problems and experiences – from Roman conquest to European integration – more closely than most separate states have done. But it is hard to write a history of the Benelux area without writing a general history of Western Europe, for the Low Countries have been the battlefield, crossroads, marketplace and microcosm of half the continent.

1

From Pagans to Crusaders, 57 BC to AD 1100

THE BELGIANS ARE THE BRAVEST OF THEM ALL, 57–13 BC

The earliest historical record concerning the Low Countries is in Julius Caesar's account of his conquest of Gaul. In a much-quoted passage describing the Gauls at the beginning of his *Commentaries on the Gallic War* he wrote, 'The Belgae are the bravest of them all', with the much less often quoted continuation, 'living furthest from the culture of the province, being least visited by merchants, . . . and constantly warring with the Germans'.

Caesar refers to the Belgic Gauls as inhabiting the area bordered southwards by the Seine and the Marne, westwards by the ocean, and northwards and eastwards by the Rhine. This corresponds roughly to present-day Belgium, Luxembourg, north-eastern France, the Dutch provinces of Zeeland, South Holland, North Brabant and Limburg, and Germany west of the Rhine. For military purposes Caesar needed intelligence about the numbers, territory and organization of the peoples he was facing, but how reliable this intelligence was there is no way of knowing, for there is no independent account against which his own can be checked. At various points in the *Gallic War* he refers to merchants, diplomatic hostages, Gaulish allies and prisoners of war as informants. The material record shows only that the inhabitants of the area Caesar describes as Belgic belonged to the much more broadly diffused late Iron Age Celtic culture that archaeologists call 'La Tène'.

Power in this culture was held by aristocratic families controlling large areas of land, on which their subjects ('tribe') lived dispersed in small agricultural communities under local chieftains. Crops were supplemented with extensive salt-working all along the coast, and sheep-rearing and the fabrication of woollen cloth further inland. There are signs of pottery production, of iron-working, and of panning for gold in the streams of the Ardennes. Some rulers had begun to mint coins, modelled on those of the Macedonians, but these were just prestige tokens: the economic life of the society was almost entirely agricultural. The great aristocrats, whose possessions might include Greek pottery and Italian bronzeware as well as Celtic work of high quality, could increase their prestige and extend their territory through war, exacting tribute from their defeated enemies but dedicating any immediate plunder to the gods. These local wars were a frequent feature of life in Gaul. Here and there in the Low Countries, especially in the Ardennes, archaeologists have uncovered the remains of late La Tène fortified settlements, hill-forts with drystone defences, or timber-framed stone and earthworks (what Caesar calls 'Gaulish walls' in his account of the siege of Alesia).

Caesar identified two social groups as distinct from the commoners (who were bound to the service of their lords as little more than slaves): druids and warriors. The druids were a body of judges and priests whose organization was the main institutional expression of the common Gaulish culture. For the Romans the most disturbing thing about the druids was that they would sometimes sacrifice humans to the gods. The endemic warfare and shifting alliances of the Celtic aristocracy encouraged a warrior ethic of honour, courage and personal loyalty, but no political cohesion among the various Belgic, let alone Gaulish, tribes.

Rome's opportunity for expansion, and Caesar's opportunity for the glory and plunder that would boost his political career at home, came through the in-fighting of the Gauls. Caesar was appointed proconsul of the Roman province of Gaul (the Po Valley and Provence) in 59 BC. The next year a tribe allied to the Romans, and settled in the region north of the Alps, appealed to Rome for aid against their enemies. The legions were sent north, and successfully intervened in this local war before encamping for the winter far beyond the boundaries of the Roman province. The Belgic tribes, naturally uneasy, concluded a league for mutual defence should the Romans move further northwards, and Caesar took this as reason enough to invade their territory the following year, 57 BC. His army consisted not only of Romans, but also of Numidian, Cretan and Balearan auxiliaries.

Among the Belgic tribes, the Treveri (in the area around Trier) and the Remi (around Rheims) saw alliance with Rome as the most profitable path and aided Caesar, who was full of praise for their cavalry. The first action in the new campaign was against the Nervians and their allies. The Nervians brought their old-folk, women and children into safety in the marshes, and engaged the Roman invaders and their allies on the river Sabis (probably the Selle, a tiny tributary of the Scheldt now in France). The struggle was fierce, and Caesar himself fought sword in hand, but by the end of the day the Nervians were defeated and their army virtually annihilated. As the battle turned against the Belgae, their warriors stood atop the fallen bodies of their comrades until they were fighting on a great mound of corpses, still catching Roman javelins and flinging them back. The few survivors were spared enslavement and given guarantees of autonomy under Roman patronage.

The Aduatuci, whose force was still on its way to support the Nervians when they heard of the defeat, retreated to what Caesar calls *oppidum Aduatucorum*, 'the walled town of the Aduatuci'. Scornful at first of the Romans' elaborate siege preparations, the novel sight of a mobile siege tower filled them with apprehension, and they offered to parley. The Roman demand for disarmament they met by throwing piles of weapons over the walls, keeping back a third of their arms in conceal-ment. That night they broke the truce by sallying out against the Roman encampment. After confused fighting in the darkness, the Romans stormed the gates of the fort at dawn, finding it virtually abandoned. Those Aduatuci who could be found were rounded up and sold into slav-ery. At the end of the year 57 BC, Caesar somewhat prematurely informed Rome that all Gaul had been subjugated. The following year he defeated the Veneti of north-western Gaul at sea, then moved against their allies on the Belgic coast, the Morini and Menapians. Rather than face his army these small tribes retreated into the woods and marshes, harassing the Romans with guerrilla tactics. Caesar blamed his failure to subjugate them on the bad weather, but the following year he had little better success. During the general Gallic Revolt of 53–51 BC, the Morini and Menapians allied themselves with Vercingetorix.

More distant tribes also presented Caesar with problems. To warn them off he undertook short expeditions across the Rhine and the Channel in 55–54 BC before resuming his campaign in Gaul. The harvests of 54 BC were poor, and as a result no single location could supply the needs of all the Roman troops. The legions went into winter quarters in a number of fortified camps which were dispersed over the Belgic region. Within a few weeks, one of these camps had been attacked and a legion and five cohorts defeated and destroyed. The perpetrators were the Eburones, under their princes Ambiorix and Catuvolcus. They went on to lay siege to another of the camps, in the lands of the Nervians, where a single legion was lodged. They built siege engines to the specifications of Roman prisoners. They were joined by the Nervians and the remnants of the Aduatuci. Soon Gaulish tribes further afield, such as the Armoricans in north-west Gaul, saw their chance to throw off Roman rule. The Treveri, who had initially allied themselves with Rome, now sided with the Belgic 'rebels', their pro-Roman prince Cingetorix having lost a factional struggle for influence to the anti-Roman Indutiomarus.

Caesar's response was swift and brutal. The Armoricans and then the Treveri were defeated in battle. Indutiomarus was captured and beheaded. Ten legions systematically devastated the lands of the Eburones, and Catuvolcus, too old to fight or flee, hanged himself from a yew. There is no later record of the existence of either the Eburones or the Aduatuci, but this does not necessarily imply effective genocide. The Gaulish tribes were as much political as ethnic groups, and it may be that large numbers of survivors took on new allegiances. Ambiorix himself escaped with four guards and was never found.

A nineteenth-century statue of Ambiorix stands in the marketplace of Tongeren, in Belgian Limburg, to commemorate the heroic leader of the 'Ancient Belgian' fight for freedom. With the change in educational fashions, many of today's youngsters will only have heard of the Ancient Belgians through admonishments from their elders not to eat like them, or from the pages of *Astérix chez les Belges*. For centuries past, though, Caesar's *Gallic War* was a schoolboy's primer in Latin and history. It was still giving some people their sense of the enduring characteristics of the Belgians as recently as the Second World War. The lesson which a primary schoolbook of 1947 drew from the story of Ambiorix was that 'The Belgian loves liberty: it is a heritage of our forefathers.'

Publius Cornelius Tacitus, writing almost 150 years after Julius Caesar's conquests, gives the historic justification for the rule of the Romans in Gaul: they had been invited in to defend the warring Gauls from one another and from the Germans. In return for Roman pacification and protection, the subjected Gauls were expected only to pay taxes and to provide military manpower. But during Caesar's lifetime the confusions of Rome's civil wars in Italy and North Africa delayed the establishment of structures for assessing and collecting tax and for recruiting auxiliaries. Caesar's adopted son, Gaius Octavius, emerged as the victor in these wars, and on 17 January 27 BC the Roman Senate conferred on him imperial powers and the title of Augustus. After spending most of the year re-establishing order in Rome and Italy, Augustus went to Gaul, where he remained for several years and instituted a series of administrative reorganizations. First, the government of Caesar's conquests of 30 years before was separated from the older province of *Gallia Transalpina* (Provence), under the name *Gallia Comata* ('long-haired Gaul'). An altar to Augustus and Rome was erected in the new provincial capital at Lugdunum (Lyons), where the Gaulish leaders were to swear allegiance and make annual sacrifices. In a later stage, *Gallia Comata* was subdivided into the provinces *Aquitania* (from the Pyrennees to the Loire), *Gallia Lugdunensis* (from the Loire to the Seine) and *Belgica* (from the Seine to the Rhine), although the 'Three Gauls' were still linked in some respects, such as the annual sacrifices to the deified Augustus at Lyons.

The province was divided into districts, called *civitates*, according to the tribe dominant in the area. In the Low Countries there were a *civitas Morinorum*, a *civitas Menapiorum*, a *civitas Nerviorum*, a *civitas Tungrorum* and a *civitas Treverorum*. These districts were largely self-governing, as long as they adopted the outward forms of Roman administration and magistracy, respected the *Pax Romana*, submitted to Roman tax assessments and provided auxiliary troops. Each tribe had its own administrative centre, the Morini *Tarvanna* (now Thérouanne), the Menapians *Castellum Menapiorum* (Cassel), the Nervians *Bagacum* (Bavay), the Tungrians *Aduatuca Tungrorum* (Tongeren), and the Treverans *Augusta Treverorum* (Trier). The great cities of the province, Rheims, Trier and Cologne, are now in France or Germany, but numerous towns and villages in the Benelux area date from Roman times, including Arlon, Maastricht, Namur, Nijmegen, Tournai and Utrecht.

BEYOND THE RHINE, 13 BC TO AD 80

At the time of Caesar's invasion, Belgic settlement extended to the 'Old Rhine', further north than the present course of the great rivers. When the Romans fixed the Rhine as the boundary of Gaul, they allowed a number of Germanic tribes, the Cananefates, Batavians and Frisiavones, to settle the delta area. North of the Rhine, the lands of the Frisians stretched along the North Sea coast as far as the Ems. This was a region of marshes and lakes, the largest of them Lake Flevo (the Zuider Zee did not form until the late Middle Ages). The material culture of the Frisians was distinct from that of the Gauls. The period of Celtic culture labelled 'La Tène' corresponds with the 'Proto-Frisian' and 'Frisian' periods to the north, the distinction resting on a number of factors but mainly the different styles of earthenware produced locally.

In 13 BC Augustus launched the Roman invasion of Germania. The first stage was an amphibian operation against the Frisians, who almost immediately allied themselves with the invading Romans. Their lands were to become a military gateway: troops and supplies could be transported by water through Frisia to the mouth of the Weser, and thence upstream into the heart of Germania. To aid this, Augustus's step-son Drusus had his men dig out a channel, the *fossa drusiana*, connecting the Rhine to the IJssel, and the IJssel to Lake Flevo. At first the subjugation of the Germans went well, but in AD 9 three legions and their auxiliaries, totalling 27,000 men, were lost in an ambush in the Teutoburger Wald (just to the east of the Low Countries). In the hour of defeat the commander of the army of the Rhine fell on his sword in true Roman fashion. The Rhine again became the border. The Frisians remained allies of Rome, perhaps fearing the tribes to their east more than they did the Romans. Over the course of the next 40 years there were six more Roman invasions through Frisia, none of which led to any permanent success beyond the Rhine. The *provincia Belgica* was to remain a frontier province, with a heavy military presence, until the fall of the Roman Empire.

The Frisians were very much the junior partner in their alliance with the Romans. They were not ruled or taxed by Rome, but they did have to pay tribute and a garrison was installed to collect it. The tribute was set at a certain number of cowhides for military uses, the size and quality of which was left undetermined. In the year AD 28 Olennius, the leading centurion commanding the garrison, decreed that the standard for tribute was to be the hide of the aurochs, the now extinct wild ox, larger and tougher than the local domestic cattle. Declaring the Frisians to be in default of tribute, the soldiers appointed to collect it seized cattle, land, women and children. The Frisians rose in arms and crucified the tax collectors. Olennius took refuge in the fort of Flevum (Velsen), which the Frisians besieged in vain. The army of the Rhine was sent in, but was unable to deploy effectively in waterlogged country and after rescuing their cavalry from encirclement the legions called it a day. Only later was it discovered that 900 men had failed to withdraw and had been killed in the Grove of Baduhenna, and another 400 had holed up in a retired soldier's villa and committed suicide *en masse* to avoid capture. Roman influence in Frisia was ended for 20 years.

In AD 47 the Chauci, who lived to the north-east of the Frisians between the Ems and the Elbe, launched a series of piratical raids into Gaul. The Romans were keen to secure the frontier, and the Frisians seem again to have favoured Roman influence as a counterbalance to the tribes to their east. The legate of the frontier army, Corbulo, finalized a new treaty of alliance with the Frisians, fixing and recognizing their borders and reorganizing their goverment on the model of a provincial *civitas*. This was in preparation for the use of their territory as a staging post for an invasion of the lands of the Chauci. The Emperor Claudius forbade the invasion, however, and Corbulo instead turned to consolidating the Rhine defences by having his men dig a canal between the lower reaches of the Maas and the Rhine to facilitate the supply of the frontier forts.

Roman extortions were the source of the most famous of the revolts on the lower Rhine, that led by the Batavian Julius Civilis. The Batavians inhabited a large 'island' of the Rhine, usually identified as the Betuwe between the Waal and the Lek, now the two main streams of the delta. In his *Germania* Tacitus describes the Batavians as 'foremost in manliness' among all the German tribes of the Rhine. Presumably the Romans had fixed their borders by treaty and encouraged them to adopt a Roman-style magistracy, as they had done with the Frisians in AD 47. As an independent client people the Batavians were not subject to taxation, but were expected to tolerate a garrison and provide auxiliary troops. They had done so since 12 BC, shortly after Augustus's invasion of Germania, and unlike most subject peoples their cohorts served under their own officers. The height of Batavian men soon had the emperors using them as ceremonial guards.

Rome's first imperial dynasty came to an end in AD 68 when Nero, faced with what looked like becoming a successful rebellion led by Servius Sulpicius Galba, committed suicide. The senate recognized Galba as Nero's successor, but in the course of AD 69, 'the Year of Four Emperors', the frontier legions proclaimed their commanders as emperor: those on the Rhine Aulus Vitellius, those on the Danube Marcus Silvius Otho, and those in the Levant Vespasian. Galba himself, and his designated heir, were murdered. The press-gangs which Vitellius sent into Batavia to recruit for the civil war displayed an unusual degree of avarice and licentiousness. According to Tacitus, they rounded up the aged and infirm for ransom, and dragged off the best-looking adolescents to quench their lust. The one-eyed Julius Civilis was a Batavian prince and a veteran auxiliary commander. The provincial use of the name Julius probably indicates an imperial grant of Roman citizenship. Civilis invited the leaders of his people to a banquet in a sacred grove, where he called upon them to reclaim their ancient freedom, 'For we are no longer regarded as allies, but as slaves.' Oaths and sacrifices sealed their secret determination to break the alliance with Rome. Messengers were sent to neighbouring tribes, and to the commanders of Batavian auxiliaries in Britannia and Germania.

In the first battle of the revolt, on the Rhine, the Batavians, with their neighbours the Cananefates and the Frisians, overcame the Romans sent against them. During the battle a cohort of Gaulish auxiliaries switched sides, and Batavian rowers in the Rhine fleet overwhelmed their officers and delivered their ships to Civilis. In the second encounter, the Belgic auxiliaries refused to fight for the Romans and the Batavian cavalry which the Romans had deployed went over to Civilis on the field of battle. The Romans were now facing veteran auxiliaries who knew their techniques and shared their discipline, as well as bands of Germans from over the Rhine. In the first siege of Civilis's campaign, that of the forti-fied camp Vetera (Xanten), the Roman defenders were terrified by the sight of both Roman standards and 'the images of wild beasts taken from the woods and groves' combined against them. But they were given fresh courage by the sight of columns of smoke rising from burning farmsteads, the sure sign of an approaching Roman army.

The relief of Vetera was far from the end of the revolt. Up until then Civilis had led his Roman opponents to believe that he was acting against the legions of Vitellius in support of Vespasian. Towards the end of the year, with Vespasian's men in command of the legions, it became apparent that his goal was the destruction of Roman power on the Rhine and in north-eastern Gaul. With the clarification of Civilis's intentions a number of disaffected Belgic chiefs met at Cologne and formed an alliance to co-ordinate with the Batavians. This was led by two Treveran officers, Classicus, prefect of auxiliary cavalry, and Julius Tutor, prefect of the Rhine shore. Both of them were former supporters of Vitellius who now joined with Civilis against Vespasian. During the street-fight-ing in Rome between troops loyal to Vitellius and to Vespasian the capi-tol had been set on fire by German auxiliaries, and Belgic druids declared this an omen of the end of Roman power. Classicus proclaimed a 'Gallic Empire', and exacted oaths of loyalty to it from his Belgic supporters and from some of the Roman legions still opposed to

17

Vespasian. Julius Sabinus, a great-grandson of Julius Caesar by a Gaulish mistress, laid claim to the imperial title.

The Batavians remained an independent force, allied to German tribes from over the Rhine in a confederation which drew its inspiration from the mysterious prophetess Veleda. She lived secluded in a tower, her oracles communicated by a boy. There was an element of aristocratic nostalgia in the German ranks: Civilis himself grew his hair long and dyed it red. The leaders of certain Belgic tribes, notably the Nervians, Tungrians and Menapians, retained their alliance with Rome until forced to submit to the Batavians or the Treverans. Matters were soon complicated by a Batavian guerrilla movement in favour of Rome led by the auxiliary cavalry commander Claudius Labeo, a rival of Civilis for authority among his people. For all Tacitus's simple rhetorical scheme of barbarian liberty versus Roman order, the Batavians, the Belgic tribes and the Rhine army itself were all divided by power struggles which a century of Roman rule had inextricably intertwined.

Despite the simultaneous distraction of the Jewish Revolt, Vespasian soon had a new army of eight legions in Gaul, under Petilius Cerialis. Cerialis quickly reconciled the Roman troops still opposed to Vespasian and defeated the Belgic alliance. He was an impetuous commander, exposing himself to personal danger on many occasions, but his narrowest escape had little to do with courage. One night part of the Rhine fleet was surprised and towed away, and Cerialis would certainly have been captured had he not already secretly gone ashore for an assignation with a German mistress. The Batavians sent his flagship to Veleda as a gift, perhaps in continuation of the custom of dedicating booty to the gods, and Civilis deployed the rest of the captured vessels in the Rhine delta to intercept Roman supply convoys. He also had his sappers divert part of the Rhine to flood the country through which Cerialis was attempting his advance. Civilis, in command of capable bodies of infantry, cavalry, navy and engineers, could see that Vespasian was re-establishing imperial power and decided that now was the time to negotiate from a position of strength. Civilis met with Cerialis on a bridge, the middle of which was cut away so that the two commanders could approach one another closely enough to converse in person without fear of treachery. The rest of Tacitus's *Histories* is missing and nothing is known of what happened to Civilis. Veleda was captured by the Romans in one of their incursions into Germania later in the decade and was carried to Rome in triumph. Julius Sabinus, 'Caesar of Gaul', survived in hiding in a cave for nine years before he was found and put to death.

The Batavians as a people seem to have made their peace with Rome and returned to being a client state on their former terms, subject to military levies but not to taxation. Around AD 80 the militarized zone on the Rhine frontier was converted into the provinces of Upper and Lower Germany (*Germania superior* and *Germania inferior*), the border between the two being near Bonn. In what is now the Netherlands, the *civitates* of Lower Germany were those of the Frisiavones, the Cananefates, and the Batavians. The chief town of the Batavians was *Noviomagus* (Nijmegen). The Dutch Revolt of the late sixteenth century coincided with a vogue for Tacitus among the humanists who dominated intellectual life. From then onwards Civilis for the Dutch, as later Ambiorix for the Belgians, came to symbolize an ancestral love of liberty and opposition to arbitrary taxation. Strikingly, both these ancient warriors who loomed so large in the national imaginations were men who disappeared from history.

ROMANIZATION, AD 80–396

Tax assessments and levies were certainly resented, but other benefits brought by the Romans were more highly valued. The general adoption of Roman technologies, luxuries and styles of life within the Empire fades away among the Frisians beyond the frontier into the piecemeal use of Roman coins, glassware and jewels, and techniques of well-building and poultry-farming. The Frisians had allied themselves with Rome for purposes which did not include becoming Romans, but they were happy to adopt whatever seemed useful or attractive. The military frontier was not by any means the outer limit of Roman cultural influence. At Wijster, in Drenthe, there was a sizeable village which by the fourth century was selling its surplus produce to the Rhine forts 60 miles to the south.

The main problem with the earliest history of the Low Countries is that it was written by metropolitan Romans, who were only interested when incursions, revolts or provincial reorganization brought the area to their attention. The gradual spread of Roman ways has to be inferred from settlement patterns, inscriptions and other material remains. One clear change is the adoption of Roman styles and techniques (such as the potter's wheel) by Belgic potters, who supplied the whole of northern Gaul and the garrisons of the Rhine with imitative 'Belgic ware' as a cheap alternative to Roman goods. Nevertheless, surprisingly large amounts of quality Italian pottery were imported, especially the warm dull-red *terra sigillata*, and are to be found even in Frisian territory. Rescue excavations carried out in Nijmegen between 1986 and 1995 turned up cavalry stables and signs that the garrison consumed not only beef, fish, grain, poultry and salt from the immediate locality and from northern Gaul, but also fish sauce, wine and olive oil from Spain and Italy, and Egyptian dates. The Romans introduced the domestic chicken to Northern Europe, and Nijmegen has some of the oldest remains. The town was the site of a military tile works, turning out red roof tiles of the sort which were rapidly displacing thatch all over Roman Gaul. The forts of the Rhine *limes* such as those at Nijmegen and Xanten, or of the Saxon Shore such as at Aardenburg and Oudenburg, contributed greatly to Romanization but were not the only centres of the process.

Setting aside the great fortified camps and the towns which grew up to service them, the evidence of Roman influence decreases as the land gets lower in the Low Countries. In the Ardennes, Trier became a bustling imperial city. The hills further north were dotted with towns and villas built in stone. In the century after the Batavian revolt mosaics made their appearance in the luxurious town houses and villas of the region. In the lowlands, where stone was much harder to come by than in the uplands, towns, villages and villas were built mainly of wood and the signs of Romanization are much harder to spot. Nevertheless, even here Roman culture and Roman roads fundamentally altered the Belgic and Batavian ways of life. The town now called Tienen, for instance, was probably the most important rural settlement in the lands of the Tungrians. It grew up as an unfortified agricultural township at a junction in the road network, where lesser roads from north and south joined the main road from the Tungrian capital Tongeren to the Menapian capital Cassel. The town throve from the early first century to the late third century and was thoroughly Roman in organization and lifestyle. Without the presence of a garrison to account for them, the material remains of the place include pots and amphorae from southern Gaul, Italy and Spain.

At Echternach a palatial villa was constructed in the last decades of the first century. Lying away from the main roads, fortifications and centres of trade or administration, it seems to indicate a Treveran nobleman adopting the lifestyle of a wealthy Roman in a grand manor. In the troubles of the later empire, a little private hill-fort was built less than a mile away. This sort of personal decision to take on Roman ways wholesale was probably not the norm. Romanization was generally a more gradual assimilation. Settlements which were already major towns in the second and third centuries show the combined influence of the three main forces of the process: integration in the larger economic system, interaction with soldiers from all over the Empire through the presence of a fort or recruitment to the auxiliaries, and the adoption of Roman-style justice, administration and ritual.

Religion is one of the most complex areas of Roman influence. Caesar had seen the gods of the Gauls as recognizably similar to those of the Graeco-Roman pantheon, with Gaulish equivalents of Mercury, Apollo, Mars, Jupiter and Minerva. Particular groves or springs were seen as holy, but this was not an unfamiliar concept to the invaders. Once Roman rule was established, those who gained citizenship were encouraged to worship the gods of Rome. At certain times they might be required to sacrifice to deified emperors, and they were forbidden to take part in druidic rituals, but the Romans otherwise respected the gods of the locality. Gods with syncretic names appeared, such as Lenus Mars worshipped by the Treverans in a massive Roman-style temple outside Trier, or Hercules Magusanus of the Batavians, possibly worshipped in the large temple complex built at Elst in imported stone. These existed side by side with the official and unofficial cults of Rome, and with entirely native deities such as Nehalennia, a goddess of plenty along the Rhine and in its delta to whom merchants and mariners dedicated many inscriptions and altars.

The ease of communications within the Empire helped the spread of Mithraism and of Christianity, despite a lack of official encouragement. The remains of a mid-third-century temple of Mithras were dug up at Tienen in 1998. The sanctuary itself is a small room which might hold a dozen or so initiates, partly dug into the earth to give the effect of a cave. But the complex also contains a ritual deposit of the remains of a single midsummer banquet of chicken, pork, lamb and wine for up to 100 guests. Even a Persian mystery religion could be given its Belgian touches. Christians, who like Jews and some philosophical sects refused to sacrifice to the emperors, had a harder time of it. Later traditions suggest a scattering of Christian martyrs in the towns of Belgica around 290, during Diocletian's reign, and the victims are usually described as the first to bring Christianity to the area. The first certain indication of Christian communities established in Belgica is that the bishops of Trier and Rheims attended the Council of Arles in 314, shortly after Constantine had made Christianity respectable.

This was after a century of deep crisis. In 235–84, one of the worst periods of Roman civil war, when 50-odd imperial claimants arose in as many years, the military organization of the border was weakened to the point of collapse. In 256 the Franks crossed the Rhine at Cologne and plundered through Gaul and into Iberia. The Batavian general M. Cassianus Latinius Postumus, legate of Lower Germany, had some success in withstanding them. In 258 he proclaimed himself emperor, and he obtained recognition from the provincial governors of Gaul, Britain and Iberia. Two hundred years after the Roman conquest, a Batavian had gained the much fought-over title of Caesar. The Western Empire was divided into a 'Roman Empire' under Gallienus, and a 'Gallic Empire' under Postumus, who died in 269. Postumus overhauled the defensive structures of the Belgic province, giving greater depth to the military frontier by constructing a series of watch towers combined with fortified store bases along the road from Cologne to Boulogne, and possibly on other routes. This was also a period when many of the unfortified townships of the northern provinces were given walls, and hill forts came back into use as temporary refuges from plunderers. The Gallic Empire outlived Postumus by only five years. In 274 one of his successors, Tetricus, was defeated and deposed by the 'Roman' emperor Aurelian. Almost immediately another Frankish invasion, more destructive than the first, swept over the Gaulish provinces. It was beyond a doubt that the effective organization of the frontier defences required a supreme commander on the spot.

With the rise of Diocletian stability began to return to the Empire. In 286, two years after being proclaimed Augustus, Diocletian appointed Maximian as his co-emperor with special responsibility for the defences of the northern frontiers. A third co-caesar, the Menapian general M. Aurelius Maesaeus Carausius, was appointed soon afterwards. Initially proclaimed by his own troops, Carausius was accepted as joint caesar only after Maximian had failed to defeat him. Carausius was the second native of the Low Countries to bear the imperial title, and like Postumus before him he owed his rise to his success against Frankish and Saxon pillagers. He commanded the Roman fleet at Boulogne and developed the defences of the 'Saxon Shore' in south-eastern Britain and along the Continental coast from Boulogne to the mouth of the Rhine. In 293 Diocletian and Maximian withdrew recognition from Carausius and appointed two other co-caesars, Galerius and Constantius Chlorus. The latter was entrusted with rule over Gaul. Before the year was out he had taken Boulogne, and Carausius had been murdered by one of his own officers. Constantius Chlorus marched to pacify the Frankish settlements in the Rhine delta in 294 and 295, and in 296 he invaded Britain and deposed Carausius's successor there. Amazingly, the Roman Empire had survived and was reunified.

Diocletian revised the governing structures of the reunified Empire, among other decrees splitting many existing provinces into two and increasing the number of high officials within each province. The Belgic province was accordingly divided into *Belgica Prima* and *Belgica Secunda*. The capital of *prima* was Trier, that of *secunda* Rheims, and the Tungrians were incorporated into the remodelled Lower Rhine province, *Germania Secunda*. Much of *Germania Secunda* was now inhabited by Franks, settled there by treaty, and the names of the former tribes were no longer in use. There was also a reorganization of *civitates*, with Boulogne, Tournai and Cambrai becoming the administrative centres of streamlined districts (see Map 2). The word *civitas* was now coming to mean the district capital rather than the district itself. The forest of the Ardennes became an imperial possession, part of a tendency for imperial managers to take over the exploitation of large businesses and natural assets, such as quarries and forests.

As the main imperial residence north of the Alps, Trier flourished considerably in the late third and the fourth centuries. The city had the main mint of the Western Empire, the largest bath complex outside Rome, an imperial palace, a circus and a magnificent amphitheatre. The rulers brought with them courtiers, administrators and soldiers from all over the Empire, and Trier attracted Syrian and Jewish merchants. The city's glory days began shortly before Constantine's adoption of Christianity as the imperial religion, and it accordingly features in the Christian writings of the fourth century. There were still many pagans in Trier, even among the educated, but the dominant tone was Christian and fiercely orthodox. Athanasius, bishop of Alexandria, was exiled to Trier when his ecclesiastical enemies brought him into disfavour with Constantine, who was then establishing his new capital at Constantinople. Athanasius's rivals were Arians, holding that God the Father had in some sense created God the Son and thereby denying the full divinity of Christ. It was a controversy which tore the Mediterranean churches apart. The orthodox three-in-one Holy Trinity was firmly established in the Belgic Church, in large part by the influence of Athanasius. An Armenian friend of his, Servatius, became bishop of Tongeren. Another friend, Paulinus of Trier, was one of the few western bishops who suffered exile rather than support Constantius II's attempt to have Athanasius declared a heretic. His alleged heresy was insisting that God the Son was, in the words of the Nicean Creed, 'begotten not made, of one being with the Father'. Christianity in the city had a very high profile, which is likely to have encouraged rapid acceptance of it in the immediate area. The emperor's mother Helena is said to have given her house for the building of the cathedral, which was indeed built over part of the imperial palace. The prose stylist and Christian controversialist Lactantius was summoned from Asia Minor to Trier by Constantine to tutor his son Crispus. A famous visitor to the imperial court in Trier was Ambrose of Milan, who may have been born in the city. But Christian life was not mainly focused on palaces and great men. In his *Confessions*, Augustine refers to the impact made on him by a friend's report of a visit to Trier, where he found monks establishing themselves in a simple house among the gardens by the city wall, a manuscript of Athanasius's Life of the Egyptian hermit St Anthony among their few possessions. There was a thriving Christian culture in the Ardennes, centred on imperial Trier, and in some of the western Belgic towns now in France, but otherwise there are few signs of Christianity in the Benelux area before later in the fourth century.

Valentinian I, emperor from 364 to 375, ruled from Trier as the last of the great Roman Emperors of the West. A professional soldier from Pannonia, he liked to appoint professionals and soldiers to administrative posts. Two figures who were often at Trier during his reign were Martin, bishop of Tours, a Pannonian old soldier turned preacher and holy man, and the Gaulish Latin poet Ausonius, tutor to Valentinian's son. In his *Mosella*, an encomium of the river Moselle (now the southeastern border of the Grand Duchy of Luxembourg), Ausonius describes the landscape and activities he beheld when accompanying Valentinian on his return from a campaign against the Germans. In a shorter work on great cities, the *Ordo Urbium Nobilium*, he lists Trier in sixth place, after Rome, Constantinople, Carthage, Antioch and Alexandria, and describes it as feeding, clothing and arming the forces of the Empire. The imperial workshops at Trier produced shields, engines of war, woollen goods and cloth embroidered in silver and gold. There were shipyards in Trier which maintained part of the Rhine fleet. Their raw materials were drawn from the vast imperial estates of the Ardennes, which also produced food crops.

After Valentinian's death, official positions generally became the family possessions of the leading families of Italy and Gaul. The great landowners were increasing their power in every respect. By the third century the agrarian economy of the northern provinces was in crisis: population was declining, wealth was concentrated in fewer and fewer hands, and the poor were selling themselves into slavery to survive. As early as 297 Diocletian had ordered the payment of taxes in goods rather than in coin, which was consistently losing value. Long before the end of the Roman Empire, the aristocratic-agricultural society that underlay the feudal order was already taking shape.

THE END OF ROMAN RULE, 396–500

For centuries the northern frontier was one of the most fruitful recruiting grounds of the Empire. Britons, Gauls, Frisians and Batavians served from the Mediterranean to Hadrian's Wall, and the Low Countries were linked even to the Middle East by a system of military roads which was in constant use. As time passed, however, military recruitment increasingly took place beyond the Rhine, among Germans and eventually Huns. In 357 a treaty was concluded with certain of the Franks, providing them with land further within the border, between the Maas and the Scheldt, in return for their military service on the frontier. In 373 these Franks destroyed an army of Saxon plunderers, and in 388 they drove back a non-federated Frankish group. The federated Germans were not reluctant fighters for the Empire they had joined. Gradually the influx of soldiers and settlers from beyond the Rhine and their integration into the life of the Empire Germanized much of the West.

German migration peaked with the 'Great Invasion' of the winter of 406, when Vandals, Burgundians, Swabians and Alamans crossed the frozen Rhine at Mainz and the military frontier collapsed. The Franks, their numbers increased by new immigrants, maintained their control of *Germania Secunda* and expanded it into parts of *Belgica Secunda*. There was no longer any civilian provincial government to speak of. By this time both Roman and Belgic aristocrats were often absentee landlords in Italy, far from the troubles of the borders.

Aetius is one of the many who have been called 'the last of the Romans'. He had served for years as a diplomatic hostage among Germans and Huns before rising to be supreme commander of the army in Gaul. It was Aetius who briefly restored the Rhine frontier, and it was under his authority that the last coins minted in Trier appeared. He commanded the army of Visigoths, Burgundians and Franks which defeated Attila's Huns in 451. In 454 he appeared before Valentinian III to demand the emperor's daughter as bride for his son, whereupon Valentinian slew him with his own hand. The following year the emperor himself was killed by officers loyal to Aetius's memory. It was to be another 20 years before the last Emperor of the West was deposed, but when Valentinian III died whatever was left of direct Roman rule in the Low Countries died with him.

By the middle of the fifth century the Franks were the dominant group in the Roman Low Countries. After Valentinian III's death their war-leader, Childeric, obtained imperial recognition as head of the provincial government. He established his capital in the Nervian *civitas* Tournai. The Franks may not have fully understood the principles of Roman government, but they whole-heartedly desired its continuation. Childeric died in 481 and was given a Frankish royal funeral at Tournai, in a tomb discovered in 1653. Among his grave goods were both his battleaxe, symbolizing his identity as a warrior leader, and the signet ring which showed his authority as the representative of imperial power.

Unlike the Germanic peoples who were coming to dominate most other parts of the Western Empire, the Franks were not yet Christians. The Goths in Spain and Italy and the Vandals in North Africa were Arians, which cut them off from the orthodox religious culture of their Romanized subjects and impeded intermarriage with them. As pagans the Anglo-Saxons and the Franks were at a slightly different disadvantage. The Angles were to remain religiously distinct from the Britons for another century, but for the Franks the problem was shorter lived. Childeric's son and heir Chlodovech (Latinized 'Clovis') unified the Franks and extended his rule over much of Gaul. At some time after 496 he was baptized by the bishop of Rheims, and the fusion of the Gaulish and Frankish aristocracies could begin. After Clovis's death in 511 his successors went on to complete his work: by 550 Childeric's descendants ruled all of what had been Gaul, and large stretches of southern and central Germany.

The north-Netherlandish coastal region of swamps and terps remained a Frisian stronghold, while the Saxons dominated the landward area north of the great rivers. In their push into Gaul, the Franks even surrendered to the Frisians parts of the delta which had been under Frankish rule since their first federation by the Romans. The Rhine delta was once again the most obvious boundary in the frontier zone between two interacting, but distinct cultures. In the high Middle Ages, the Dutch language itself grew from the interaction and convergence of Old Lower

Frankish, Old Saxon and Old Frisian. Gradually, from a frontier or a bridgehead, the Low Countries became a crossroads.

THE AGE OF SAINTS, 500–800

In the early Middle Ages the Christian Church replaced the Empire as the institutional vehicle of Roman culture. Monastic communities became the main source of historical narratives. The bishops, abbots, abbesses and hermits who mediated the transformations from Germanic paganism to Latinate Christianity were remembered after their deaths as the heavenly patrons of the new societies they brought into being. Rheims, where Bishop Remigius had baptized Clovis, became the spiritual capital of Francia, but, with the extension of Frankish power southwards and eastwards, Tournai was replaced by Paris and other towns as the main royal residences. The kingdom of Clovis's grandson Chlothar I encompassed all Gaul, but was repeatedly divided and reunited by the vagaries of Frankish inheritance. After Chlothar's death in 561, the Frankish Low Countries belonged to the north-eastern sub-kingdom Austrasia, which for much of the time was ruled separately from Neustria in the north-west, Aquitaine in the south-west or Burgundy in the south-east.

The baptism of Clovis did not mean the immediate conversion of the Franks as a people. Christianity was closely identified with the Romano-Gaulish aristocracy and with the Frankish royal house. Most inhabitants of the Low Countries remained vigorously pagan. The work of converting them was a slow one, but the Frankish kings firmly desired that the one true God who gave them victory should be worshipped by all who recognized their authority. The beginnings of this work in the Low Countries came around 500, when Remigius of Rheims sent an Aquitanian named Vedastus (or Vaast) to the derelict see of Arras. By the time of his death in 540 Vedastus had rebuilt Christian life in the town, although his success did not extend far into the surrounding countryside. A slightly younger contemporary of Vedastus was Nicetius, bishop of Trier, another Aquitanian who similarly rebuilt the church life of his see, as well as reviving wine production in the Moselle valley. Tongeren also had an active bishop at this time, Donatius, who preached in the valley of the Meuse and reportedly overcame a dragon that was infesting a pool near Huy – presumably indicating his success against a pagan cult.

Despite such local recoveries, Christianity in the Low Countries made little headway in rural communities. Even in the towns it may have been losing ground to paganism. In the course of the sixth century the see of Arras was combined with Cambrai, that of Tournai with Noyon, and Tongeren for a time with Cologne. Although the major churches were maintained, there was not the Christian presence to support a resident bishop in the Low Countries. The original placename of Nivelles near Brussels, *Niuwiala* meaning 'the new place of sacrifice', may bear witness to the revived spread of pagan rituals. In the seventh century the retreat of Christianity was ended, and reversed, by monastic missionaries in the Irish tradition.

Irish monasticism made much of the concept of 'exile for Christ', leaving behind one's native land for a life of prayer or pilgrimage among foreigners. Irish monks founded exile monasteries on the edges of Christendom, first among the Scots at Iona, later among the Franks. These monasteries soon became mission stations to the countryside and to neighbouring pagan peoples. The foremost of the Irish pilgrim missionaries on the Continent was Columbanus, who left Ireland in 590. His main foundation was at Luxeuil, in Burgundy. This monastery soon attracted recruits from across the kingdom, and they carried on the missionary tradition of the founder. During the reign of Dagobert I, a long-reigning king of Austrasia who briefly (628–37) brought all Francia under his sway, preachers trained in the Irish missionary tradition made their first attempts to Christianize the Low Countries. One such was Omer (or Audomarus, Omaar), who became bishop of Thérouanne, a see refounded by Dagobert, and with his companion Bertin spread Christianity in what is now north-eastern France. Another was Eligius (or Elooi, Eloy). A goldsmith by training, Eligius was a famously able craftsman and eventually became the patron saint of metalworkers and their guilds. He is usually represented with a workman's hammer. He was the first to preach in the villages of what is now the Flemish coast. Eligius also patched up a quarrel between King Dagobert and the most active of all these early missionaries in the Frankish Low Countries, Amandus.

Although not himself a product of the Irish monasteries, Amandus did grow to adulthood and live 15 years as a hermit in areas where the influence of Columbanus, and the memory of St Martin of Tours, were strong. After obtaining ordination as a missionary bishop not attached to a particular see, he set off to preach the Gospel in Austrasia and wherever else he saw an opening. The nature of his quarrel with Dagobert is not clear, but it has been plausibly suggested that the king disapproved of Amandus's preaching to peoples who did not recognize Frankish overlordship. After all, where would the king be if his enemies were also praying to the God who granted victory? Once Eligius had brokered a settlement, apparently on Dagobert's terms, Amandus enjoyed full royal support. With the king's backing he not only preached to the pagans of the Low Countries, the Danube and the Pyrennees, but also tore down temples and idols to build churches and chapels where they had stood.

Like many of these early missionaries, Amandus founded monasteries. He was involved in establishing more than a dozen in the Low Countries alone. These included the nunnery of Nivelles, where the 'new place of sacrifice' was transformed into a centre of Christian prayer and learning under the Frankish noblewoman Gertrude. The near-contemporary *Life of Saint Gertrude* and other writings relating to the saint are vital documents for late seventh-century Frankish history. They are the only sources giving convincing detail about the family relationships and political career of her father, Pepin of Landen, the founder of an aristocratic dynasty later known as the Carolingian. Late in life Begga, Gertrude's widowed sister, founded a monastery at Andenne near Namur, with a colony of nuns from Nivelles. Their brother Grimoald died childless (murdered by a Frisian) and the Pepinide line was continued by Begga's son Pepin of Herstal.

The endowments of noble monasteries made them substantial forces in the economic life of the localities where they were built or owned land, quite apart from the social, intellectual and moral prestige of the members. For hundreds of years, such establishments were to play an important role in every aspect of life in the Low Countries. Two of the most powerful ecclesiastical institutions of medieval Flanders were the abbeys of St Peter and of St Bavo in Ghent, both founded by Amandus. The second of these was dedicated to one of his earliest local associates on the mission, a widowed nobleman who dedicated himself to a life of solitary prayer under Amandus's direction and whose tomb became a place of pilgrimage shortly after his death. Within two or three years of Amandus's own death, the Christian mission spread beyond Austrasia into Frisian and Saxon lands.

The inundations of the fourth century had for a time made Frisia much less hospitable to human habitation. It is not clear what continuity, if any, there was between the Frisians of Roman times and those of the Middle Ages. They left no written records of their own and are mentioned only in foreign sources. The bias of the Frankish perspective which provides most of the written record is indicated by consistent reference to the rulers of the Frisians as 'counts' or 'dukes', where the scantier English sources speak of 'kings'. In the late seventh and early eighth centuries Utrecht was the main residence of the Frisian kings. Concentrations of finds of gold and luxury craftsmanship dating from the fifth to the seventh century seem to indicate that the earlier royal centre was in the very north of the Netherlands, in what is now the vicinity of Franeker. The rise of Utrecht may reflect the growing importance of river trade to Frisian royal wealth. The occasional clash of arms dominates the historical sources, but constant and well-organized trading relations are more typical of the archaeological record. The close economic links between Frisia and Francia made 'Frisian' synonymous with 'trader'.

There is a hint that the Franks may have aided the Frisians against the Danes, in how the death of Hygelac (if the identification is correct) is recounted by Gregory of Tours and in the Anglo-Saxon epic *Beowulf*. Another reference in *Beowulf* shows a moment of strained relations between Frisians and Danes: at the celebrations after Beowulf's slaying of the monster Grendel, the royal bard of the Danes sings of a legendarily disastrous family visit. At the conclusion of a peace treaty the Danish king Hnaef had travelled to visit his sister Hildeburg, wife of Finn, king of the Frisians. Tempers frayed in close proximity to recent enemies, and after a fight in Finn's hall Hildeburg ended up consigning her Frisian son and Danish brother to the same pyre. The following year the Danes returned, killed Finn and carried Hildeburg back to Denmark. The fight at Finn's hall was described in detail in another Old English poem, only a few lines of which survive, the *Finnesburg Fragment*. There is archaeological as well as literary and linguistic evidence for the closeness of Angles and Frisians. Primitive silver coins known as *sceata* circulated in Frisia and England alongside or instead of the coins from Frankish mints. Excavations of a terp at Wijnaldum in the early 1990s turned up amazingly rich finds (mainly now in the Frisian Museum at Leeuwarden) which include a 'royal' brooch stylistically related to jewellery from the Sutton Hoo burial hoard.

The English themselves would not accept Christianity from the Britons, a defeated and despised people, but embraced it when it was brought by Roman missionaries in the wake of Frankish royal brides. Within two generations of the Anglo-Saxon conversions, Northumbrian missionaries set out to preach to the Frisians and Saxons, who had so far rejected Christianity as tainted by its identification with the

Frankish royal house. A central inspiration for the Anglo-Saxon mission was the sharing of the good news of Christ with their not so very distant kin. The first of the English missionaries to the Frisians was the Northumbrian bishop Wilfrid of Hexham. Travelling to Rome to appeal against a decision to split his diocese, Wilfrid landed in Frisia in 678 and stayed the winter. He enjoyed the protection of the king, Aldgisl, and by the time he resumed his journey in the spring of 679 numerous Frisian noblemen and commoners had been baptized. The Anglo-Saxon mission to Frisia thus predates even the mission to Sussex, which Wilfrid initiated in 681.

Aldgisl's successor, Radbod, was a determined pagan, but after his defeat in the Battle of Dorestad (689) he agreed to admit missionaries to his kingdom. A century later it was recounted of Radbod that he had himself agreed to accept baptism. It was to be administered by the Frankish missionary Wulfram, who had already impressed the king with his interventions for the intended victims of human sacrifice. On one occasion, when a man was hanged for the gods, Wulfram prayed for him and after two hours the rope snapped and the man was found to be still alive. Another time Wulfram braved the elements to cut loose two boys who had been tied to stakes at low water to appease the anger of the sea. At the moment of Radbod's intended baptism, the king with one foot already in the font, Wulfram congratulated him on escaping the eternal damnation reserved for all idolaters. The king removed his foot and stated that he would rather follow his ancestors to Hell than gain Heaven without them.

The title 'Apostle of the Frisians' goes to the Northumbrian missionary Willibrord, a monk of Wilfrid's monastery at Ripon. He arrived in Frisia in 690. He worked under the protection of the Austrasian mayors of the palace, the 'Pepinides', whose effective power eclipsed that of the Merovingian kings they were eventually to replace. In 689 Willibrord received the land for a monastic foundation at Echternach from Pepin of Herstal's mother-in-law, and further endowments followed from other members of the family. It was he who baptized Pepin the Short, Charlemagne's father and the first Carolingian king of the Franks. Willibrord's main base of operations was Utrecht and he seems to have had considerable success among the Frisians living in the vicinity of the rivers, but was unable to penetrate the northern parts of the kingdom. When Pepin of Herstal died in 714, Radbod again tried to throw off Frankish overlordship, and Willibrord retreated to Echternach until Radbod's death in 719. Then he renewed his forward policy, installing an Irish companion at the head of a monastery at Antwerp, in the front line of the mission.

A contemporary of Willibrord's probably from Wessex in the west-country of England was Winfrid, who was given the Roman name Bonifatius by the pope who ordained him bishop. Boniface was a bishop among the Thuringians of central Germany. He established the beginnings of an organized Church in Germany, undertook reforms of the aristocratic Frankish Church to increase papal control, and after Willibrord's death was entrusted with the church of Utrecht and the mission to the Frisians. It was he who anointed Pepin the Short as king of the Franks in 751. In 754, while trying to bring the Gospel to northern Frisia, Boniface and his companions met their deaths in the wilds. They were attacked by a war party which mistook their chests of books for more earthly treasure. The battered Gospel book which Boniface held over his head to ward off the blows is still preserved in the minster treasury of Fulda, where his body was eventually taken for burial. A mound was thrown up on the place of his martyrdom, and the site eventually became the town of Dokkum. The curing of a child's persistent cough in 1990 has reinvigorated Dokkum as a centre of pilgrimage, with other healings reported since.

The Frisians themselves were as quick to evangelize among related peoples as the English had been. By the late eighth century Frisia was within the frontiers of Christendom, and was the staging post for the missions to Danes and Saxons. Ludger was one such missionary to the Saxons. Two of his great-uncles had been among the first Frisians to be ordained as priests. He began his education in Utrecht under Gregory of Utrecht, one of Boniface's Frankish disciples and his successor as administrator of the see. Under Gregory's direction the school in Utrecht had become a centre of learning, attracting students from far afield. Ludger completed his studies in York under Alcuin, who later brought the Northumbrian traditions of monastic learning to the court of Charlemagne. Ludger's Latin account of Gregory's life is the oldest substantial piece of writing known to have been produced by a Dutchman. It contains severe criticism of the reluctance of Frankish bishops – in contrast to their kings – to support the northern missions.

After Gregory's death in 777 the new bishop, Alberic, sent Ludger to Deventer to take charge of a church which had been founded there by a recently deceased Englishman. Among Ludger's converts was the Frisian bard Bernlef, who sang the deeds of ancient kings, and after baptism exchanged his traditional repertoire for the Psalms of David.

Ludger's preaching beyond the IJssel took him into Saxon lands, and he eventually became the first bishop of Münster in Westphalia. In 782 the Saxons revolted against Charlemagne's rule. The Christian missionaries, identified with Frankish power, were foremost among the targets of Saxon resentment. During these disturbances Ludger travelled to Italy. He visited Rome, as many of his missionary predecessors had done, and studied at Monte Cassino, eventually returning to his Saxon flock after Charlemagne reimposed order in 785.

Scores more – Irishmen, Englishmen, Franks and Frisians – have been remembered as saints of the early medieval Low Countries, often only in the locality where they preached and prayed or where they were buried. The men and women reverenced as saints, and their often far from saintly royal backers, together brought about a cultural synthesis which lies at the basis of all subsequent social developments. Often by force, they ended the practice of sacrifice, including human sacrifice, in the pools and groves of the Low Countries, and replaced it with the Mass, a re-enactment of Christ's unique sacrifice on the Cross. All the arts became concentrated on the Mass and on the singing of the Psalms: architecture in the building of churches, painting and carving in their decoration and furnishing, music in the chanting of the services, calligraphy and illumination in the copying and embellishment of service books, and the arts of goldsmiths and jewellers in the making of processional crosses, candlesticks, chalices and many other liturgical objects.

Not only the arts were greatly changed by the acceptance, or imposition, of Christianity. Ordinary Christian life entailed a new ordering of priorities. One of the most important changes, commented on by Scandinavian visitors to the Low Countries, was regular poor relief organized through monasteries or associations of pious ladies. A dole of alms is represented among the images in the famous Utrecht Psalter, produced around the year 800. Gift-giving was already an important element in the social, political and economic life of the Germanic peoples, and arguably the main source of royal authority. This giving of gifts was, however, always intended to bind the recipient to the giver. Nobody would ever give a gift without recalling or expecting some reciprocal benefit, and this did not change with the coming of Christianity. What did change was the perception of what the poor could offer. Dhuoda, a ninth-century noblewoman from southern Francia, wrote in a book of advice to her teenaged son William: 'If you should meet a penniless pauper, help him not only with words, but also with deeds . . . . Do not, son, forget to have compassion on the poor, for as the Psalmist says, God frequently hears their voices.'

THE EMPIRE OF THE WEST RENEWED, 800–1018

One of the most large-scale medieval renovations of Roman life was the reinstitution of the Western Empire as the Holy Roman Empire, first under the Frankish Charlemagne, and later under the Saxon Otto. In each case, the pope crowned the emperor in Rome, but the emperor claimed supreme authority over the whole Christian people, bishops and pope included. As Charlemagne put it in a letter to Pope Leo III: 'Your task, most holy father, is to lift up your hands to God, like Moses, so as to aid our troops.' Although in practice imperial power was often very limited, the Holy Roman Empire lasted for almost 1000 years, up to the French Revolution. Until then considerable parts of the Low Countries were subject to it, albeit often only in name.

The Frankish custom of dividing an inheritance among all the heirs meant that their kingdom was in constant flux, reunited and redivided according to variations in royal fertility and survival. Nor does family affection appear to have done much to prevent the in-fighting kings and queens of the Franks from speeding their rivals to childless deaths. Members of the nobility who were felt to be a threat were no safer, and nor were bishops and hermits who got in the way. One of the many attractions of monastic life for the Frankish elite must have been its relative insulation from the literally cut-throat world of the court. Two or three saintly nuns were repentant murderous queens.

Out of the tangled feuds of the Merovingian kings the victor to emerge was Pepin the Short, mayor of the palace. The Low Countries provided the basis for Pepin's triumph, but did not become the centre of politics. Once crowned, Pepin was no keener to rule from his original powerbase than Clovis had been two centuries before. Nevertheless, his estate at Herstal (near Liège) did become one of the many royal residences and it was not unusual for his heir, Charlemagne, to spend Christmas or Easter there. Charlemagne established unified rule over most of what is now France, the Benelux, Germany, Switzerland, Austria and northern Italy. On Christmas Day in the year 800 Pope Leo III crowned him emperor in Rome, restoring the Western Roman Empire. Charlemagne's palace of choice was at Aachen, a few miles from the point where the Belgian, Dutch and German borders meet, and the city of Liège has claimed to be his birthplace.

Charlemagne was survived by only one son, Louis I (814–40), to whom his empire passed entire. But in 843, after three years of civil war, the kingdom of the Franks was divided between his three grandchildren. Charles 'the Bald' became king of the West Franks, ruling western, central and northern France, including the Low Countries west of the Scheldt; Louis 'the German' was king of the East Franks, ruling most of western Germany; the eldest son, Lothar, got the imperial title and the Middle Kingdom, which included most of the Low Countries and stretched from the North Sea to central Italy so as to include the imperial cities of Aachen, Trier, Milan and Rome.

The Middle Kingdom was in turn divided between Lothar's three sons in 855, the eldest getting northern Italy, the youngest Provence, and the middle child, Lothar II, getting the northern areas. Part of this territory, Burgundy, went to France after Lothar II died childless in 869. The rest became a duchy of the East Frankish kingdom (Germany) under the name 'Lotharingia'. In 959 the duchy of Lotharingia was subdivided into Upper Lotharingia (Lorraine) and Lower Lotharingia (the Low Countries east of the Scheldt). This was the least well-integrated part of East Francia. The historic links with Roman and Frankish Gaul, which still played a part in patterns of land-holding and possibilities of inheritance, meant that the family connections of the Lotharingian nobility and the traditions of their churches tended to draw them westwards. Although it was short-lived as an independent kingdom, the existence of Lotharingia gave some later rulers in the Low Countries a semi-fictional dynastic identity as descendants of Lothar, 'true' Carolingians rightfully distinct from both the Ottonians who came to rule Germany and the Capetians who came to rule France.

The Fury of the Norsemen

Scandinavians were a familiar sight in the eighth-century Low Countries. Links were so strong that in 829 the bishop of Hamburg established a school at Torhout in Flanders to train priests for the Scandinavian missions. The great merchant town, or *vicus*, of Dorestad (now Wijk-bij-Duurstede) was the main point of contact between the maritime trade of England and Scandinavia, and the river trade of the Rhine and Maas. Dorestad, perhaps more than any other early medieval town, shows the flourishing trade between all the kingdoms around the North Sea. The goods traded could even include Chinese silks and Russian furs brought from Kiev by Scandinavians. This booming economy went through some sort of crisis in the second half of the eighth century, and those who had been traders looked for alternative ways to maintain their lifestyles. In the 790s Scandinavian seafarers began raiding the isolated monasteries of the northern British Isles, and soon extended the practice to other coastal areas on a larger scale. During the reign of Charlemagne the military reputation of the Franks discouraged large-scale raids into their realm, but in 810, four years after his death, came the first major attack on Frisia, with 200 ships. In following years raids got more daring. With a largely agrarian population weakened by cycles of crop-failure and disease, it was difficult to resist the power of Viking armies fed on a high-protein diet of herrings. Dorestad was plundered three times in the years 834–36 and what had been a bustling international marketplace was left desolate.

In the 860s and 870s, their numbers swollen by desperate men from the regions they had devastated, the Vikings embarked on wars of conquest. In 878 the Danelaw was established across central and eastern Britain. Norsemen were granted control of half of England in return for accepting baptism and keeping new raiders at bay, while the kings of Wessex ruled the remainder. Lothar I had tried the same accommodating tactic in the Middle Kingdom soon after coming to power in the 840s, granting the Danish adventurers Harald and Roric control of the Rhine delta and what is now the coast of Holland. After Roric's death the experiment was not repeated immediately, but the issue of Viking settlement was to come up again.

Viking incursions set the scene for the emergence of Flanders as a powerful county. In 861, while still a royal officer in the lands immediately to the west of the Scheldt, Baldwin 'Iron Arm' eloped with Charles the Bald's teenaged daughter Judith. She was already twice the widow of kings of Wessex, and step-mother of Alfred the Great. Once the furore had died down and the wedding was properly solemnized, King Charles established Baldwin as count of the coastal defences west of the Scheldt. He is traditionally regarded as the first count of Flanders. Baldwin and Judith's son and heir, Baldwin the Bald, married Alfred the Great's daughter Elftrude. The marriage alliances of the kings of Wessex, the kings of France and the counts of Flanders cemented their co-ordinated resistance to the Vikings.

The major raids of the Vikings often came shortly after the deaths of local rulers, an indication of their effective intelligence-gathering. When Baldwin I died in 879, the Vikings sailed up the Scheldt to Ghent, wintered there, and laid waste much of Flanders. In 881 they were defeated by the West Frankish king in a battle on the Somme, but not badly enough to prevent them from moving their operations east of the Scheldt. They wintered near Nijmegen and Roermond, and sacked several towns in the valleys of the Maas and the Rhine. In 882 they made it as far as the walls of Trier but the archbishop directed a successful defence. This enabled the newly crowned East Frankish king, Charles the Fat, to gather an army and besiege the main Viking camp at Asselt. There an agreement was reached whereby the lands once held by Harald and Roric were granted to the leader of the Viking army, Godfrey 'Sea-King'. Godfrey accepted baptism and was married to Gisela, an illegitimate daughter of Lothar II. Although Lotharingia was now part of Germany, Godfrey began to lay claim to the inheritance of Lothar II in his wife's right. In 885 a meeting was arranged at Lobith to discuss the matter and there Godfrey was killed by Gerulf, Count of Frisia. Gisela's brother Hugo, who had allied himself to Godfrey, was blinded but was allowed to live out the remainder of his days in a monastery. The widowed Gisela herself became abbess of Nivelles. The lands which Godfrey had briefly ruled were turned over to Gerulf, and in time they passed to his younger son Dirk (Diederik, Theoderic). Around the year 1100 this territory came to be called Holland, and it will be referred to as such (somewhat anachronistically) from this point onwards. Before 1100 it was known as the county of West Frisia, but there were plenty of West Frisians who did not accept the rule of the counts.

The murder of Godfrey Sea-King put a stop to Viking settlement in the Rhine delta, but not to Viking raids. In 891 another invasion of Lotharingia was launched. Charles the Fat had now been succeeded as king of the East Franks by Arnulf. Arnulf's illegitimate son Zwentibold, who died in 900, was duke (from 895 styled 'king') of Lotharingia. After an initial military setback, Arnulf brought the Vikings to battle on the river Dijle, near Leuven, and resoundingly defeated their army. There were still occasional incursions thereafter, such as that of King Gorm of Denmark into Frisia in 934, but they were without lasting impact. In the century after 891 the military organization of the counties of Flanders and Holland, and of the area which was eventually to become the duchy of Brabant, put an end to Scandinavian ambitions along the Rhine, Maas and Scheldt. Trade began to recover. The Old Rhine was now silting up, but Tiel, on the more navigable Waal, replaced Dorestad as the main marketplace of the Low Countries.

The Arrows of the Hungarians

The last Frankish king of Germany, Conrad I, was succeeded by Henry, Duke of Saxony, in 918. Henry was presented with the regalia and elected king by the 'whole people' of the Franks and Saxons of the East Frankish Kingdom. The ancient Germanic institution of elective monarchy, mentioned by Tacitus, henceforth replaced descent from Charlemagne as the source of legitimacy. At Henry's death his son Otto was elected to succeed him. After an uprising in Lotharingia Otto appointed Conrad the Red, an outsider, as duke, with a brief to combat West Frankish political influence and see that imperial decrees were followed in the duchy. Although Conrad had a high reputation as a military leader, the appointment was not a success. In 953 he too rose in revolt against Otto. Never popular in the duchy, he was driven from Lotharingia by the native nobility but returned the next year with a Hungarian army. The Hungarians had been raiding deep into Germany for decades, but they had never before made an appearance in the Low Countries. With the exiled Conrad the Red as an ally and guide, they traversed Lotharingia as far as Cambrai, on the very borders of France, plundering as they went. Conrad himself lost his life in the campaign and it is not at all clear what he hoped to achieve.

Otto immediately appointed his own younger brother, Bruno, as the new Duke of Lotharingia. This was a natural choice in so far as he was an able and reliable relative, but unusual because Bruno was a clergyman. He had been destined for the church at an early age, and educated in Lotharingia by Baldric, Bishop of Utrecht. After serving as Otto's chancellor and private secretary, Bruno became both archbishop of Cologne and duke of Lotharingia, combining the highest ecclesiastical and secular authority in the region. He was active, according to his admiring biographer Ruotger, 'not only in study and discussion, but also in the line of battle'. Not everybody was uncritical of a bishop being a duke but Ruotger insisted that Bruno's warlike proceedings were entirely justified by the peace and security which his Lotharingian subjects enjoyed as a result. This generally meant imposing order on feuding or predatory lords, but it could also mean taking an independent line from royal policy. In 955 Otto summoned an army from all parts of his kingdom and broke the Hungarian threat with a victory on the River Lech on the border with Bavaria, but the Lotharingians took no part in the battle. Bruno had detained their contingent at Cologne, for the defence of Lotharingia should his brother fail.

The Ottonian System

In 962, after a series of successful campaigns against the Hungarians and against the pope's political opponents in Italy, Otto was crowned emperor in Rome. As emperor he favoured the development of 'imperial churches', granting land and jurisdiction to minsters and abbeys. Since ecclesiastical offices could not become hereditary, and the emperor appointed the prelates, a body of educated and dedicated local power-holders could be put in place whose first loyalty was to the emperor as the head of Christian society. Bruno became the archetype of a new sort of bishop. A later bishop in the same mould as Bruno was Egbert of Trier, one of the greatest churchmen of the late tenth century. During his time as its archbishop (977–93) Trier began to be called 'Roma Secunda'. Egbert's father was Count Dirk II of Holland; his mother, Hildegard, was the daughter of Count Arnulf I of Flanders. Egbert was a famous patron of learning and the arts. Among the works he had compiled was a new *Life of St Adalbert* which is the most important narrative source for the early history of Holland: the monastery at Egmond where Adalbert's relics were housed had been founded by Dirk I in 922 and was the burial place of the counts.

The two great centres of the Ottonian System within the Benelux area were the bishoprics of Utrecht and Liège, both in the archdiocese of Cologne. The see of Maastricht (originally Tongeren) had been moved to Liège by St Hubert in 717. Hubert's immediate predecessor, Lambert, had been a forthright pastor who intervened in aristocratic feuds and denounced the adulteries of Pepin of Herstal. Having spent years in exile from his see, during which time he preached to pagans in the valley of the Meuse, Lambert was finally murdered near Liège in circumstances which never became clear. Hubert, having been converted from a life of courtly frivolity (according to later legend, after a vision of the Cross while stag-hunting on Good Friday), was determined to widen the distance between his see and the court, especially after 714 when Pepin of Herstal's son Grimoald was murdered in his cathedral. He moved Lambert's tomb to Liège, close to the site of his murder, as the focal point of a new cathedral there. Two hundred and fifty years later, under the Ottonian emperors, the bishops of Liège became lords temporal in their own right. The founder of this power was Ansfrid, count of Huy, who after his son's death gave his lands to the bishop of Liège and retired to a hermitage. The emperor confirmed the gift, and hauled

Ansfrid out of retirement to implement imperial policy as bishop of Utrecht. Eventually the territory ruled by the bishops became known as the Prince-Bishopric of Liège. It was only united to the rest of what is now Belgium by French annexation in 1794. The bishops of Utrecht similarly became great temporal lords, at roughly the same time. The bishops actively espoused the imperial cause, and later emperors added to the territorial power of their churches, but they were not always able to master the counts.

Although they delegated day-to-day rule to dukes and bishops, the emperors did sometimes take a personal interest in Lower Lotharingia. Perhaps once in a decade, or more frequently if affairs required their presence, the emperors would celebrate Easter at Utrecht or hold court in the old palaces at Maastricht and Nijmegen. In 1018, when Henry II was holding court at Nijmegen, Bishop Adelbold of Utrecht and the merchants of Tiel appealed to him to give them justice against Dirk III of Holland. Dirk was a nephew of both Egbert of Trier and the Empress Cunegunde. He had built a castle in the Rhine estuary to levy tolls in his own name. This was a clear infringement of the imperial regalia and an oppression of the bishop's subjects, particularly the merchants. Henry despatched an army under the duke of Lotharingia and Bishop Adelbold, including contingents raised by the bishops of Liège and Cambrai. After a first defeat the army regrouped for a second attempt. According to the Ottonian chronicler Thietmar of Merseburg this was on an island in the peat bogs, thought to be safe, where they were ambushed by the Frisians. The imperial army was all but wiped out, those not dying by the sword drowning in the rout. A peaceful settlement was mediated by Walbodo, Dean of Utrecht, who later became bishop of Liège. The losses incurred by the forces of the bishops meant that Dirk would now have to be relied upon to guarantee the security of the coast. Thietmar's characteristically gloomy assessment was that crimes could no longer be punished.

In the mid-eleventh century, Bishop Bernold of Utrecht led Emperor Conrad II's more successful campaign against Dirk IV of Holland, who had invaded the bishop's territory. In recognition of his many services and capable rule, Conrad granted Bernold a collection of lands east of the IJssel, at some distance from the core territory of his lordship and administered from Deventer. Counts and dukes increasingly ignored the emperor's overlordship, but the imperial bishops were a brake on the fragmentation of the Empire.

FEUDALISM

Feudalism is a word which is sometimes used of almost any formalized relationship of dependence or subjection. Were it not a useful technical term, it would be better to do without it altogether. Strictly speaking, feudalism had two elements. The first was that one free man (the vassal) gave his personal service to another free man (the lord) in return for maintenance and protection. This was a practice dating back to the late Roman Empire, and in Merovingian times it was called commendation. The second element, which only became associated with commendation in Carolingian times and is the distinctive mark of feudalism, was that the lord should fulfil his duty to maintain his vassal by granting him a benefice or fief, preferably in the form of landed estates. By the tenth century feudalism was the dominant form of social organization. The reciprocal obligations of protection and service, which later centuries saw as inherent in the relationship of crown and subject or nation and citizen, were privatized on a massive scale. This was not the cause of political fragmentation, but a way of dealing with it. By the eleventh century even kings expected their great subjects to be bound not so much by their duty to the crown as by their fealty as vassals.

Although the legal heart of the system was a man-to-man exchange of vows, in principle entered into freely, there were generally good reasons for renewing the agreement with the vassal's son when the vassal died. In this way the obligations of lord and vassal virtually became hereditary. Lords did however charge a fee, called a 'relief', when taking the homage of a deceased vassal's son, as a constant reminder that this was a favour rather than a right. Feudalism was thus a historically unique amalgam of contractual, status and kinship relations. Northern France, the Low Countries and post-Conquest England were the areas in which strictly feudal relationships reached their fullest form and greatest extent.*

Under the Frankish kings counts were the local representatives of royal authority, and in many ways bishops were too, although not yet to the extent that Otto made them. Dukes were another German addition, the organizers of regional defences and the commanders of royal armies. As the power of kings was curtailed, counts, dukes and eventually bishops

---

* The classic historical introduction to feudal obligations and ceremonies, drawing many examples from the Low Countries, is by the Belgian medievalist F.L. Ganshof. The third English edition of his *Feudalism* (first published in French in 1944) has recently been reissued by Toronto University Press.

became rulers in their own right. They raised armies in their own name, built castles, levied tolls and taxes, granted immunities, took abbeys and collegiate churches under their protection, minted coins, and exploited the mineral, forest and water resources which since Roman times had been considered a state monopoly. They were the holders of delegated royal authority and they were feudal lords granting land in return for service from lesser lords and mounted warriors. From the tenth and eleventh centuries onwards the Benelux area was dominated by these great lords, whose territories were the 'counties' which made up the Low Countries. One royal power the counts and dukes of the Low Countries never acquired was the nomination of bishops. None of them quite had an episcopal see within his dominions. The bishops of Liège, Utrecht, Cambrai and Tournai were all politically independent, while the bishop of Thérouanne resided in France, outside his see. The archbishops over them sat in Rheims and Cologne. The secular authority of the bishops extended over substantial areas. Their ecclesiastical jurisdiction was even wider. The distinction between the two was observed precisely by their subjects and their neighbours, but the bishops themselves sometimes crossed the line.

The personal, contractual relationship of vassal and lord had become increasingly widespread in Carolingian times. Typically, the service expected in return for maintenance was military. The need of Frankish kings to respond over long distances to incursions by Saxons, Frisians and Saracens, and later Vikings and Hungarians, required highly mobile mounted armies under the command of local representatives of royal power. These armies were very small, but made up of men whose lives were dedicated to honing their battle skills. A soldier needed horse, lance, shield and sword to be effective, and would bind himself in life-long service to the lord who would maintain the expense, or better yet who would grant him the land to do so.

By the end of the tenth century the debilitating cycles of famine and disease had ended, and agriculture continued to expand in the eleventh century. This was partly due to improving weather conditions, partly through projects of land clearance. Other important factors were the improvement of agricultural techniques, most importantly the three-year rotation of crops, and the wider dissemination of productivity-boosting technologies, such as the heavy plough, windmills and watermills, wheelbarrows, and the horse collar. This was true of much of Europe, but it was particularly important in the increasingly densely populated Low Countries. Those who worked the land were peasants. Slavery, the main source of labour from Roman times into the early Carolingian era, had all but disappeared and agricultural labourers were now either free peasants or serfs tied to a particular estate. Free peasants did not work entirely for themselves. They too entered into contractual relationships of service and protection, for instance working a lord's land two or three days a week in return for tenure on a piece of land for themselves. Successful enterprise did not go unrewarded at any social level: from the eleventh century onwards, peasant colonists could obtain tenures relatively free of such duties by taking part in projects of drainage and forest clearance. Even serfs could serve as warriors, and so partake in the rising esteem in which knighthood was held. In Lotharingia the servile descent of such knights was marked by them being called 'ministerials', but in Flanders the social distinction was more blurred.

Feudal relationships were only the dominant form of social organization from the tenth century to the thirteenth, but they remained strong even thereafter and have had long-lasting effects in the Low Countries. Outside the modern conurbations (themselves almost always spreading around a medieval city centre), the broad outlines of the landscape still reflect patterns of land use and settlement which developed in the feudal age. Communities of scattered farmsteads tended to become nucleated villages clustered around a parish church wherever a lord established a castle or fortified manor house. In much of the Low Countries lords of the manor retained legal dominance of community life until the French invasions of the 1790s, and their considerable social influence and commitment to serving as local leaders lasted far longer.

THE ELEVENTH-CENTURY REFORM, 1018–1122

The eleventh century saw profound changes in almost every aspect of life. So far as the idea of Christendom was concerned, these changes included a new sense of the dignity of the priesthood, a new emphasis on peace and poverty, and a desire to set clear limits to the powers of laymen in the affairs of the Church.

One of the most remarkable movements in European history was that to establish the 'Peace and Truce of God'. This called for an end to wars of aggression, feuds, banditry, the despoiling of churches, the oppression of the poor, the burning of crops and other crimes of violence. In the course of the period 1024–43 councils decreed the Peace of God in the dioceses of Cambrai, Tournai and Thérouanne. This was apparently at the instigation of the counts of Flanders: none of the bishops resided in the county, but the peace councils were each held in a part of the diocese that lay within it. The counts and dukes of the Low Countries, busy extending their powers, had good reason to support the movement. Opposition to feuds and banditry helped establish their own authority, while opposition to war discouraged their royal superiors from taking up arms to bring them to heel. Monks promoting the peace might, with a fine sense of the dramatic inspired by their liturgical expertise, interpose the relics of saints between factions at daggers drawn. Those with reputations for holiness tried, not always without success, to mediate peaceful settlements. In a few notable cases battles were avoided and feuds ended. In the longer term, an important element in the chivalric ideal, emerging in these years, was that the only legitimate use of force was to defend the innocent (stereotypically widows, orphans, wayfarers and the clergy) from oppression by tyrants, outlaws and infidels. Mounted warriors still had an eye for the main chance, but there was generally a higher idea of their social role, and higher expectations of their conduct. One knight who stole a peasant woman's two cows was boiled alive in armour in a great kettle to demonstrate just how seriously Baldwin VII of Flanders (1111–19) took his duty to protect the powerless.

Besides peace, the eleventh century saw a great demand for poverty. Famines were less frequent, foreign enemies less threatening, and wealth was accumulating in castles and monasteries. Those wanting to dedicate themselves to prayer might become not monks but hermits. In imitation of the hermits of ancient Syria and Egypt this usually meant finding a desert in which to live in solitude or in small like-minded groups. In the Low Countries the 'desert' could be scrubland, woodland, a river island or a marshy valley. Hermitages sprang up all over the countryside. One hermit among many was a knight called Gerlach who had made a pilgrimage to Jerusalem and spent his final years living in a hollow tree in Houtem, now in Belgian Limburg. The eremitical movement also included wandering preachers, who lived outside settled society in a rather different way.

Secular (non-monastic) clergymen who wanted lives of prayer in community had since Carolingian times been able to organize themselves as chapters of canons serving a collegiate church, praying as a community but living independently and keeping their own incomes. There were seven such churches in Liège alone, besides the cathedral itself. Under the impulse of the eleventh-century ideal of poverty, many of these canons 'secular' became canons 'regular': they not only prayed together, but lived under a common rule and shared their goods. St Augustine, who had once been so impressed by a description of the monks of Trier, had drawn up an outline rule for religious communities and this generally served as the rule for canons regular. In the county of Flanders 21 chapters of canons secular became regular between 1070 and 1155. In addition to these, 12 new regular chapters were founded, six of which grew out of communities of hermits. This regularization of hermit communities was not uncommon, and like monasteries, collegiate churches could become powerful centres of scholarly, economic and artistic life. Monasticism was itself still an option: the Benedictine monastery of Affligem, which in future centuries was to be one of the most influential institutions in Brabant, was originally founded as a hermitage by six laymen inspired by a wandering preacher.

One result of the more elevated view of priestly dignity was that even parish priests were required to practise celibacy, setting them apart from all worldly connections. Another new emphasis on the other-worldliness of the priestly state was an attack on simony, insisting that spiritual benefits (such as ordination) could not be bought and sold. Both were long-standing ideals which had never before been rigorously enforced. This heightened sense of the distinctiveness of the priesthood was soon to lead to a momentous breach between the pope and the emperor.

The imperial appointment of bishops now came to be seen as undue interference in priestly affairs. As supreme rulers of a Christian society the Ottonians had never distinguished clearly between State and Church. Pope Gregory VII did make the distinction, so in 1076 Henry IV (emperor 1054–1106) had the imperial bishops declare the pope deposed. Gregory in turn excommunicated Henry, who at Canossa had to recognize on his knees that the pope was the earthly head of the Church. But this was only one particularly striking episode in a much longer struggle. The conflict came to focus on the investiture of bishops, when they received a staff and a ring to symbolize their authority. The reformers insisted that even if rulers continued to play a role in choosing bishops, the symbols of their authority could only be conveyed by priestly power after their ordination, not by royal command beforehand. The kings of France and England gave in after a short struggle, but the emperor still insisted that he, as the head of Christendom, should invest the imperial bishops.

The bishopric of Liège was one of the fiercest battlegrounds of the controversy. Lotharingia was at that time renowned for its schools and those of Liège were among the best of them. Mathematics and music were the great strengths, but important Latin works of history, poetry and canon law also came from the schools of the various churches and monasteries in and around the city. At mid-century, particularly under Bishop Wazo (1042–48), intellectual opinion in Liège was firmly set against imperial interference. Wazo had a very clear idea of the separation of powers. When a fellow bishop asked his advice about the punishment of heretics he wrote back that, 'The bishop does not receive a sword at his consecration.' In 1046–47 he even refused to raise a contingent for the emperor's campaign against Dirk III of Holland. Two influential writers from Wazo's Liège, the chronicler Anselm of Liège and the anonymous author of a treatise on priestly offices, show nothing but disdain for imperial claims.

The situation had changed entirely by the end of the century, when the bishopric was divided by schism and excommunications. Bishop Otbert (1091–1119) was an imperial appointment and tried to impose the imperial way of thinking on his diocese. He encouraged the writing of polemical treatises against papal claims about investiture and priestly marriage. When the pope called a council at Rheims, Otbert attended but when the matter of simony was brought up he walked out. He had paid the emperor a hefty fee for his own appointment and saw nothing wrong with the practice as long as it was clear that ordination itself was not for sale. In 1105 Henry IV's son led a rebellion and imprisoned his father, but the emperor escaped and fled to Bishop Otbert as his last support. Liège was where he made his last stand against papal claims and against his son's rebellion, at the head of an army raised by the bishop. It was there, in 1106, that he died. The Investiture Conflict continued under Henry V (1106–25), but German bishops were ever more inclined to give ear to papal claims. When Henry V was excommunicated in 1115, Otbert was one of the last imperial bishops to stand by him, and he continued to do so until his own death in 1119. In 1122 the conflict was ended in the pope's favour by the Concordat of Worms. With their powers over the Church curtailed, the emperors lost perhaps the most important remaining element in their control of the Low Countries.

THE FIRST CRUSADE, 1095–1099

Religious experience is now often considered a peculiarly inner thing, but in the early Middle Ages one of the highest expressions of devotion imaginable was an arduous and uncomfortable journey to the Holy

Land. Rome might be the earthly head of the Church, but its heart was in Jerusalem. When the Holy City had fallen to Arab invaders in 638 a *modus vivendi* had been found which preserved Christian pilgrimage. The conversion of the Hungarians around the year 1000 allowed the reopening of the land routes from Western Europe to Constantinople, and pilgrims began making the journey to Jerusalem in unprecedented numbers. Many still went by sea, from Sicily. Two of the most popular saints of the Low Countries of this period were Guido of Anderlecht and Poppo of Stavelot. Both came from poor backgrounds, but both made the pilgrimage to Jerusalem, Guido more than once. Eventually Guido became a hermit and Poppo a monk, even an abbot, but at the time of their travels they were laymen. Their claim to spiritual authority lay precisely in their status as returned pilgrims.

The increasingly popular pilgrimage came under threat after 1076, when the Seljuk Turks conquered Jerusalem. The Byzantine emperor appealed to the West for military aid against the Seljuks and Pope Urban II passed on the Byzantine appeal in 1095, decreeing that joining the campaign for the security of the pilgrimage to Jerusalem was sufficient to replace any and all punishment due under canon law. The following year four armies set off, one from southern France, one from Norman-ruled southern Italy, one from northern France and one from the Western Empire. The Low Countries contributed greatly to two of these armies, both in leadership and in manpower. Robert II of Flanders was one of the commanders of the northern-French contingent, and in the course of the campaign the horde of poor Flemish footsoldiers gained much notice for their ferocity. The German contingent was mainly a Lotharingian affair, and was commanded jointly by Godfrey of Bouillon, Duke of Lower Lotharingia, and his brother Baldwin. Otbert, Bishop of Liège, financed Godfrey's army, taking the lordship of Bouillon as security for the loan. Although most crusaders were setting off into the unknown, their leaders must have had some idea of their destination. The lie of the land in Palestine could be gauged from the reports of earlier pilgrims, such as Robert II's father, Robert the Frisian, or Bishop Lietbert of Liège.

In Northern Europe the most striking promoter of the crusade was Peter the Hermit. He came out of seclusion near Liège for a rabble-rousing preaching tour, and made it all the way to Jerusalem at the head of a rapidly dwindling peasant contingent. His charismatic influence was such that in Constantinople he was mistakenly thought to have inspired the whole venture. When the crusaders took Jerusalem in 1099, Godfrey of Bouillon was proclaimed Guardian of the Holy Sepulchre. After his death, in 1100, his brother Baldwin became King of Jerusalem. Another Baldwin, the count of Hainaut, took part in the First Crusade but died before reaching Jerusalem.

The social, political, religious and economic changes of the eleventh century coalesced to make the remarkable phenomenon of the crusade possible. Perhaps most significantly, Aquitanians, Normans, Flemings and Lotharingians were marching beyond the frontiers of Christendom not behind the banners of their kings, but under their own command and at the behest of the pope. At the highpoint of the feudal period a much wider international dimension was suddenly added to the world in which the rulers of the Low Countries moved.

The military orders of the Temple and of the Hospital of St John, founded to protect pilgrims in the Holy Land, established priories for recruitment and fund-raising in the Low Countries. So too did the Teutonic Order, founded to spearhead the German 'crusade' against the pagan peoples of the Baltic coast. As a result of the crusades, thousands of more modest individuals from the Low Countries – knights, simple soldiers or peaceful pilgrims – travelled to Palestine or died along the way. In 1270 alone a large Frisian contingent went to fight in North Africa alongside Louis IX of France. When Louis died and the French went home, the Frisians instead joined England's Prince Edward in the Holy Land.

Frankish noblemen ruled semi-feudal kingdoms and principalities in the Levant – in Jerusalem for almost 100 years, until it fell to Saladin in 1187, and for almost 200 in Antioch, Tripoli and Acre. After the loss of Acre in 1291, the hope of one day re-establishing these Christian kingdoms continued to dominate the ideals of Western knighthood to the end of the Middle Ages. Even thereafter, the concept of a Christian Holy War, born in 1095, continued to inspire the response to the Ottoman Turkish advances of the fifteenth and sixteenth centuries, and fed into the religious wars of Christendom in the sixteenth and seventeenth centuries. To later generations, Godfrey of Bouillon was one of the greatest exemplars of chivalry, one of the 'Heroes of Christendom' alongside King Arthur and Charlemagne.

2

Patterns of Power and Piety, 1100–1384

As the poverty and chaos of the tenth century gave way to increasing wealth and security, trade expanded and towns grew. A new type of urban life developed which was more concentrated in the Low Countries than anywhere else north of the Alps. This period saw the rise of the counts, dukes and bishops of the Low Countries to the height of their power as independent rulers of separate principalities. These small countries began to emerge in the break-up of the Carolingian Empire, and were fully formed by the end of the twelfth century. Although some of these principalities were joined in personal unions, they each retained their own laws, customs, tolls and institutions until the end of the eighteenth century. The main sources of revenue of the territorial princes were feudal dues, judicial fines and tolls on trade. Their power rested on control of farm land, woodland jurisdictional rights, roads and waterways. Seemingly paradoxically, the growth in the power of princes went hand in hand with the towns gaining large measures of internal self-government.

THE COUNTY OF FLANDERS, 1037–1157

The first of the principalities of the Low Countries to take clear shape, in the ninth century, was the county of Flanders. This was one of the most successful feudal principalities, with barons and knights proliferating but the count's administration keeping a tight hold on his rights and revenues. Control was maintained through the workings of the count's feudal court, the systematic organization of the territory into castellanies held directly from the count, and the count's position as 'advocate' or 'guardian' of almost every important church and monastery in Flanders. Around 1100 the count of Flanders could field an army of 1000 knights, comparing very favourably with the count of Hainaut's 700, the king of France's host of 500, or the 300 that the bishop of Liège could raise. In the eleventh and twelfth centuries Flemish counts, lords and knights played a significant role in the affairs of France, England and the Empire, as well as in the Holy Land.

In 888 Baldwin II did homage to the king of France, and from then on the counts of Flanders were vassals, as well as subjects, of the kings of France. Although the king of France was suzerain or feudal overlord of Flanders, he had very little say in how the county was run. For much of the tenth and eleventh centuries, the kings of France directly controlled only a small territory stretching no more than a few dozen miles in any direction from Paris. Most of northern France was ruled by the far more powerful counts of Flanders and dukes of Normandy, whose zones of influence overlapped just north of the Somme. When King Henry I of France died in 1060, Count Baldwin V (1035–67) became guardian of the 8-year-old son and heir, and effective ruler of the kingdom. When William of Normandy and his Flemish wife, Matilda, became king and queen of England in 1066, there seemed little chance that French royal power would ever be more than notional.

Flanders became a power in the Empire when Baldwin V invaded the area between Scheldt and Dender (around Aalst and Dendermonde) in 1047. Despite facing a coalition of the emperor, Edward the Confessor of England and the king of Denmark, he managed to keep a toehold beyond the Scheldt. In 1056, after a failed imperial invasion of Flanders and a failed Flemish counterattack into the marquisate of Antwerp, Baldwin V did homage to the emperor's widow for this patch of territory, 'imperial Flanders'. Henceforth, the counts of Flanders were vassals of the German emperor as well as of the king of France.

After France and the Empire, England was an important element in the political calculations of the Flemish counts. Their role in England's affairs can be dated from 1037, when Baldwin V provided refuge to the exiled Queen Emma, the daughter of a duke of Normandy, widow of both Ethelred the Unready and Canute, and mother of Edward the Confessor. In the 1040s and 1050s Baldwin gave refuge to a number of prominent English exiles. This culminated with his son-in-law Tostig, the disaffected brother of Harold Godwinson, using Flanders as a base in the winter of 1065–66. It was from there that Tostig sailed to combine forces with Harald Hardrada of Norway and meet defeat at Stamford Bridge. Numerous Flemings joined the successful campaign of Baldwin's brother-in-law, William of Normandy, later in 1066. Baldwin himself died in 1067, too soon to pluck the fruits of Flemish involvement in the Conquest, but individual participants were more fortunate. The Domesday Book shows that Flemings were well represented among the landholders of post-Conquest England, and the largest gainer among them, Gilbert of Ghent, became one of the dozen greatest lay landowners in the country.

After Baldwin V's death, the main concern of the counts of Flanders, especially Robert the Frisian (1071–93), was to prevent Normandy from becoming overwhelmingly powerful in northern France. They offered refuge and succour to William's English opponents, and Robert married his daughter Adela to Canute II of Denmark, a dynasty opposed to the Norman. When England and Normandy were ruled separately, from 1087 to 1106, the counts sought alliance with the kings of England. By a secret treaty agreed at Dover in 1101 Robert II of Flanders became a vassal of the king of England in return for a hefty money fief. This arrangement was renewed by several of his successors. There was constant political interaction and intermarriage between the nobility of Flanders and England for almost a century after the Conquest, and Flemings spearheaded the Anglo-Norman colonization of Wales. In the 1130s, while the count of Flanders backed Matilda in the civil war for the English crown, numerous Flemish knights led by his unsuccessful rival for the countship, William of Ypres, fought for Stephen. When Matilda's son, Henry II, came to the throne in 1154, he banished most of the Flemings who were not merchants, bringing the close ties between the nobility of Flanders and England to an end just as the commercial links were blossoming.

When feudalism worked it kept peace and order in the absence of the effective rule of law. The tensions which it contained became evident when this fragile peace failed. One of the most spectacular breakdowns in feudal relationships took place in Flanders in 1127 when Count Charles, the son of Canute II and Adela, was murdered. Charles the Dane (or after his murder 'the Good') was killed as a result of his attempts to impose the rule of law on personal feudal relations. This was not an aim born of idealism for justice. He was trying to bring to heel the Erembalds, the most powerful family of landowners and office-holders in his territory. The family was of servile descent, so Charles decided to humble them by taking legal steps to have them declared his serfs.

The castellan of Bruges, Bertulf, was a member of the Erembald connection, as was Charles's own chamberlain, Isaac. The count refused to be bought off, so in desperation the Erembalds plotted to murder him, and carried out the plan while he was attending Mass in the church of the castle of Bruges.

Charles had no children and no designated successor. His unexpected death, and the manner of it, unleashed a disordered settling of scores and jostling for advantage among all the forces in the county: barons, knights and towns. At the highest level, William of Ypres tried to seize power but was out-manoeuvred by William Clito (a grandson of William the Conqueror). Clito himself ruled for only a year, dying of his wounds after a battle with the ultimate victor, Thierry of Alsace. Galbert, notary of Bruges, recorded the daily detail of the anarchy in one of the most revealing narrative documents of his times, an English translation of which has recently been reissued. Count Thierry ruled Flanders until 1157 and then handed power to his son to become a crusader.

EAST OF THE SCHELDT

Eastwards of Flanders, the Low Countries were a patchwork of principalities and lordships, in what on formal occasions was still sometimes called the duchy of Lotharingia. Here, imperial authority delayed, but ultimately failed to prevent the emergence of territorial rulers who could rival the counts of Flanders in power and independence. By the twelfth century the dozens of counties and scores of lordships had mostly been consolidated under the power of a handful of territorial princes (see Map 3), although a few fiefs, institutions and jurisdictions retained some form of independence, or direct dependence on the emperor, for far longer. By 1200 the main rulers of the Low Countries were the dukes of Brabant and Limburg, the counts (later dukes) of Guelders and Luxembourg, the marquis of Namur, the counts of Flanders, Holland-Zeeland, Loon and Hainaut, and the bishops of Liège and Utrecht. The bishops of Cambrai and Tournai each ruled a small territory immediately around their cathedral city. A final area was Frisia, a case to itself.

Frisia was the northernmost of the 'low countries by the sea', stretching from what is now North Holland all along the North Sea coast to Denmark. In this region there was no overall princely rule. In a manner reminiscent of the Iceland of the sagas, an oligarchy of the wealthier families continued the use of Germanic customary law in the *liudthing*, a regular public meeting of the free menfolk of a district. The village or district headmen, living in tower houses called *stins* and keeping armed retainers, also organized defence against invaders and against the encroaching sea. From the twelfth century there were annual national assemblies of district representatives, meeting under the Upstal Tree on a hill beside a prehistoric burial mound near Aurich (now in Germany). These meetings would settle major disputes or co-ordinate large-scale operations. Feudal customs made little impact on the area, since the Frisians were fishermen, stock breeders and traders, rather than knights and agriculturalists. In the fourteenth century Geoffrey Chaucer referred to Frisia to indicate both untold wealth – 'all the gold in Rome and Frise' (*Romaunt of the Rose*) – and (in 'Lenvoy de Chaucer a Bukton') cruelty to captives:

> Experience shall thee teach, so may hap,
> That thee were liever to be take in Frise
> Than eft to fall of wedding in the trap.

Private warfare was a part of life, largely in the form of blood-feuds carried on by headmen and their retainers. It generally lacked the courtesies and ransoms of chivalric battles. In 1268 a monastic chronicler noted the newsworthy fact that the Fivelgo district (near Groningen) had enjoyed a full 12 years of peace.

In the eleventh century the bishops of Utrecht gained lordship over the city of Groningen and the lands around it (the Ommelanden). The city itself effectively became independent in 1251, but the anomalous status of Groningen and the Ommelanden separated what was to become the Dutch province of Friesland (west of the Lauwer) from German Friesland (east of the Ems).

What had once been known as 'West Frisia' was by 1100 definitely 'Holland'. The heartland of the counts of Holland was the mouth of the Rhine and the coastland immediately to its north. They soon began to expand their territory, eventually dominating the whole of the Rhine/Scheldt delta area, the North Sea coast above it and the west coast of the Zuider Zee. The expansionism of the counts of Holland was not into a political void and did not go unchallenged. Their rivals for control of the Scheldt estuaries were the counts of Flanders, to whom they did homage for Zeeland whenever it became unavoidable. Along the Zuider Zee, the counts faced the established interests of the residually independent West Frisians and of the bishops of Utrecht. Ultimately their expansion brought them into conflict with Guelders.

Holland was to be the dominant province by the end of the Middle Ages, but before then the bishops of Utrecht were the most important rulers north of the Rhine. Their ecclesiastical jurisdiction covered almost all of the Netherlands north of the rivers. As temporal lords their rule was more restricted, but still considerable. Their worldly jurisdiction comprised the Sticht (or Nedersticht), a compact territory around the city of Utrecht, and more extensive possessions over the IJssel – the Oversticht northwards and eastwards of Deventer. After 1122 the bishops were no longer imperial appointees, but were elected by the canons of the five collegiate churches of Utrecht. They were generally drawn from the noble and princely families of the Low Countries, and their rule was enmeshed in the dynastic calculations of their lay neighbours, especially the rulers of Brabant, Holland and Guelders. Like all territorial princes the bishops in the later Middle Ages had to face fractious cities and overmighty vassals, as well as scheming neighbours. Their tendency to run up debts to secure election and their standing as spiritual lords both seem to have weakened their power to deal with challenges to their authority. For much of the time Deventer and the lands beyond the IJssel were ruled by the bishops in name only.

One factor weakening the worldly power of the bishops of Utrecht was the geographical separation of the Nedersticht and the Oversticht. Between them lay the Veluwe and Zutphen. There was no over-all political authority here, but after 1190 the main power in the area was the count of Guelders. The county of Guelders proper (now largely in Germany) was separated from the Veluwe and Zutphen by the German county of Cleves. In the lands between the Maas and the Rhine lordship was much more tenuous and fragmented than in the western Low Countries, where Holland, Brabant, Flanders and Hainaut developed into relatively compact territorial powers. The standing of the counts of Guelders (dukes from 1339), ruling disparate territories with varying legal powers, was greatly enhanced by their wealth. In the course of time they accumulated lordship over a range of choice locations controlling the river trade of the Maas (Venlo and Roermond), the Rhine (Arnhem on the Lek and Tiel on the Waal) and the IJssel (Kampen and Zutphen).

South-west of Zutphen and Veluwe, south of Holland and Utrecht, and east of Flanders, was the marquisate (or march) of Antwerp. South again of Antwerp was the county of Leuven. After 1100, the count of Leuven was awarded the marquisate of Antwerp and the title Duke of Lower Lotharingia. The House of Leuven united the marquisate of Antwerp and the county of Leuven as a single territory, the duchy of Brabant. This was the foremost in prestige of all the medieval principalities.

The ducal title of Lower Lotharingia had previously been granted to the count of Limburg, who was thereafter known as the duke of Limburg. This duchy (now mostly in Germany but partly in the Dutch province of Limburg) was a disparate collection of scattered territories and legal claims on a comparatively small scale. One important source of income for the dukes was the toll on the road from Cologne to Flanders, which passed through their town of Herzogenrath. In 1289 Brabant and Limburg were united, and for a time the ruler of both was the only duke in the Low Countries. Between the two duchies lay the county of Loon.

The counts of Loon were a dynasty renowned for their courage in war, but they ruled a poor and poorly organized county. Throughout the 1170s the count of Loon was at war with the count of Duras, procurator of the abbey of Sint-Truiden. In 1179 the bishop of Liège, Rudolph of Zähringen, intervened militarily on behalf of the abbey, and burned down the castle of Loon. The counts of Hainaut and Berg mediated a settlement, after which the count of Loon became a vassal of the bishop. Their vassalage notwithstanding, future counts of Loon often sided with Brabant against Liège in order to maintain their freedom of action. In 1366 the bishops finally took over Loon and thenceforth ruled it directly, being sworn in as count in Borgloon after being installed as bishop in Liège.

The main territory of the prince-bishopric lay immediately southwards of Loon. From 1121 onwards the bishop was usually elected by the cathedral chapter. The first bishop so elected was the brother of the duke of Brabant, but the emperors could still sometimes impose an outside candidate. The principality of the bishops was bordered westwards by the German principality of Jülich, on the Rur. Jülich, and the nearby counties of Cleves, Mark and Berg, were in the Middle Ages closely involved in the affairs of the eastern Low Countries. The languages of these areas lay close together on the spectrum of dialects shading from Dutch to German. Eventually Jülich, Cleves, Mark and Berg became part of the German complex of states, while Guelders and Limburg were drawn into the Low Countries, but this distinction dates from later times.

The westernmost county of the Holy Roman Empire was Hainaut, directly to the south of Flanders. The counts were also margraves of

Valenciennes, in the kingdom of France, which made them (like the counts of Flanders) vassals of both the king of France and the Holy Roman Emperor. Although not as powerful as the counts of Flanders, the counts of Hainaut could raise impressive armies of knights and intervene to their advantage in the war and diplomacy of France and the Empire. Their court at Valenciennes was one of the most brilliant of the pre-Burgundian Low Countries.

Sandwiched between Hainaut (to its west), Brabant (to its north) and Liège (to its east and south) was the county of Namur, centred on the confluence of the Sambre and the Meuse. Despite their extensive personal lands and the revenues from the Meuse river trade, the counts of Namur never quite mustered the degree of political clout attained by their neighbours. In the years around 1200, when it was elevated to a marquisate, Namur was briefly a focal point of territorial aggrandizement, succession disputes and imperial politics. Thereafter it again became the least significant of the great principalities.

In extent, the greatest of these was the southernmost, Luxembourg. The founding moment in the history of the county was in 963, when a count named Sigfrid exchanged lands near Echternach for the castle of Luxembourg. His descendants extended their rule to nearby counties. Longwy, Durbuy, Laroche and Luxembourg were brought together under the single rule of Henry IV (1136–96). After some dispute they were inherited by his daughter, Ermesind (1199–1247), who by her second marriage added the marquisate of Arlon to the collection. In the later Middle Ages, this collection of counties was unified as the duchy of Luxembourg. Of all the principalities of the Low Countries, Luxembourg was perhaps the one most oriented towards Germany, in part because it was the only one where a variant of High German was spoken.

TOWN AND COUNTRY

One reason that the rulers of the Low Countries were able to maintain relatively tight control of fragmented feudal territories was that their income from feudal dues was supplemented, even surpassed, by that from exactions made on trade. Counts, dukes and bishops granted the towns ever-wider freedoms of self-government in return for their monetary and military support. If these towns never quite became independent city states, it was not for want of trying. The citizens of Liège and

Ghent were the most fractious, often contesting the powers of bishop and count but never managing to escape them permanently. Groningen was the most successful: the hereditary prefect of the bishop of Utrecht was driven out in 1251 and the city remained independently self-governing for 150 years.

The great Belgian medievalist Henri Pirenne thought that towns disappeared with the Romans and made their reappearance with the recovery of international trade after the age of the Vikings. More recently Adriaan Verhulst, from the study of material remains and a more careful reading of the historical sources, has shown that urban life never quite vanished entirely, and began to flourish again even in Merovingian times (c.500–750 AD). The urban centres of the Frankish Low Countries lay along the three main river systems. On the Meuse were Dinant, Huy, Namur, Liège and Maastricht; in the Rhine delta Nijmegen, Dorestad and Utrecht; and on the Scheldt and its western estuary Valenciennes, Tournai, Ghent, Antwerp, Middelburg and Bruges.

Merchants and craftsmen tended to congregate round existing castles and major churches, not so much for protection as because this was where the money was. More important than mere growth in the size of urban settlements was that townspeople began to demand legal guarantees and exemptions, and even the status of self-governing corporations. The first signs of the process are in the episcopal towns of Cambrai, Tournai and Liège in the later tenth century. The oldest surviving civic charter from north of the Alps is that granted to Huy by Bishop Theoduin of Liège in 1066. The townspeople were exempted from trial by combat or ordeal, promised speedy decisions in suits and trials, prohibited from taking private vengeance, and guaranteed a presumption of free status (so that any lord claiming a townsman as a serf had to provide irrefutable evidence). The first town to make itself an internally self-governing corporation was Cambrai, in 1077. The towns of Flanders and of the episcopal lordships mostly gained their charters in the twelfth century, those of the other principalities in the thirteenth century and slightly later.

Patricians, who might be either merchants or landowners or both, took the lead in demanding self-government. They dominated the life of the towns, often in conjunction with a sheriff or bailiff representing the count or duke, or with a prefect or provost exercising the bishop's worldly powers. The mayors and aldermen came from patrician ranks and they controlled the fairs and markets. 'Free market' would have seemed a contradiction in terms, as the very purpose of a market was that it was somewhere where the quality, quantity and prices of goods could be policed. The aldermen appointed supervisors to inspect goods, and cloth, bread, beer, meat and fish all had to meet standard requirements.

The wealth of the merchants was greatly enhanced by local manufactures that could be exported. In Wallonia, most famously in Liège, metal was the foremost manufacture. Particularly notable was the brassware, made from German copper alloyed with tin from Cornwall and local zinc. From the early twelfth century it was exported to neighbouring countries on a considerable scale. Elsewhere in the Low Countries, the mainstay of economic growth was cloth. Villagers might make simple homespun cloth for their own uses, but production for international sales required numerous specialized skills: spinning, carding, dying, weaving and fulling might take over a dozen separate processes, with increasing specialization in the towns which made the most reputable quality cloths. Quality varied according to the wool used and the methods of working. Each locality had its own traditional working methods, and cloth of Ghent, or Ypres, or wherever, meant a particular length and weave as well as simply where it was from. Anybody producing inferior cloth was not simply cheating a customer but disgracing the town, so stringent controls were imposed.

Something approaching capitalist organization of cloth production developed in twelfth-century Flanders, with master drapers as the key figures in the trade and other master craftsmen earning their living by working to their orders. By then Flemish cloth was being traded in Winchester, Novgorod and at the fairs of Champagne. It was in Champagne that Flemish merchants acquired the goods brought northwards by Italians. The link between the Low Countries and Italy was to be one of the most fruitful commercial ties in medieval Europe. Silks and spices were the most glamorous of the goods which Italians provided, but the most important were exotic dyestuffs, such as kermes, brazil wood and saffron, and the dye fixer alum, which gave faster and brighter colour to many sorts of cloth. The importance of alum in the history of industry and commerce is hard to overstate.* Long after competition from foreign weavers was being felt, Flemish dyers kept their position at the forefront of the market.

---

* See Charles Singer, *The Earliest Chemical Industry*, 1948.

The aldermen tended to meet in the cloth hall, the largest public building of most towns and the place where cloth was brought to be sold. Towards the end of the twelfth century they began to build belfries (belforts), great square towers to house the town's charters and the bells which dominated city life, ringing the fixed times of work and rest and sounding peels for celebration and tocsins for danger. These then became the meeting place of the magistrates, and their balconies the place where proclamations were published. The model for many such belfries was that of Tournai. Those of Ypres and Bruges, built in the late thirteenth century as the focal point of symmetrical cloth halls, were by far the most imposing. The thirteenth century also saw the building of town halls separate from the cloth hall, which was generally a sign that the cloth merchants had lost their monopoly of power or had failed to establish it in the first place. The most impressive medieval town halls still in use are those of Brussels, Leuven and Gouda, all built in the fifteenth century – those of Brussels and Leuven in a fairytale flamboyant style known as Brabantine Gothic.

The emergence of an urban market economy had profound repercussions on the countryside, stimulating more intensive and specialized forms of agriculture and transforming feudal relations. At first the cloth trade relied on local wool. In the ninth and tenth centuries the coastal saltmarshes, the Kempen heath and the downs of Artois and Hainaut were covered with immense flocks of sheep, but by about 1100 the merchants of the cloth towns were importing wool from England, and pastures began to be turned over to cows for meat and milk. Basic dyestuffs were also grown locally: woad for blue, madder for red, weld for yellow. The increasing urban population meant a growing market demand for basic foodstuffs. In the course of the eleventh and twelfth centuries the saltmarshes of the Flemish coast, and later of Holland, were diked, drained and converted to arable land. Woods and wastelands were cleared for new fields in eleventh-century Flanders and twelfth-century Brabant and Hainaut. The success of peasants in the Low Countries in clearing forests and draining marshes and polders led to invitations to carry out similar ventures in Germany, in return for tenures on easy terms. In 1113 the bishop of Bremen called upon colonists from Flanders and Holland to develop wastelands around Hamburg, and the count of Holstein issued a similar call in 1143. Others followed their example, and the 'Flemish manse' became a standard measurement of land as far away as Poland and Prussia.

Rural life was far from unchanging. Agricultural improvements provided the conditions for the rise of towns, and in turn the close urban network of the Low Countries gradually changed agricultural practices in the region. No village was more than a day's walk away from the nearest town, and most were much closer. In the eleventh century agricultural surpluses had been brought to village markets: by the fourteenth century these had disappeared and peasants headed for town from all over the surrounding countryside, to buy and sell on a much greater scale. Some smallholders might concentrate on producing just one of cereals, mutton, salt, ale, peat, wool or leather for the market, besides a fringe of basics for their own use. Others, particularly those with tiny holdings, might concentrate on growing everything they needed for subsistence, and sell a range of surpluses. Flax in particular became a favourite market crop that could be grown on marginal lands, and the process of breaking it down into fibres for linen weavers was a welcome source of supplementary cash. In Holland fishing, fowling, reed gathering and dike work were supplementary employments for smallholders, and besides food crops they produced hops for brewing, flax for linenweaving and salt for preserving fish. The 'waterships' that organized and oversaw communal dike building and repairs were the seeds of civil society in the rural Netherlands.

The towns contributed more than mouths to feed. They were also a rich source of fertilisers: chimney soot, shavings of leather, household garbage, compost, rags. Even human excrement was recycled: urine was collected in great vats by dyers and tanners; solid waste (called 'city earth' or 'privy manure') was sold to peasants, who would come with carts to collect it. In the interests of smooth disposal a few of the larger towns in the late Middle Ages licensed intermediaries who would collect the waste and sell it on. But a great deal of manure was still produced in the countryside, mainly from cattle and dovecots.

Stock-breeding became possible even to smallholders by the growing of feed crops, such as beets, cabbages and turnips. Linseed and rapeseed were grown as winter fodder but also to produce oil for sale. Livestock generally meant cattle, the polders of Flanders, Frisia and Holland providing excellent grazing. In the countryside pigs were kept as scavengers in wood and wasteland, which were at a premium in the Low Countries – unlike today, pork was a luxury meat. Increased livestock ownership meant more manure and hence higher crop yields. Intensive manuring meant that three-yearly crop rotations with a year lying fallow could be abandoned, and in the late Middle Ages peasants in the Low Countries began to sow complementary crops on the same ground, for summer and winter harvests. The rest of Europe adopted the same techniques in the eighteenth century. The 'Flemish system' of intensive manuring and year-round growing of diverse crops provided variety, but it also meant a reduction in the amount of grain that could be sown. From the thirteenth century grain was imported in large quantities from Artois, Hainaut and Picardy. The Baltic coast became the bread-basket of the fourteenth century, and by the fifteenth century Flanders was also importing grain from East Anglia and the Rhineland. Townspeople across Europe and beyond were clothed by the weavers of the Low Countries, who themselves were fed by the peasants of many lands.

Sir Richard Weston, a Royalist refugee in the Low Countries during the English Civil War, wrote a *Discourse of Husbandry used in Brabant and Flanders, shewing the wonderful improvement of Land there, and serving as a pattern for our practice in this Commonwealth* (1650). The heart of his message was that on heathland which would be considered inferior in England:

> one acre of good flax is worth four or five acres of the best corn . . . and after the flax is pulled, it will bear a crop of turnips, which may be better worth, acre for acre, than the best corn in the country. After that crop is off, about April following you may sow the same land with oats, and upon them clover-grass seed . . . which will come up after the oats are mowed, and that year yield you a very great pasture till Christmas, and the next year following you may cut that grass three times, and it will every time bear such a burden, and so good to feed all sorts of cattle, as the best meadows in the country . . . .

When tillers of the soil could be growing cash crops, or colonizing land of their own, or moving to the towns, it was natural that they were reluctant to spend up to half their productive time working their lords' fields. Labour services were frequently converted to cash rents, either to attract new tenants or in response to organized resistance to the customary corvées. Even the landlord's own domain was increasingly leased out to rent-paying tenants. The lord could put the squeeze on villagers in other ways: through fines in the manorial court, and his monopoly of the mill, the brewhouse, and sometimes even the plough animals. Hay-making obligations and rights of pasture were kept up the longest, as the system was still supposed to maintain mounted warriors. Serfdom was not legally abolished until the 1790s, but with the exception of parts of

Guelders and the Oversticht it survived only in very residual form after the thirteenth century.

Feudal forms were absorbing, or being absorbed by, a money economy. The same process worked further up the social scale. A thirteenth-century inquiry in Flanders found that only a third of knights' fiefs were actually held by knight service; the rest had been converted to cash or symbolic payments. The management of the rights and domains of the rulers had long been carried out by their personal servants – clerks of their chapel or the servile knights known as ministerials. By the thirteenth century administration was in the hands of professionally organized chanceries. Ministerials had lost all taint of servile status and merged with the patrician and land-owning classes. A nuisance to the bishops of Utrecht throughout the thirteenth century were the lords of Amstel, whose forefathers had been ministerials of the bishops. In the second half of the thirteenth century the river Amstel (part of one connection between the Zuider Zee and a branch of the Rhine delta) was dammed to prevent flooding, and a town grew up on the Amstel Dam. Gijsbrecht IV of Amstel (1235–1303) started levying tolls in his own name, and his son claimed Amsterdam as a fief. For decades the counts of Holland, the lords of Amstel and the bishops of Utrecht were to fight for lordship over the town and its revenues, with Holland finally victorious.

The Zuider Zee itself was a result of a particularly devastating flood in 1163, which transformed the Almere, the great lake at the centre of the northern Netherlands, into an arm of the sea. What had been a landscape dominated by lakes and bogs was transformed into one of creeks, islands and peninsulas. Fish were an important source of nutrition, and fishing in the sea was free for all (unlike fishing in lakes and rivers), so the sudden availability of an inland sea rich in flounders partly made up for the loss of fertile land. The shores of the Zuider Zee were soon dotted with fishing villages. The sheltered sailing conditions of the Zuider Zee made it the ideal route for north-bound vessels (this was the route which Scandinavian shipping to Dorestad had once followed, over the Almere). As trade with northern Germany, Denmark and the Baltic grew, the towns along the IJssel, which linked the Zuider Zee to the Rhine, gained importance. Deventer and Zwolle in the Oversticht, and Zutphen and Kampen in the lands of the counts of Guelders, all joined the Hanseatic League in the later thirteenth century, as did Stavoren on the north-eastern shore of the Zuider Zee.

The desire for an income from tolls on the Zuider Zee shipping goes

a long way to explain the determination of the counts of Holland to dominate its southern coast, at the expense of the bishops of Utrecht, and its
northern reaches at the expense of the Frisians. The Zuider Zee was full
of shallows, so many cargoes were reloaded on to vessels of lighter
draught at Stavoren, Enkhuizen or Hoorn. These were all Frisian towns
which the count of Holland eventually came to rule. West Frisia (a name
now used only of the northern parts of what was to become the province
of North Holland) was almost completely cut off from the rest of Frisia
as a result of the twelfth-century inundations. The counts of Holland
began a series of earnest attempts to impose their rule on the area.
William II of Holland, King of the Romans (emperor-elect), lost his life
in a winter campaign against the West Frisians in 1256. His horse fell
through the ice, but he was not drowned: Frisians dragged him out of the
water and killed him on the spot. Their final subjection was brought
about by William's son, Floris V, who was only two when his father died.

THE NEW MONASTICISM, 1098–1147

In 1098 a new sort of monastery was founded at Cîteaux in Burgundy.
Here the Rule of St Benedict, commonly used as a guideline for monastic life, would be lived to the letter, with no relaxations. After a shaky
start the monastery gained fame through the influence of Bernard of
Clairvaux, who entered in 1112. Two of his journeys to the Low
Countries were particularly important, since they led to the founding of
the first Cistercian abbeys in the region. The order continued to grow
rapidly to the end of the century. Like hermits, Cistercians sought waste
places and sought to make them fruitful – often by the labour of lay
brothers who lived under a less strict rule and had no say in the government of the community. Although they were not the first to be active in
the clearance and draining of new land, the Cistercians of the Low
Countries somehow acquired particular fame for it. Abbeys noted for
their polders on the coastal plain of Flanders were Our Lady in the
Dunes (now a museum near Koksijde) and its daughter house Ter Doest,
the tithebarn of which still stands. In Friesland the Abbey of Klaarkamp
built a number of dikes and developed the island of Schiermonnikoog
('schiermonnik' meaning lay brother); its daughter house at Aduard
became the kernel of a flourishing trading community.

Another new order was founded by Norbert of Xanten, a
Rhinelander. Norbert travelled to Prémontré in northern France and in

1120 founded a house of canons regular there. The life of his followers (known as Norbertines or Premonstratensians) was to be based on the rule of St Augustine. The second foundation was at Floreffe, in the county of Namur. Others soon followed. By the end of the century there were another twenty-two throughout the Low Countries. From the fourteenth century, the Premonstratensian abbots in Brabant were among the most important lords spiritual in the estates of the duchy. Two of the abbeys in Frisia, Mariëngaarde and Bloemhof, became centres of Frisian history-writing.

Like Bernard, Norbert travelled in the Low Countries and founded monasteries there in person. In 1131 both men were in Liège for the meeting of the emperor-elect Lothar with Pope Innocent II. Together they contributed to the reconciliation of Pope and Emperor. The meeting culminated with the imperial coronation, the only one to take place in the Low Countries. One of Norbert's earlier trips to the Low Countries was in 1124, when he took possession of the collegiate church at Antwerp (St Michael's) to reform it as a Premonstratensian abbey. The provost of the church transferred it to him because of the need to combat the heresies which had taken hold in Antwerp through the preaching of a certain Tanchelm, who seems to have died in 1115.

In a letter written around 1113 the canons of Utrecht complained to the archbishop of Cologne that a man called Tanchelm, then in Cologne, had been teaching that only he and his followers were the true Church; that the offices of pope, bishop, archbishop, priest and clerk were meaningless; that it was the sanctity of the minister, not ordination, that made a sacrament valid; that churches were places of evil where empty motions were gone through; and finally that since he himself had received the plenitude of the Holy Spirit, he was little less than divine. Tanchelm's followers venerated his bathwater as 'a blessed drink and salutary sacrament', and on one occasion he had gone so far as to have a statue of the Virgin Mary brought before his congregation, and taking it by the hand declare: 'My most dear friends, see how I give myself in marriage to the Blessed Virgin; as for you, bring up your wedding gifts.' The haul was allegedly immense.

The canons of Utrecht were not entirely unbiased reporters. Tanchelm was on his way to Rome to petition the pope on behalf of the count of Flanders that diocesan borders be rationalized by transferring the parts of the diocese of Utrecht lying west of the Scheldt to the diocese of Tournai. As matters stood Bruges was in the diocese of Tournai, but its outport at Damme was in the diocese of Utrecht. The loss of Damme would have harmed Utrecht's revenues, and the canons were certainly hoping (they said as much) that the archbishop would prevent Tanchelm from reaching Rome. There are one or two later references to Tanchelm's misleading sermons, but no reliable details of his opinions. A *Life of St Norbert* mentions that Tanchelm's teachings gained credence because the people of Antwerp were in effect pastorless. It was a populous town with only one parish priest, and him living in concubinage with his niece. Before St Norbert took over the church, the canons of St Michael's were tonsured but unordained clerks whose main job was to collect the tithes and pass two-thirds of them on to the duke.

THE RENAISSANCE OF THE TWELFTH CENTURY

Bernard's and Norbert's idea that ancient texts could provide exact rules of life, rather than simply guidelines to be worked out in community, is one aspect of a wider intellectual movement, known for convenience as the twelfth-century renaissance. Other important aspects of this renewal of learning were the revival of the study of Roman law and ancient philosophy, the systematization of canon law and theology, and a more self-conscious sense of human individuality.

A few of the great twelfth-century thinkers born in the Low Countries show something of the impact of the new learning. One is Rupert of Deutz (*c.*1075–1130), a monk of St Laurence's in Liège who spent 40 years or more in its school, first as pupil and later as teacher. In his final years he was called to Germany to be abbot of Deutz, where he died. He was a commentator on liturgy and scripture, a mystic and a poet. Book 12 of his commentary on Matthew, recounting his own struggles to understand and live the Gospel, is one of the most self-reflective pieces of medieval autobiography. When interpreting scripture, Rupert attached particular weight to parallels of imagery in the Old Testament and the New, rather than to the logical distinctions of the more fashionable schools. The poetic parallels he perceived in different parts of the Bible became a standard part of monastic education in the Low Countries and the Rhineland, and influenced the choice and juxtaposition of biblical scenes to be painted or carved in churches. Generations, even of the illiterate, unknowingly drew their basic understanding of the Bible from Rupert's commentaries. In the 1520s his books were put into print and the first generation of Lutherans in Cologne and Antwerp cited them to show that there was nothing very novel about their own attitudes to biblical interpretation and to Scholasticism.

Alan of Lille (d. 1203) was a poet and theologian who had a very different career. He studied in the schools of Paris, which were at the forefront of the new learning. He extended the boundaries of twelfth-century theology. His systematic surveys of biblical terminology and of the main theological problems of the day, together with his comprehensive manuals for preachers and confessors, earned him a reputation for 'universal' learning. Less universal, but even more clear and systematic, was Simon of Tournai, a master of Paris who set out disputed points in physics and metaphysics. Such men could not blossom fully in their native Flanders, where learned clerks were expected to use their skills in the service of administration rather than speculative thought.

The renewal of legal learning had perhaps more direct impact on broad sections of the population. In 1127 Galbert of Bruges wrote of 'customary laws', but by 1205 a charter distinguished between 'law' and 'custom', the one rational and written, the other possibly recorded in writing but not at all the same sort of thing. The distinction had partly grown from the Peace of God and the Gregorian Reform, which emphasized justice in the abstract regardless of what was usual. In 1092 Pope Urban II pointed out to Robert the Frisian that Christ had said 'I am the truth', not 'I am usage or custom'. Another source was the codified law of the later Roman Empire, which regarded the ruler as the fount of the law rather than simply its guardian. In 1170 Philip of Alsace, count of Flanders (1157–91), no longer ruling on behalf of his father Thierry III (d. 1167) issued the Great Charter giving uniform legal codes to the towns of Arras, Bruges, Douai, Ghent, Lille, Saint-Omer and Ypres. The ruler no longer simply confirmed customs or conferred exemptions, but could make new law.

Philip of Alsace patronized another aspect of the twelfth-century renaissance, the flourishing of secular literature. The foremost poet of the time was Chrétien de Troyes, a Frenchman in the service of the count who dedicated his grail legend, *Perceval*, to Philip. The fashion for courtly love was also embraced by the highest circles in Flanders, for Philip's countess, Elizabeth of Vermandois, ran a 'court of love' in the French style. Another of the great courtly poets was Henric van Veldeke (*c*.1150–1210). He was a ministerial from the county of Loon and wrote in a dialect midway between Dutch and German, which enables speakers of both languages to claim his *Eneit* (a reworking of the story of Aeneas) as their first chivalrous romance. Scraps of Dutch survive from earlier times: an eighth-century baptismal formula from Utrecht, two verses of a ninth- or tenth-century Lower Frankish psalm translation, a line from a West Flemish love song doodled on a parchment in Kent around 1100. Henric van Veldeke's life of St Servatius, written around 1170, is the first substantial piece of Dutch verse to have survived. He also wrote love poetry, complete with shooting buds, green leaves and birds singing in the trees.

Around 1148 a Master Nivardus wrote the *Ysengrimus*, a series of comic anecdotes in Latin verse recounting the disasters befalling the wolf Isengrim, incidentally satirizing clerical and monastic abuses. Isengrim's frequently fatal misfortunes were often brought about by his cunning rival Reynard. Towards the end of the century a beast epic in Flemish verse was written, *Reynard the Fox*. This tells how the wily and antisocial Reynard gets away with robbery, rape and murder by playing on the vices of his opponents: the avarice of King Noble the lion, the greed of his officers, Brun the bear and Tybalt the cat, and the nepotism of his counsellor Grimbert the badger. The poem remained popular throughout the rest of the Middle Ages, and Caxton's translation of 1481 (the source of the versions of the names given here) was among the earliest English books in print. In the nineteenth century Reynard became an important political symbol of the antiquity and high achievement of Flemish literature, as well as inspiring Michel Rodange's *Renert*, the best known work of literature from Luxembourg.

The bulk of literary production in Dutch relied on translations or adaptations of French originals. These include Dutch versions of the *Song of Roland* and of *Renaut de Montauban*. This last was a romance, tremendously popular on the Continent right up to the nineteenth century, telling of Charlemagne's attempts to punish the four falsely accused sons of Aymon, who evade capture on their magic horse Bayard. A Flemish Charlemagne romance without known French original is *Karel ende Elegast*, about 'how the emperor went out robbing'. Commanded by an angel to take to crime for one night, the disguised emperor teams up with the outlaw knight Elegast and together they discover and foil a plot against his life.

THE EMPIRE AND THE LOW COUNTRIES, 1155–1256

Imperial authority in the Low Countries recovered somewhat under Frederick Barbarossa (1155–90). He restored the imperial palace at

Nijmegen and from time to time held court there. The emperor might no longer be able to invest bishops, but in 1156 he did travel to Utrecht to preside over the election of Godfrey of Rhenen, and in 1167 he saw to it that his friend and ally Rudolph of Zähringen, a veteran of the imperial wars in Italy, became bishop of Liège (1167–91). In 1189 the Emperor Frederick, along with Philip Augustus of France and Richard Lion-Heart of England, established royal control over the crusader movement by leading the Third Crusade. They failed to regain Jerusalem. The crusade was of great importance for the history of the Low Countries because of the death toll. Philip of Alsace, Count of Flanders, and Rudolph of Zähringen, Bishop of Liège, died of disease during the siege of Acre. Floris III of Holland died of exhaustion at Antioch, in the arms of his younger son William. Frederick Barbarossa himself drowned in a river in Asia Minor.

At the time of the emperor's death the succession to the county of Namur was being disputed. From 1139 Namur was ruled by Henry the Blind, who was also count of Luxembourg, Longwy, Durbuy and La Roche. In 1163, as a childless widower, Henry designated his sister's son, Baldwin the Brave, as his heir. Baldwin became count of Hainaut in 1171 and count of Flanders (in his wife's right) in 1191. Frederick Barbarossa agreed to the nomination of Baldwin as the heir to Luxembourg, and to the integration of the various counties stretching from the Moselle to the confluence of the Sambre and Meuse as the marquisate of Namur, to be joined to Flanders and Hainaut in a personal union. Had things gone as planned the political unification of the Low Countries would have taken a very different course, but in 1186 the 72-year-old Henry the Blind (who had remarried in 1168) was unexpectedly blessed with a daughter, Ermesind. He accordingly changed his will, and in 1188 Baldwin the Brave invaded and occupied the county of Namur. Before departing on crusade the emperor raised the county to a marquisate and confirmed Baldwin's title to Namur, Durbuy and La Roche, but reserved the county of Luxembourg to his own brother. In 1195 Baldwin the Brave was succeeded in Flanders and Hainaut by his older son, Baldwin, and in Namur by his younger son, Philip. Henry the Blind lived until 1196, still seeking to have Ermesind's right of inheritance recognized. The cause was then taken up by Ermesind's betrothed, Theobald of Bar.

With greater difficulty than his father Frederick, and less finesse, the Emperor Henry VI (1190–97) continued to maintain imperial power. In 1191 news reached Liège of the death of Bishop Rudolph at the siege of

Acre. The Brabantine party in the cathedral chapter pushed through the election of Albert of Leuven, brother of Henry I, Duke of Brabant. The emperor tried to impose Lothar of Hochstaden instead, but Albert appealed to the pope and his election was confirmed. Banned from Lotharingia by Henry VI, Albert was ordained bishop of Liège in Rheims in September 1192. He was murdered by three imperial knights shortly afterwards and became celebrated as a martyr for the liberty of the Church. After Albert of Leuven's murder, the chapter elected Simon of Limburg as his successor, but the validity of the election was disputed. In 1194 a group of canons inclined to the count of Hainaut elected a rival, Albert of Cuyck. The result was civil war, with the dukes of Limburg and Brabant backing Simon, while Baldwin the Brave, Count of Flanders and Hainaut, backed Albert. In 1195 the two candidates travelled to Rome to present their cases to the pope. Simon died before judgement was given, so Albert was confirmed in the see.

In 1196 there was a similarly disputed election in Utrecht. The clerical candidate as bishop was Arnold of Isenburg, supported by Count Otto I of Guelders (1184–1207). The emperor and Dirk VII of Holland backed one of Dirk's relatives, Theoderic. The counts of Holland and Guelders each sent an army in support of their candidate. Guelders was defeated in Utrecht, but managed to install Arnold in Deventer. In 1197 Arnold and Theoderic both travelled to Rome to seek papal confirmation of their election. The exhausting journey to a malarial city had a way of solving such disputes: both died with their case unresolved. The churches of Utrecht, divided between Holland and Guelders, settled on a compromise candidate in Theoderic of Ahr (1198–1212), a former imperial chaplain.

Henry VI died in 1197 and left only an infant son as heir. The princes of the empire proceeded to elect a successor but ended up with two candidates, each proclaimed by a rival faction. These were Henry VI's younger brother, Philip of Swabia (1198–1208), and Otto (1198–1218), son of Henry the Lion, Duke of Saxony and Bavaria, who had been driven into exile by Frederick Barbarossa in 1181. Each found supporters in Germany, Italy and the Low Countries. Otto IV's family were the Welfs, Philip's the Hohenstaufens. The conflict between their clans was to last a century. It was particularly important in the Low Countries in its first 50 years (1198–1248), when it coincided with, and complicated, a number of succession disputes.

Henry I of Brabant (1190–1235) was titular duke of Lower Lotharingia and had an important ceremonial role as the imperial sword-bearer. He became kingmaker of the Low Countries, determining which candidate was recognized by the princes of Lotharingia. Initially he swung several of the counts to the Welf party. Then in 1203 he made a marriage alliance with Guelders, and together they switched allegiance to Philip of Swabia on condition that he confirm all the grants and concessions that Otto IV had already made to them. They returned to the Welf camp after Philip was murdered in 1208.

Holland similarly changed sides, but only because it also changed rulers. Dirk VII died in 1203 leaving only a teenaged heiress, Ada. Her mother immediately married her off to Louis, Count of Loon, so that she would have a man to support her claim to the county and frustrate the ambitions of her uncle, the returned crusader William. Before his brother's body was buried, William crossed from Frisia to Holland in a fishing boat and incited a rebellion against rule by the 'foreigner' Louis of Loon. Ada and Louis sought the support of the Hohenstaufen party, William of the Welf. By the end of 1204 William had established himself in Holland and had sent Ada into captivity in England. In 1206, with Brabant and Guelders having gone over to the Hohenstaufens and giving Louis of Loon diplomatic backing, Ada was released and Louis confirmed in the title of count of Holland. The collapse of the Hohenstaufen cause in 1208 changed everything, and from 1210 William I was again issuing charters as 'count of Holland' even though nobody had yet recognized him as such.

The rivalries for imperial power also affected the relations between Flanders and France. The Welf emperor Otto IV had an English mother, and had grown up in exile at the court of his uncle, Richard Lion-Heart. Philip Augustus of France accordingly inclined to the Hohenstaufens. This was enough for Baldwin IX of Flanders (1194–1205) to abandon his family's long-standing loyalty to the House of Hohenstaufen for an Anglo-Welf alliance against France. Baldwin IX was the son of Margaret of Alsace, Countess of Flanders, and Baldwin the Brave, Count of Hainaut. When Philip of Alsace had died at Acre in 1191, Philip Augustus abandoned the crusade to rush back to France, where he confirmed Margaret and Baldwin in royal Flanders only after claiming for himself a number of border towns and charging the unusually high feudal relief of £20,000. Upon succeeding as count in 1194, Baldwin IX's first priority was to regain the border towns lost in 1191. In 1199, in the interests of a united front against the French-Hohenstaufen coalition, the dispute over Henry the Blind's legacy was settled. The county of Luxembourg, which the Hohenstaufens had sought to keep for themselves, Otto IV awarded to Ermesind. Baldwin also made his peace with

Ermesind, relinquishing the counties of the Ardennes to her and even part of his brother's marquisate of Namur. His policy of concentrating on France paid off in 1200, when Philip Augustus returned the towns seized in 1191 in exchange for Baldwin abandoning his alliance with King John of England. In the same year the count's first child, Joan, was born. By 1202 his second, Margaret, was on the way.

In 1202 Baldwin, having settled his territorial disputes to his satisfaction, departed on the Fourth Crusade. As soon as Margaret was born his wife followed him, dying on the journey. Having run short of money, the crusaders *en route* hired themselves out as mercenaries and never reached the Holy Land. Instead, in 1204, they took service in a dynastic struggle in Constantinople. When their client failed to pay them, they brutally sacked the city and declared Baldwin emperor. The following year he went missing during a battle with the Bulgars and was never seen again. News that he was dead reached France and Flanders in 1206. Philip Augustus demanded the unheard-of relief of £50,000 to recognize Baldwin's orphans as his heiresses and also claimed his feudal right of wardship over them. The infants Joan and Margaret were taken to Paris. Philip Augustus ruled Flanders until 1212, when he married the 12-year-old Joan to Ferrand of Portugal and the 10-year-old Margaret to Burchard of Avesnes, a man four times her age. King Philip hoped to install Ferrand as a puppet ruler of Flanders but in this he was disappointed. French insults led Ferrand to refuse to join the planned invasion of England; then pressure from the cloth towns pushed him into alliance with the English crown. The Flemings took and sacked Tournai, and the French fleet was destroyed at Damme, but soon French knights were laying waste the countryside of Flanders.

Otto IV was crowned emperor in Rome in 1209, but conflicts with territorial princes and with the pope persisted. In 1212 a gathering of princes at Nuremberg declared Otto deposed and elected Henry VI's son, now 18, as Frederick II. This renewal of the Hohenstaufen cause was a serious blow to Otto, who began to rally support outside Germany. In 1212 he backed the election of a younger son of the House of Guelders as bishop of Utrecht. In 1213 he finally confirmed William I as count of Holland and heir to all the fiefs of Floris III. In 1214 he married the duke of Brabant's sister, Maria. Then he led an international coalition of Germans, Englishmen and Lotharingians to drive the French from Flanders. Otto was the feudal overlord of Joan and Ferrand for imperial Flanders and thus owed them his protection. The Anglo-Welf army met resounding defeat at Bouvines, on 27 July 1214.

The Battle of Bouvines was the death-blow to Otto's authority in the Low Countries. William I of Holland was captured, but was released when he transferred his loyalty to the Franco-Hohenstaufen cause. The duke of Brabant, Otto's brother-in-law, similarly abandoned the Welf interest. In 1215 the see of Utrecht went to Otto of Lippe, a distant cousin of Frederick II. The most profound effects were felt in Flanders. Count Ferrand was captured at Bouvines and was held prisoner for over a decade. In order to obtain his release Joan was forced to follow the political directives of the king of France. King Philip, ever cavalier about matrimonial law, even made her go through a wedding ceremony with the count of Brittany – a marriage she repudiated as soon as her husband was free. In 1224–25 she had to cope with the bizarre challenge of the 'False Baldwin', an unbalanced hermit who became convinced he was her father returned from the East and who garnered a surprising amount of support from the townspeople of Flanders. In the aftermath she imposed such enormous fines on the cities that in 1226 she was able to buy Ferrand's freedom.

The chaos of the years around 1200 shows how weak imperial power had become in the Low Countries, but also how important it still was. Might was only right if it received imperial sanction, and in the fight between Welf and Hohenstaufen imperial sanction was for sale. That was soon to change. Frederick II, needing the support of the territorial princes of the Empire to pursue his schemes in Italy, in 1231 issued the *Statutum in favorum principum*. This confirmed the erosion of the imperial regalia, admitting the right of the princes to levy tolls, mint coins, build castles, administer justice and collect judicial fines and fees. The rulers of the Low Countries continued to play their part as princes of the Empire, but they were no longer subject to imperial overlordship in any meaningful sense. When Frederick II was excommunicated in 1245, the Welf party elected first Henry of Thuringia (1246–47) and then William II of Holland (1247–56) as counter-emperor. When Frederick II died, the Hohenstaufens elected his son as Conrad IV (1250–54). The rivalry dragged on, but it had lost much of its interest for the rulers of the Low Countries.

RELIGIOUS LIFE IN THE THIRTEENTH CENTURY

The thirteenth century saw the most radical of the new religious movements of the Middle Ages, seeking to supply answers to the desperate

72

spiritual needs arising in an expanding market-oriented and urban society. Such groups included those condemned as heretics and those acclaimed for their sanctity.

The Cathars ('the Pure') emerged in the eleventh century as a sinister alternative to Christianity. They drove to extremes the distinction between the flesh and the spirit, teaching that the physical world was entirely evil. A favourite argument was that a good creator would not have made wolves. This bleak system of belief spread across much of Continental Western Europe, but outside southern France, where Cathars became known as Albigenses, it was very much a minority cult. Cathars turned up in Flanders as early as the twelfth century. Numbers were never large, but the appearance of groups inspired by French Albigensians was persistent. In 1155 the bishop of Cambrai declared a clerk named Jonas no longer to be in good standing with the Church because of his *Cattorum heresi*. In 1162 Louis VII of France, trying to put pressure on Flanders, wrote to the pope that heresy was rife there. In 1163 eleven Flemings were arrested near Cologne and after much questioning and disputation were burned as heretics, the penalty under criminal law.

In order to maintain some sort of ecclesiastical control over who was deemed a heretic, a new response to heresy was devised in 1184: the officials of the bishops were to carry out formal inquiries ('inquisitions') into the beliefs of suspects, the secular courts only becoming involved once an individual had been formally identified as a heretic. In 1232 Frederick II argued that these episcopal inquiries should be under imperial control, and the papacy responded in 1233 by appointing special papal inquisitors with roving commissions. In 1235 Robert le Petit was appointed papal inquisitor for the whole of France. Wherever he went there turned out to be large numbers of unsuspected heretics. In 1236 and 1237 he toured Flanders, and in 1238 the diocese of Liège, having dozens burned at the stake. Shortly afterwards complaints were made to the pope, and Robert was condemned to perpetual imprisonment for his oppressions and injustices. Over-enthusiasm was curbed, but inquisitors were to become a familiar part of life. Most of their energy went into hunting Waldensians and Brothers of the Free Spirit, fundamentally Christian sects that denied the role of the Church as a vehicle of God's Grace.

Mendicant Friars

In Italy, the urge to renounce the riches and pleasures of the world inspired Francis of Assisi (1182–1226), the son of a merchant. After a worldly youth he adopted a life of poverty and humility, but at the same time he affirmed the dignity of creation, insisting that Jesus was born a little child of flesh and blood, and preaching to birds and beasts – even, it was said, to a wolf. Francis not only rejected personal property, he also rejected communal ownership. He and his companions lived by begging, and travelled from place to place proclaiming the Gospel. Francis's order of Friars Minor (Little Brothers) was given papal approval in 1229. By then they already had half a dozen houses in the Low Countries, and many more were to follow. As time passed the order made a distinction between 'owning' and 'using', and some communities used goods on a grand scale without claiming to own them.

A similar group of mendicant friars was the Order of Preachers founded in 1214 by Dominic de Guzman (1170–1221). Their *raison d'être* was preaching as a way of communicating the teachings of the Church to those in danger of being misled by heretical teachers. Dominicans, and later other friars, were closely involved in the papal inquisition. One order of friars originated in the Netherlands, near Huy: the Brothers of the Cross, also known as Crutched Friars. According to legend the founder, Theodore of Celles, was a canon of Liège who had accompanied Rudolph of Zähringen on the Third Crusade and returned with a determination to dedicate his life to proclaiming salvation through Christ's death on the Cross. Houses were founded in other parts of the Low Countries, and even in a few towns in France, England and Germany, but they were never a big order so their history is very poorly documented.

Rather than seek the desert, the mendicant friars congregated in the towns, where they had more chance of living by begging. By 1350 there were six houses of friars in Bruges alone, five in Ghent, four each in Ypres and Valenciennes, and at least one in every major town in the Low Countries. From the towns they undertook regular preaching tours through the countryside. A particular speciality of the friars was enabling rural parishioners to celebrate the great feasts of the year with a special sense of Christian community. While a parish priest was himself often involved in local feuds, the friars would come in from outside and with finely honed preaching skills exhort the people to live in the love and peace of Christ, then proceed to hear confessions and mediate restitution and reconciliation. The new emphasis on confessing and receiving communion at least once every year (decreed by the Fourth Lateran Council in 1215) meant that Christians were obliged to be at peace with their neighbours at least around Easter.

Friars were members of international organizations not tied to particular houses, and could thus be highly mobile. In 1234 Emo, abbot of the Premonstratensian monastery of Bloemhof in Frisia, remarked that the Dominicans 'fly here and there like clouds'. Around 1300 a French jurist noted that nobody was better informed of the affairs of the world than the friars. Membership of a mendicant order was often a gateway to a wider world, both in terms of distance and in terms of intellectual achievement. Because of the importance that the friars attached to preaching and hearing confessions, they often sought the best education available. Already in the thirteenth century there was increasing Flemish and Lotharingian participation in the intellectual life of the University of Paris. Under William II, Count of Holland and King of the Romans, the Dominican Albertus Magnus founded the University of Cologne (1248), which provided further educational opportunities for Lotharingians. One among the first generation of students there was the natural philosopher Thomas of Cantimpré, a Brabantine nobleman who had already been through a traditional course of studies in Liège but became a pupil of Albertus after joining the Dominicans. By the fourteenth century the Franciscans, Dominicans and Augustinians all had international houses of studies in Bruges, but these were only for training members of the order and could not grant degrees.

Theology and Philosophy

The most important intellectual development of the thirteenth century was the rediscovery of Aristotle. His thought presented a profound challenge to the theological and philosophical learning systematized in the twelfth century by such figures as Alan of Lille. The extent of Aristotle's intellectual achievements began to become apparent to Western Christians through Latin translations of the Arabic versions of his works available in Spain and Sicily. In the mid-thirteenth century the Brabantine Dominican William of Moerbeke translated most of Aristotle's known works from the Greek, as well as a number of ancient Greek commentaries on Aristotle. The magisterial synthesis of Aristotle's thought with the existing doctrines of the Schools was the work of the Italian Dominican Thomas Aquinas (c.1225–1274), who lectured in Paris and Cologne.

The Low Countries had never before produced such a clutch of philosophers as in the mid-thirteenth century, and it would be centuries more before the achievement was repeated or surpassed. Among

Franciscan graduates Walter of Bruges wrote on the psychological primacy of free will over reason, while Gilbert of Tournai wrote on rulership and peace. The secular priests Godfrey of Fontaines, Henry of Ghent and Henry Bate of Mechelen were among the foremost intellects of the late thirteenth century. The most influential thinker from the thirteenth-century Low Countries was another secular priest, Siger of Brabant, whom Dante places beside Thomas Aquinas in his *Paradiso* (Canto 10). Siger and Thomas took very different approaches to the problem of reconciling Aristotle with established doctrines, and in life they were bitter opponents. Thomas saw philosophy and theology as distinct, but complementary disciplines: since truth is one and indivisible, philosophy can provide statements proved by reason, with the aid of which one could interpret divine revelation. Siger denied the singleness of truth, arguing that religious truths were beyond the reach of philosophical discussion, while sound philosophy might not be valid theology. Siger gained quite a following in the Paris Faculty of Arts. His stance was abhorred by academic theologians, and especially by Thomas. Siger bears the distinction of having elicited some of the most insulting epithets applied by the generally serene Aquinas. In 1277 he was charged with heresy by the bishop of Paris, but in a personal appeal to the pope he was vindicated of contradicting any article of faith. He spent three years in the papal household at Orvieto before he was murdered there by his secretary.

Beguines

The Cathars, Waldensians, Franciscans and Dominicans originated in southern Europe and spread to the Low Countries through France. A movement which seems to have been indigenous, and which was exported across northern France and Germany, up the Rhine as far as Switzerland, and possibly over the North Sea to East Anglia, was that of the Beguines and Beghards. Beguines were women, and Beghards men, who dedicated their lives to supporting one another in prayer and works of mercy. Since they did not hold their goods in common, or renounce the world and live by begging, they were in most respects indistinguishable from other secular laypeople. They took simple (rather than solemn and perpetual) vows, from which they could at any time be released to marry or otherwise break with involvement in the movement. The ecclesiastical authorities looked on with unease at groups which in their anonymity and loose organization bore a marked resemblance to the networks of secret heretical conventicles then spreading across urban Europe. 'Beguine' seems at first to have been a term of abuse, possibly derived from 'Albigense'. Beguines were repeatedly banned by Church decrees, but exceptions were always made for 'praiseworthy' Beguines, and a tendency towards enclosure, or semi-enclosure, in beguinages took the edge off official mistrust. Very often there was social or functional differentiation, with two different beguinages in the same town, one specifically for poorer beguines, or for those running a hospital. In fourteenth-century Groningen there were three, perhaps even four beguinages. Beguines maintained their own church, or at least employed a priest of their own to say Mass and hear confessions, making them independent even of parish structures.

The late thirteenth-century Flemish narrative poem *Beatrijs* brings out the new importance attached to personal confession.* With beautiful embellishments of incidental detail and psychological depth, it recounts a commonplace miracle story. The stock tale is of a nun who leaves her habit at the foot of a statue of the Blessed Virgin to run off with her former boyfriend; he later abandons her, and eventually she returns to the convent in shame, only to find that Mary has been filling in for her and her absence has not been missed. One of the poet's most telling additions is a coda in which the nun learns that the return of surface normality is not enough to restore her relationship with God. Expressing heartfelt penitence in confession is what makes the final difference, not a life of outward piety concealing inner guilt.

Mysticism

This new emphasis on interior religiosity coincided with a new mystical spirituality. One of the first great mystics of the high Middle Ages was the Cistercian nun Lutgart of Tongeren, whose visions and ecstasies were recorded for posterity by Thomas of Cantimpré. The first mystic authors in Dutch – the writers of the oldest substantial prose works in Dutch to have survived at all – are the nun Beatrice of Nazareth and the Beguine Hadewijch. Hadewijch, who also wrote verse, drew on the literary conventions of courtly love to convey the feeling of God's loving presence. The mystics' experiential understanding of this did not always agree with the definitions and distinctions of theologians. One who fell

---

* Published in an English translation by Adrian Jacob Barnouw as *The Miracle of Beatrice*, New York: Pantheon, 1944.

77

foul of inquisitors was Margaret Porete, a Beguine from Hainaut who became a solitary. In 1310 she was burned as a heretic in Paris because she refused to withdraw or clarify certain passages in her mystical treatise *The Mirror of Simple Souls*.

The literary expression of Flemish mysticism reached its peak in the fourteenth century, in the writings of Jan van Ruysbroeck (1293–1381). Ruysbroeck lived as a hermit at Groenendael, just outside Brussels. In a reprise of the development so common in the eleventh century, a community gathered around him and what had begun as a hermitage soon became a priory. In the course of the following two centuries Ruysbroeck's Flemish writings were translated into Latin and profoundly influenced the spiritual life of Europe. It may seem a paradox that this flowering of mystical spirituality was in a part of Europe where urban life and a money economy were becoming most pronounced, but William Blake would no doubt have appreciated the relationship.

The thirteenth century's eucharistic piety played an important part in the visionary experiences of Hadewijch, among others. Her first vision occurred when communion was brought to her in her private room because she was incapable of attending church. This more intense veneration of the eucharistic presence originated in large part in the diocese of Liège. There, the mystical experiences of the Cistercian nun Juliana led her to press for the institution of a new feast in special celebration of the presence of Christ under the appearance of bread and wine. In 1246 the bishop of Liège decreed the feast in his diocese. After Juliana's death in 1258, her friend Eva, a recluse, lobbied to make it a general feast of the Church, and a papal bull to that effect was issued in 1264. Thomas Aquinas was commissioned to compose the office for the Feast of Corpus Christi (the Body of Christ). The processions and public ceremonies which grew up around the feast transformed what had originated as a personal, ecstatic experience of Christ's presence into a communal ritual of inclusion and exclusion. The processions to celebrate Corpus Christi particularly emphasized the unity of Christian communities as the mystical body of Christ. Towns with Jewish inhabitants might banish them for the duration of the celebration, so that the civic community could be entirely one in Christ.

Jews

By the beginning of the thirteenth century there were Jewish groups living in several of the towns of the Low Countries. None appear to have settled in the county of Flanders in any organized form, but there were Jewish communities all along the land route from Flanders to Cologne: in Brussels, Leuven, Tienen, Zoutleeuw and Sint-Truiden. Later in the century, Jews expelled from France established communities in Hainaut. Jewish religious and intellectual life in Brabant has left a few traces. The learned German rabbi Eliezer ben Joel ha-Levi, known as Ravyah (1140–1225), appears to have lived for a while in Leuven. In 1309 the Jewish copyist Isaac, son of Eliyahu Chasan of Oxford, completed a codex of the Hebrew Bible in Brussels. In the fourteenth century Leuven had a Jewish cemetery and at least one synagogue. There is speculation as to whether 'Moyses Judeus, presbyter of the Jews in Leuven', living around 1312, was a rabbi or some sort of community or financial official. Guild and other regulations effectively excluded Jews from most forms of productive labour. They made their living from trading not monopolized by the merchant guilds (such as dealing in second-hand goods), from the practice of medicine and from money-lending. In the Low Countries Italians were far more numerous as money-lenders, and 'lombard' became a synonym for usurer.

Henry III of Brabant, who died in 1261, decreed in his will that all Jews and Lombards involved in usury be driven from the duchy. By waiting until his death Duke Henry avoided facing the fiscal consequences of his piety: charges on money-lenders were a source of ducal income not subject to feudal custom, canon law or civic consent. Faced with this problem Henry's widow consulted Thomas Aquinas about the fairest treatment of her son's Jewish subjects, and his answer was the *De Regimine Judaeorum*. Thomas advised that Jews should not be driven out or forcibly baptized, but suggested that contact between Christians and non-Christians should be minimized and that it should be decreed that Jews do productive work, while those who persisted in usury should be heavily taxed. The final stipulation is perhaps the only one to have been followed, Aquinas having given a shadow of theological sanction to ducal patronage of Jewish money-lenders. During a popular pogrom in 1309, Jews found refuge in the castle of Duke John II at Genappe.

WAR, MARRIAGE AND MURDER, 1246–1305

The years around 1300, like those around 1200, saw an interconnected set of dynastic crises in the Low Countries. Imperial confirmation of title was no longer the main element in the growth of principalities: it had

79

been replaced by marriage. This was followed by war, only resorted to when marriage alliances or feudal custom gave some pretext, and at a greater distance by purchases and exchanges of territory. Imperial over-lordship, already weakened by internal divisions, was pushed into irrel-evance by the diplomatic and military resurgence of the French monarchy.

The marriages of Baldwin IX's younger daughter, Margaret, were among the most thorny matrimonial issues of the thirteenth century. When she was 10 years old, Philip Augustus of France had married her off to the subdeacon Burchard of Avesnes in a ceremony with no shadow of canonical validity. In 1215 Countess Joan obtained a decree of nullity for her sister, but Burchard for years refused to give Margaret her freedom. In 1223 Margaret, free at last, married William of Dampierre, and bore him a son also named William. But when it became apparent that Margaret was likely to succeed her sister Joan as countess of Flanders, her firstborn son, John of Avesnes, sought to assert his legit-imacy. Quarrels which drew public declarations from popes, emperors, and kings of France smouldered and flared, with Margaret's longevity delaying the necessity of a solution. When she finally died in 1280, Flanders passed to her grandson, Guy of Dampierre, and Hainaut to another grandson, John (II) of Avesnes. This division of the inheritance between Avesnes and Dampierre, ending the century-old personal union of Flanders and Hainaut, had been agreed in 1246, but the parties concerned never considered it entirely satisfactory. In the meantime the Avesnes had obtained a marriage alliance with the count of Holland, the Dampierres with the duke of Brabant, three small wars had been fought, and Margaret's son, William of Dampierre, had been murdered at a tour-nament in Trazegnies. More wars were to follow, for the enmity of the houses of Avesnes and Dampierre was to be an element in the political life of the Low Countries for decades to come.

In an attempt to encircle Hainaut, Guy of Dampierre had in 1263 bought the marquisate of Namur for £20,000. In selling his title the marquis was not exactly selling the marquisate: in 1256 a revolt had delivered effective rule to Henry V of Luxembourg, whose grandmother Ermesind had been done out of Namur in 1199. After a short war Guy and Henry settled the matter by an alliance which involved Guy marry-ing Henry's daughter Isabella. The Luxembourg claim to Namur became Isabella's dowry, with a stipulation that it was to pass to Guy's descendants by her rather than to his heir by his first marriage. Guy lived until 1305 but in the late 1290s, whilst imprisoned in France, he formally relinquished rule of Namur to his oldest son by Isabella, John of Dampierre, and of Flanders to his heir by his first marriage, Robert of Béthune. Far from bringing the principalities of the Low Countries together, marriage alliances seemed to be breaking them apart.

John the Victorious

War, on the other hand, could be successful. John I, 'the Victorious', Duke of Brabant (1267–94), was the acme of chivalry. He was a crusader and leader in war, a dispenser of justice, a patron of the Church and the arts, a renowned jouster, and a courtly poet who wrote in praise of wine, women and song. Chroniclers liked to recall that his mother had once consulted Thomas Aquinas, so he even basked in that reflected glory, while some have suggested that Gambrinus, legendary king of drinkers, is a corruption of 'Jan Primus'.

When the last duke of Limburg in the direct male line died in 1280, the candidates for succession included the count of Guelders (in his wife's right), the count of Berg, the count of Luxembourg and, at some remove, the duke of Brabant. The emperor invested Guelders with Limburg, but his decision was ignored. Luxembourg sold his rights to Guelders, and Berg sold his to Brabant, considerably simplifying the contest. The bishop of Liège was a Dampierre, tied to John I by marriage, so he backed the duke, as did the counts of Jülich and Cleves. Guelders was supported by Luxembourg and by the archbishop of Cologne, the main prince in the Rhineland. The citizens of Cologne sided against their bishop, who was disputing their liberties. On 5 June 1288 the armies of the duke of Brabant and the archbishop of Cologne met near the Rhine, north of Cologne, at Worringen (in Dutch, Woeringen). The knights of Brabant, the peasant levies of Berg and the city militia of Cologne faced the knights of the count of Guelders, the archbishop of Cologne and the count of Luxembourg. In the course of the battle the archbishop and the count of Guelders were both captured. The count of Luxembourg and his three brothers fought to the death, immortalizing the bravery of their house even as a generation of it was virtually wiped out. Hostilities did not end with Worringen, but it was the decisive battle. By the end of 1289 the liberties of Cologne and John I's title to Limburg were recognized by all concerned. John I was now the only duke in the Low Countries, and master of the road from Cologne to Flanders.

In 1279 John I's son, the future John II, had become affianced to

King Edward I's daughter Margaret. The marriage was solemnized in 1290. The medieval national epic of Brabant was a tendentious verse account of the Battle of Woeringen which John I commissioned from Jan van Heelu as a way of familiarizing his English daughter-in-law with the language and glorious achievements of her new family. In 1294 Margaret's sister Eleonora married the count of Bar in London. The couple then travelled through Brabant to Bar, where a magnificent tournament was to be held. John I and a small company of his knights joined them on the final stage of their journey, to take part in the tournament. It was the 41-year-old duke's seventy-second such competition, and his last. On 3 May 1294 he suffered a fatal fall while jousting.

The Murder of Floris V

A younger contemporary of John I was Floris V, who became count of Holland at the age of two and ruled for 40 years, until his murder in 1296. His father was William II, the King of the Romans hacked to death by the Frisians in 1256. Floris's concessions of liberties and legal guarantees after peasant revolts in 1272 earned him the nickname 'the god of the peasants'. At the age of 23 he was knighted by John I of Brabant at a tournament held in 's-Hertogenbosch for the occasion – tournaments providing opportunities for diplomacy, as well as for exercises in courtesy and the martial arts. In the following years Floris completed the conquest of West Frisia, marking it with a line of castles the northernmost of which was that at Medemblik, finished in 1285. In 1292 he gained Stavoren, a toe-hold on the north-eastern shore of the Zuider Zee.

King Edward I's marriage alliances with Brabant and Bar were part of a wider network being built up on the northern and eastern frontiers of France. In 1281 Floris V of Holland affianced his daughter Margaret to Edward I's son and heir Alfonso, offering half his county as dowry. The wedding was prevented by the prince's early death, so Floris was not to see a grandchild on the English throne. In 1286 Alexander III of Scotland was thrown over the cliffs of Kinghorne by his horse. His daughter, the wife of Eric II of Norway, had died three years before. His only living descendant was his granddaughter Margaret, 'the Maid of Norway'. In 1290 the ship carrying her to Scotland failed to arrive, and the Scottish succession was thrown open to about a dozen claimants. Floris V, a great-great-grandson of Alexander III's great-aunt Ada (sister to William the Lion), travelled to Scotland in 1291, and again in

1292, to promote his own claims. In 1292 John de Balliol secured the crown. Floris attended his coronation to show that there were no hard feelings, and to be confirmed in the earldom of Garioch (his inheritance from Ada). Floris's father had been elected King of the Romans, but hopes of a royal crown for his descendants were never to be realized.

In the course of his journeys to Scotland Floris visited the king of England, with whom he was quite friendly. It has even been suggested that he was King Edward's candidate for the crown of Scotland. The upshot of the visits was that Floris's infant son and heir John was affianced to Edward's daughter Elizabeth, and was sent to be raised at the English court. The marriage was solemnized in 1297, the year after Floris's death.

In 1294 Edward I added Guy of Dampierre, count of Flanders, to his allies on France's northern border. Floris V was already put out that the English had moved their wool staple from Dordrecht to Mechelen. He had a mortal hatred of Guy, who in 1290 had humiliatingly held him hostage, and was disputing his suzerainty over Zeeland. Accordingly he abandoned his allies in England and Brabant and sided with France against Flanders. At once an international conspiracy against him was set on foot. The go-between appears to have been Gerard van Velsen, a minor landowner in Holland who was also a vassal of the duke of Brabant and of the bishop of Utrecht. The outcome is narrated here (with spelling modernized) from Edward Grimestone's *Generall Historie of the Netherlands* (1608), which largely follows the chronicle of Willelmus, procurator of Egmond, and the verse chronicle of Melis Stoke, one of the count's clerks, who saw the behaviour of the count's greyhounds for himself:

In the same year 1296 Count Floris (being ignorant of this conspiracy made against him at Cambrai, by the deputies of the King of England, the Duke of Brabant, the Count of Flanders, and the lords of Amstel and Woerden) at the instance and suit of Gerard van Velsen . . . went to make good cheer with the Noblemen and Prelates of Utrecht. After dinner, being laid down to rest a little, thinking to spend the remainder of the day in sport and pleasure, the Lord of Amstel went to wake him, inviting him to ride abroad with his hawks, saying, that they had found a goodly flight of herons, and other wild fowl (but they were such fowl as no hawk could take, and were lodged there to take the Count himself) who loving hawking exceedingly, went to horse with a merlin on his fist, being very slenderly accompanied of his followers. Riding about half a mile out of Utrecht, he was led into the midst of the ambush of these conspirators . . . . Gerard van Velsen (who held himself much wronged) was the first that offered to lay hold on him: but like a courageous prince (casting away his merlin which he carried) he laid hold of his sword to defend himself, desiring rather to die than to yield. But not able to make resistance, he was taken, they meaning to carry him secretly that night to the castle of Muiden, and from thence to send him into England by the river Vlie.

This was on 23 June. Watch and ward was raised and the men of the districts of Waterland, Kennemerland and West Frisia came to arms to liberate the count. The chronicle continues with the events of 27 June:

the conspirators being advertised of their coming, departed suddenly, leading the count through marshes and unknown places. Those of Naarden (who first went in search of him) encountered them full in the teeth: they being much perplexed, knowing that the Kennemers pursued them, were doubtful what way to take. The count's horse whereon he was mounted, and bound, . . . not able to leap like the rest, he fell into a ditch, where they laboured to get him forth, but could not, having no leisure by reason of the pursuit of them that followed. Gerard van Velsen full of fury and rage, . . . played the part of a desperate man, giving him one and twenty wounds with his sword, most of which were mortal: then mounting upon a good horse he saved himself in his castle of Croonenburch. In the mean time the Kennemers arrive, who found their count half dead in this ditch, speechless, drawing only his breath. They took some of these conspirators' servants, whom in the count's presence they cut in pieces, and having drawn him forth of the ditch, they carried him up to the mount of Muiden, whereas he breathed out his last gasp, after that he had governed Holland, Zeeland and Friesland, as well by himself as by his tutors, two and forty years. He was a generous prince, of a goodly stature, and lovely countenance, gracious and eloquent in his speech, a good musician, stately and liberal. . . . His body was carried by boat to Alkmaar, where his bowels were buried in the church, and his body being embalmed was laid in the choir, until that Count John his son was returned out of England. Count Floris had two greyhounds, the which had always followed him, going in and coming out of the Castle of Muiden, and which were found lying by him in the ditch where he was slain: carrying him into the boat, they followed and leaped into it, and would never eat nor drink although it were offered them; yea they would have starved themselves if they had not been drawn away from the count's dead body.

Floris V was succeeded by his son John, who died childless – himself only 15 – in 1299. The house which had ruled Holland for almost 400 years was extinguished in the male line. The new count was to be John of Avesnes, a first cousin of Floris and already count of Hainaut. To win the support of the merchants of Holland for his claim, John of Avesnes made Dordrecht a staple market: all foreign goods passing through the county had to be offered for sale in the city. As bitter enemies of the Dampierres who ruled in Flanders, the House of Avesnes could also be relied upon to assert Holland's claims over Zeeland.

Enjoying the backing of the kings of France, the House of Avesnes was in the ascendant. In 1300 the Emperor Albert I came to Nijmegen to invest John of Avesnes with the county of Holland, but John had no interest in being bound by further oaths of fealty and chased the emperor away. The following year the bishop of Utrecht died while making war on the Avesnes, and John sought to impose his brother Guy as bishop. The canons of Deventer elected their dean, Adolph of Waldeck, but at the same time Liège fell vacant and the Avesnes cut a deal that Adolph would get Liège if he resigned Utrecht in favour of Guy. Utrecht and the Oversticht belonged to the Avesnes until 1317, and they ruled Hainaut and Holland-Zeeland until 1345.

The Battle of the Golden Spurs

In 1297 Guy of Dampierre, count of Flanders, renounced his feudal loyalty to the king of France, Philip the Fair. The French at once invaded and overran much of Flanders. Pope Boniface VIII dispatched the general superiors of the Franciscan and Dominican orders to mediate a settlement, the result of which was a separate French–English peace which left Guy out in the cold. The artisans of the cloth towns Ghent, Ypres and Douai backed the count who had promised them a share in urban government, but the patricians of Bruges and elsewhere sided with Philip the Fair to maintain their pre-eminent position. By the end of 1300 Guy of Dampierre was languishing in a French dungeon and Philip the Fair had appointed Jacques de Châtillon as his own governor over all of Flanders. On 17 May 1302 the craftsmen of Bruges struck against the French in what came to be called the 'Bruges Matins', the church bells being the signal for the attack. Under the leadership of the master weaver Pieter de Coninck and the nobleman William of Jülich (a grandson of Guy of Dampierre) they rampaged through the city slaughtering over 200 Frenchmen and francophiles. Châtillon and his personal guard barely made it out of the city.

Philip the Fair despatched an army, the cream of French chivalry, to put down the rebellion. Small forces of knights came from Namur and Zeeland to support the townsmen, but the bulk of the Flemish army consisted of the craftsmen of Bruges, reinforced by peasants from the surrounding countryside and a few detachments of militiamen sent from other towns. The armies met outside Kortrijk on 11 July 1302. The Flemings slightly outnumbered the French, but were an army of commoners fighting on foot against an army of knights. The battle was a massacre. The horses quickly got bogged down in the mud, and countless knights were slaughtered by artisans and peasants wielding pikes, halberds and cudgels. The partisan historical vision of nineteenth-century Flemish nationalists turned the battle into a victory of Dutch speakers over French speakers, and 11 July is now the 'national' holiday of the Flemish Region. But this was not the end of the war. The French fought on until 1305, when Guy died and they could force more favourable peace terms on his son, Robert III.

CIVIC CULTURE AND GOVERNANCE AROUND 1300

The connection between the rise of the towns and the rise of the Dutch language, although out of place in a discussion of the Battle of Kortrijk, is not simply fiction. The writings of Jacob van Maerlant, who died probably shortly before 1300, were the first basis of a coherent literary tradition in Dutch. The Dutch medievalist Frits Van Oostrom has suggested that with a lifetime's output probably not much short of a quarter of a million lines of verse, Maerlant may well have been the most prolific vernacular author of medieval Europe. Maerlant was neither mystic nor mendicant, but a churchwarden at Maarland on the island of Voorne in Zeeland. Later he returned to his native Flanders, and there is a tradition that he worked as a clerk for the magistrates of Damme. Besides his humdrum daily occupations, he enjoyed the literary patronage of the highest in the land. His crowning achievement, dedicated to Floris V, was the 90,000-line *Spiegel historiael* (Historical Mirror), a world chronicle from the Creation to the First Crusade. His other writings – and like the *Spiegel historiael* these were all adaptations of French and Latin originals – were Arthurian romances, lives of St Francis and St Clare, various works on the wonders of nature, a verse paraphrase of biblical history, and accounts of the Trojan War, Alexander the Great and the Destruction of Jerusalem.

The word most often used to characterize Maerlant's work and the literary tradition that sprang from it is 'didactic'. Informing and improving were unquestionably central to Maerlant's concept of his role as a poet. It was this conviction that led him to renounce the 'false' romance tradition of his early works, and turn to writing on natural philosophy, political morality and religious history. In the work of Maerlant and his followers, histories, chronicles, bestiaries, herbals and lapidaries, moral reflections and lives of saints displaced the fantastic adventures of knights, damsels and talking beasts as the central concerns of literature. Although Maerlant wrote for noble patrons, his readers included the urban middle classes, who were just as keen on improving their knowledge of the world's history and marvels. Burghers commissioned copies of his works, and they were among the earliest printed books in Dutch. Literate urbanites were coming to be as considerable a market for Dutch texts as the Church and the court had long been for Latin and French.

A new sort of literature which began to appear in the thirteenth century was civic and secular drama. Some sort of religious drama had been performed in monasteries since Ottonian times, particularly around Easter, and from the early thirteenth century passion plays were performed in the major churches, and later on marketplaces and carts. By the end of the Middle Ages an element of pageant had attached itself to most religious processions, and numerous mystery, miracle and morality plays were being performed at set times of year in the cities of the Low Countries, as elsewhere in Western Europe. The English morality *Everyman* is an adaptation of the fifteenth-century Dutch play *Elcerlyc* or *Den spyeghel der salicheyt* (The Mirror of Blessedness).

Among the oldest known secular plays in post-antique Europe are *Le jeu de la feuillée* and *Le jeu de Robin et Marion* by Adam de la Halle, a clerk of Arras who died in 1288. In the fourteenth century Dutch-speaking performers put on 'abele spelen', able (or artful) plays on serious themes. Four survive: *Esmoreit* (with the same basic plot that Shakespeare was to use for *A Winter's Tale*), *Gloriant* (a tale of love triumphing over pride), *Lanseloet van Denemerken* (a tragi-comedy of love dishonoured and honour redeemed) and the more allegorical *Vanden Winter ende Vanden Somer* (in which Winter and Summer, with their followers, nearly come to blows in a debate of their respective merits, but Venus mediates an amicable settlement). In performance one of these serious plays would be followed by a farce, the knock-about comedy of which is still apparent although it takes a medievalist to spot the more subtle jokes.

The pretext of Guy of Dampierre's war with Philip the Fair could not have been more typically feudal: the count's abjuration of his homage to a lord who oppressed him. The course and outcome of the war demonstrated the new power of the towns, and especially of the craft guilds. By intervening in political affairs in the count's absence, and defeating the chivalry of France, the craftsmen of Bruges had established that they were now a force to be reckoned with. By slaughtering the francophile patricians of their city, the most essentially mercantile of all the towns of Europe, they had shown that those who lived off rents and trading could no longer lord it over those who worked with their hands.

Craft guilds had been pressing for a greater say in the affairs of their towns throughout the thirteenth century. The example of their success in Flanders in forcing the patricians to share, or even surrender, civic power inspired similar movements in neighbouring principalities. In some cities in Liège and Brabant artisans were admitted to power as early as 1303, but were unable to dislodge patrician dominance until much later if at all. In Utrecht the artisans seized power in 1304. As time went on the demand for craft-guild participation in civic government spread to every town in the Low Countries, meeting varying degrees of success. The craft guilds were transformed from instruments of economic regulation into self-governing corporations which quickly developed their own traditions of urban governance and military training. City laws and civic militias were used to maintain the economic interests of the dominant trades. The weavers of Ghent, for instance, regulated cloth production in the lesser towns of the vicinity and prohibited the selling of cloth made in the countryside within two miles of the city. From the beginning guilds served to perpetuate the social position of established master craftsmen and their families, and this became clearer as time went on. Fees for mastership became higher; numbers of masters might be restricted; except in certain guilds in some of the Flemish towns, only masters could elect or be elected as deans. Wages and conditions were set more often in conflict than in consultation with journeymen and apprentices, whose hopes of one day becoming master of their own shop grew ever more slender.

Another new element in urban government was the professional administrator. From the thirteenth century onwards, the constantly changing magistracies of the towns – elected in rotation by patricians and craft guilds – employed permanent civil servants to give continuity to their administration. At first these were simply called *clerc*. One of the most famous is Jan van Boendale, clerk to the aldermen of Antwerp. In his free time he was a writer in the mould of Jacob van Maerlant (whom he described as 'the father of all Dutch poets'), and among other works he produced a rhyming chronicle of Brabant called *De Brabantsche yeesten* (The Deeds of Brabant). Towns were now producing their own versions of history, to supplement and rival those of monasteries and courts. From the end of the Middle Ages clerks were lesser functionaries and the heads of the administrative staff were the 'secretary', who drafted edicts, kept records and managed the official correspondence; and the 'pensionary' or 'syndic', a lawyer on permanent retainer to advise the magistrates and represent the town to outside powers.

The patricians did not give up their monopoly on power without a fight. Most notoriously, in 1312 the patrician party tried to reclaim power in Liège by setting fire to the Butchers' Hall. The coup failed and the conspirators took refuge in the tower of the church of St Martin. In what became known as the *Mal de Saint Martin* (St Martin Disaster) the artisans set fire to the church tower, killing hundreds and briefly ensuring the total exclusion of the patricians from power.

Opposing patrician and craft-guild interests were not the only sources of tension in the towns. The crafts themselves were not always allies: in Ghent in 1345, for instance, fighting broke out between weavers and fullers. Factional struggles of the sort portrayed between Montagues and Capulets in *Romeo and Juliet* were rife in the later medieval Low Countries, from combinations of motives. Factions tended to seek support from other quarters, as in 1302 the artisans of Flanders had sided with the count against the patricians and the king. Thus did social, dynastic and personal rivalries become entangled in lasting enmities. The local variants on the Guelphs and Ghibbelines were the Lilies and Claws in Flanders, Lichtenbergers and Fresings (and later Lichtenbergers and Lokhorsts) in Utrecht, Bronkhorsts and Hekerens in Guelders, and the Schieringers and Vetkopers in Friesland. Most securely institutionalized as 'parties' were the Hooks and Cods in

Holland, factions which for a century or more chanelled all the varied in-fighting of the towns and noble families of the county. A further source of violent confrontation was trade rivalry between the towns: once the craft guilds established their dominance, civic militias battled to do down their competitors.

THE DISMAL CENTURY, 1305–1384

By the end of the thirteenth century there was more land under cultivation than ever before or since. There was less woodland than at any time before the nineteenth century. The need for timber and firewood led lords, abbeys and village communities to give up marginal lands which were yielding ever leaner returns in order to start reforestation. Land was also lost to flooding, and to sand drifts: on the Flemish coast alone over 1000 hectares of agricultural land disappeared beneath the dunes. As harvests worsened the population was increasingly poorly fed, resulting in chronic malnutrition, occasional famines and the spread of epidemics. From May 1315 it rained uninterruptedly for a whole year, ruining a harvest so that grain prices tripled and there was terrible famine in the Low Countries.

In the struggle of 1302 the peasants of Flanders had played almost as important a role as the craftsmen of Bruges, but with no corresponding rewards. From 1323 to 1328 there was a bloody peasants' revolt in maritime Flanders, finally suppressed with great brutality. More untimely deaths followed with the coming of the Black Death, which reached Flanders in 1349 and the rest of the Low Countries in 1350. The death rate in the Low Countries seems to have been lower than in many places, but mortality was still considerable. The pestilence became endemic, recurring periodically until the 1660s. Throughout the fourteenth century population fell, and so did incomes from land and from the cloth trade. There were nine serious floods in the course of the century, three in the years 1373–76, with Holland and Zeeland suffering the most damage. But worse was to come: on 19 November 1421 the 'St Elizabeth' Flood submerged 34 parishes in the vicinity of Dordrecht. In the course of the fourteenth century, flooding, famine and disease were supplemented by war and economic recession.

The English royal family was tied to the counts and dukes of the Low Countries by a web of marriage alliances built up since the 1290s. Edward III continued the tradition in 1328 by marrying Philippa of

Hainaut, a daughter of William of Avesnes, count of Holland, Zeeland and Hainaut. In the same year William married off another daughter, Margaret, to Louis of Bavaria, Holy Roman Emperor, and his own brother-in-law, Philip of Valois, unexpectedly inherited the kingdom of France. Almost at a stroke, William of Avesnes was an in-law of the crowned heads of the three surrounding kingdoms. The Hundred Years War began in 1338, and Flanders was to be one of its many theatres. In the first move, Edward III forged an alliance with the emperor Louis and landed his army at Antwerp, to link up with his allies in the Low Countries. His achievements were memorialized by Jan van Boendale in the 2018-line *Van den derden Eduwaert* (Of the third Edward), particularly stressing the deeds of his ally John III of Brabant. One of those who attended upon Philippa of Hainaut in the 1360s was Jean Froissart (*c*.1338–*c*.1404), a native of Valenciennes. Froissart wrote a set of *Chronicles of England, France, Spain and the Adjoining Countries* which gives an incomparable account of the Hundred Years War. This was one of the most popular works of the late Middle Ages. More than a hundred manuscript copies survive and it was repeatedly printed after 1495.

Edward's allies did not include the count of Flanders, Louis of Nevers, who remained loyal to his suzerain Philip of France. The importance of the English wool trade to the Flemish cloth trade meant that the great cloth towns favoured England's side in international affairs. With the count failing to support their interests, the weavers and merchants of Ghent formed an unstable alliance and established a republican regime headed by Jacob van Artevelde. Soon the men of Ghent, rather than the count, were ruling Flanders, and Jacob van Artevelde was their increasingly autocratic leader. On 26 January 1340 Edward III was proclaimed king of France in Ghent. A few months later the entire French fleet was destroyed in a naval battle at Sluis. This success was not followed up on land, and fighting was suspended until 1346. In the meantime the fragile internal alliances in Flanders were crumbling. In May 1345 the weavers and fullers of Ghent fought a pitched battle against one another on the city's Friday Market. In July Van Artevelde arrived back in the city from a shipboard meeting with Edward III at Sluis. He was mobbed and slaughtered. In 1346 Louis of Nevers died fighting for the king of France at Crécy. His successor, Louis of Male, soon restored comital authority in Flanders. Bruges, Ypres, and the lesser towns threw off the rule of Ghent and admitted Louis of Male as count. In 1349, the very year that plague struck, the men of Ghent were defeated in a battle fought within the walls of their own city.

The local dynasty perhaps least concerned with events in the Low Countries was that of the counts of Luxembourg. The reason for their general absence was the growth of their power elsewhere. In 1308 the princes of the Low Countries formed the Alliance of Nivelles to prevent the king of France's brother being elected King of the Romans, with the result that Henry VII of Luxembourg was elected instead. Henry was the first emperor actually to be crowned in almost 100 years, and he travelled to Rome for the purpose. On the way he was crowned king of Lombardy. Dante was ecstatic, rather prematurely hailing Henry as the saviour who would pacify the domestic turmoils of Italy, and reserving a seat for him in the *Paradiso*. In the event the pope stayed away from Rome and Henry was crowned emperor by two cardinals. He died near Siena in 1313 and was buried at Pisa. Henry VII's imperial election was the beginning of the remarkable rise of the House of Luxembourg to the forefront of international affairs. They attained not only the imperial crown, but the royal crowns of Bohemia and Hungary.

In 1345 William IV of Holland and II of Hainaut, the last of the Avesnes in the male line, invaded Frisia and fell in the Battle of Warns. His death opened up the succession to Holland, Zeeland and Hainaut. One well-placed contender for the title was Edward III of England, in the right of his wife Philippa of Hainaut. In the event, Margaret, William IV's other sister and the wife of Louis of Bavaria, inherited the Avesnes lands. In all, the House of Bavaria ruled Holland, Zeeland and Hainaut from the 1350s to the 1430s. These 80 years were the most brilliant in the court life of The Hague and Valenciennes. In 1371 the House of Guelders also died out in the male line, to be replaced by heirs whose court has recently been studied in detail by Gerard Nijsten.

As in earlier centuries, the growth in princely brilliance was paralleled by a growth in the power and independence of their subjects. To finance their wars and courtly displays, princes were obliged to give formal recognition to the privileges of the towns and of the provincial nobility. As they did so, a clearer sense of a contract between ruler and subjects developed. The fourteenth century saw the first involvement of representative assemblies in the rule of the principalities, the earliest being the Council of XXII in Liège and the Council of Kortenberg in Brabant. In the course of the fourteenth and fifteenth centuries fully fledged parliamentary institutions, known as 'states' or 'estates', began to meet. In Brabant the great abbeys, the nobility and the four cities Leuven, Brussels, Antwerp and 's-Hertogenbosch had a say in the counsels of the duke, particularly when it came to taxation and the redress of grievances. In Flanders the only voting members were to be the cities of Ghent, Bruges and Ypres and the rural Liberty of Bruges. In Holland the cities and nobility shared power; in Utrecht and Liège, the cities, nobility and clergy. In Hainaut, Namur and Guelders the nobility predominated, while in Luxembourg the nobility and the five boroughs (Luxembourg, Arlon, Thionville, Echternach and Bitburg) were represented at the first meetings of the States, supplemented with representatives of the clergy from 1378.

When John III of Brabant died in 1355 he left three daughters as heiresses. Their husbands were the duke of Luxembourg, the count of Flanders, and a pretender to the duchy of Guelders. The States of Brabant insisted that the inheritance pass inviolate to the eldest daughter, Joanna. She brought her husband Wenceslas, duke of Luxembourg, to reign by her side. Before they would admit a foreigner to rule, the noblemen and cities of Brabant required that Joanna and Wenceslas subscribe to a charter of the main privileges of the duchy, swearing to uphold them or forfeit the obedience of their subjects. They were sworn in as rulers in 1356. This Great Charter was the clearest and most far-reaching statement of the ideal of government by contract and of the duty of the prince to uphold the liberties of the subject. Louis of Male, count of Flanders (1346–84), invaded Brabant to secure his wife's share of the inheritance and managed to conquer Antwerp and Mechelen. In the political crisis that followed the Great Charter of Brabant was almost immediately breached and nullified by both rulers and subjects. Nevertheless, it was to play a legal, political and mythical role in the history of the Low Countries somewhat akin to that of Magna Carta in the English-speaking world. Future dukes, or their personal representatives, were required to swear to some version of this Great Charter upon entering into their rule, and jurists in Brabant came to call the charter itself 'the Joyous Entry' (a term used throughout the Low Countries for the festive reception of a new ruler).

The development of parliamentary institutions in Brabant (as earlier in England) coincided with the end of the ruler taxing Jews for supplementary income. In the search for culprits in the disasters of the fourteenth century, the Jews of Brabant had suffered special blame. In 1350, after rumours that Jews had caused the plague by poisoning wells, most were driven out in a wave of popular violence. German Jewish martyrologies record up to 700 deaths. Refugees from Brabant made Guelders the most important centre of Jewish life in the late-medieval Low Countries, but also founded or augmented communities in Zeeland and Luxembourg.

By 1370 there were six Jewish households left in Brabant, four in Brussels and two in Leuven. In that year the six heads of household confessed to desecrating eucharistic hosts. They were put to death, their families banished and their goods seized. There are good circumstantial reasons for doubting the truthfulness of the confessions, and it has even been suggested that the affair was got up by a couple of dodgy characters in the clerical establishment to cover their tracks in a usury scandal, but no direct evidence survives beyond the bare facts stated.

The damaged hosts, from 1402 mentioned as having bled miraculously when stabbed, were preserved in the collegiate church of St Michael and St Gudula (now Brussels Cathedral). The shrine of the Sacrament of Holy Miracle became a ceremonial focal point of national life in the duchy of Brabant. In the sixteenth century a separate chapel was built to house it, and in the course of time this was richly adorned with paintings, tapestries and stained-glass windows. For the clergy and the faithful what mattered was that Christ's presence in the eucharist had been miraculously manifested. Similar eucharistic miracles, such as the Sacred Blood at Boxtel, or the Miraculous Host at Douai, were said to be due to priests treating the eucharist with culpable carelessness. In Amsterdam there were consecrated wafers which had miraculously escaped damage when a church burned down in 1345, and in Enkhuizen pilgrims venerated a crucifix said to have sprouted from a hollow tree into which a young woman had vomited shortly after receiving communion. As far as later pilgrims were concerned the anti-Semitic component in the reputed eucharistic miracle of Brussels was incidental, but it cast a long shadow on the history of Brabant.

There is no record of a formal perpetual banishment of the Jews from Brabant (as had occurred in England in 1290), but there was a persistent later tradition that Jewish settlement was contrary to the laws of the duchy. At the height of Antwerp's prosperity in the early sixteenth century, Jews were only admitted to Brabant on a temporary basis and if they could demonstrate that they were visiting for economic reasons and not fleeing persecution. In the seventeenth century there were attempts to give more secure legal protection to Jews in order to take advantage of economic down-turns in Amsterdam and of the flight of Jewish capital from Portugal, but these were shipwrecked on the determination of the duke (who was then also the king of Spain) to maintain the 'purity' of Brabant.

THE BEGINNINGS OF BURGUNDIAN RULE

From 1379 Ghent was again in rebellion against Count Louis of Male and the king of France. In a replay of Jacob van Artevelde's seizure of power in 1338, his son Philip gained control of the government of Ghent in 1382. He was soon proclaimed *ruwaard* (governor) of Flanders. At the beginning of the rebellion Count Louis had called in the aid of his son-in-law Philip the Bold, duke of Burgundy. A new power was felt in Flanders. The combination of king of France, duke of Burgundy and count of Flanders working closely together was ultimately too much for the men of Ghent. They met crushing defeat at Westrozebeke at the end of 1382, a battle in which Artevelde himself died. The rebels held out in desperation, fighting a losing war.

The situation was not improved by a brief English 'crusade' to Flanders in 1383. Since 1379 there had been two opposing claimants to the papal crown: Urban VI in Rome and Clement VII in Avignon. In the Low Countries not only different princes but even different towns recognized one or the other as the rightful pope. The pretext of the English invasion was that winning Flanders from France would enable Urban VI, rather than the French anti-pope Clement VII, to exercise papal jurisdiction there. Billing the war as a crusade meant that the clergy could be taxed to pay for it. After an unsuccessful siege of Ypres (which in any case already recognized Urban VI) the English army went home.

In 1384 Louis of Male died. His daughter Margaret succeeded to the county, with her husband Philip of Burgundy ruling on her behalf. Philip's combination of military supremacy and generous clemency soon had him in firm control of Flanders. In the course of the next 50 years the dukes of Burgundy were to extend their rule over most of the Low Countries, transforming the balance of power in Western Europe.

3

The Low Countries United and Divided, 1384–1609

The dukes of Burgundy gradually established themselves as rulers of much of the Low Countries, a process of unification completed in the sixteenth century by the Habsburg emperor Charles V. Almost at once, this fragile composite state was torn apart into two hostile blocs, the Dutch Republic and the Habsburg Netherlands.

THE BURGUNDIAN CENTURY, 1384–1477

The dynasty founded by Philip the Bold of Burgundy (d. 1404) lasted only a century in the male line, dying with his great-grandson in 1477, but the House of Burgundy set its mark on the Low Countries like no lineage since the Carolingians. In one form or another, the link between the Low Countries and Burgundy was to last for 300 years.

Philip the Bold, youngest son of King John the Good of France, earned his nickname at the battle of Poitiers (1356), after which he spent four years in English captivity. In 1363 his bravery was rewarded with the duchy of Burgundy. In 1369 he married Margaret of Male, heiress of Flanders, and from 1384 he ruled the county in her right. In 1385 Philip arranged a marriage between his own children (John and Margaret) and those of Albert of Bavaria (Margaret and William). As a result, Philip's grandson could lay claim to Holland, Zeeland and Hainaut when the Bavarian line failed. In the meantime, other weddings and financial arrangements were to lead to Burgundian rule over Brabant and Limburg, and Namur. But Philip was more occupied with France than with the rest of the Low Countries. He was effectively regent of the kingdom during the minority, and later the madness, of Charles VI. Despite the focus on France, Burgundian rule was soon extended to Brabant and Limburg, albeit only collaterally. In return for Philip the Bold's support against the duke of Guelders, the childless Duchess Joanna bequeathed Brabant to her niece Margaret of Male on condition that it not become part of the Burgundian dominions but pass instead to a cadet. This happened in 1406, with Philip the Bold's younger son Anthony of Burgundy becoming duke of Brabant.

Philip's elder son, John the Fearless (1404–19), had by then already inherited Burgundy and Flanders. Like his father he focused his political energies on France. His main achievement in international affairs was, however, when still count of Nevers, to help Sigismund of Luxembourg lead the flower of Western European chivalry to defeat against the Turks in the Crusade of Nicopolis. Again like his father, he knew what it was to be a prisoner of war. His ransom was paid by the cities of Flanders. Thereafter, his overriding concern was always to try to control the government of France. This meant heavy involvement in the Hundred Years War, which Henry V of England had resumed. In 1407 Louis of Orleans, his main rival for power in France, was murdered by John's hirelings in the streets of Paris. By 1419, when John was murdered in turn, France was divided into three zones: the Lancastrian north, the Dauphinist south and the Burgundian east.

It was Philip the Good (1419–67) who plucked the fruits of his grandfather's marriage alliances, and put Burgundian power on a par with that of any kingdom in Europe. In 1421 he paid John III of Namur a considerable sum to be declared his heir, and in 1429 Namur passed to Burgundian rule. Brabant had passed to Philip the Good's uncle, Anthony of Burgundy, in 1406, after whose death it was ruled in turn by his sons John IV (1415–27) and Philip of St Pol (1427–30). When Philip of St Pol died childless, his cousin, Philip the Good, successfully laid claim to Brabant and Limburg. Almost as soon as becoming duke of Brabant, Philip transferred his main residence from Dijon to Brussels and founded the Order of the Golden Fleece, soon to be one of the most prestigious orders of knighthood in Europe.

Holland, Zeeland and Hainaut were added to the collection of territories in 1433, in circumstances which will be treated in more detail below. In 1434 the first common currency in the Low Countries was minted, the *vierlander*, which was to be of the same size, weight and value in Flanders, Brabant-Limburg, Holland-Zeeland and Hainaut. Philip extended his rule southwards, to Auxerre, Bar-sur-Seine and

Mâcon, in 1435. The last of his acquisitions was Luxembourg. In 1441 he badgered the ageing and childless duchess into designating him as her heir. When she died in 1443, Philip invaded Luxembourg to drive out William of Saxony, a rival claimant, and by 1451 he was undisputed master of the duchy. Although Burgundian image-makers celebrated the peacefulness of their aggrandizement – through marriage, purchase and inheritance rather than conquest – their claims always had to be backed up with the sword and the siege gun.

The most involved dynastic struggle was for the inheritance of the Low Countries branch of the House of Bavaria, rulers of Holland-Zeeland and Hainaut (see Map 4). John of Bavaria was nominated prince-bishop of Liège in 1389 and ruled Liège and Loon for 28 years without ever being ordained beyond the level of subdeacon. He was driven out by the townsmen of Liège in 1406, but returned at the head of troops lent by his brother William VI of Holland and his cousin John the Fearless of Burgundy. 'Bishop' John put down his opponents with such severity that he became known as John the Pitiless.

The last independent ruler of Holland, Zeeland and Hainaut was Jacqueline (or Jacoba) of Bavaria. She was born in 1401, the daughter of William VI of Holland. At the age of 14 she was married to the dauphin of France. In 1417 her father died of an infected dog-bite. At the age of 17 she was a widow and an orphan, countess of Holland, Zeeland and Hainaut, and had obtained a papal dispensation to marry her cousin, John IV of Brabant. Jacqueline's uncle, John of Bavaria, resigned his bishopric, married the duchess of Luxembourg, and claimed wardship over Jacqueline, challenging the validity of her marital dispensation. Her husband, John of Brabant, was notably lax in defending her interests and allowed John of Bavaria (who was backed by the power of both Burgundy and Luxembourg) to gain control of Holland and Zeeland as *ruwaard*, the countess's official lieutenant. In 1421 Jacqueline took matters into her own hands by repudiating her husband and travelling to England. There she married Humphrey, duke of Gloucester, and in 1424 they landed at Calais with an army and marched to Hainaut, to secure at least that part of her inheritance. The following year Gloucester ran off with one of Jacqueline's ladies-in-waiting. The devastated countess, still only 24, surrendered to Philip the Good.

John of Bavaria had died suddenly earlier in the year, of a slow-acting poison smeared on the pages of his prayer book. He had made Philip the Good his heir, so Philip now ruled Holland as *ruwaard*, with the approval of John IV of Brabant. Jacqueline soon revolted against this situation. She escaped from Ghent disguised as a man, and held out in a patch of Holland dense with castles garrisoned by those loyal to her. It took Philip four consecutive summers of military campaigning (1425–28) to bring her to submit to his terms. Matters then settled down until 1432, when Jacqueline secretly married Frank van Borselen. The Borselens were a powerful noble family in Zeeland and Frank had leased the government of Holland and Zeeland from Philip. The secret wedding breached the conditions of 1428 and when it became known Philip imprisoned Frank van Borselen and declared Jacqueline's title to her counties forfeit. The countess agreed to abdicate and retire to one of her castles in return for her husband's release. In 1436, aged only 35, she died of tuberculosis and Burgundian control of her inheritance was finally assured.

The only territories that the Burgundians could not inherit were the bishoprics, but these they sought to control in other ways. In the crises of the fourteenth century the political authority of the bishops of Utrecht had crumbled. Bishop Frederik of Blankenheim (1393–1423) set about restoring the power of the mitre with notable success, even restoring episcopal lordship over Groningen. In a local replay of the recently ended Great Schism, two candidates claimed the newly powerful position of bishop of Utrecht at Frederick's death. One was backed by Philip the Good, the other by Arnold of Egmond, Duke of Guelders. The Nedersticht and the Oversticht each came under the control of one of the rivals. Through a series of nominations, elections and shifting alliances the split was kept up until 1450, so that for 27 years the diocese was divided for control of the lordship.

In 1455, just a few years after the bishopric was reunited, Philip the Good tried to force his legitimized bastard David on the see. The canons had other ideas but a quick invasion deposed their elected nominee. David of Burgundy ruled as bishop of Utrecht until 1496. In 1456 the reigning bishop of Liège, John of Heinsberg, was forced to resign and Philip the Good's nephew, Louis of Bourbon, ruled the see from 1456 to 1482. The bishoprics of Utrecht and Liège were thus in the duke's pocket. A similar fate befell Cambrai, but Tournai resisted Burgundian influence by accepting French patronage.

The Burgundian dukes inherited each principality separately, and their territories formed a composite state, each part being ruled by a different title through different institutions and with different laws, customs and liberties. Nevertheless, as early as 1386 Philip the Bold began to consolidate the financial administration of Burgundy and

Flanders, and the process continued with the dynasty's expansion into neighbouring territories. One of the most important steps towards forging the various counties and duchies into a loosely federalized whole capable of co-ordinated action was taken in 1464. In that year Philip the Good summoned representatives of the Estates of Brabant, Flanders, Walloon Flanders, Artois, Hainaut, Valenciennes, Holland, Zeeland, Namur, Mechelen and the Bourbonnais to Bruges for joint consultation. Such meetings of what came to be called the Estates General became increasingly frequent, and were held almost annually from 1477 to 1576. They gave the territories of the Burgundian Netherlands a sense of the 'common good' intermediate between the whole of Christendom and their own county or duchy.

When Philip the Good died, his son Charles the Bold (1467–77) inherited Burgundy, Flanders, Artois, Namur, Brabant, Limburg, Holland, Zeeland, Hainaut and Luxembourg. He maintained proxy rule of Utrecht, Liège and Cambrai through the family members appointed to those sees (see Map 4). Charles loved the visual arts and music, but above all books, and especially history books. His father's collection was one of the great libraries of Europe, and Charles added to it considerably. He was particularly enamoured of stories of Alexander the Great and Julius Caesar, and was an enthusiastic patron of writers, translators and illuminators. Bad-tempered throughout his life, he was a studious child, a vindictive man and a cruel ruler. In 1465 his cousin Louis of Bourbon was driven from Liège, but in 1468 Charles savagely put down the rebellion and plundered the city. The *perron*, a column representing the city's liberties, was removed and set up in Bruges as a trophy. When the citizens again took up arms, Charles had Liège put to the torch.

It was Charles's ambition that the disparate lands he ruled should become one kingdom. With this aim he launched wars of conquest against many of the territories which bordered on and separated the two parts of his inheritance, Burgundy and the Low Countries. He took Sundgau and Breisgau in 1469, Guelders in 1473, Lorraine and Bar in 1475. On the eve of his death it was possible to travel from the North Sea to within sight of the Alps on land he had either inherited or conquered. In 1473 Duke Charles got as far as meeting with the emperor Frederick III at Trier to arrange a marriage between their heirs, Mary of Burgundy and Maximilian of Habsburg, and to negotiate for the title 'King of Burgundy' or 'King of Lotharingia'. The emperor, dismayed at Charles's exorbitant demands, broke off negotiations and secretly fled Trier. The duke had failed to gain a royal crown, but he pressed ahead with his plans for the unification of his territories. In December 1473 he issued the Edict of Thionville, creating four central institutions for all his lands: the *Parlement* (supreme law court) at Mechelen, the Chamber of Accounts, the Chamber of the Treasury and the Chamber of Subsidies. The centralization and rationalization of the duke's finances was desperately needed to keep up with the cost of his constant wars.

Seeking to free himself from feudal dependence on France for Burgundy and Flanders, Charles in 1475 agreed to recognize Edward IV of England as king of France, in return for being released from vassalage. The plan fell through because the defeated duke of Lorraine again made war on Charles to reclaim his duchy, and the town of Nancy rose in his support. Charles laid siege to Nancy and was thus unable to back an English invasion of France. In January 1477 he died in battle outside the town. His body was found days later, frozen in a ditch, stripped by looters, the face gnawed off by wolves, and identifiable only by his old war wounds.

THE ARTS OF PEACE

The Burgundian Low Countries are even more famed for their trade, artistry and piety than for exploits of arms. Two important innovations in diet in the Burgundian Netherlands were the consumption of hopped beer and salt herring. The great leap forwards in Dutch brewing came in the early fourteenth century, when hopped beer (copied from the Germans) replaced spiced ale. Hops were both a flavouring and a preservative, giving the beer a crisper taste and enabling it to travel well. By 1340 the Dutch were exporting beer to Germany. Particularly after 1396 they were a major force in the international beer trade and remained so until the early seventeenth century, when the distilling of brandy and gin began to displace brewing. The herring has long been a vital component in Northern European diets. In the late thirteenth century, fishermen from Flanders and Zeeland adopted and perfected a Swedish technique for salting herrings. The gills, heart and gut were removed through a narrow cut by the left gill, and the herring packed in salt. Previously each day's catch had to be put ashore for curing. Now it could be preserved in barrels as it was brought up, and fishing fleets could follow the herring for weeks at a time. The Dutch quickly came to dominate the herring fisheries and even built a special type of boat, the *buis*, for the purpose.

Bruges the Fair

Other developments in shipping were to make Flanders the centre of Europe's trade. In 1278 Italian galleys sailed to Bruges, by-passing the old trade routes through Champagne. It was a precocious exploration of the viability of long-distance sea-borne trade, not repeated until it became a regular trip for Genoese and Venetian galleys a century later. Overland trade remained important (increasingly through the Rhineland rather than through war-torn France), but the direct link with Italy meant a new commercial importance for Bruges. Merchants from all over Europe travelled there to do business. At first they went simply to take advantage of the enormous demand for necessities and luxuries which the success of the Flemish cloth industry had created. This made Bruges an international meeting place, reinforcing the incentive for foreign merchants and bankers to maintain a presence there. As early as 1300, Italian banking houses were moving their northern offices from Troyes to Bruges. Merchants could go to the city to buy wool from all over the British Isles, lead and tin from Cornwall and coal from north-eastern England; copper from Ireland; hawks, skins, peas and butter from Norway; horses, salted herrings and smoked hams from Denmark; furs from Sweden and Muscovy; precious metals from Bohemia and Hungary; wines from the Rhineland, metals from southern and eastern Germany; ermine and sable from Bulgaria; leather, olive oil, canvas, silk, figs and grapes from Spain; and rice, dates, figs, sugar, pepper, spices, gold wire, silk and alum from North Africa and Asia Minor. This besides the produce of the Low Countries and the Italian wares brought by Florentines, Venetians and the Genoese.

The long depression of the fourteenth century delayed the development of Bruges, but when the international economy picked up again around 1380, the city was ideally placed to be the commercial metropolis of northern Europe. Bruges was linked to the Scheldt estuary by the Zwin, and even as it silted up trade continued to focus on the city. The first outport was Damme, but when that became inaccessible for sea-going ships, cargoes were unloaded at Sluis and brought to Bruges by small boats. When even these began to run aground in the growing shallows, carts were used for the final stage of the journey. The importance of Bruges's trade networks, for a few decades at least, made the added expense worthwhile.

Bruges was not entirely without rivals. Other towns maintained important commercial activities and whenever political tensions threatened any nation's trade in Bruges, Dordrecht in Holland, Middelburg in

Zeeland and Antwerp in Brabant were all ready to offer incentives to merchants willing to move their offices. But the foreign merchants returned to Bruges whenever the political tensions eased. The first crack in the city's dominant position showed in 1471, when the Scots left for Middelburg, never to return. In the 1490s other nations of merchants were drawn away to Antwerp, and by 1540 only the Castillians maintained their consulate in Bruges, where the bulk of their business was selling Spanish wool for Flemings to turn into cloth.

Burgundian rule happened to coincide with economic recovery: in the course of the Burgundian period the volume of trade in the Low Countries more than doubled. In the mid-fifteenth century the standard of living of the common people was probably higher than at any other time before the nineteenth century. The remarkable wealth of the merchants and master craftsmen of the Low Countries allowed indulgence on a scale unimaginable elsewhere. Luxury and display were at their most sumptuous at the courts of the Burgundian dukes. When Charles the Bold married Margaret of York on 3 July 1468, it was without doubt the wedding of the century. Those in attendance included the bishops of Cambrai and Utrecht, half-brothers of the groom. John Paston the younger, an East Anglian gentleman, was roped in to make up the numbers in Margaret's entourage. His breathless letter home to his mother shows the effect (and effectiveness) of Burgundian courtesy and display:

> my Lady Margaret was married on Sunday last past, at a town that is called Damme, 3 miles out of Bruges, at 5 of the clock in the morning; and she was brought the same day to Bruges to her dinner; and there she was received as worshipfully as all the world could devise, as with procession with ladies and lords, best beseen of any people that ever I saw or heard of. Many pageants were played in her way in Bruges to her welcoming, the best that ever I saw. And the same day my Lord the Bastard [Anthony, another of Duke Charles's half-brothers], took upon him to answer 24 knights and gentlemen . . . and they that have jousted with him unto this day, have been as richly beseen, and himself also, as cloth of gold, and silk and silver, and goldsmiths' work, might make them; for of such gear . . . they of the Duke's court, neither gentlemen nor gentlewomen, they want none; . . .
>
> And as for the Duke's court, as for ladies and gentlewomen, knights, squires, and gentlemen, I heard never of none like to it, save King Arthur's court. And by my troth, I have no wit nor remembrance

to write to you, half the worship that is here; but that lacketh, as it cometh to mind I shall tell you when I come home.

We depart the sooner, for the Duke hath word that the French King is purposed to make war upon him hastily, and that he is within 4 or 5 days journey of Bruges, and the Duke rideth on Tuesday next coming, forward to meet with him; God give him good speed, and all his; for by my troth they are the goodliest fellowship that ever I came among, and best can behave them, and most like gentlemen.

(James Gairdner (ed.), *The Paston Letters* (reprinted Alan Sutton, 1986), pp. 297–9)

This courtly ceremonial did not exclude the civic elites whose cities provided the backdrop and the money for such display. A smooth relationship between the court and the upper reaches of urban society was acknowledged to be necessary to ducal power. At times the intertwining of interests was so great as to make it moot whether an event was a courtly or a civic ritual. The Burgundian dukes (and their Habsburg successors) by no means felt themselves above taking part in civic ceremonies, particularly those of a military or religious nature. Patrician youths had long delighted in displaying their horsemanship and martial skill in jousts, and the militia guilds held regular shooting competitions in which their rulers occasionally took part.

Art and Music, Literature and Learning

The Burgundian culture of display relied on craftsmen whose job was to produce images and sound. Builders, tapestry-makers and goldsmiths were the best paid, but those whose fame has lasted are the painters and musicians. Jan van Eyck, for instance, began his career in The Hague, at the court of John of Bavaria, but was soon in the service of Philip the Good. He remained a courtier of Philip until his death in 1441, and worked for the duke as a painter and as a diplomat. The two roles were combined when he was sent to negotiate a wedding treaty and bring back a portrait of the intended bride. Jan van Eyck, and his elder brother Hubert about whom almost nothing is known, are reckoned first among the painters called Flemish Primitives. They are primitive in the sense of being first, but not in any negative sense: their work is the fountainhead of much modern painting. Their greatest masterpiece, produced jointly, is the altarpiece in the church of St Bavo in Ghent, sometimes called the Adoration of the Mystic Lamb. The Van Eycks were followed by others, most famously Hugo van der Goes, Rogier van der Weyden and Hans Memling. Jan van Eyck's *Marriage of Arnolfini* and Hugo van der Goes's *Portinari Altarpiece*, among many other works, show the importance of the wealth of Bruges, and its trading links with Italy, in stimulating the cultural efflorescence of the fifteenth century.

The Flemish 'secret' was eagerly sought after by French and Italian artists, who travelled to Flanders to learn the techniques of such vibrant colour. Depth was suggested not by a geometrical calculation of perspective (an Italian trick), but by the gradation of hues, achieved by the painstaking application of multiple layers of paint and gloss. The revolutionary impact of fifteenth-century Flemish art led Giorgio Vasari, the chronicler of the art world of the Italian Renaissance, rather inaccurately to credit Jan van Eyck with the invention of oil painting. The art of the Flemish painters did not come from nowhere, although nothing like it had been seen on such a scale before. Besides panel painting, the Low Countries were justly famed throughout Europe for manuscript illumination. The *Très-riches heures du Duc de Berry*, a prayer book illuminated in the 1410s by the 'Limbourg brothers' Pol, Herment and Jehannequin, is just the best known of an unbelievable wealth of artistry. To meet demand from the growing market of readers at home and abroad, workshops in the Low Countries produced on what, for hand-copied books, must be considered a massive scale. Whether it was in dyed cloth, tapestries, painted panels or illuminated books, fifteenth-century Flemings were the acknowledged masters of the mysteries of colour.

In sound, too, the fifteenth-century Low Countries led Europe. From Guillaume Dufay and Gilles Binchois in the first half of the century, through Jean Ockeghem at mid-century, to Josquin des Prez, Heinrich Isaac and Jacob Obrecht around 1500, the flowering of late-medieval polyphonic music owed an immense debt to the 'Flemish school'. The artistry of these musical composers developed from the traditions of the cathedrals of Cambrai and Tournai, but their breakthrough to European influence was due at least in part to the wealth and connections of the Valois dukes. In the sixteenth century the tradition was continued by Adriaan Willaert, Nicolaas Gombert and Clemens non Papa, to culminate with Orlandus Lassus.

Besides images and music, words were an important element in the ceremonies of cities, courts and churches. The verbal element in the display went by the name of rhetoric. Amateur societies, known as Chambers of Rhetoric (a term first found in 1441), were set up in most towns of the Low Countries to promote the practice of rhetoric through theatrical performances and poetry competitions. These institutions were unique to the Low Countries, and were patronized by the magistrates to uphold their public image. The aim was to hone the skills of public speaking which civic life and ceremonial culture required, and to provide honest and edifying entertainment. Urban rhetoricians were often responsible for planning public ceremonies. The Chambers of Rhetoric dominated the literary life of the towns through the fifteenth and sixteenth centuries.

The first university of the Low Countries was founded in Leuven in 1426. The town already had a school which could attract masters and students from beyond Brabant, even from Germany. To reinvigorate a flagging urban economy, the city magistrates applied to the duke and the pope to have the school chartered as a university. The defunct cloth hall became the university hall, and the duke granted Leuven a monopoly on the issuing of degrees for the whole of the Burgundian Netherlands. One of the first graduates of the university was the poet and courtier Georges Chastellain. He served at the courts of Philip the Good, Charles VII of France and Charles the Bold, ending his career as chronicler of Burgundy. He was one of many memoirists and historians to thrive at the Burgundian courts and follow in the footsteps of Jean Froissart. Charles the Bold's chamberlain, Philippe de Commynes, was another. Commynes went over to Louis XI of France in 1472 and for the next five years enjoyed great favour as an adviser with inside knowledge of the Burgundian court and close acquaintance with the duke. After 1477 he sank into relative obscurity, his usefulness ended with the death of Charles the Bold. In retirement he wrote acid memoirs of the reign of Louis XI which have been compared to the writings of Machiavelli for their cynicism. Alongside chronicles and histories the ducal court also had a taste for reworkings of old romances of chivalry, and a great deal of late-medieval French literature is Burgundian in patronage and inspiration.

The first printing presses of the Low Countries were set up in the early 1460s, less than a decade after Johannes Gutenberg had invented the new technology. The earliest books to be printed in any numbers were the basic didactic and devotional compilations of the thirteenth and fourteenth centuries. Printers first established themselves in cities like Utrecht, Deventer and Zwolle which had strong ties with Germany. Only later did more westerly commercial centres such as Bruges, Antwerp and Amsterdam catch up. It was in Bruges that William Caxton learned the skills, and there that he produced the first printed book in English: *The recuyell of the historyes of Troye* (1473), translated at the behest of Margaret of York from a French compilation made by Philip the Good's chaplain Raoul Lefèvre.

The 'New Piety'

The Burgundian age saw the appearance of a 'new piety', or *devotio moderna*, that initiated and popularized criticisms of moral laxity, folk religion and excessively sumptuous liturgical display. Its dissemination among the burghers and artisans of the Low Countries in some respects made them more readily receptive to Protestant ideas in the early sixteenth century, although it also fed into a Catholic evangelicalism that was hostile to doctrinal innovation. A new body that was to have considerable impact on the moral awareness and social attitudes of the burghers of the Low Countries was the Brethren of the Common Life. The foundation of the Brethren of the Common Life owed much to the preaching and advice of Gerard Groote (1340–1384). A native of Deventer, Groote became a career ecclesiastic in minor orders, amassing canonries and university degrees. After a conversion experience around 1373 he resigned his benefices, gave away the house he had inherited in Deventer, and spent three years in a monastery. Then he was ordained as a deacon and embarked on a campaign of hell-fire preaching against hypocrisy, heresy and clerical laxity. This was a great age of building, and in 1382 Gerard denounced the newly completed cathedral tower of Utrecht as witnessing to the city's pride rather than its piety. Shortly before his death the bishop of Utrecht invited him to address the assembled clergy of the diocese, and he took the occasion to berate those present. The result was a ban on preaching, which he was in the process of appealing when he died. His Dutch translation of the Book of Hours was copied in more than 800 manuscripts and a hundred years after his death it was a best-seller in print.

The most famous pupil of the Brethren of the Common Life was Groote's biographer, Thomas Hemerken (*c*.1380–1471), also known as Thomas à Kempis. He was a German Rhinelander, educated in Deventer, who later joined a house of the congregation of Windesheim near Zwolle. He spent the rest of his life there, and was in great demand as a spiritual advisor. His *De Imitatione Christi* (Of the Imitation of Christ) began circulating anonymously in 1418. It became the most frequently copied work of the fifteenth century, later a steady seller in print, and is still among the best known works of Christian spirituality.

FROM BURGUNDY TO HABSBURG, 1477–1515

The sudden death of Charles the Bold cast the Low Countries into confusion. In several towns the artisans rebelled to demand or reclaim a share in civic government. To win recognition of her succession Mary of Burgundy made one concession after another, ratifying the privileges of states, towns and guilds in the fullest form possible. At her lowest ebb, the duchess was held captive by the men of Ghent while two of her father's councillors were executed before her eyes on charges of bribe-taking and oppression. Unpopular centralizing institutions were abolished, the provincial States and the Estates General were granted the privilege of meeting on their own initiative, war was not to be waged without the consent of the Estates General, and 25 representatives of the Burgundian territories were to be admitted to the Great Council alongside the councillors appointed by the duchess.

These concessions weakened the power of the ducal crown at a time that the duke of Guelders, the city of Liège and the king of France were united in their determination to put an end to the threat of Burgundian expansionism. The life was barely out of Charles's body before Louis XI of France invaded and annexed the duchy of Burgundy. Louis then entered into negotiations with the men of Ghent and invaded the Low Countries. The civic militias succeeded in frustrating French expectations of an easy victory, but the cities pressed Mary to provide a strong ally by marriage. She offered her hand to Maximilian of Austria, son and heir of the Habsburg emperor Frederick III, and the Estates General gave their consent to the match.

Mary died in 1482, after falling from her horse while hunting, and in accordance with her will Maximilian became regent until their son Philip, born in 1478, should come of age. It took until 1490 for Maximilian to have his regency recognized throughout the Low Countries, and to break French-backed opposition in Guelders, Utrecht and Liège. In 1493, when he handed over to Philip, Habsburg rule in the Low Countries was an established fact. During the regency those who rose against rule by the foreigner Maximilian had claimed the underaged Philip as their true lord and natural prince. Philip exploited this to the full when he came to power (1493–1506), restoring many of the centralizing policies of his

Burgundian grandfather and great-grandfather. At the same time he abandoned their expansionism, in 1498 relinquishing any claim to Guelders, which his parents had managed to bring under their direct rule from 1478 to 1492. His dynastic interests lay in other directions. In 1496 he married Joanna of Castille, who by a series of royal deaths became heiress to the Spanish kingdoms of Castille and Aragon. When Isabella of Castille died in 1504, Philip declared himself king of Castile in his wife's right, but his father-in-law, Ferdinand of Aragon, claimed regency of the kingdom. After a brief struggle Philip was recognized as king, but almost immediately died. His wife, Joanna, went mad with grief. Their heir, Charles, was only six years old. Charles's paternal grandfather, Maximilian, again became regent of the Low Countries.

Charles was born in Ghent in 1500, and was named after his great-grandfather Charles the Bold. He and his three sisters were raised in the Low Countries by their aunt, Margaret of Austria. Maximilian insisted that his grandson and heir be familiarized with the lives of his subjects by frequent walks through the city streets. Ambassadors and courtiers always found Charles stately, reticent and immobile at audiences, but his 'common touch' when hunting or travelling is the theme of countless anecdotes in Early-Modern jestbooks. From the age of 9 Charles had his own household and was under the tutelage of William of Croy, lord of Chièvres. His academic education was entrusted to the scholar Adrian of Utrecht, chancellor of Leuven university and later Pope Adrian VI.

THE RENAISSANCE

The age of Charles V was one of great intellectual and artistic achievement in the Low Countries. As early as the 1460s Rudolph Agricola, a grammarian from Groningen, was making waves even in Italy with the purity of his Latin. But this was nothing in comparison to the international buzz caused by the later humanist Desiderius Erasmus of Rotterdam (1466–1536), the most influential figure of the northern Renaissance. Erasmus became a monk as a young man, but hated the life and managed to get the bishop of Cambrai to take him out of the monastery. Thereafter he travelled widely throughout Western Europe. He taught in Leuven, in Cambridge and elsewhere but eventually settled in Switzerland. In every centre of learning he made both friends and enemies.

Erasmus's constant concern was to return to the ancient sources of classical and Christian learning. In his *Adagia* (1500) he provided a compendium of the wit and wisdom of the ancient pagans; in his *Enchiridion* (1502) he presented a 'philosophy of Christ' that prefigures much of modern Christianity; in the *Praise of Folly* (1511) he mercilessly satirized the superstitions and shortcomings (real or perceived) of his contemporaries. Despite its deficiencies his edition of the Greek New Testament (1516) was to be the basic scholarly text until the nineteenth century. In his almost contradictory love of both classical elegance and evangelical simplicity, he succeeded remarkably in combining the wisdom of the serpent and the gentleness of the dove.

From the early sixteenth century to the mid-seventeenth the Low Countries were among the leading areas of scientific discovery. One of the most remarkable figures of Renaissance science was Andreas Vesalius, personal physician to Charles V. As an anatomist Vesalius surpassed all his predecessors in the study of how the human body fits together. The illustrations of his lavishly produced *De humani corporis fabrica* (1543) combine his exact observation with superb artistry, although at a price few can have afforded. Another great physician was Rembert Dodoens, whose richly illustrated *Cruijdeboeck* (literally 'herb book') appeared in 1554. It was a masterful exposition of European botanical knowledge, with an emphasis on the medicinal uses of plants. It was translated into Latin in the 1580s and into many other vernaculars thereafter.

Geography was another field in which new knowledge was cast into beautiful images. Gerald Mercator (1512–1594) produced the first topographical map of Flanders in 1540. After an unrelated spot of trouble with the inquisitors he moved to Germany. There, in 1569, he published the first map of the world on the 'Mercator projection'. Another important cartographer was Abraham Ortelius (1527–1598), whose collection of maps published as a book, the *Theatrum Orbis Terrarum* (Antwerp, 1570), was the first atlas of the world. From 1579 Ortelius's publisher was Christopher Plantin of Antwerp, who also printed the Latin edition of Dodoens's herbal. The Plantin house, continued after his death by his son-in-law Jan Moretus and by his descendants down to 1866, was one of the foremost printing houses of Europe. The palatial premises are now a museum. Plantin's most impressive achievement was the printing of the eight-volume *Biblia Regia*, a polyglot Bible in Latin, Greek and Hebrew (all with different alphabets) commissioned by Philip II of Spain.

WORLD MARKET – WORLD EMPIRE

In the course of the fifteenth century, towns in Holland (Amsterdam, Enkhuizen and Hoorn) replaced the IJssel towns as the main transporters of northern goods. At the end of the century a further shift in the patterns of trade took place: Antwerp replaced Bruges as the metropolis of Northern Europe, the 'commercial capital of Christendom'. One of the key elements in the shift from Bruges to Antwerp was alum. In 1462 alum was discovered in the papal states, but Italian merchants in Bruges continued to deal in Turkish alum in competition with the pope's commercial agents. The staple for the sale of papal alum north of the Alps was established at Antwerp in 1491. Maximilian of Austria had commanded foreign merchants to leave Bruges in 1488, during the city's rebellion against him, but they may well have returned in 1492 (as they had so often in the past) had the move to Antwerp not been thus fixed by alum. Another nation to contribute to the city's commercial dominance was England. From the 1490s onwards most English trade with the Continent went through the Company of Merchant Adventurers in Antwerp. English cloth was sent to Antwerp to be dyed and finished, and distributed throughout the known world.

From 1501 Antwerp became the northern staple for the colonial goods of Portugal, of which spices were the most important. The Portuguese merchants chose Antwerp because they needed bullion for their trade in Asia, and it was the most convenient location for them to acquire silver from the mines of Central Europe. Antwerp was also an important market for wines from France and the Rhineland, non-precious metals from the German mountains, grain and timber from the Baltic, Spanish leather, and soon Spanish colonial goods. In the Middle Ages sugar had been an expensive luxury, imported from the Eastern Mediterranean. In 1508 the first ships carrying sugar from the Canaries arrived in Antwerp, knocking the bottom out of the market. It was the beginning of the sweetening of the Northern European diet. From the 1520s onwards Antwerp was a major centre of international finance, with extensive private dealings in instruments of credit as well as loans to crowned heads in many parts of Europe. Antwerp's merchant community systematized maritime insurance and the endorsement of bills of exchange, patchy practices at best in the Middle Ages. The city was a by-word for best business practice. A French guide to the arithmetic needed to calculate shares, interest rates, exchanges and other matters of concern to merchants (including ransoms paid in instalments) was translated into English in 1591 as *The Practize of Cifering ... Conteyning all sortes of Accompts daily used amongst the Merchants in the citie of Andwerpe.*

Finally, the manufactures of Antwerp were not inconsiderable. Cloth-dyeing was most important, but fish-curing, soap-making and sugar-refining were also located on the edges of the city. Antwerp roodscreens, altarpieces, tapestries, paintings, stained glass, prints and illuminated and printed books were in wide demand, at first as providing reliable quality at a reasonable price, later as the best quality available. Quentin Massys (or Metsys), who died in 1530, was among the first Antwerp painters to gain fame for his artistry. His older contemporary Hieronymus Bosch worked outside the artistic mainstream but with great success. His giving grotesquely 'lifelike' representation to hidden evil, both human and preternatural, won the patronage of many high noblemen, and spawned a host of sixteenth-century admirers and imitators.

When he came of age in 1515, Charles V ruled the largest empire the world had ever seen. By his father, Philip the Fair, he was the heir of Burgundy and Habsburg; by his mother, Joanna, he was heir to the Spanish kingdoms of Castile, with its possessions in the Americas, and of Aragon, with its possessions in southern Italy. Throughout his reign his Spanish subjects extended their power in the Americas and the Far East. In the Low Countries, Charles completed the Burgundian conquests. In 1515 he bought the lordship of Friesland, and only nine years later had established with the Frisian estates a mutual understanding that enabled him to exercise real power. In 1521 he conquered the episcopal city of Tournai, which had become a French enclave in Flanders. The bishop of Utrecht, Henry of Bavaria, in 1528 surrendered his temporal lordship to Charles. This was a bid to escape the perpetual warfare between Habsburg and Guelders over the territory of Utrecht, but Charles of Egmond, duke of Guelders, would not allow such a massive extension of Habsburg power to go unchallenged. He appointed the *condottiere* Maarten van Rossum as governor of Utrecht, and Van Rossum promptly plundered The Hague. In 1538 Charles of Egmond died and Charles V established Habsburg rule over the lands of Utrecht. William II, the new duke of Guelders, accepted the situation but Van Rossum continued the war under French colours, plundering through Brabant in 1542 and seizing Amersfoort in 1543. In that very year William II, the last independent duke of Guelders, died and left Charles V his heir. Van Rossum entered Habsburg service.

Having brought all of the Low Countries except the prince-bishopric of Liège under his rule, Charles V set about ensuring that he would be able to pass them on to his son entire. In 1548 he made the Netherlands independent of imperial jurisdiction. By the Pragmatic Sanction of 1549 it was decreed that a single heir would inherit them. In 1550 Charles imposed a unified heresy law on the whole of the Low Countries. In 1555 he retired to a monastery, transferring power to his son, Philip II, who had been raised in Spain and was to rule from Madrid.

THE REFORMATION, 1517–1566

In the 1520s the Flemish Franciscan Thomas van Herentals, in his sermons on the first commandment ('I am the Lord your God . . .') warned his hearers against atheism, heresy, superstition, satanism, divination, and trusting more in the saints than in God. He was clearly aware that ordinary Christians were facing basic problems of belief. He concluded with the lament (implicitly referring to Erasmus and Luther) that 'the right service of saints and good pilgrimages are blamed and despised, because of the false superstitions which are attached. And nobody puts out their hand to maintain the virtuous in honour and to put down and destroy the superstitions.'

One who did seek to restore and maintain what was good in medieval religion without succumbing to novelty was Adrian of Utrecht. He had been a professor in Leuven and tutor to the young Charles V, as well as regent of Spain during the crucial years when Charles established his claim to the throne. Adrian was elected pope in January 1522 and died in September 1523. In his 20-month pontificate, during which he retained his baptismal name as Adrian VI, he sought to head off the emerging Protestant reformation by initiating reforms from the centre and by uniting Christendom against the advancing Turks. He arrived in Rome only in September 1522, unveiled his plans at once, and met a hostile reception from the people of Rome and the curia. All his efforts were frustrated. He was the last non-Italian to be elected to the papacy until the twentieth century.

Desire for a purer life and teaching in the Church coincided with changes in the relationship between lay and clerical authority. Even perfectly orthodox magistrates were dissatisfied with the ways in which Church privileges caused inequality before the law. One point of friction between lay rulers and the Church was matrimonial law. Jurisdiction was claimed by the Church, which insisted that marriage was a sacrament which the two partners conveyed on one another, preferably with a priest and at least two others as witnesses. The repercussions for property relations meant that magistrates liked to have marriages arranged and witnessed in a way that guaranteed parental consent and social recognition. To take just one example of disputes, late in 1525 the dean of Amstelland was accused of performing secret weddings and the bishop of Utrecht refused to take action against him. The aldermen of Amsterdam decreed criminal punishments for anybody who officiated at weddings without having thrice pronounced the banns. Now the bishop did react, since this was an intrusion of the city into clerical discipline. He threatened an interdict and cited the magistrates in the church courts, but the Court of Holland applied its own pressure (threatening confiscation of Church goods) and the bishop had to back down.

Lutherans

Martin Luther, a monk and university lecturer, had broken with the Catholic Church in 1519. He was already an influential figure in certain circles in northern Germany. In 1517–22 his public stance against the power of the Pope and the teaching of the bishops made him the leader and spokesman of a reforming movement which sought not to change the established Church, but to abolish it. His supporters were soon numerous in the Low Countries, particularly in the merchant cities trading with Germany. The first formal condemnation of Luther's views came from the University of Leuven in 1519. In 1521 Charles V prohibited Luther's writings and criminalized his adherents. The first Lutherans to be put to death for their beliefs were Hendrik Voes and Joannes van Essen, executed by burning in Brussels in 1523. They were both, like Luther himself, Augustinian hermits of the Congregation of Saxony. They had been members of the Antwerp house of the congregation, which was closed down as a hotbed of heresy. On 15 September 1525 the Court of Holland had Jan de Bakker, pastor of Woerden, burnt as a heretic in The Hague, the first Protestant martyr of the northern Netherlands. Another Lutheran died in Antwerp the same year, the first in that city. Thereafter persecution subsided for a time. In the later 1520s and the 1530s Antwerp developed into the main international centre for Lutheran printing outside the German-speaking lands. Works not only in Latin, Dutch and French but also in English and Danish – even in a few cases in Italian and Spanish – were printed in Antwerp for distribution abroad. It now seems certain that the first complete English bible in print, the 1535 Coverdale Bible (previously thought to have been printed in Germany or Switzerland), was a product of this clandestine trade, the backdrop to which was a thriving legitimate trade in printed books and images.

Law Reform

Charles V's proclamation of 1521 had left a loophole for local magistrates to impose fines, the pillory, banishment and penitential pilgrimages instead of burning at the stake, and these were the usual punishments meted out in places such as Antwerp and Amsterdam. When a case came to the attention of royal officers, bodies such as the Council of Brabant in Brussels or the Court of Holland in The Hague were much more likely to give a death sentence. In 1531 the loophole was closed and death was decreed the only punishment for Lutherans. This meant that city magistrates became more reluctant to bring heretics to trial, at least until the Anabaptist panic of 1535.

The law against Lutherans of 1531 was just one part of a general attempt at moral and legal reform. From 1530 to 1531 Charles V resided in the Low Countries in person. He divided the Great Council into three 'collateral councils' of equal standing, but with separate remits: the Council of Finance oversaw the financial administration, the Privy Council was a body of jurists which advised the prince on matters of law and policy implementation, and the Council of State was made up of great noblemen who advised on the highest policy of state. Charles also issued new laws on the currency, public order, vagrancy and poor relief. Poor reform went furthest in Ypres, where the emperor licensed an amalgamation of the numerous 'poor tables' into a central municipal institution. There was some nervousness about putting what were generally ecclesiastical institutions under direct civic control, but the theologians of Paris gave the plan their blessing. It seemed the only way to cope effectively with the growing numbers and desperation of the city's paupers. Although the experiment was short-lived, it was publicized across north-western Europe, in England in a pamphlet entitled *The form and manner of subvention or helping for poor people, devised and practised in the city of Ypres in Flanders* (1535).

Anabaptists

The most radical of the religious movements of the early sixteenth century, and the only one to gain rapid support among the lowest social classes, was Anabaptism. Unlike Protestants, Anabaptists denied that they had been validly baptized as children and insisted on rebaptizing one another. The Anabaptist Thomas Münzer was preaching the violent overthrow of the established social order as early as 1523, perhaps even 1520. After the German Peasants' War he was captured and executed. From 1530 to 1533 another German Anabaptist, Melchior Hoffmann, was preaching the end of the world in the Rhineland, Holland and Friesland. His followers, 'Melchiorites', were most numerous in the towns of the Zuider Zee: Amsterdam, Kampen, Zwolle, Deventer. After Hoffmann was imprisoned in Strasbourg, their leadership fell to the Haarlem baker Jan Matthys. In the spring of 1533 Matthys led a group of Anabaptist refugees to Münster and somehow gained control of the city council. The troops of the bishop of Münster were soon attempting to encircle the city. Matthys instituted community of goods and decreed that all men who refused to be rebaptized should depart the city. Both were measures to prepare for a siege, but tinged with apocalyptic expectation. When Matthys died in a sally against the bishop's men in 1534, the journeyman tailor Jan Bockelson (1510–1536) took over. John of Leyden, as he came to be known in English, abolished the city council, appointed 12 elders in its stead, and proclaimed himself king. He also decreed Old Testament polygyny, and took 16 wives.

In March 1534 it came to the attention of the Court of Holland that a number of ships were being prepared in Amsterdam to carry supporters to the new Kingdom of Münster. Four of those involved were executed as ringleaders, and the rest, adjudged to have been 'seduced and deceived', were cautioned and released. In April there were rumours of a new revolt in Amsterdam. House searches were carried out and arrests were made. Two victims were chosen for exemplary execution: they were condemned by the bench of aldermen, rather than the Court of Holland, the city magistrates now for the first time deciding that heretics were dangerous enough to be killed. Matters came to a head in the winter of 1534–35, as the Kingdom of Münster reached its most radical stage. In December 1534 Anabaptists tried to seize control of Deventer. In Friesland a little band on their way to Münster occupied the Norbertine monastery Oldeklooster and it took an eight-day siege to dislodge them. In February 1535 12 Anabaptists (seven men and five women) ran through Amsterdam proclaiming the imminence of the Kingdom of the Saints. To underline the point they ran naked. More arrests were made, and in the night of 10–11 March an

Anabaptist crowd stormed the Town Hall. In the course of the turmoil one of the city's mayors was killed. Over the next few months 62 Anabaptists were condemned to death, and 21 to lengthy periods of banishment.

After the blood-soaked failure of the Kingdom of Münster, the Anabaptists of the northern Netherlands were shepherded by Menno Simons (1496–1561). Simons was a former parish priest from Friesland who taught pacifism and non-resistance. He also insisted that Christians should take no part in government and judging over others. His followers came to be called Mennonites and they have been a relatively small, but intellectually influential group in the Netherlands. They rejected doctrinal formulas and Church structures, and just about the only uniting factor among them is the belief that baptism should be the expression of mature faith.

Calvinists

Another priest with new ideas was John Calvin, a Frenchman who had studied in Paris. In 1534 he resigned his livings and may have been briefly imprisoned. In 1535 he fled France for Switzerland, where his *Institutes of the Christian Religion* was printed in 1536. He stressed the absolute authority of God, the total depravity of man, and the Bible as the basis of belief. In 1541 Calvin became head of the Church of Geneva, and had the opportunity to put his ideas of reformed discipline and doctrine into effect. Calvin's teachings reached the Low Countries through Picardy. The cloth towns of Hainaut and French-speaking Flanders soon had secret Calvinist congregations, often among skilled workers. Soon the towns of Dutch-speaking Flanders and Brabant, especially Ghent and Antwerp, saw similar developments. Calvinists had sympathisers and even members among the urban middle classes and patricians, and clearer discipline than the Mennonites, with presbyterian ideas about the organization of congregational life. This meant that magistrates tended to leave them alone as long as they kept their heads down. They quickly became by far the largest and best organized Protestant group in the Low Countries.

The minister to the underground Calvinist community in Antwerp, Adriaan van Haemstede, built up a reputation as a discreet man who would not get his secret sympathisers on the town council into trouble. But in 1558 he decided that the time was ripe for public witnessing and he preached to a crowd on the Meir, the main thoroughfare of the city (now one of the highest-paying squares on a Belgian 'Monopoly' board). Grandstanding like this could hardly go ignored, and a bloody repression of Calvinists followed. Haemstede himself escaped to Germany, and eventually to England. While in hiding he began to compile a history of martyrs, beginning with the early Christian martyrs of ancient Palestine and Rome, and ending with his close friends burned in Antwerp. It was printed in 1559 and went through dozens of editions and revisions in the course of the following century. This Book of Martyrs was one of the key texts of the Dutch Reformed communion and a defining document of Dutch Protestant identity.

The Witch Craze

Heretics were not the only ones in danger of death by burning. Various beliefs about magic and witchcraft seem to have been common through the Middle Ages. Rumours and taunts within village and ward were apparently fairly commonplace. At the end of the fifteenth century some learned minds began to discern an international conspiracy of diabolists. In the Low Countries the view that witches were a threat to society was enshrined in law in 1532. The usual punishments were fines, the pillory or banishment, but burnings also took place and became more frequent after 1570. Cases that came to the attention of the central councils of justice, or made it to appeal, were almost always quashed. One way of counteracting rumours of witchcraft was invented by the enterprising souls of Oudewater. Since it was widely believed that Satan made his servants lighter than the Bible (how else could they fly?) the town magistrates of Oudewater set up a *heksenwaag*, 'witch scales', and obtained a licence from Charles V for its operation. For a fee somebody facing slanderous accusations of witchcraft could obtain a certificate that they had been weighed against the Bible and found heavier. This would not have satisfied a serious demonologist, but it could quash malicious gossip and might even impress some country magistrates.

One of the first to take a public stand against the witch craze, in his *De praestigiis daemonum* (On the Tricks of Demons, 1563; English translation by John Shea, 1991), was Johan Wier (or Weyer), a Dutchman who was physician to the duke of Cleves. One of the most emphatic and learned writers to spread alarm at the danger of witches was the Jesuit Martin del Rio, a lecturer in Leuven. His three-volume *Disquisitiones magicae* fanned the flames of witch-burning throughout

Europe.* It also gives testimony to the attempt of Cornelis Loos, a Catholic from Gouda who became professor of theology at Trier, to counteract the trend: Del Rio recorded with satisfaction that when Loos tried to publish a book denouncing fear of witches (whom he held powerless to harm people except by natural means), it was suppressed and he was forced to recant his opinions.

Witch-burnings tended to cluster in time and place. Although the criminal courts generally only acted in response to complaints and denunciations, an increase in witch trials can often be traced to the appointment of a public prosecutor with strong views. To some extent the same is true of other crimes: when Cornelis Dobbenzoon was sheriff of Amsterdam (1535–42), prosecutions of family offenders (wife-beaters, disobedient children) doubled, often on charges of public disorder. In the case of witchcraft, the determined use of torture meant that judges looking for witches usually found them. Even when no individual prosecutor can be indicated, the pattern suggests it was a matter of limited concern in high places. In Groningen, for instance, there were three spates of witch trials in the mid-sixteenth century, all in the aftermath of larger witch-hunts in German Friesland. The Dutch province of Friesland seems to have seen no executions for witchcraft at all.

Tridentine Reform

Calls for reform were not limited to those convinced that the Pope was the Antichrist. Catholic reformers had been active before 1500, and grew in strength and numbers even as Protestant reformers assaulted the Church. Erasmus of Rotterdam and Adrian of Utrecht had both, in their different ways, been reformers within the Church. The various uncoordinated movements of Catholic reform were given structured content and direction by the twice-interrupted Council of Trent (1545–63), the final decrees of which were published in the Low Countries almost immediately.

The decrees of Trent were to be implemented in the Low Countries by the bishops, and these were no longer limited to Liège, Cambrai, Tournai and Utrecht. One of the most important ecclesiastical developments in the sixteenth-century Low Countries had been the founding of a dozen new bishoprics in 1559. Throughout the Middle Ages the relationship

---

* *Investigations into Magic, 1599–1600*; English translation by P. G. Maxwell-Stuart, Manchester University Press, 2000.

between worldly rule and episcopal authority had been problematic. Now every major city was to have a bishop who was in no position to challenge royal power. Only the duchy of Luxembourg was left out, the prince-bishops of Trier and Liège adamantly maintaining their own episcopal jurisdiction in the Ardennes. This was the culmination of Charles V's determined drive to leave the Low Countries to his son, Philip II, as a united patrimony free of the taint of heresy.

ICONOCLASM TO ABJURATION, 1566–1581

The new bishoprics set up in 1559 were resented by the great abbeys and collegiate churches, which saw their freedom of action and finances curtailed by the obligation to submit to bishops and pay for their maintenance. At the same time, the king's reliance on the advice of Cardinal Granvelle to the exclusion of other Councillors of State irritated the great noblemen of the Low Countries. The intensification of persecution after 1550 drove Calvinists to desperation while alienating the civic magistracies who saw inquisitors infringe upon their jurisdictions. Very few of the powerful elements in society were entirely happy with royal policy in the 1550s and 1560s. Added to this, Antwerp's commerce was meeting its first major setbacks. The Portuguese spice trade had left the city in 1548, as Spanish America had replaced Central Europe as the main source of silver. The English cloth trade went elsewhere in 1564, after a trade dispute, and in general the city was going through a recession.

In April 1566 a group of discontented noblemen presented the king's regent in the Low Countries, Margaret of Parma, with a petition requesting, among other things, that the heresy laws be suspended. A hostile courtier's scornful reference to the petitioners as 'gueux' (beggars) was taken up as a party name, a battlecry and symbol of the downtrodden demanding justice. The count of Egmont was sent to Madrid to confer with Philip II, and came away with the impression that he had won the king round. Hopes were raised in the Low Countries, only to be dashed when royal letters arrived in Brussels which insisted on a strict application of the heresy laws, contrary to what Egmont had taken to be the king's verbal assurances.

In August 1566 Calvinist frustration burst out in the Iconoclastic Fury. Small gangs of image-breakers toured the Low Countries smashing up churches, defacing carvings, statues and paintings, and burning and soiling books and vestments. Priests, monks and nuns were assaulted, sometimes murdered, and prominent Catholic laymen were intimidated and publicly humiliated. The civic militias were seldom willing to intervene. Calvinists seized power in Valenciennes, 's-Hertogenbosch and a few other towns, but order was soon restored. The reports reaching Philip II in Spain had caused him such grave concern that he had already dispatched an army of Spaniards and Italians, under the command of the duke of Alva, to reassert his control of the Low Countries. They marched from Milan through Switzerland and Lorraine, along a route that came to be known as the 'Spanish Road', the crucial strategic link between Habsburg Italy and the Habsburg Netherlands.

Once Alva had arrived in the Low Countries and found the disturbances settled, he was not content to let sleeping dogs lie. His mission as he saw it was to destroy those responsible for the threat to royal authority. He set up an emergency tribunal called the Council of Troubles, popularly known as the Council of Blood, which put thousands to death. Although these were not the tens of thousands alleged by partisan chroniclers, it was a shocking enough procedure. At times he delayed the publication of royal and papal pardons by months so that there would be fewer rebels and heretics left alive to take advantage of them. It is not without reason that the dark-robed and long-bearded figure presiding over Brueghel's *Massacre of the Innocents* has been thought to represent the duke of Alva.

The Revolt

The greatest nobleman among the gueux, William, Prince of Orange, did not tarry in the Netherlands, but made away to his German estates and began to collect troops and allies. In 1568 he invaded the Low Countries. On 23 May the rebels had their first victory in battle, at Heiligerlee in Friesland. Among the dead was one of the foremost loyalists of the Netherlands, Jean de Ligne, count of Aremberg and Stadholder (Lord Lieutenant) of Groningen and Friesland. But it was a false dawn. The rebel cause soon crumbled again. Many of the noblemen whose petition was blamed for setting off the troubles had been rounded up, and in the weeks after the Orangist invasion several of them were executed. Even the counts of Egmont and Horne, entitled to trial before their peers as knights of the Fleece and councillors of state, were sentenced like common criminals and beheaded on 5 June 1568. Public opinion never recovered: clearly nobody was safe. Neverthless,

Calvinist exiles in Germany, England and France kept the flame of hope burning.

The duke of Alva's policy of terror alienated large sections of the population, but also instilled fear. The strategy might even have worked in the long term if he had been able to pay his troops. But with the expected silver from Spain not coming through, Alva resorted to demanding that the Netherlanders pay a 10 per cent sale tax, the 'Tenth Penny'. This was heavy by the standards of the time, but not unheard of. During Charles V's wars with France the Estates General had agreed to a Tenth Penny for a limited space of time and on certain terms. Alva, however, was determined that the tax would be collected with or without the consent of the Estates, and would set no limit to its duration. The combination of bloody repression and arbitrary taxation was too much. Alva forfeited all sympathy for the royal cause and drove many into open defiance.

To give the rebels naval capabilities the Prince of Orange had issued letters of marque which enabled Calvinist privateers to attack Spanish shipping under his princely authority, and hence escape prosecution as pirates by neutrals. Many privateering 'Sea Beggars' operated from English ports and were such an embarrassment to Elizabeth that in the spring of 1572 she ordered them out of the country. On 1 April 1572 the Sea Beggars landed at Brielle (Brill) and seized the town. It was the first territorial conquest of the Revolt. In succeeding weeks more towns in and around the estuary opened their gates to the Beggars, the inhabitants preferring anything to continued subjection to the Duke of Alva. Soon most of Zeeland and southern Holland were in rebel hands, although Middelburg valiantly withstood a two-year siege before the town could resist no longer.

From 1569 to 1573 the Frisian farmer Rienck Hemmema kept an accounts book that has survived. It is a unique source concerning the rural life of the Low Countries in the sixteenth century. Apart from its interest in recording the fate of Hemmema's crops and livestock, it shows something of the impact of the early Revolt in the countryside. The continual rise in prices may have been what prompted Hemmema to keep this record of his affairs. On 1 November 1570, the All Saints' Flood, one of the worst of the century, swept over the dikes of Friesland. Hemmema lost half his winter barley, and the following summer had to provide two or three men and a cart with two horses to help with dike repairs. Further floods in 1573 meant that he had to harvest his peas from salt water, and the cows waded into the fields and ate the barley where it stood.

The commander of the royal garrison in Groningen was Don Caspar de Robles. He managed to re-establish royal control over Friesland and Groningen's Ommelanden. As provincial governor, his attitude to privileges was purely practical. He did not go out of his way to break them, but he refused to respect them when what he saw as the common good was at stake. When the States of Friesland refused to grant extra taxes to pay his Walloon troops, he took the money unconstitutionally to prevent the soldiers from mutinying. When noblemen presented their patents of exemption from dike-building, he told them that if the patents would stop a spring flood their exemption could stand.

In Friesland in the early 1570s, the floods seem to have been far more devastating than the wars. At the beginning of July 1572 the Sea Beggars landed in Friesland, and for the next 12 months Rienck Hemmema paid a great deal to rent a room in Franeker, presumably to store his surplus away from looters and as a refuge of last resort for himself. In the event the military operations in Friesland had little impact on his business. The rebels occupied Franeker on 28 August 1572, but had to abandon the town on 26 November. The day that Franeker fell into their hands, Hemmema was there selling two rams to a butcher. In September he was in town to sell his harvest and dairy products as usual. In early October he was in Leeuwarden, still under royal control, to sell a colt. There was no 'front line' for him to cross, just zones of influence radiating out from fortified places.

The Revolt quickly bore the appearance of a religious war, although it was never entirely that. Foreign mercenaries from all over Europe served in the Low Countries, and sometimes carried confessional militancy home with them. The Privy Council of Scotland, for instance, in 1573 licensed John Adamson to go to the Low Countries with 130 fully equipped soldiers of fortune 'for serving in the defence of God's true religion, against the persecutors thereof', stipulating a fine of 5000 marks if they were found to have served 'with papists against the protestants'. There were to be Scots in Dutch service until 1782. Englishmen, Frenchmen and, most importantly, Germans also fought alongside the rebels as well as, in smaller numbers, for the king of Spain. As far as the royal pikemen from Spain and Italy were concerned, the war was a crusade against heretics.

The mobile element in the war was made up of small commando groups which looted the peasants in enemy-held territory to deny forage to their opponents. From 1568 to 1576 the Sea Beggars had their inland counterparts in the Wood Beggars. Gangs of Calvinists took to the woods and operated as bandits, especially targeting churches and the houses of priests and outspokenly Catholic laymen. As the rebels established bases on the ground, the Wood Beggars disappeared to make way for another sort of irregular looter: freebooters who would cross into enemy territory in lightning raids, then head back to safety in the fortified towns of Zeeland or the Flemish coast. The royal forces did much the same, operating into rebel-held territory from their garrisons on the Maas and in Friesland. Major operations were usually sieges. The strategic landscape of the Low Countries was made up of dense constellations of great cities and small towns, almost all walled and fortified, and increasingly surrounded by brick-fronted earthworks that rendered artillery ineffective. Even villages and manor houses were given rough-and-ready fortifications. An army could not operate on any scale across the countryside, and the few pitched battles of the early years of the Revolt soon gave way to one weary siege after another.

Short of the money and manpower to win a war of protracted sieges, the duke of Alva adopted a policy of intimidation against towns which attempted to withstand his forces. He sanctioned plundering and atrocities at Mechelen, Zutphen, Naarden and Haarlem. These examples did encourage some towns to surrender more readily to escape a like fate, but also meant that once a siege had started the citizens would resist to the end. The most famous of the many sieges is that of Leiden, which held out against royal forces from December 1573 until October 1574. In the spring of 1574 Louis of Nassau led his last invasion of the northern Netherlands, in the hopes of diverting royal forces from before Leiden. Together with his brother Henry he fell in the battle on Mook Heath on 14 April, and his army was driven away. The siege was resumed, but the desperate measure of breaching the dikes forced the withdrawal of royal troops. In 1575 the patent for Holland's first university was granted to the city in recognition of its determined resistance.

The Revolt entered an entirely new phase in 1576. The bankruptcy of Spain's royal treasury in 1575 meant that the loyal troops in the Netherlands could not be paid. There were widespread mutinies, and the king's soldiers were now the biggest threat to peace and security. The Estates General took control of the country. There was no repudiation of royal authority, but the Estates were determined to settle matters on their terms. A ceasefire, or 'pacification', was negotiated and proclaimed in Ghent. It failed to end the war, but the Pacification of Ghent stands as the eternal might-have-been of the historiography of the Low Countries, a golden moment of universal concord and rational compromise.

The Estates General also outlawed mutineers, and bounties were offered for those who brought them in, dead or alive. In desperation, the mutineers banded together and cast about for a strong place of safety. They settled on Antwerp citadel, built on Alva's orders and only recently completed. The city of Antwerp was sacked, in an orgy of violence and rapine ('the Spanish Fury') which shocked Europe. The mutinies and rapacity of royal troops had the same source as Alva's Tenth Penny and his attempt to impose order by fear: the inability of Philip II to pay for his policy of reconquest in the Low Countries.

In 1577 Don Juan de Austria repudiated the Pacification of Ghent and ensconced himself in Namur. The Estates General in turn declared him deposed as governor general and appointed their own: Matthias, Archduke of Austria. Matthias had been brought to the Low Countries by the moderate rebels opposed to the Prince of Orange, but he failed to establish his authority and returned to Austria in 1581. Throughout 1578, and on into the early 1580s, there was a series of Calvinist and Orangist *coups* in the cities of the Low Countries. These were in defiance of the terms of the Pacification of Ghent and alienated much of the Catholic population from the Revolt. Early in 1579, a number of provinces formed closer unions for mutual support and defence. Polarization was complete in 1580 when mercenaries in rebel pay took and sacked Mechelen ('the English Fury') and Catholic worship was suppressed there. The saying of Mass was also prohibited in the churches of Utrecht. The Utrecht canonries became secular positions, their holders maintaining a role in public life without having any religious duties.

The Return to Loyalty

In 1579 the States of Artois, Walloon Flanders and Hainaut combined in the Union of Arras, to preserve royal government and the Catholic faith. They entered into negotiations with the king's new governor general, Alessandro Farnese, Prince of Parma, to co-ordinate their military response to Calvinist insurgents, but they still excluded foreign troops from their territory. In 1580 they forced the withdrawal of the king's foreign troops from the Low Countries as a condition of continued co-operation, but soon the Spaniards and Italians were invited back as a counterbalance to the German, Scottish, English and French mercenaries in rebel pay. Parma was already in direct control of Namur, Limburg and Luxembourg, which had so far been untouched by the Revolt.

Luxembourg had not even been represented in the Estates General of 1576, since the States of the Duchy claimed the liberty of deciding their own affairs without being influenced by the common decisions of the other provinces. The governor of the province from 1545 to 1605 was Peter Ernest count of Mansfeld, who briefly served as acting governor general of the Seventeen Provinces in the 1590s.

The provincial States of Holland and Zeeland joined with Utrecht, Friesland, Gelderland and Groningen's Ommelanden in the Union of Utrecht (1579). This was also joined by those towns in Flanders and Brabant which came under Calvinist control in the course of 1579–81, including the great cities Antwerp, Brussels and Ghent. The articles of union were the constitutional foundation of the Dutch Republic. As Parma's reconquests progressed, the territory of the Union of Utrecht rapidly shrank, but this was to prove only a temporary setback.

In 1580 the States of Holland and Zeeland offered rule over their counties to Francis, duke of Anjou, the brother of the king of France, on certain limiting conditions. In 1581 the Orangist rump of the Estates General drew up the Act of Abjuration, a formal declaration of the deposition of Philip II. Anjou, impatient at the limits to his powers, attempted a *coup* in 1583 ('the French Fury') and was set aside. With monarchical power gone in the northern Netherlands, sovereignty came to be seen as vested in each of the seven provinces of the union. Matters of common concern were decided in The Hague by the States General (as it will henceforth be called), but members of the States General still had to refer back to their provincial States before voting. There was a problem with expecting sympathetic foreign princes, such as the queen of England or the king of France, to deal with commoners. Since the tiny principality of Orange was a sovereign state, certain executive and military powers were delegated to the Prince of Orange as Stadholder of Holland and Zeeland, and captain-general of the Union. The 'stadholder' was now not the lord lieutenant of the king, but executive officer of the sovereign States.

Political power, and especially the power of the purse, was in the hands of the States, made up of representatives of the nobility and the towns. Except in a few small towns in the eastern Netherlands the craft guilds were excluded from power. The patrician merchants who monopolized most city governments came to be called 'Regents'. The old practice of royal confirmation of elections, or of the prince choosing appointees from lists voted by the aldermen and guilds, was replaced by straightforward co-optation. The Regents became a self-perpetuating class increasingly distant from commoners. There was no body in the United Provinces which could issue patents of nobility, but they took care to marry their children into noble families, or bought up estates with titles attached. This patrician oligarchy was to rule the Republic, with or without a Stadholder, for the next 200 years.

THE NETHERLANDS DIVIDED, 1581–1609

The Union of Arras responded to the Union of Utrecht's Act of Abjuration by recognizing in full the king's sovereignty and Parma's authority as governor general. The three positions of 1579 (loyalty, conditional loyalty and revolt) had narrowed to two. The Low Countries were divided into two blocs which were to be at war until 1648. At the crisis of the Revolt, with royal authority recovering and the sovereignty of the United Provinces in question, William of Orange was assassinated. The prince had been declared an outlaw, with 25,000 gold crowns on his head, and Balthasar Gerard, a young man from the Franche Comté, decided he would risk all for the reward. On 10 July 1584 he approached the Prince in his house in Delft, apparently a petitioner, and shot him. Gerard was apprehended trying to make his escape, and the bounty was eventually paid out to his mother. The Revolt had lost the greatest of its leaders and his death could not have come at a worse time.

To see the Republic through the crisis Elizabeth increased England's commitment to the rebels. She refused to accept the sort of limited sovereignty the United Provinces were willing to offer, but did for the first time make a formal declaration of support and alliance. She even provided a new governor and captain-general in the person of her favourite, Robert Dudley, earl of Leicester. In 1586 Leicester established his seat of government in Utrecht, but the following year he returned to England to take part in the preparations to meet the Spanish Armada, and he died there. The Dutch were by no means sorry to see the back of him.

The six loyal provinces, and a scattering of loyal towns in Flanders, Brabant and Gelderland, served as the basis for the Prince of Parma's reconquest of most of the Netherlands. For over a year the army and the royal administration were paralysed by internal division, but in 1583 the main campaign of reconquest was launched. At the end of the year the Admiralty of Flanders was re-established in newly reconquered Dunkirk, restoring naval capabilities to royal forces in Flanders. Parma's advance culminated in the reconquest of almost the entire county of Flanders in 1584, and the lordship of Mechelen and much of the duchy of Brabant (including Brussels and Antwerp) in 1585. With a second royal army operating in Overijssel and Gelderland, the number of provinces under loyalist control had almost been doubled since 1582. Parma's offensive ground to a halt after 1585, as Philip II's attention and resources were diverted first to the unsuccessful enterprise against England and then to intervention in the civil wars of France. Parma himself died in 1592 and was succeeded as governor general by Philip II's nephew the archduke Ernest of Austria (1594–95), and then by the archduke Albert (governor 1596–98) – both of them brothers of the archduke Matthias who had once attempted to intervene in the affairs of the Low Countries.

After the fiasco of Leicester's governorship William of Orange's second son, Maurice of Nassau, came to the fore as the military leader of the Revolt. Maurice had been appointed Stadholder of Holland and Zeeland in 1585. Appointment in Overijssel followed in 1589, in Utrecht in 1590 and in the same year he was appointed captain-general and admiral-general of the Union. He became Stadholder of Gelderland in 1591. Friesland elected to appoint a Stadholder of its own, a cousin of Maurice. In 1590 Maurice's first major success was the taking of Breda, where a commando of crack troops concealed in a boat shipping peat opened the gates to his forces. A similar attempt at Lier in 1595 was foiled by the citizen militias of Antwerp and Mechelen, who sped to the town's rescue. In 1591 Maurice took Zutphen and Deventer, to secure the line of the IJssel, and further south Nijmegen. In the east and north – Overijssel, Gelderland, Groningen – the rebel losses of the 1580s were reversed by Maurice's campaigns, culminating in 1594 with the taking of the city of Groningen itself. In a further campaign in 1597 Maurice succeeded in reducing the last royalist garrisons in the northern Netherlands, establishing that the division of the Low Countries would be into North and South rather than into East and West.

A major *coup* for royal prestige on the intellectual front was the return to Leuven of one of Leiden's star professors, Justus Lipsius, in 1592. This was the man hailed by his followers as the saviour of Europe for his response to the horrors and instabilities of the time. The direction of his thought was towards the revival of Stoicism, the great Roman philosophy of constancy in misfortune. In 1582 he published the dialogue *On Constancy*, putting the case that a life of steadfast virtue was its own reward, regardless of exterior circumstances and physical misfortunes. He followed this with *Six Books on Politics*, as well as many other works. The 'Neo-Stoic' Lipsius was a hypochondriac who moved from Catholic Leuven to Lutheran Jena to Calvinist Leiden and finally back to Leuven, but despite his own inconstancies he was an influential teacher and writer whose philosophy caught on. He presented himself simply as a student of the ancients, and was most famous for his editions of the works of Tacitus and Seneca, and his handbook on Stoic philosophy. He taught two generations of intellectuals in the Netherlands how to express themselves in Latin, developing the outlook of men who became councillors, jurists, preachers, teachers, and pensionaries and secretaries of cities and provinces. His works were sold, reprinted and translated across Europe, and in the seventeenth century were the educational reading even of future kings and their ministers.

Philip II died in 1598. One of his last political acts was to make the Netherlands the dowry of his eldest daughter, Isabella, and marry her to the governor general, her cousin Archduke Albert of Austria. Philip III inherited Spain and Portugal, the Habsburg lands in Italy and the overseas empire, but not the Netherlands. Albert left the Netherlands to collect his bride in Barcelona, travelling via Italy, and they returned together in 1599. With them they brought William of Orange's eldest son, Philip William, who had been raised at the Spanish court by his godfather, Philip II, and whose presence symbolized the restoration of loyalty. Dynastic continuity was guaranteed by clauses in the transfer stipulating that the Netherlands would revert to the Spanish monarchy if either Albert or Isabella died without issue. There were further secret clauses guaranteeing the king of Spain indirect influence. Spanish field troops and garrisons were to be maintained at his expense, which reduced the financial burdens of the archdukes but did not overly please their subjects. The extent to which this was an army of occupation is easily exaggerated: there was a greater degree of local control over the foreign troops in the service of the United Provinces, but soldiers were never a welcome sight. In 1616 Albert replaced the Spaniards in the highest positions in the military judiciary with Netherlanders, and even though Philip III complained about his troops being put under foreign judges the appointments were not reversed.

Under the archdukes customary law and civic privileges were codified, and the constitutional understanding with the nobility and urban patriciate was restored, beginning with a series of magnificent Joyous Entries in 1599–1600. As in the North, civic life was coming to be dominated by the patrician elite, who in the Habsburg Netherlands could purchase patents of nobility and increasingly displaced the traditional nobility in the governing councils. The great difference with the United Provinces was that anything touching foreign policy was subordinated to wider Habsburg dynastic ambitions.

Soon after their arrival the archdukes were faced with a Dutch invasion of Flanders. Taking advantage of on-going Spanish mutinies, and hoping to destroy the threat that Dunkirk posed to Dutch shipping, Maurice landed his army on the Flemish coast. Isabella, a Spanish princess, rallied the Spaniards to the colours and Albert led the royal army to meet the invaders. They clashed in the dunes outside Nieuwpoort on 2 July 1600. Maurice's Scots mercenaries and the troops of Zeeland distinguished themselves particularly, both in a preliminary engagement at the bridge of Leffinge and in the main battle. At the end of the day the Dutch held the field, but the archdukes had forced Maurice to abandon his planned campaign. Both sides claimed victory.

The Dutch campaign of 1600 fixed the attention of the archdukes on the Flemish coast, as did a petition from the States of Flanders that the taking of Ostend, a nest of privateers and freebooters, be made a military priority. Isabella, in imitation of her forebear and namesake at the Siege of Granada, resolved not to change her underwear until Ostend was retaken, thus giving her name to a shade of yellow. The siege was to last until September 1604, with the town reduced to little more than a smouldering ruin in the mud. Operations were at first directed by Archduke Albert in person, but in 1603 command was handed over to Ambrogio Spinola, a newly arrived *condottiere*. Spinola was a Genoese nobleman from a banking family who was determined to use his wealth to seek military glory. He completed the siege and was to remain the foremost military commander in the Low Countries until 1627.

By 1605 the end of the war, at least temporarily, was in sight. France had made peace with Spain in 1598. England followed in 1604. Volunteers from France, Scotland and England continued to fight in the Netherlands, but the United Provinces were now without public allies. Spinola led a successful campaign in Gelderland in 1605, taking a few small towns of some strategic importance, but the Spanish royal treasury was exhausted. The States General were also deeply in debt. In 1607 a ceasefire was agreed and negotiations were opened with French and English mediation. The sticking points were the Dutch demand that they be recognized as independent, and the Habsburg demands that the Dutch abandon their incursions into the Spanish colonial empire and allow Catholic worship in the United Provinces.

In 1609 a Twelve Years Truce was agreed at Antwerp, and it was ratified at The Hague a few months later. Without going so far as to grant independence, Philip III and the archdukes agreed to treat the United Provinces 'as though' they were sovereign states. Direct Dutch trade with Philip III's overseas possessions was tolerated – the merchants of the loyal provinces had to wait until 1640 for the same concession, but already had strong business ties with intermediaries in Lisbon and Seville. The Catholics of the United Provinces were not granted freedom of worship, but their safety from persecution was guaranteed by the king of France. The issue of navigation on the Scheldt was left open and the following year a clarification by the States of Zeeland determined that there would be no change to the wartime practice of trans-shipping all goods for Antwerp in Zeeland. This was not quite the death-blow to Antwerp's trade that it is sometimes made out, but it was a brake on further recovery or expansion. It also demonstrated the political clout and determined self-interest of the merchants of Holland and Zeeland, already making the Dutch Republic the leading commercial power in Europe.

4

From Delftware to Porcelain, 1609–1780

THE REPUBLIC AS A WORLD POWER

In the sixteenth century the northern provinces dominated the shipping and fisheries of the Low Countries, and Dutch linen weavers and brewers exported internationally. In the late sixteenth and early seventeenth centuries financial and commercial expertise and a range of new industries moved north. Tin-glazed pottery, to take but one example, had been made in Antwerp since before 1512. It was produced in Delft from 1584 and in English soon came to be called Delftware. Delft blue was among the closest European imitations of Chinese porcelain in the seventeenth century, before real porcelain began to be manufactured at Meissen in 1711. By 1670 there were 28 faïence factories in Delft alone, with more in Haarlem, Rotterdam, Gouda, Dordrecht and elsewhere. Other forms of pottery, particularly Dutch tiles, were produced at Middelburg and Leeuwarden.

By the middle of the seventeenth century, Leiden was the largest European centre for the manufacture of woollens, as Haarlem was for linen. Leiden's weavers invented 'camlet', a comparatively light and hard-wearing worsted cloth mixing woollen thread and camel hair. They also developed an improved loom known as the ribbon frame. Dutch cloth, especially worsteds and linens, became an important part of colonial trade and was shipped to the Americas and to Africa in return for exotic produce and slaves.

The fame of Dutch cheese and butter is much marked in the literature of the period. Another area of Dutch dominance, the cod and herring fisheries, was supplemented with whaling in northern waters. In the seventeenth century the herring fleets of half a dozen towns would sail out in June and come home in September, spending the whole of the summer following the herring. The fishermen of the villages dotted along the coastal dunes, and of towns not included in the cartel (even Amsterdam), might put out for cod, flounder, salmon, sole, turbot or whiting, but they were prohibited from intruding into the herring grounds. Alongside fish and cheese, beef became more readily available with the development of an international system whereby cattle bred in Denmark were shipped to the Netherlands to be fattened for slaughter. Dutch dominance of shipping from the Baltic to Western and Southern Europe also brought control of the international grain trade. Dutch artisans and labourers were among the best fed urban populations in Europe.

The wealth of the seventeenth-century Netherlands, and of Amsterdam in particular, was the wonder of the world. A predominantly Catholic city, Amsterdam had held out against the rebels until 1578 and was one of the last towns in Holland to fall. Once out of the fighting it was soon swamped with Calvinist, Mennonite, and even Catholic refugees seeking a more stable environment. They brought with them capital, connections and business techniques from Antwerp and elsewhere. The relative decline of Antwerp was not immediate, but over the decades after 1585 Amsterdam developed its existing strengths while drawing ahead in almost every field for which the older metropolis had been famed. It became the commercial and financial centre of Northern Europe, and of European trade with the wider world. The monumental new town hall (now the royal palace), begun in 1648 and completed in 1655, was a fitting and deliberate expression of the city's wealth and self-confidence. This was not a delusional prestige project. The rows of stately townhouses on the canals, and the many 'pleasure houses' which burghers owned in the surrounding countryside (sometimes amounting to small castles), testify to the solid basis of the city's prosperity.

The transactions of the Amsterdam Wisselbank (bank of exchange), founded in 1609, were of a new order in international finance, and institutionalized the direct bank transfer. At the other end of the scale, the Amsterdam Bank van Lening (loans bank) provided the sort of basic individual and business credit vital to healthy economic development. Marine insurance was further refined in Amsterdam by the first insurance companies. All these developments in banking and insurance built on Antwerp's earlier systematization of medieval Italian business practices. One big difference was that Antwerp's merchants had run their own houses, sometimes working in 'companies' which were little more than temporary partnerships, while an important element in the financing of Dutch trade was the formation of long-term joint stock companies. Another major difference was that Bruges, and even to some extent Antwerp, had been passive centres of commerce. They attracted foreign traders by offering special privileges, a convenient meeting place and a large local market. Holland and Zeeland were far more proactive as commercial powers, going in search of new markets and aggressively competing with established colonial powers at source.

On the relatively short runs of the Baltic and North Sea trades a new type of cargo ship was used, the long and flat-bottomed *fluyt* or flyboat. The flyboat was sluggish and (when not convoyed) easy prey to pirates and privateers, but large numbers could be built cheaply and quickly and it was ideal for transporting bulky cargoes. Dominance in Baltic shipping, the 'mother trade' of the Republic, was supplemented with direct sailings to Italy and the Levant through the Straits of Gibraltar, to the East and West Indies, and to the Arctic North. Contraband trade with Spain and the Spanish colonies flourished. Dutch habits, speech, cities and museums are scattered with souvenirs of their centuries as a colonial trading power.

In the 1590s the intrepid Willem Barentsz led a number of expeditions into the Arctic Sea, with the aim of discovering whether the English route to Muscovy could be extended as a route to China. In 1596–97 Barentsz and his crew were forced to winter on Nova Zembla, in what is now called the Barents Sea. Accounts of their months in a makeshift driftwood cabin measuring 16 metres by 10 set the standards for all later stories of wilderness survival and instilled the heroic importance of thrift, grit and ingenuity in generations of Dutch schoolchildren. No North East Passage was found, but the Dutch did gain access to the Russia trade through Archangel (in competition with the English Muscovy Company) and (in competition with the Danes) to the Arctic whale fisheries. As an image of frostiness, Shakespeare's now mystifying 'You are sailed into the north of my lady's opinion; where you will hang like an icicle on a Dutchman's beard' was once highly topical.

Jan Huygen van Linschoten, another explorer of the North, had already pioneered the Dutch presence in the East Indies. After serving as a clerk aboard a Portuguese merchantman, he returned to his native town of Enkhuizen in 1592 and began publishing his observations. The fabulous profits of the spice trade were what drew Dutch merchants eastwards. In 1596 they first reached what is now Indonesia. In 1602 the

Vereenigde Oost-Indische Compagnie (United East India Company) was formed, VOC for short. The readiness of the VOC to use force, and of the States General to give them diplomatic backing, soon made them masters of the Moluccan spice trade. They seized Jakarta in 1619 and established the administrative centre of the Netherlands East Indies there. After a fort, they built canals, town houses and a town hall in the Dutch style, naming the city Batavia. Most of the population was soon Chinese.

The Portuguese were driven out of trading post after trading post, and even the English and Japanese in Amboina were given short shrift. Ceylon and Malacca were seized from the Portuguese by Anthony van Diemen, who oversaw Abel Tasman's expedition to the Australian coast in 1642. By the end of the century the trading cities of Indonesia were almost all under the direct or the indirect control of the VOC, which dominated the trade in pepper, nutmegs, cloves and other spices. Soon they were establishing sugar plantations, and later coffee: in the eighteenth century they ran the trade from Mocha and Java. From 1636 the VOC had a station in Bengal, and silk and opium entered the range of goods traded. The last of the Portuguese bases on the Sri Lankan coast were taken in 1658, after half a century of pressure, and remained Dutch until 1795.

In June 1598 five ships set sail from Rotterdam with the intention of reaching Japan. Just one of them, the *Liefde* (Charity), finally arrived in April 1600. Among the officers was the Englishman William Adams, on whose adventures James Clavell's *Shogun* is loosely based. The Portuguese Jesuits and their Japanese converts were falling into disfavour, and the sudden appearance of anti-Catholic European navigators was warmly welcomed by the Shogun. Regular trading relations were established in 1609, and from 1641 until 1853 the Dutch were the only Europeans permitted to trade in Japan. Those posted to the lonely island of Deshima in Nagasaki Bay grew rich on Japanese silver, gold and lacquered goods. Incidentally to their main trade, they introduced the Japanese to the finest European cartography and to Dodoens's herbal, gave them the word *biiru* for beer, and were eventually to supply them with their first steamships.

In 1624 the VOC founded Fort Zeelandia on Formosa (now Taiwan). The Company was generally lax in promoting evangelization – this being one of the reasons for their favour in Japan – but on Formosa Dutch Reformed missionaries found an encouraging governor and receptive natives. By the time they were driven out by Ming loyalists in

1662 the Dutch had made considerable progress in converting the aboriginals to Christianity.

Pepper first drew the Dutch to the East Indies, but what brought them to the West Indies was salt. The Dutch herring fleet was in constant need of fine salt to preserve the catch, and the vast saltpan of the Venezuelan coast could supply the quality needed at low cost. The other attractions of the West Indies were contraband trade with Spanish settlements and privateering against Spanish ships. In 1621 the Dutch West India Company (WIC) was formed to finance such profitable incursions into the Spanish and Portuguese Americas.

Around 1609 the English navigator Henry Hudson had explored the North American coast for the VOC. In 1624 the WIC established the colony of New Amsterdam on the Hudson river and seized Bahía on the Brazilian coast (lost again the next year). In the 1630s they established a more substantial foothold in the Caribbean. The Caribbean islands functioned as trading depots, the mainland colonies in Guyana (1625–1803), Brazil (1630–1654), Surinam (1667–1975) and Demerara (1667–1814) provided plantations. What had brought the Dutch was salt, but what kept them was sugar.

Thanks to cigarette manufacturers, Peter Stuyvesant (1592–1672) is probably the most famous colonial Dutchman. He was a Frieslander in the service of the WIC and in 1643 became governor of Curaçao. In 1644 he lost a leg in a failed raid on the island of St Martin, then still Spanish. In 1647 he was appointed director general of New Netherland and governor of the Leeward Isles. Company policy for populating New Netherland was a neo-feudal system called 'patronage', in which any 'patron' who could bring over 50 adult men as tenant farmers was allocated what amounted to a fief held from the Company. Stuyvesant had a great deal of trouble with these overmighty subjects, and with policy towards the Indians and the position of the Dutch Reformed Church in the colony. In 1655 he managed to conquer the Swedish colony on the Delaware for the WIC, but in 1664 he had to surrender New Netherland to the English. Like most Dutch colonists he stayed on as a farmer in what became New York.

Until 1796 the Dutch also ruled the Cape Colony, established by Jan van Riebeek under the auspices of the VOC in 1652. Van Riebeek founded Cape Town, the oldest colonial town in Southern Africa, but for decades it was little more than a watering place for ships sailing to or from the Far East. Towards the end of the seventeenth century the Cape became a colony of settlement, with Huguenot refugees and Dutch orphans arriving in hopes of a better future. The VOC put a stop to this in 1707, forbidding further immigration. Existing planters stayed on, the ancestors of the Boers. A string of forts and trading posts were established along the West African coast as watering stations, but these soon functioned as slave markets. The Dutch plantations of the East and West Indies were in constant need of forced labour, and the Dutch also sold slaves to other nations. From 1663 to 1701 the Dutch ran the Atlantic slave trade not only on their own account, but also as holders of the state contract for the transportation of African slaves to the Spanish colonies of the New World, and as agents for Portuguese and Italian firms. In the eighteenth century they had to make way for the merchants of Bristol and Liverpool.

THE MULTI-FAITH NORTH

One early seventeenth-century commentator suggested that the Netherlands were one-third Catholic, one-third Protestant, and one-third indifferent. The years of religious strife and devastating warfare had taken their toll on religion. In the village of Ritthem, on Walcheren, the last Catholic priest had fled in 1572 during the siege of Middelburg. The first Dutch Reformed minister was appointed in 1612. In the meantime two generations had grown to adulthood without immediate access to an officially vouched-for teacher of religion. Some Christians thirsted for the sacraments they were denied – in 1609 thousands streamed to Antwerp and 's-Hertogenbosch for Confirmation and First Communion – but the general result was a growth in indifference, self-help and folk religion.

One self-help phenomenon in the northern provinces was Bible-study groups whose members were sympathetic to Calvinist doctrines, but reluctant to submit to the discipline of the Reformed Church. There was not the same pressure to conform as was common under Protestant state churches or under most Catholic governments: the Dutch Reformed Church was the only public Church of the United Provinces, but it was not quite a state church and not at all keen to be swamped by a mass of lukewarm members. Within the Dutch Reformed Church there were the 'precise' (*precies*) and the 'flexible' (*rekkelijk*), whom the precise called 'libertines' – a term also used for a seventeenth-century form of atheism.

A later English ambassador to The Hague, Sir William Temple, wrote in his *Observations upon the United Provinces* (1673) that 'the great care of this state has ever been, to favour no particular or curious inquisition into the faith or religious principles of any peaceable man, who came to live under the protection of their laws.' This was in fact a constitutional principle. Article 13 of the Union of Utrecht decreed a 'don't ask, don't tell' form of freedom of conscience, which provided space for alternative religious groups to maintain a low-key presence in the Republic. This was true even of Catholicism. Although the Mass had been declared illegal, priests continued to serve their congregations in secret, supported by an underground network of pious women, 'klopjes', who were successors to the Beguines. Not that Beguines had vanished entirely, even though there were few sixteenth-century women interested in the lifestyle. In Haarlem, for instance, the beguinage and its church had been confiscated by the city authorities, but the Beguines bought up houses in a nearby street until an unofficial beguinage, with a secret church, had been created. In Amsterdam, unusually, the original beguinage was allowed to remain in place. In the provinces under Habsburg rule there was a reflowering of Beguine life in the seventeenth century.

Other denominations had a legally shadowy but socially substantial existence on the fringes of public life: Mennonites, Lutherans, a wide variety of small *sui generis* congregations known (without pejorative intent) as sects, and in some places Jews. Amsterdam was particularly noted for its large and active Jewish community, tolerated on the condition that Jews take care of their own poor, refrain from proselytizing, and not intermarry with Christians. Many towns still barred Jews from citizenship, and some even prohibited Jewish settlement, but in most towns gypsies were the only ethnic group to be expressly excluded from habitation.

Doctrinal deviants within the public Church were tolerated less readily than other faiths. That the Dutch Reformed Church was a strictly Calvinist church was established only in 1619, after Holland had teetered on the brink of civil war. The Calvinist view of salvation was that God's grace was everything, and human action nothing, and that God's decision as to whether a person was saved or damned was fixed even before their conception. An early seventeenth-century correspondent of the 'Antwerp gazette' cried out against those who could teach 'that God would pluck an innocent babe from its mother's breast to cast it into the depths of hell!' and this was no misrepresentation of the strict Calvinist view. The 'precise' Leiden professor Antonius Thysius had used the example in all seriousness in his *De praedestinatione* (1613),

138

and he was not alone in doing so. For pastoral reasons Dutch Reformed teaching was that the deceased children of church members should be assumed to have been saved, but theologians writing of abstract cases were not bound by this sensitivity to parental concerns.

Even though the best human act was a sin in God's sight, this did not mean that personal behaviour was entirely irrelevant. Those assured of their place in heaven were 'called to the practice of godliness'. This meant to conform their lives to divine standards, with the comfort that when they fell short, it could not lead to their damnation. There was no sense that humans were in any way free to accept or reject the grace that God offered: free will might play a role in daily life, but not in salvation.

Remonstrants and Counter-Remonstrants, or: the Arminian Controversy

A different opinion, closer to the usual Catholic belief, found its spokesman in Jacobus Arminius (1560–1609). In this view, a sort of conditional predestination, there was an element of free response to God's saving grace. Arminius was appointed a professor of theology at Leiden in 1603, but his opinions on grace and salvation were heavily attacked by his colleague Franciscus Gomarus (1563–1641), a hard-line Calvinist refugee from Bruges who had been appointed in 1594. After Arminius died, an even less strictly Calvinist follower was appointed to his chair, and Gomarus resigned in protest. The first round may have been lost by Gomarus in academic politics, but the contest was only just beginning. Arminians and Gomarists were soon battling it out in the pulpits, and even fighting in the streets. The mass of faithful Reformed church-goers were inclined to Gomarist views. Feelings ran so high that Gomarist mobs attacked those leaving services led by Arminian preachers. In 1610 Arminians drew up a remonstrance and appealed to the States of Holland for protection; hence they would come to be known as Remonstrants, their opponents as Counter-Remonstrants.

Disputes about the relationship between grace, faith and salvation were not simply theoretical, but touched the heart of Calvinist religiosity: the sense of invincible security in God's favour. A particularly poignant case (recently examined by Willem Frijhoff) was recorded by Aert van Rijnevelshorn, a leading Lutheran citizen of the town of Woerden. In the plague year 1636 Rijnevelshorn wrote a pamphlet to demonstrate that the Fourth Monarchy of the world (see Daniel 2: 31–45) was drawing to its end and that the age of the everlasting Fifth

Monarchy would soon dawn. In the course of this work, and in more detail in a later pamphlet, he wrote of a Dutch Reformed villager he had known, and visited in his final sickness, who despite a large and happy family, a successful farm, regular church-going and a godly life lacked assurance of salvation. Around 1617 this farmer had become convinced that he was predestined to damnation, and his crisis of faith was much discussed in Woerden. In the opinion of the foremost Dutch Reformed minister in the town 'the problem is not with his soul, but his head'. He was quite possibly right, but even deep-seated melancholy was then considered more a physical than a psychological affliction. That it could be experienced as certainty of damnation shows something of the temper of the time. This was certainly how Rijnevelshorn took it, despair and doubt together being one of his 15 signs of the End Times.

It was in 1617, the year of the Woerden farmer's crisis of faith, that the public controversy came to a head. In February a Gomarist mob attacked a Remonstrant congregation in Amsterdam. The regents of Holland were generally inclined to flexible views, and even those who were not were averse to theological disputes being decided by the disorders of *hoi polloi*. The States of Holland empowered the towns to levy troops (*waardgelders*) to keep public order. Precisians saw the regents of Holland as attempting to force a heresy on the public Church, and appealed to the Stadholder. Maurice had thus far been reluctant to get involved, but now decided that intervention was necessary to maintain his position as the head of the armed forces. He marched through the United Provinces, purging the town councils of Remonstrants. Many suspected him of intending an attempt on the sovereignty of the States. Johan van Oldenbarnevelt, Grand Pensionary of Holland, authorized the civic levies to fire in defence of the privileges of Holland or any of its towns, but in the event no resistance was offered.

Johan van Oldenbarnevelt had long been the pilot of the ship of state. As pensionary of Rotterdam he had been one of the main drafters of the articles of union in 1579, and he had played a leading role in public life ever since, particularly after becoming Grand Pensionary in 1586. His authorization to the *waardgelders* to fire upon the Stadholder's troops, although never put into effect, became the basis of a treason trial. He was beheaded in 1619. Charges were also brought against Gilles van Ledenberg, secretary of the States of Utrecht. Ledenberg cut his own throat with a breadknife to save his family from being dispossessed, but was condemned posthumously and symbolically his coffin hanged on the gibbet. Hugo Grotius, pensionary of Rotterdam, was sentenced to life imprisonment in the castle of Loevestein, the usual place of detention for prisoners of state, but in 1621 he was smuggled out in a bookchest and escaped to France.

From November 1618 to May 1619 a National Synod of the Dutch Reformed Church met at Dordrecht. It concluded with a condemnation of Arminian theology and the demand that Remonstrant preachers subscribe to a strictly Calvinist understanding of predestination. Over 200 ministers of religion were deprived of their livings and 80 were banished from the country. As long as they caused no public scandal, these Remonstrant exiles were tolerated in Catholic Antwerp as an embarrassment to the Stadholder. It was there that exiled ministers formed the Remonstrant Brotherhood to continue to serve now-clandestine congregations in the United Provinces, formalizing a schism which has persisted to the present day. The victory of the 'precise' at the Synod of Dort carried over into other spheres of life. Increasingly after 1619, towns and provincial States took measures to limit the civil rights of religious dissidents, or to exclude them from citizenship. The United Provinces became a Calvinist country in a way it had not been before, but Article 13 of the Union continued to provide cover for dissent.

THE CATHOLIC SOUTH

The years of the Truce saw the rebuilding of Catholic life in the Habsburg Netherlands. Under the auspices of Archdukes Albert and Isabella (1598–1621) a self-consciously Catholic and loyalist society was created. Those parts of the Archducal Netherlands conquered by the Dutch from 1629 onwards (North Brabant, Limburg and parts of Gelderland) have remained largely Catholic to this day, despite a vigorous protestantizing policy in the mid-seventeenth century.

The archdukes were rulers on the spot, whose main interest was in the welfare of their subjects, as long as it was understood that continued Habsburg rule and the Catholic faith were good things. During the Truce they did all they could to help the process of recovery from the devastations of the Revolt. Economic and monetary measures were taken to stimulate an economy which was rapidly regaining momentum, although it never attained the glories of before the Revolt and nowhere came near to Holland's meteoric rise. Antwerp's money market was boosted by its reintegration into the monarchy's financial system, and the trades in silk and other luxuries started up again. The canal network of Flanders, linking Ghent, Bruges and Ypres to Ostend, Nieuwpoort and Dunkirk, was extended for military and commercial purposes. To combat usury, the archdukes patronized low-interest loan banks known as Mounts of Mercy, to answer the perennial social problem of making affordable credit available to the poor.

The two most clearly novel elements in the Tridentine Church in the Low Countries were the new bishoprics and the Society of Jesus. Although Jesuits are sometimes spoken of as synonymous with Catholic reform, they often met opposition from reforming bishops, monks and friars with equal zeal and conflicting priorities. They were undoubtedly important, but not the dominant force that later myth-making, both admiring and hostile, has made them. They had no particular pull at the court of the archdukes, who had Franciscan and Dominican confessors and entrusted prestigious new foundations to Oratorians and Augustinians. The one Jesuit to have Albert's ear was Leonardus Lessius, an influential moral theologian whose work drew on his sensitivity to the questions of conscience of Antwerp's merchants. Lessius's ideas about practical religious toleration and licit interest on loans were not shared by many members of his order. The Jesuits did have enthusiastic supporters among the nobility and the urban elites, mainly because of their reputation as excellent teachers. Towns were soon vying with one another to have a Jesuit college established. The English government and the States General of the United Provinces both felt it necessary to prohibit the sending of boys to Jesuit schools in Flanders, and Lutheran bishops as far away as Norway complained about the same thing. The Jesuits also organized Sunday schools and prayer clubs known as 'sodalities' which quickly put them at the centre of associational life in the cities. The social influence of the order somewhat made up for its lack of friends at court.

The challenges facing the new bishops in combining Catholic restoration and reform have recently been set out by Craig Harline and Eddy Put. Their *A Bishop's Tale* is a series of vignettes based on the diaries of Mathias Hovius, Archbishop of Mechelen from 1596 to 1620. The most basic issues were funding and discipline. Without money suitably qualified candidates were difficult to find (since those called to poverty would as soon join an order as become diocesan priests), but without tight clerical discipline the money was spent in vain. Religious houses were valued supplements to the bishop's forces as long as they did not become competitors for alms or recruits: a minor crisis in relations with the Jesuits came in 1615, when their school in Mechelen poached the star pupil Jan Berchmans (a future saint) from the bishop's college. The Dutch Mission was an ark tempest-tossed by similar rivalries.

THE GOLDEN AGE

Catholic life in the Habsburg Netherlands was rebuilt in a much more literal sense. The damage done by iconoclasts and by wartime ravages and neglect had to be repaired. In many cases this meant completing the destruction of medieval art so that new works could be installed. Some entirely new churches were built, such as the heptagonal basilica at Scherpenheuvel, a Marian pilgrimage centre promoted by the archdukes. Restoration and construction provided employment for architects, builders, masons, carpenters, tilers, sculptors, painters and many other craftsmen. Seventeenth- and eighteenth-century statues and pulpits are among the most striking sights in major Belgian churches. The early seventeenth century was a golden age of artistry in the Habsburg Netherlands. Beyond the highly remunerative commissions for churches and guild chapels, and those from the archdukes' court, there was a burgeoning art market at all levels of society. Inventories in Antwerp's notarial archives show that artisans might tie up spare cash in decorative works, which livened up a room and could always be sold on at need. Some even had family portraits.

Painting

Archduke Albert's favourite artist was Otto Vaenius, or Van Veen, a Catholic refugee from rebel Leiden. Although primarily a painter, Vaenius gained greatest fame for his books of emblems. The 'emblem', a combination of a poem, a picture and a caption, all in some way related, was a fashionable genre in the seventeenth century, and was nowhere more popular than in the Low Countries. Internationally bestselling collections of such emblems were Vaenius's 'love is . . .' *Amorum emblemata* (1608) and 'divine love is . . .' *Amoris divini emblemata* (1615). These influenced illustration, decoration and design not only throughout Europe, but wherever Europeans settled. Vaenius's pupils included Peter Paul Rubens (1577–1640). Rubens's parents fled the war-torn Low Countries and he was born in Germany. He was educated first in Cologne and later in Antwerp, and at the age of 23 entered the service of the dukes of Mantua. He returned to Antwerp in 1608 and quickly established himself as the foremost painter of the age. He received major commissions for Antwerp churches, and from courts throughout Western Europe. A phenomenal rate of production was maintained by having apprentices do most of the laborious work, the master himself sketching the design and adding the finishing touches. Rubens worked closely with the finest engravers to ensure that his designs were given the widest and most remunerative circulation, and the contractual arrangements he sought show a precocious concern for intellectual property. He also designed frontispieces for the most prestigious publications of the Plantin Office, including the collected works of Justus Lipsius.

Contemporaries of Rubens in Antwerp were John Brueghel and Peter Brueghel the younger, who continued the family tradition begun by their father, Peter Brueghel the elder. John, nicknamed 'Hell', specialized in Boschian religious themes; Peter the younger, nicknamed 'Velvet', in still-lifes and landscapes. Others were Sebastian Vranckx, best known for his battle scenes, and Frans Snyders, a master of still-lifes and hunting scenes. One of Rubens's pupils was Anthony Van Dyck, who began his career in Antwerp but later became attached to the Stuart court. Van Dyck started a new fashion in high-society portraiture, eagerly copied by contemporaries in England and the Low Countries. Among his contemporaries who stayed in Antwerp was Jacob Jordaens, a crypto-Calvinist who did well out of church commissions but is best known for his drinking scenes. The greatest figure of the following (and final) generation of the seventeenth-century 'Antwerp school' was David Teniers the younger, whose landscapes and scenes of peasant life were in demand even among foreign royalty. These are just a few of the more famous talents in a craft at which many laboured in poverty and obscurity.

Painting was one of the areas in which Antwerp held its own longest, but even this speciality trade flourished in the seventeenth-century Republic. Like so much else, this was by a combination of established and imported skills. The first historian of Netherlandish art was Carel van Mander, an Antwerp Protestant who moved to Haarlem after 1585. He catalogued the lives and achievements of Flemish artists, recording a tradition and a canon on which new artists built. The central concept of painting was emulation. The aim was to imitate the artists who had gone before, in order to master their techniques and surpass them. 'Lifelike' was among the highest term of praise, but the ultimate goal was to transform and surpass nature by invention. With Calvinism dominant, the big commissions in the North were not religious paintings but group portraits of regent office-holders: magistrates, officers of the watch, the boards of charitable foundations. Colour was the great strength of the tradition of Flemish painting, but the best Dutch painters typically excelled in conveying the play of light.

With the possible exception of Vincent Van Gogh, the best known Dutch painter is Rembrandt Harmensz van Rijn (1606–1669). A native of Leiden, where he began his career, Rembrandt moved to Amsterdam in 1631 and spent the rest of his life there. Fame came in 1632, with *The Anatomy Lesson of Dr Tulp*, and commissions for portraits flowed in. Like Rubens, Rembrandt was at his most imaginative and versatile in the monumental genre of history painting, often drawing on biblical narratives. Perhaps his single most famous work is the *Night Watch* (1642), commissioned as a group portrait but looking more like a history piece. He was in some respects a wayward painter, whose notorious stubbornness led to falling earnings and eventually bankruptcy. His *Conspiracy of Claudius Civilis*, commissioned in 1660 for Amsterdam's new town hall, was rejected by the aldermen for failing to conform to the accepted iconography of the Batavian Revolt. Rather than a noble youth of pleasant aspect, Civilis was shown as the one-eyed, battle-hardened veteran described by Tacitus.

Far more than the art of the Habsburg Netherlands, the painting of the Dutch Golden Age turned to representations of everyday life and objects. The range of such pictures was immense, and immensely rich, with portraits, still-lifes, landscapes (with some painters specializing in winter landscapes or moonlit landscapes), paintings of low-life, festive gatherings and brawls, church interiors, images of rural domesticity, and perhaps now most famously the bourgeois domestic interiors of Pieter De Hoogh and Johannes Vermeer. In the northern provinces the market for art started later, but grew to even wider proportions than in the South. The traveller Peter Mundy, in Amsterdam in 1641, commented on how everybody, including bakers and smiths, could be seen to be 'striving to adorn their houses'. The diarist John Evelyn, in Rotterdam the following year, was surprised to see the interiors of farmhouses hung with paintings. With this flood of highly imitative artistry to meet a range of budgets, connoisseurship became a commercial asset. A reputable artist like Frans Hals of Haarlem, a childhood refugee from the South and a pupil of Van Mander, could supplement his income from painting and teaching by advising the magistrates about their purchases, and providing expertise at auctions.

Views of the world

Painters were not the only crafters of new ways of seeing. There was great interest in the use of words and numbers to create meaning and change the world – uses which could take many forms. Not to be confused with witchcraft was the 'natural' magic of the learned, including alchemy, numerology, astrology and cabbalism. Learned magic relied not on demonic powers, but on supposed hidden ('occult') correspondences between numbers, words, the stars, the elements and the orders of angels. One of the most lastingly influential of natural magicians was Heinrich Cornelius Agrippa (1486–1535), a German physician whose final years were spent as archivist and historian to the Brussels court. His encyclopedic *De occulta philosophia* was printed in Antwerp in 1531. One of the most successful alchemists of the Low Countries was Jan Baptist van Helmont (1577–1644), who studied a variety of subjects at Leuven before taking his doctorate in medicine. His interest in transmutations from solid and liquid to vaporous states led him to coin the word 'gas'. He was the first to identify the chemical composition of a number of gases, and also demonstrated experimentally that plants use water in their growth, transforming liquid into solid. But his lifetime's ambition, never realized, was to find the philosopher's stone. His son Frans Mercurius (named after the element mercury) was a less successful scientist but a more daring speculator in the arcane, and part of the circle that produced the *Cabbalah Denudata* (1677). Several seventeenth-century secret societies, such as the Rosicrucian order and lodges of Freemasons, were rooted in this sort of natural mysticism.

The passing of the scientific and cultural initiative from Antwerp, Leuven and Brussels to Amsterdam, Leiden and The Hague is embodied in the life of Rembert Dodoens (1517–1585). Once physician to the city of Mechelen and to the Habsburg court, he ended his days as a professor in Leiden. Another scientist who made the move north, in his case from Bruges, was Simon Stevin (1548–1620). Besides his contributions to mathematics (including a decimal system) and to military and hydraulic engineering, Stevin was an early linguistic purist who lastingly replaced terms such as 'paralel' and 'geometrie' with 'evenwijdig' and 'meetkunde'. In Amsterdam Willem Janszoon Blaeu continued the Netherlandish tradition of cartographic publishing with his maritime atlas (1608) and his *Theatrum Orbis Terrarum* (1634), an achievement surpassed only by the nine-volume world atlas published by his son,

Joan, in 1664–65. The Elzeviers of Leiden replaced the Plantin office of Antwerp at the forefront of more general quality publishing.

The most versatile 'pure' scientist from the Netherlands, and in his lifetime the most famous, is probably Christiaan Huygens (1629–1695), the grandson, son and brother of successive secretaries to the stadholders. A mathematician, physicist and astronomer, Huygens was a figure of international standing, a member of the Royal Society and of the Académie Française. His contemporary Antonie van Leeuwenhoek (1632–1723) laid the foundations of microscopic research, discovering bacteria, spermatozoa, capillary circulation and various other wonders of nature too small to behold with the naked eye. In medicine, Jacob Bontius's posthumous *De Medicina Indicorum* (1642) revealed to Europeans some of the hazards of life in the tropics. The celebrated Herman Boerhaave (1668–1738), who turned to medicine when a career in the Church was blocked by scandal, showed little originality but a flair for explaining the latest discoveries. Medical students from across Europe journeyed to Leiden to attend his lectures and demonstrations, and his *Institutiones medicae* (1708) was translated into every major European language.

One important reason for Dutch pre-eminence in the intellectual life of seventeenth-century Europe was the relative tolerance and freedom of thought in the Republic. Just how relative this was can be seen from cases like that of Adriaan Koerbagh, an atheist condemned to ten years hard labour after a heresy trial. He died with broken health in 1669, before completing his sentence. An earlier victim of intolerance was Hugo Grotius, the Arminian pensionary of Rotterdam who fled to France in 1621. Banished from his own country, he was from 1631 Swedish ambassador in Paris. His standing as a jurist had once led the magistrates of Amsterdam to seek his advice when considering whether, and on what terms, to give formal permission for Jewish residence in the city: the measures taken were essentially those which Grotius had proposed. His *Mare liberum* (1609), written at the VOC's behest, argued for the freedom of the seas, at a time when on land the Republic maintained its medieval particularism of staple towns, tolls and tariffs. His most influential work was *De jure belli ac pacis* (1625), on the law of war and peace, which provided the first developed statements on international law to be framed as jurisprudence rather than moral theology.

The main institution of learning was still the university. The seventeenth century saw the expansion of higher education in the Republic: Leiden was joined by new universities in Franeker (1585), Groningen

(1614), Utrecht (1636) and Harderwijk (1648), and *Athenae Illustria* (liberal arts colleges) in more than half a dozen towns, most importantly Deventer (1630), Amsterdam (1632) and Breda (1646). In the Habsburg Netherlands there was soon only one university. Douai, where a second university had been founded in the 1560s, was lost to Louis XIV in 1668; Leuven fiercely defended its monopoly on higher education, especially against Jesuit colleges. Novel speculations stimulated learned interest in the South as in the North, albeit with less public debate, but while intellectual life was not as stagnant as is sometimes assumed, it was undeniably less vibrant than in the Republic.

In logic and natural philosophy all the universities of the Low Countries were once more taking Aristotle as their point of departure. Gijsbrecht Voetius (1589–1676) set his mark on seventeenth-century Dutch culture perhaps more than any other individual. Voetius was a precise Calvinist, and insistent on the need to repress Arminians and Catholics, but he was influential in shifting the emphasis of Dutch Calvinism from doctrinal dispute to godliness of life. He insisted on strict observance of the sabbath, and lobbied for laws against gaming and prostitution. As a professor of theology at Utrecht, he developed a Calvinist scholasticism which put Aristotle at the service of Reformed Christianity. Through the influence of his students this system became academic orthodoxy not only in the Netherlands but also elsewhere in Protestant Europe, most significantly providing the intellectual formation of those active in the Scottish Enlightenment. Scholastic Aristotelianism in its more traditional Catholic form remained strong in the southern Netherlands.

The most novel thinkers of the time worked outside academia. Menasseh ben Israël was a talmudic and biblical scholar of great renown, and the person to whom Dutch humanists turned for advice on the Hebrew language or for a Jewish perspective on a passage in Scripture. Among other works, Menasseh wrote the much-consulted *El Conciliador*, reconciling apparent contradictions in the Hebrew Bible. It was, like most of his writings, in Spanish. He had been born in Madeira in 1604 but his family fled to Amsterdam when he was a child. In 1655, two years before his death, Menasseh succesfully petitioned Cromwell for the readmission of Jews to England. He also encouraged Jewish settlement in Brazil, the spreading of the Jewish people throughout the world being part of his understanding of the messianic scheme of history. English criticism of Cromwell's decision he met in 1656 with his greatest work, the *Vindiciae Judaeorum* (Vindication of the Jews).

Another foreigner among the most influential thinkers to work and publish in the Low Countries was René Descartes, who lived in Amsterdam from 1628 to 1649. In his *Discours sur la méthode* (1636) Descartes exalted rationalism to new heights and changed the way that philosophers went about their thinking. The tradition of humanism dating back to Erasmus and before had been based on the study of ancient texts (the Classics, the Bible, the Church Fathers) and their application to life; the philosophy of Descartes relied on mathematical abstraction, and a thoroughgoing divorce between mind and body, experience and thought.

A controversial figure of similarly lasting influence was Baruch Spinoza (1632–1677), a pupil of Menasseh ben Israël. When he was only 24, before he had yet given his unorthodox views clear expression, he was expelled from his synagogue and banished from the city of Amsterdam. After his death his books were banned by the States of Holland. Spinoza saw the universe as an intricately interconnected whole which might be called either God or Nature. He thought of traditional religion as useful for keeping the ignorant in their place, but as encoding, rather than revealing, fundamental truths. His basic assumptions about man and his place in the world owed much to medieval Jewish Aristotelianism, but his philosophical method was entirely new. In the fashion of Cartesian logic and Rosicrucian numerology Spinoza attempted to draw out the necessary consequences of ethical principles in the form of geometrical propositions. In doing so he refracted traditional ideas about life, liberty and the pursuit of happiness into unrecognizable patterns. Spinoza's thought was influential on developing notions of freedom and reason, and is fundamental to modern secular humanism. His views did much to shape the Deism of the Enlightenment and the Pantheism of certain Romantics.

Literature

In 1637 the crowning book of Dutch Calvinism was completed: a new, official translation of the Bible, licensed by the States General. The role of this *Statenvertaling* (States Translation) in the development of Dutch prose was similar to that of the King James Version in the English-speaking world. Also like the King James Version, the Statenvertaling was a deliberately archaising product of an age of high literary achievement. The period of late Shakespeare and Milton in English literature corresponds with that of Pieter Cornelisz Hooft and Joost van den

Vondel in Dutch. Hooft, a poet and historian, was from 1609 to 1647 a country magistrate just outside Amsterdam with his official residence at the castle of Muiden. He often had literary friends to stay at the castle, so that several of the writers of the time are for convenience grouped as the 'Muiden circle'. These poets include the sisters Anna and Tesselschade Roemers Visscher, and Constantijn Huygens, secretary to the stadholder and father of the scientist Christiaan Huygens.

The opening of the Amsterdam *Schouwburg*, the first (and long the only) purpose-built playhouse in the Low Countries, speeded a shift from the drama of amateur rhetoricians to that of professional poets. Joost van den Vondel (1587–1679) was the prince of poets and an unsurpassed playwright, but his writing did not pay enough to keep him from working as a clerk at the Bank van Lening. Vondel was the grandchild of Mennonite refugees from Antwerp but was received into the Catholic Church in 1639. Throughout his career he faced Calvinist criticism of his plays, either for staging biblical figures in works such as *Lucifer* (banned after the first performance in 1654), or for having characters in history plays, such as *Gijsbrecht van Aemstel* (1637) or *Maria Stuart* (1646), express clearly Catholic religious sentiments. His worst offence was in 1625, with *Palamedes*, an attack on the late Oldenbarnevelt's enemies thinly disguised as an adaptation of an episode from Homer. He went into hiding when the Court of Holland requested his extradition from Amsterdam, but in the end the city magistrates refused to have him apprehended.

The best-selling Dutch writer of the time was Jacob Cats, a lawyer (pensionary of Middelburg, then Dordrecht, and finally Grand Pensionary of Holland) whose collections of poems and of emblems illustrated biblical, classical and folk aphorisms to teach morals and manners to his readers. In the twentieth century Cats was discounted as 'didactic' and 'the original bourgeois moralist', but for almost 300 years he was considered the epitome of fluently expressed and memorably illustrated prudence. A strict Calvinist himself, his writings appealed to readers of all denominations.

In Antwerp Richard Verstegan (an English Catholic refugee of Dutch descent) was a prolific satirist of hypocrites, usurers, Calvinists and other dangers to society, but in the southern provinces sacred letters were more favoured. The greatest achievement was the *Acta Sanctorum*.* At the suggestion of Heribert Rosweyde (who died in

* On which see David Knowles, *Great Historical Projects* (London: Nelson, 1964), pp. 3–33).

150

1629) the Antwerp Jesuits set up a still ongoing project to publish the lives and legends of the saints on the basis of the fullest source materials treated with the best text-critical scholarship. Those involved in the work are known as Bollandists, from the first director of the project, Jean Bolland. The volumes are arranged by the festive calendar of the Church: the two volumes on the saints whose feastdays are in January first appeared in 1643; by 1940 the beginning of December had been reached, and since then the assimilation of scholarly advances and the rate of new canonizations have kept the work from completion.

THE EIGHTY YEARS WAR CONTINUED, 1621–1648

Hoping that the Low Countries might be spared further fighting the archdukes pressed the king of Spain to prolong the Truce, but neither he nor the Dutch would pitch their demands low enough for there to be a realistic chance of agreement. Maurice himself had signalled a readiness to negotiate, but according to some historians this was a deliberate attempt to string the Habsburgs along. Philip III and Archduke Albert both died in 1621, and as the archdukes remained childless the Habsburg Netherlands reverted to Philip IV of Spain. Isabella stayed on as Governess General until her own death in 1633.

The renewal of war in 1621 was half-hearted at best. It was only with the Siege of Breda, in 1624–25, that the war on land was again begun in earnest. Breda was strategically important, commanding the lands between the Scheldt estuary and the mouth of the Maas, but also of great symbolic value: Lord of Breda was one of the titles of the house of Orange. The surrender of the city to Ambrogio Spinola, the Italian in over-all command of the Army of Flanders, was commemorated in painting, song and history, most famously by Velázquez.

The war at sea was faster to pick up again. The WIC was a trading company, but it had been founded in 1621 as a weapon of war to undermine the Habsburg hold on the Spanish and Portuguese bases in the Americas. The Spanish government retaliated by sponsoring a Spanish-Flemish commercial company, based in Seville, to try (without much success) to cut Holland out of the Baltic–Mediterranean carrying trade. The Habsburgs and their allies controlled the German Rhineland and the middle Maas. Work was begun on a canal linking the Maas and the Rhine, but progress was slow. The archduchess and Spinola both hoped that the regents could be forced back to the negotiating table by a blockade of the river trade combined with a vigorous campaign of privateering at sea, out of Ostend, Nieuwpoort and above all Dunkirk. Their ships were built to a new design, narrow and low in the water: the frigate. The ferocity with which Dunkirkers attacked Dutch shipping, including the precious herring fleet, became notorious. In 1622, when the encircled Captain Jan Jacobsen put his match to the powder rather than surrender one of the king's frigates to the Dutch, he set a level of determination for his fellows to emulate.

The new Habsburg strategy of commercial warfare had much to recommend it, but after Breda the fortunes of the land war turned. When Maurice died in 1625 it seemed to set the seal on a remarkable run of Habsburg victories in the Low Countries, Spain, the Americas and Central Europe. But Maurice was succeeded as stadholder and captain general by his much younger half-brother Frederick Henry (1584–1647), an experienced commander who was eager for military glory. In 1627 Spinola was removed from the Low Countries, as the result of a Spanish court intrigue. The commanders of the army of Flanders fell to jockeying for position. In 1628 a Spanish silver fleet was captured off Cuba by a WIC flotilla commanded by Piet Heyn (who was to die the following year in a fight with Ostenders off the Scottish coast). It took a week to reload the booty on to the Dutch ships, and 1629 was a very good year for WIC shareholders. A popular song about Piet Heyn can still be heard at football matches. When the loss of the silver fleet became known there was a crisis of credit at Antwerp and the Army of Flanders, already divided at the top, was paralysed.

In 1629 Frederick Henry, who came to be called the 'stedendwinger' (forcer of cities), began a series of conquests by taking 's-Hertogenbosch. This was one of the four chief cities of Brabant and had withstood numerous assaults and sieges since 1579. For years Dutch royalists had made up the most prominent part of the garrison, and the city had above all others come to represent battle-hardened loyalty. Quite apart from the psychological consequences, the fall of 's-Hertogenbosch meant the loss of much of northern Brabant, and a new bridgehead for the Republic south of the Maas.

The collapse of Habsburg prestige was so total that in 1632 a conspiracy of noblemen in the Loyal Provinces planned an uprising. In the event the only conspirators to move were Count Henry of Berg, a leading commander frustrated at the promotion of Spaniards over his head, and René de Renesse, count of Warfusée, a councillor of finance suspected of malfeasance. Both fled to Liège and issued manifestos against the 'Spanish yoke'. Frederick Henry, informed in advance of the conspiracy, fulfilled his part of the plan by marching up the Maas, taking Venlo, Roermond and Maastricht. Royal dominance between the Maas and the Rhine was broken. The strategy of river blockades and the plan for a Maas–Rhine canal became unworkable. As at 's-Hertogenbosch in 1629, Frederick Henry was willing to encourage these Catholic cities to surrender by granting religious guarantees that the States General later refused to honour. The States of Zeeland, in particular, were adamant that to tolerate 'the blasphemous idolatry of the Mass' would call down God's wrath on the Republic.

To defuse political tension the Infanta in 1632 summoned the Estates General of the loyal provinces to meet in Brussels, the first such meeting since 1600. The loyal provinces insisted that peace talks be resumed, sending envoys to Madrid and to Bergen op Zoom, but the intransigence of the Republic was now the main obstacle to a settlement. The Estates General was disbanded in 1634, never to meet again. At the same time Habsburg fortunes briefly revived. In 1634 Philip IV's younger brother, Don Ferdinand, led a Habsburg army from northern Italy to Flanders. On the way he defeated the Habsburg emperor's German and Swedish enemies in pitched battle at Nordlingen, where the battlecry was 'Viva Spania!'

Richelieu had long kept France out of direct involvement in the wars against the Habsburgs, while giving substantial support to their enemies in the Low Countries, Germany and Italy. When a Spanish strike-force abducted the archbishop-elector of Trier, who had accepted French rather than Habsburg protection for his principality, it was impossible to stand idle. The French army invaded the Habsburg Netherlands in 1635 – the first in a series of French invasions ending only in 1815. They linked up with the Dutch to lay waste Tienen and besiege Leuven. Any chance that the invaders might be welcomed as liberators, as the noble conspirators had planned in 1632, was destroyed by the sack of Tienen. Events in the town also showed up divisions in the French–Dutch alliance, when French officers drew swords on their Protestant allies to secure the safety of nuns. Over 1000 peasant families, with their livestock, took refuge from pillagers in the ducal hunting forest of Soignes (Zoniën), between Tervuren and Brussels. Don Ferdinand was able to halt the invaders and go onto the offensive, but while battles might still be won the war was slowly to be lost.

The prince-bishop of Liège from 1612 to 1640 was Ferdinand of Bavaria, also archbishop of Cologne and strategically one of the most important allies of the Habsburgs. He had spent much of his youth at the court of the archdukes. His only open intervention in the Eighty Years War was at Maastricht in 1632, to safeguard his share in the lordship of the town. As bishop of Liège he was officially neutral, but he was definitely a sympathetic neutral. There was an anti-Habsburg party in Liège, opposed to the bishop's policy, which was led by the mayor, Pierre de La Ruelle, and looked to France for backing. The Count of Warfusée, in exile in Liège since 1632, conspired with de La Ruelle to depose Ferdinand as prince-bishop and install Cardinal Richelieu, but nothing came of the plan. After five years of kicking his heels, Warfusée sought to reingratiate himself with the Habsburgs by murdering the mayor. He invited de La Ruelle to a banquet on 16 April 1637, and had him slaughtered by a party of 60 Spanish soldiers brought to Liège for the purpose. Everything went as planned but the murder did not have the expected consequences. Far from the 'French party' being left cowed and leaderless, an outraged mob laid siege to the house, killed the assassins, strung up Warfusée's corpse on the gallows, and went on the rampage against the 'Spanish party'. Even religious orders with Spanish associations suffered: the rector of the Jesuit college was murdered and the Carmelite convent was set on fire.

The borders which were to be fixed in 1648 largely took their final shape in 1637. In that year the neutrality and independence of Liège were reaffirmed. Venlo and Roermond, taken by Frederick Henry in 1632, were retaken by royal troops and became Habsburg enclaves on the Maas (until 1715 and 1794 respectively). Meanwhile Frederick Henry regained Breda, lost in 1625, and the strategic river fortress Schenkenschans, lost in 1635. Thereafter the Habsburg military position deteriorated rapidly. The Spanish Road from Italy had become untenable, and the alternative of sending troops by sea suffered a major blow in 1639 when a Dutch fleet under Maarten Tromp destroyed a Spanish troop convoy in the Battle of the Dunes. The outbreak of civil wars in the British Isles stopped the recruitment of mercenaries in Ireland. In 1643 the French, for eight years little more than a nuisance, wiped out the cream of the Army of Flanders in pitched battle at Rocroi. The 1640s saw revolts against Spanish Habsburg rule in Portugal, Catalonia, Naples and Sicily, making the Low Countries a low military and financial priority for the Spanish Monarchy. In 1644 and 1645 Frederick Henry consolidated the Dutch position on the southern shore of the Scheldt estuary and probed the defences of Bruges and the approaches of Antwerp. The States General called him back: the regents of Holland discovery in 1842 of great deposits of iron ore around Esch-sur-Alzette in south-western Luxembourg led to a rapid development in metallurgy there in the 1850s.

Although in other respects slow to industrialize, the Dutch got off to an early start with steamships. A Nederlandsche Stoombootmaatschappij was founded in Rotterdam in 1823, and an Amsterdamsche Stoombootmaatschappij in 1825. Railways also made a speedy appearance in the Low Countries. The first on the Continent, five years after the first in England, was the line from Brussels to Mechelen. It was opened in 1835 and was soon extended to Antwerp. The first Dutch railway line, from Amsterdam to Haarlem (and subsequently to Rotterdam), was finished in 1839. Luxembourg was much slower, with the first railway being that from Luxembourg to Thionville in 1859. Belgium and the Netherlands quickly developed state oversight of the railways, but the rulers of Luxembourg relied on concessions to foreign companies to do the job for them.

THE BELGIAN REVOLUTION, 1830–1839

Belgian opposition to William I's rule was divided between Catholics, who took particular exception to his measures to impede the reconstruction of Catholic education and religious life, and liberals, who objected most strongly to his autocracy. In 1828, at the instigation of the moderate liberal Luxembourger Jean-Baptiste Nothomb, they formed a common front in the Union for the Redress of Grievances.

In July 1830 a revolution in Paris replaced the restored Bourbon monarchy with the constitutional monarchy of Louis-Philippe of Orleans. The example was infectious. On the evening of 25 August 1830 the Brussels opera house, La Monnaie, put on Esprit Auber's *La Muette de Portici*, an opera about the Neapolitan revolt against Spanish rule in 1647. The grand finale was a chorus of 'Amour sacré de la patrie'. After the performance there were disturbances. A citizen militia was formed 'to restore order', and took control of the city. The black, yellow and red of the Brabant Revolution made its reappearance, now as a tricolour.

William, Prince of Orange (the future William II), and his uncle Frederick jointly commanded an army sent to subjugate the revolutionaries. Prince William tried to seize the leadership of the revolution, but failed to win the confidence of the Belgians and disgraced himself with the Dutch. After three weeks of negotiations Prince Frederick launched and Zeeland were more concerned to equip a fleet to force the reopening of the Sound, closed by the Danes during a war with Sweden. They certainly had no desire for territorial gains which would bring more Catholics into the Republic, and potential commercial rivals at that.

In 1643 an international conference had begun at Münster, to restore peace to the Holy Roman Empire in its broadest sense. The French envoys arrived in 1644, having travelled via Holland to get a Dutch guarantee not to make a separate peace. It was to take two more years for the composition and powers of the Dutch delegation to be agreed on. Each province, being sovereign, had its own representation. Frederick Henry, the leader of the war party, died in 1647. By 1648 most of the United Provinces were willing to make peace despite their previous guarantee to the French. The only fly in the ointment was that the States of Zeeland refused to contemplate a treaty with Spain. It was finally arranged, with the connivance of the envoy of Zeeland, that the peace would be signed 'unanimously by those present' while he was out of the room. In this way the principles of the States of Zeeland were uncompromised, while the peace was a *fait accompli* which they would have to accept. The Eighty Years War in the Low Countries and the Thirty Years War in the Empire were brought to an end. The war between France and the Spanish Monarchy continued for another decade. Amsterdam now openly replaced Antwerp in serving the financial needs of the Army of Flanders.

THE FIRST 'STADHOLDERLESS' PERIOD, 1650–1672

At Frederick Henry's death in 1647 his 20-year-old son, William II, succeeded him as stadholder of five provinces and captain-admiral-general of the union. Once peace was made, the unsolved constitutional conflicts of the Republic resurfaced. The immediate issue was the army, which was paid for by the States but commanded by William. The attempts of the regents of Holland to reduce the size and cost of the army were met with obstruction by the States General, where the stadholder still wielded considerable influence. William was in any case bent on dragging the Republic back into war, either by renewing the alliance with France against Spain, or by intervening in England to revenge the murder of his father-in-law, Charles I, and restore the crown to his brother-in-law Charles II. In 1650 he had six deputies of the States of Holland imprisoned at Loevestein and attempted to make himself master of Amsterdam. The plot was foiled but neither the States of Holland nor the Stadholder wanted a civil war and an unsatisfactory compromise was reached. An attack of smallpox prevented further ruptures by carrying off William II in November 1650, a week before his heir William III was born.

The States of Holland decided that they could do without a stadholder in peacetime, and by-passed the States General by calling a Great Assembly in The Hague, where cities and provinces were represented directly. The meeting was chaired by Jacob Cats, Grand Pensionary of Holland, and on most points left the constitution of the Union as it stood. The position of the Dutch Reformed Church as the only public Church, with the teachings of the Synod of Dort, was given a firmer legal basis. Command of the army was divided between the States, with whoever paid the troops being responsible for issuing commissions. In effect it gave the Republic seven local armies instead of one central one. The navy already functioned on this model, under five Admiralty Colleges – one in Friesland, one in Zeeland and three in Holland.

The States of Holland made it clear that they had no intention of appointing a Stadholder, and pressured several other provinces to do likewise. Hence the term 'stadholderless period' for the following years. But not all the States of the Union decided to do without a stadholder. A cadet branch of the Nassaus had been stadholders of Friesland since the 1590s, and continued to be so throughout both of Holland's 'stadholderless' periods (1650–72, 1702–47). It was only in 1663 that the States of Holland got around to instructing preachers to omit prayers for the stadholder from public services.

The Dutch decision to do without a stadholder coincided with an English attempt to do without a king. Charles I was executed in 1649 and Oliver Cromwell quickly established a military dictatorship. Cromwell made proposals for a union of the Protestant Republics of England and the Netherlands, but the Dutch were not keen. Seeing his overtures for peaceful dominance rejected, Cromwell instituted the Navigation Act (1651). By this law foreign goods could be imported to England only in English ships or ships of the nation of origin of the goods. It was a measure aimed squarely at Dutch dominance of the international carrying trade. In 1652 fighting broke out in the Channel between a Dutch convoy commanded by Maarten Tromp and the English fleet. Diplomatic attempts to patch the affair up came to nothing. The Republic at once showed that it could fight a war without an admiral-general, although not necessarily a victorious one. Battles at sea went both ways, with contemporary reporters often at a loss as to who had won an engagement. The hero of the Dutch fleet was Tromp, the victor of Dunes in 1639, who perished in the course of the war.

Johan de Witt succeeded Jacob Cats as Grand Pensionary of Holland in 1653. It was the year that a Dutch victory off Leghorn (Livorno) drove the English from the Mediterranean, but Tromp's defeat at Portland led to a blockade of the Dutch coast which severely restricted the nation's livelihood. De Witt quickly came to terms with Cromwell, in 1654 securing the trade and safety of the Dutch in return for numerous less pressing concessions, including barring the Stuarts from Holland and perpetually excluding the House of Orange from the stadholderate. De Witt was to be the foremost figure in Dutch political life for the next 20 years.

A second Anglo-Dutch war broke out in 1663, again over trade rivalries. The English were victorious at sea, and their ally the Bishop of Münster invaded the Republic by land, but Johan de Witt had concluded a treaty with France which brought Louis XIV into the war. Louis, however, was more interested in conquering Flanders than in following up his advantage against Münster. Things turned against the English, first with plague and the Great Fire in 1666, then with the Dutch sailing up the Solent and destroying the English fleet at anchor. The Treaty of Breda (1667) ended the war with England on Dutch terms, and the Treaty of Aix-la-Chapelle (1668) confirmed Louis XIV in his conquests.

The years around 1650 saw the beginnings of economic recovery in the Habsburg Netherlands, mainly in the countryside. This was the period in which Flemish lace became famous, but in other respects the cities could not meet the commercial competition of the Dutch. Rural industry and agriculture did grow, and the area of land under cultivation began to expand again. In 1655, for instance, the 500 hectare ducal forest of Zaventerlo (now the runways of Brussels airport) was opened to exploitation. Commercial life was not quite dead, but it carried on in a low key. The closing of the Scheldt mainly benefited Holland and Zeeland, but some trade was rerouted through the ports of the Flemish coast, leading to a minor growth in the prosperity of Bruges. The canal networks of Flanders were extended to take advantage of this trade, culminating in the completion of the Bruges–Ostend canal in 1665. Although a sleepy place compared to the Republic, and much more vulnerable to French ambitions, the Habsburg Netherlands precariously managed to maintain a comfortable standard of living without spectacular new growth.

A HAPPY FEW

Cornelis Jansen, or Cornelius Jansenius (1585–1638), was a widely respected Dutch Catholic theologian. He was the first president of Leuven's Holland College, founded in 1617 to train priests for the Dutch Mission. Towards the end of his life he was appointed bishop of Ypres. Jansen developed his ideas in an austere theological tradition which had been strong in Leuven since the early sixteenth century. Dominicans, Augustinians and the theology faculty in Leuven all inclined to a gloomier view of divine grace than did Jesuit moralists, whom they criticized as lax. When leading Remonstrants were in exile in Antwerp, some Dominican theologians privately tried to convince them of a position which was closer to Calvinist orthodoxy. Jansen's life's work was the *Augustinus*, printed posthumously in 1640 and soon condemned by the papacy as too extreme an interpretation of Augustine's theology of grace. At once Jansen's followers began to put the case that the papal condemnation was a mistake.

In one way or another, arguments about the validity of the papal condemnation of Jansen's *Augustinus* dominated Catholic theology well into the eighteenth century, with Jansenists forming a strong body of internal dissent in the Church. As with predestinarian disputes in the Republic, the basic issue of whether Jesus had died for all or just for an elect few went far beyond academic debate. In the mid-1640s there was street-fighting in Ghent and Brussels when Jesuits began a preaching campaign against Jansenism. Ultimately the issues of papal authority raised by the Jansenist controversy led to another Utrecht Schism in 1723, when the Dutch 'Old Catholic Church' (a group which now has strong links with Anglicanism) repudiated its obedience to the papacy.

The 1650s saw other reconfigurations of the political-religious scene in the Habsburg Netherlands. The crown had claimed jurisdiction over heresy since 1531, but now it was relinquished to the bishops. Unofficial, or semi-official, toleration was granted to a few surviving Calvinist communities, worshipping in the 'Brabant Mount of Olives' in Antwerp, the Dutch Embassy Chapel in Brussels or the 'Flemish Mount of Olives' in Horebeke-Corsele. The Anglicanism of English Royalist exiles was tolerated, as long as it was discreet, but plans for a synagogue in an Antwerp suburb had to be shelved.

As the dust settled around the predestination controversy, Dutch Calvinism experienced a moral reawakening known as Pietism. This placed emphasis on the spiritual joys of a godly and prayerful life, often in seclusion from the world. Conventicles would meet together to study the Scriptures, edify one another by witnessing to their internal motions of faith, and encourage one another in godliness. The initial inspiration for the movement seems to have come from contact with English puritans like the 'Pilgrim Fathers' who were for some time resident in the Netherlands. A leading figure in the growth of Pietism was Gijsbrecht Voetius, already met with as a determined Aristotelian in academic controversy.

The emphasis on inner experience, private get-togethers and a sense of community with like-minded individuals unintentionally encouraged the growth of conventicles into sects outside the public Church. One of the most famous Pietist sects was that of the charismatic French preacher Jean de Labadie (1610–1674). Although educated by Jesuits, de Labadie's conviction that Christ had died for a select few led him first to Jansenism and then to Calvinism. He was invited to the Netherlands by Voetius in 1666 and installed as minister of the Walloon Congregation in Middelburg. Expelled in 1669 for his unorthodox ideas, he gathered his small body of followers and headed for the then more tolerant atmosphere of Lutheran Germany. When he died, his followers cast about for new bearings, and in 1675 a group of them settled in Friesland. There they enjoyed the patronage of the Van Aerssens, possibly the wealthiest family in the Republic. Cornelis van Aerssen was governor of Surinam, and owner of a third of the colony. The Labadists lived in a community of goods on the Thetinga estate in Friesland, which Cornelis van Aerssen had made over to his sisters. There were tentative plans to move the community to Surinam, but only a few of the Labadists ever made the trip. The group drifted apart early in the eighteenth century.

The fame of the Labadists beyond that of the countless other such sects of the time relies mainly on two female members. Anna Maria van Schuurman was an exceptionally learned individual, an adornment to literary and philosophical salons before her conversion. Her *Dissertatio de Ingenii Muliebris* (1641) argued that women were as capable as men of academic and literary studies (a view fiercely criticized by Spinoza, among others). Maria Sibylla Merian, who travelled to the West Indies after having parted ways with the Labadists, was a naturalist and artist whose illustrations of exotic plants (themselves of startling clarity) include the insects which typically feed or breed on them. It has been suggested that this innovation shows an ecological sensibility well ahead of its time.

THE RETURN OF THE STADHOLDER, 1672–1702

By the Treaty of Aix-la-Chapelle (Aachen) in 1668 Louis XIV gained ratification of his conquest of the Flemish coast from Dunkirk to Nieuwpoort, half of Flanders (including all the French-speaking part, and the city of Ypres) and great chunks of Hainaut. In the same year the Netherlands, together with England and Sweden, formed the Triple Alliance to limit Louis XIV's territorial ambitions. Initial success was reversed when France bought Sweden's neutrality and Charles II of Great Britain switched sides. Louis XIV also forged alliances with the bishops of Münster and Cologne, the eastern neighbours of the Republic.

In the *Rampjaar* (Year of Disaster) 1672, a Third Anglo-Dutch War coincided with a French and German invasion of the Republic. At sea this was by far the most successful of the Dutch wars with England. Michiel de Ruyter, the hero of the Second Anglo-Dutch War, again commanded the fleet in a couple of resounding victories. New Netherland was briefly retaken. On land, however, French and German forces overran the eastern provinces of the Republic and occupied Utrecht. The armies of the States withdrew behind the water defences of Holland. Johan de Witt's diplomatic successes of 1654 and 1667 were not to be repeated on this occasion: a warrior was needed.

In the crisis of 1672 William of Orange, aged 22, was appointed stadholder William III by the States of Holland and Zeeland, and captain-general and admiral-general by the States General. Popular reaction against the 'oligarchic arts' of the regents was extreme. Johan de Witt, and his brother Cornelis, were torn apart by a mob in The Hague and their mutilated bodies strung up on a gibbet. In 1673 the new stadholder successfully defended Holland, and brought Spain and Austria into the war against the French. He invaded the lands of Cologne and took Bonn, cutting the logistic link between the French and their German allies and forcing a French withdrawal from the Netherlands. Peace with England was made in 1674, but France was more persistent.

The war of 1672–78 saw the re-establishing of stadholderly power as the dominant element in the politics of the Republic. William was declared stadholder of Utrecht in 1674, and in the following year of Gelderland and Overijssel. The States of Friesland maintained their separate stadholderate. In 1675 William III had been declared hereditary stadholder of Holland, Zeeland, Utrecht, Gelderland and Overijssel, and hereditary captain-admiral-general of the Republic. At once he had issued Governing Regulations which enabled him to appoint many of the civic and provincial dignitaries in Utrecht, Gelderland and Overijssel, where the existing office-holders were thought to have put up too little resistance to the invaders. William did not get all his own way: in 1678 the war was brought to an end against his wishes. The Treaty of Nijmegen restored all Dutch losses and gave improved trading status to the Republic, but meant that William was forced to abandon his allies. The French got to keep Franche Comté, ending the long-standing dynastic link between Burgundy and the Low Countries.

William's growing monarchical pretensions even before 1688 can be gauged from his residence at Loo, outside Apeldoorn in the Veluwe. The castle had been the hunting lodge of the medieval dukes of Guelders, but it was torn down and replaced with something in the latest grand style. Work began in 1684 and, despite the difference in scale, the influence of Versailles on both the palace and the gardens (open to the public since 1984) is clearly apparent.

In 1688 a group of disgruntled politicians invited William to invade England. John Churchill, commanding the English army, went over to the invading forces. James II, who was both William's uncle and his father-in-law, fled the country. The change of regime was surprisingly (if not entirely) peaceful. James II had already decreed freedom of worship, but William III did so again, this time leaving out Catholics. In order not to offend the sensibilities of his new subjects, William left his Catholic courtiers at home and played down the diplomatic support that he was receiving from the Habsburgs and the Pope in his war on the Bourbon–Stuart alliance. In the winter of 1688–89 London was governed under martial law by the Dutch army. In 1689 a Bill of Rights stripped the crown of many of its powers and formally subjected dynastic inheritance to confessional considerations: the oligarchic and sectarian interests that William had counteracted in the Netherlands he buttressed in the British Isles. In 1690–91 Ireland and Scotland were forced to accept the *coup* that had delivered England to William. There, rather more vigorous measures were needed to bring the matter off. From 1691 William III was effectively ruler of the United Provinces and the British Isles, and dominated the Southern Netherlands.

The Habsburgs had now been reduced to relying on the Dutch to keep the French out of Flanders. War with France resumed in 1688. François-Henri de Luxembourg-Montmorency, a collateral descendant of the medieval dukes of Luxembourg, led Louis XIV's armies to victory at Fleurus (1690), and at Neerwinden and Steenkerque (1693). In 1695

Brussels was bombarded, and much of the town was destroyed: the medieval town hall survived, but the guild halls around the marketplace in front of it had to be rebuilt. Eventually a story spread that the *manneken pis* (a considerably older statue) represented a little boy urinating on the fuse of a French grenade.

After the defeat of the Stuarts in Ireland and Scotland, the weight of the Grand Alliance (the Republic, Britain, Austria, Spain and Brandenburg Prussia) ground the French down. The Treaty of Rijswijk (1697) was the first occasion since 1659 that France had been forced to disgorge conquered territory. Even so, the wars of Louis XIV had expanded his rule into large and strategically important parts of Flanders, Hainaut, Luxembourg and Liège. The Treaty of Rijswijk also established the 'Barrier', an arrangement whereby the Dutch could hold and garrison the fortifications of several towns in the Southern Netherlands at the expense of the locals – at times eating up 30 per cent of the country's treasury disbursements. It formalized the Royal Provinces' military dependence on the Republic in a fashion that bred resentment.

THE SECOND STADHOLDERLESS PERIOD, 1702–1747

When William III died childless in 1702, the States of which he had been stadholder decided again that the function was not necessary. So the Second Stadholderless Period began. At Johan Willem's death in 1711 Groningen also decided to do without a stadholder, and only Friesland was left to recognize the authority of Willem Friso (William IV).

The Treaty of Rijswijk in 1697 was the last occasion on which the Dutch Republic could act as an equal among the great powers of Europe. When the Treaty of Utrecht ended the War of the Spanish Succession in 1713, the Netherlands were simply the backdrop against which foreign powers thrashed out the details of the settlement. The Spanish succession had been thrown open by the death of the last Habsburg king of Spain, the sickly Charles II, in 1700. The Austrian Habsburgs claimed the inheritance, as did the French Bourbons. The French quickly established dominance in the Habsburg Netherlands, but again the Protestant powers and the Habsburgs united against them. John Churchill, duke of Marlborough, had been serving in the wars of the Low Countries since the 1670s, and had now risen to command of the allied armies alongside Eugene of Savoy. Bavaria sided with France, but an allied victory at

Blenheim (1704) neutralized that threat. Then they were ready to meet the French in the Low Countries: at Ramillies in Brabant (1706), at Oudenaarde in Flanders (1708) and at Malplaquet in Hainaut (1709) the allies won once-famous victories which until recently were considered essential information for any British schoolboy.

In 1709 a new Barrier Treaty effectively turned the Southern Netherlands over to the Republic. At the end of the war (1714) the Bourbons got Spain and her overseas dependencies, but the Austrians (in the person of Emperor Charles VI) got the old Habsburg lands in the Netherlands and Italy. The Barrier Treaty was renewed in 1715: Dutch garrisons were limited to Namur, Tournai, Ypres and a scattering of West-Flemish forts, but in return the Habsburgs ceded territory on the Maas to Prussia and the Republic.

THE AGE OF ENLIGHTENMENT, 1747–1787

Willem Friso, a direct descendant of a nephew of William the Silent, succeeded his father as stadholder of Friesland in 1711 and of Groningen (after a brief interregnum) in 1718. In 1722 he was appointed stadholder of Drenthe and Gelderland, but as he was still a child it was his mother who dominated the political life of the northern and eastern provinces. Willem Friso came of age in 1729. Princely authority was again in the ascendant. Regent wealth and power was now almost entirely hereditary, and Dutch merchants had lost the initiative in international trade. The town staples, the local tolls and tariffs, the fragmentation of economic life from town to town and province to province (with Amsterdam a law unto itself) meant that the Republic lacked the scale and co-ordination to compete with Britain or France as an equal. Domestic industries for which the Dutch had an international reputation, such as brewing and linen-making, were in steep decline (although in the case of brewing this was partly due to the success of Dutch gin). Only Baltic shipping and some parts of the colonial trade were still marked by any sort of Dutch dominance.

When the Austrian Habsburg emperor Charles VI died in 1740 he was succeeded by his daughter Maria Theresia in everything except the imperial title (which went to her husband). The Bourbons, Brandenburg and Bavaria seized upon inheritance by a woman as a pretext for their own aggrandizement. In the course of 1745–46 the army of Louis XV occupied the whole of the Habsburg Netherlands, the most successful

French invasion to date. The Dutch garrisons of the Barrier proved ineffective, despite their expensive upkeep.

In 1747 the French again invaded the Republic, taking Bergen op Zoom in September and Maastricht the following spring. As in 1672, there was a popular reaction against the government of the regents, seen as incapable of guaranteeing the international security of the Republic. There were riots against tax farmers, and the Amsterdam militia guild sought to remove itself from regent control. In the course of 1747 Willem Friso, already stadholder of Friesland, Groningen, Gelderland and Drenthe, was proclaimed stadholder of Zeeland, Holland, Utrecht and Overijssel as William IV. The 'Second Stadholderless Period' was over. What was more, for the first time in its history the Republic had the same stadholder in all its provinces at once. The positions of stadholder and of captain-admiral-general were declared hereditary, and passed to William IV's son, William V, in 1751.

In the meantime the second Treaty of Aix-la-Chapelle (1748) had ended the war and restored Austrian rule in the Habsburg Netherlands. Maria Theresia was to reign for another 30 years. Charles Alexander of Lorraine was her governor general in the Low Countries throughout these years, although real power in Brussels was coming to lie with the empress's Minister Plenipotentiary. Together they gave stability and continuity to government in what was in any case a staid enough period.

But the war had revealed underlying social tensions. Violence was still the only way for the poor to express their desperation, as in the Dutch riots against tax-farmers and regent government in 1747–48. Poverty and insecurity also led to the appearance of highwaymen and footpads. In 1745–48 south-east Flanders was terrorized by the gang of Jan de Lichte, which committed over 100 break-ins, at least 50 other robberies, ten murders and seven attempted murders. In the same years a mysterious gang began operating in Limburg under the name Bokkerijders (literally 'goat riders', meaning something akin to 'Herne's huntsmen').

Extremes of wealth and poverty were most pronounced in the South. High grain prices meant bread riots in towns, but comfortable agricultural incomes. Careful management meant that the riches of churches and monasteries and of noble households reached new heights, particularly those of the great aristocratic dynasties which had flourished since Burgundian times. Such untold wealth could give rise to a hedonistic cosmopolitanism apparent in the life of Charles Joseph, Prince of Ligne (1735–1814). Ligne served the Austrian Habsburgs as a soldier and a diplomat, which largely meant swanning about the capitals of Europe playing cards, attending balls, and notching up sexual conquests. He was to declare, 'I have six or seven fatherlands, the Empire, Flanders, France, Spain, Austria, Poland, Russia, and nearly Hungary'. The Prince was not entirely a playboy: he was also a follower of the French philosophy of daring speculation and outrageous satire which was becoming widespread among the educated. He wrote a treatise in favour of giving civil liberties to Jews, as well as one defending sodomy.

Aristocrats and clergymen of a more serious turn of mind devoted their plentiful leisure to projects for 'improvement' which owed little to fashionable French theorizing. This was the age of the European dissemination of red cabbage, chicory leaf and Brussels sprouts – all developed by husbandmen in the Low Countries – while the introduction of the potato ended reliance on Baltic grain to keep the population fed. Road and canal networks were extended. In the course of the 1770s model prisons, in which the prisoners slept in cells rather than dormitories, and were expected to do useful work, were opened in Ghent and Vilvoorde. Maria Theresia's representatives in Brussels, the plenipotentiary minister, Prince Stahremberg, and the president of the Privy Council, Count Patrice de Nény, were cautious reformers imbued with the principles of enlightened despotism radiating from Austria and Prussia, and impressed with the practical achievements of British science and technology. An *Académie imperiale et royale des sciences et belles-lettres* was set up in Brussels to stimulate theoretical and practical research, with expatriate Englishmen (J. T. Needham and A. T. Mann) in the key positions of director and secretary. As in most other countries, the Society of Jesus was suppressed in 1773. The Jesuit colleges were confiscated and turned into 'Theresian colleges', with curricula which made plenty of room for French literature and the physical sciences. It was the beginning of a showdown with established interests dating from feudal and confessional times.

Like the *abbés* and aristocrats of the Austrian Netherlands, the regents, clergymen and aristocratic remnant in the Republic lived lives of cultured ease as pauperization increased around them. Powdered wigs and knee-breeches were the defining dress of gentlemen, and the eighteenth century is known to Dutch historians as the 'Pruikentijd' (Peruke Era). The Dutch scientific academy, the Hollandsche Maatschappij der Wetenschappen, was founded at Haarlem in 1752. The thought of the French *philosophes* was fashionable, but its reception superficial. More important was the moral seriousness of the German Enlightenment.

With the successive impact of Christian Wolff in the first half of the eighteenth century, Immanuel Kant in the second half, and Georg Friedrich Hegel in the nineteenth century, the Netherlands became an intellectual satellite of Prussia. The moral tone is exemplified in the first novel in Dutch, the sharply observed *Sara Burgerhart* (1782) co-authored by Betje Wolff and Aagje Deken.

One of the new manufactures most characteristic of the eighteenth century was porcelain. Once German alchemists discovered how to make true porcelain, Netherlands maiolica ('Delftware') lost ground rapidly. With the established trade in Delftware declining and new opportunities presenting themselves, the mercantilists of the Austrian Netherlands turned to porcelain as a potential boost to the economy. In 1751 the empress Maria Theresia granted a privilege for a porcelain factory at Tournai, funded by the city council. The arcanist Robert Dubois was lured away from Vincennes as director of works, and skilled workmen were engaged from England, probably from Chelsea or Worcester. This was still not genuine porcelain but 'soft paste' (clay made translucent by mixing it with ground glass). Nevertheless, the factory was highly profitable for half a century. Charles Alexander of Lorraine established another pottery at Tervuren in 1767, but it was a less successful venture. In the Netherlands the first successful porcelain factory was established at Weesp in 1759. It ceased working around 1820, after having moved first to Oude Loosdrecht (in 1771) and then to Amstel (in 1784).

5

The Rise and Fall of the Liberal Order, 1776–1914

The first cracks in the old regime were opened in Boston. British treatment of neutral shipping during the American Revolutionary War (1776–82) led to the Fourth Anglo-Dutch War (1780–84). From a military point of view, it simply showed up how far the Republic had declined from its world-power status of the Golden Age. International finance reached new heights, most spectacularly with loans to the new USA and to Russia, but manufacturing was stagnant and trade was at a standstill. From 1780 to 1781 the Baltic carrying trade fell from over 2000 vessels to a mere 11.

Even when the American War was over, in 1782, the Republic was obliged to continue the fight with England until France would make peace. The Prince of Orange, the Republic's military leader, had been against the war from the start and was blamed for the disastrous course of events. By the 1780s there were 'Patriots' in the Netherlands who drew their inspiration from the American Revolution. The traditional Regent opposition to Orangist control made common cause with the demands of the Patriots.

PATRIOTS AND REVOLUTIONARIES, 1782–1799

In 1782 Patriot militias of citizen volunteers were formed in the Netherlands. In parts of the Republic they seized power. Meetings of Patriots from various provinces began to take place from 1783 onwards. In 1784 a national meeting of patriot volunteers was held in Utrecht, with every appearance of a National Convention; perhaps as many as

28,000 men were under arms. By 1785 the effective power of the stadholder had become negligible. Pressure for democracy on the American model increased, and the reform-minded Regents began to dissociate themselves from the radical Patriots.

In 1787 the political balance suddenly tipped the other way. William V had been driven from Holland and was exercising his functions as best he could from Nijmegen. His wife, Wilhelmina of Prussia, decided to travel to The Hague to rally the Regents behind the Orangist cause. Her style of travel was too regal to pass unnoticed and in South Holland she was detained by the Patriot volunteers of Gouda. Her captors sent to the States of Holland to hear whether she should be allowed to continue her journey. After waiting two days for an answer, Wilhelmina gave up and travelled back to Nijmegen. Her brother, the King of Prussia, seized the pretext for an invasion to obtain satisfaction for the insult to his family. In the face of resurgent Orangism and foreign intervention the Patriot cause crumbled. Five to six thousand of the most committed Patriots went into exile in France and the Southern Netherlands, many to return in 1795.

In what was soon to be Belgium the situation was virtually reversed: the initiative for social and institutional reform came from above, mainly from the emperor Joseph II, but was imposed with autocratic disregard for established customs and the will of the people. The serious-minded and self-opinionated Joseph II had succeeded his mother Maria-Theresia in 1780. In 1781 he toured the Austrian Netherlands incognito, under the name Count Falkenstein, visiting towns, councils, law courts, fortifications and garrisons. His was the first royal tour of the Habsburg Netherlands in almost 200 years. By travelling incognito he saved himself the time-consuming bother of being joyously received in each town and swearing to uphold the rights and liberties of his subjects.

There was a brief commercial boom in the Austrian Netherlands during the American and Anglo-Dutch wars, as their neutral status enabled them to trade between the belligerents. The maritime insurance agencies of Ostend and Antwerp also did well from the wars. A series of toleration edicts in 1781–82 gave non-Catholics full civil rights and freedom of worship. This fortuitously aided trade, since it gave more secure legal rights to British and Dutch merchants willing to avail themselves of neutral soil. In 1784 most of the trustees of the Protestant congregation in Ostend had Scottish names. After the peace treaties of 1782–84 the boom came to an end. Subsequent events should be seen in the light of this sudden bursting of the wartime bubble, alongside agricultural depression and urban pauperization.

In March 1783 Joseph II ordered the closing of 'useless' religious houses, meaning those not running a school or hospital. In 1784 the judicial use of torture was abolished, as were old guild regulations limiting the number of apprentices and day-labourers a master craftsman could take on. Henceforth masters could hire as many men as they liked, and capital or credit became the only restrictions on the expansion of a business. In the same year marriage was declared to be a civil contract, and burials in churches and churchyards were banned on hygienic grounds – new cemeteries were to be opened on the edges of built-up areas. In 1786 the seminaries were closed and a central, state-run institution for the training of the clergy opened. At the same time confraternities were ordered to amalgamate to a single 'charitable fraternity', Masonic groups were limited to three officially recognized lodges, processions and pilgrimages were abolished, and a decree was issued that all village fairs throughout the country should be held on the same day.

Outrage at despotic interference in religious, associational and festive life was deeply felt, but at first organized resistance was limited to the clergy. In 1787 Joseph II decreed the abolition of existing provincial councils and law courts, and the erection in Brussels of new, centralized executive and judicial bodies. It was a step too far. Constitutional opposition was led by the States of Brabant, appealing to the Joyous Entry of 1356. The civic militia guilds, long moribund as military organizations, began to enrol volunteers for the defence of liberty. Cockades and streamers appeared in the colours of the medieval arms of Brabant: black, yellow and red. With the example of the Dutch (not to mention of America) before the eyes of all, Joseph II decided to nip things in the bud. While Prussian forces restored the House of Orange to power in the Republic, Austrian troops arrived to pacify the Habsburg Netherlands. The volunteer brigades refused to disband. Early in 1788 imperial troops fired on the crowd in Brussels. The Brabant Revolution had begun.

The two main leaders of the Brabant Revolution were the lawyers Henri van der Noot and Jean-François Vonck. Van der Noot was more influenced by Anglo-American and Dutch Patriot ideas, Vonck by the French philosophers of the Enlightenment. In the crisis of 1788 Van der Noot sought refuge in Breda, setting up a Committee there which was soon to take over the leadership of the revolution, while Vonck remained in Brussels and, with financial support from the clergy (among whom radical ideas had become widespread), founded a secret society for the preservation of liberty, *Pro Aris et Focis*, 'for altars and hearths'. News of the storming of the Bastille in Paris, and the deposing of the prince-bishop of Liège by revolutionaries there, fanned the flames in the Austrian Netherlands. On 27 October 1789 the first pitched battle was fought, at Turnhout, and the Austrian troops suffered an unexpected defeat. On 31 December the States of Brabant proclaimed their sovereign independence and called upon the other provinces to join them in a union. Within a month all the other provinces except Luxembourg had done so, and the United States of Belgium was proclaimed. Simultaneously occupied with the Turks, the emperor was in no position to do anything about it. In eastern Flanders peasants and weavers formed a militia of Habsburg loyalists which the revolutionaries defeated near Oudenaarde. But the United States of Belgium failed to form an effective government. The followers of Van der Noot and Vonck were at daggers drawn over the location of sovereignty: in the States (which in practice would mean a Dutch-style Regent oligarchy with a leavening of guild masters) or in the 'whole people' (meaning all men of property).

Joseph II died on 20 February 1790. A few days before his death he exclaimed to the prince of Ligne, then serving in the army of Hungary, 'Your country has killed me!' He was succeeded as emperor by Leopold II, who made peace with the Turks and launched an invasion of Belgium from Luxembourg. By the end of the year the Austrian army had restored Habsburg power in the Southern Netherlands and put down the revolution in Liège. Vonck fled to France and issued an appeal for intervention in Belgium.

In 1792 a French revolutionary army crossed into the Austrian Netherlands under Charles Dumouriez, assisted by Van der Noot's followers and by a Batavian Legion commanded by the exiled Dutch Patriot Herman Daendels (1762–1818). The Tree of Liberty made its appearance in the Low Countries as a symbol of revolutionary fraternity. The Austrians were defeated at Jemappes (1792), but rallied their forces and achieved a Second Restoration after the Battle of Neerwinden (1793). This was no longer simply an Austrian affair: France had declared war on Britain in 1792, and a coalition of Austria, the Dutch Republic, Hanover and Britain was now fighting the French in the Low Countries. The defeat at Neerwinden failed to dispirit the revolutionary armies, which invaded again in 1794, sweeping all before them. Austrian, British and Hanoverian troops withdrew from the Low Countries, leaving the Prince of Orange to face the revolutionaries alone.

By December 1794 the French controlled all the lands west of the Rhine except the fortified cities Luxembourg, Mainz and Maastricht. General Pichegru, at the head of an army including Daendels's Batavian Legion, completed the conquest of Belgium in a bitter winter and crossed the frozen rivers into Holland. He met no resistance. The Dutch fleet, frozen in at anchor at Texel, was taken by a handful of hussars riding over the ice. William V fled to England, and a Batavian Republic was proclaimed. The States of Holland were replaced with a directly elected chamber of representatives. Referral back to the electors was abolished, as was the requirement of unanimity for a decision to be adopted. Other provinces followed the example of Holland, and in 1796 a National Assembly replaced the States General as the highest authority in the land. It was the end for centuries of Dutch particularism.

As in the short-lived United States of Belgium, the main political divide in the Batavian Republic was between unitarists and federalists. Similarly, the political differences led to violence. Herman Daendels, feeling his role as national liberator entitled his views to rather more consideration than was given, twice carried out *coups d'état* to push through his proposals. A unitarist constitution for the Republic was finally agreed in 1798. Church and State were separated, the executive branch became a five-man directorate, and a bicameral national legislature was set up with electors qualifying on the basis of levels of tax payments. The provinces became departments on the French model and judicial reforms were introduced, including the abolition of torture.

Belgium and Luxembourg were formally annexed to France in 1795. The counties and duchies were reorganized as nine *départements* of the French Republic, the basis for the current system of provinces. In the same year, by the Treaty of The Hague, the new Batavian Republic became an ally and a client state of France. The southern shore of the western Scheldt and the city of Maastricht were ceded to the French, and the Dutch revolutionary government agreed to maintain a standing French army on their own soil at their own expense. The whole of the Benelux area was implicated in France's wars, which were to dominate European affairs for the next 20 years.

After the Treaty of The Hague, Britain, already at war with France, declared war on the Netherlands. A British landing at Hellevoetsluis was beaten off in 1795, but in the course of the following years the British seized Dutch trading stations in the East Indies, South Africa and the Caribbean. The Dutch North Sea fleet was all but destroyed at Kamperduin in 1797. The first war came to an end in 1797, when among other things the Austrians renounced all claim to Belgium. The second began soon afterwards, in reaction to Bonaparte's invasion of Egypt. The peasantry resented the increasing suppression of their festive and religious culture, the closing and desecrating of churches and the banning of fairs and feast days. The introduction of conscription in 1798 was the last straw. After rioting had broken out in East Flanders, peasant armies were raised in Brabant, Limburg and northern Luxembourg. The guerrilla operations and reprisals of late 1798 and early 1799 are known to Belgian historians as the Peasant War (*Boerenkrijg*) and to Luxembourgers as the Cudgels War (*Klëppelkrig*). Not all resisters were peasants by any means. One of the leaders of the 'brigands' in the Kempen, captured and executed in 1799, was the Leuven printer Pieter Corbeels, who also printed pamphlets denouncing French tyranny.

Despite initial successes, large-scale resistance was quickly crushed. Smaller scale resistance continued. Many draft-dodgers took to the woods. These bands were sometimes simple gangs of robbers, sometimes principled opponents of the regime, and sometimes a mixture of the two. Even before the conscription law of 1798 Charles Jacqmin had led a secret society of Habsburg loyalists partly based in the forest of Soignes (Zoniën). He was captured in 1799 and guillotined on the main square in Brussels. In Flanders alone, well over a hundred members of various gangs were executed between 1798 and 1806. The most famous, led by Lodewijk Bakelandt (guillotined in 1803 with 23 accomplices), was based in French Flanders but also operated in what is now Belgium.

In the Batavian Republic organized crime similarly reached its summit in the 1790s. For the length of the decade the twin brothers Frans and Jan Bosbeeck led the Grote Nederlandse Bende (Great Netherlands Gang) in crimes throughout the Republic. Rural Brabant and Gelderland provided ample scope for robbery with violence in and around isolated farmsteads; elsewhere less obvious ploys were practised. In 1803 the court of Guelders condemned three members of the Gang of Dossain and Prudhomme (active since 1798) for robberies, assaults and murder. To set an example in troubled times, they were first hanged by the neck, then taken down alive and broken on the wheel. Torture might have been abolished, but gruesome executions were still an option.

In August 1799 combined British and Russian forces under the duke of York landed in the Netherlands near Den Helder and forced the surrender of what was left of the Dutch fleet. The fighting was some of the bloodiest and most destructive the Netherlands had yet seen. Despite being welcomed in Alkmaar as liberators, the Allies soon had to withdraw. After this, the theatre of war moved elsewhere and the Low Countries were largely spared direct devastation. More peaceful consequences of Bonapartist rule persist to this day.

NAPOLEON THE LAWGIVER, 1800–1815

In 1800 France gave the force of law to a new, standardized metric system, replacing the local variety of measurements dating back to the Middle Ages. In 1801, a concordat with the Catholic Church was signed. Bonaparte allowed all the churches not converted to other uses to be reopened as places of worship and made the local authorities responsible for the maintenance of the buildings and ministers of religion, in return for the Church relinquishing all claim to its confiscated lands. The greatest legal change came in 1803 with the publication of the Code of Civil Law. This Napoleonic Code, built around the property rights of male heads of families, abolished feudal rights and liberties, established equality before the law, and set down strict rules about marriage, inheritance and the transfer of property. Rather than allowing people to dispose of their property as they please, the Napoleonic Code contains detailed stipulations to safeguard all claims and expectations foreseen by the legislator, and making it difficult for children to be disinherited (for instance by property being left to a second wife rather than to the children of a first marriage).

Bonaparte crowned himself Emperor in 1804. The following year he appointed Rutger Jan Schimmelpenninck as Pensionary of the Netherlands, with dictatorial powers. In 1806 the Batavian Republic became the Kingdom of Holland, ruled by Bonaparte's brother Louis. The capital was moved to Amsterdam, where the town hall became the royal palace. Among his actions as king, Louis commissioned a unified Code of Commercial Law for the Netherlands. It was drafted by Mozes Salomon Asser, the first Jewish member of the Amsterdam law court. French pressure had led to the voting of full civil liberties for Jews in 1796, but it was only under King Louis that this was implemented.

In 1810 the Kingdom of Holland was annexed to France. For the first time since the reign of Charlemagne's son all the Low Countries were ruled by a single head of state. In 1811 the Napoleonic Code was introduced in full force in a Dutch version drafted by Willem Bilderdijk, a lawyer and man of letters whose name will come up again. French laws meant equality before the law and trial by jury, but also state censorship, the secret police and conscription. Fifteen thousand Dutchmen were pressed into service in the Grande Armée, only a few hundred of them returning from the horrors of the Russian campaign. With the retreat from Moscow, and after the defeat at Leipzig, French power in the Low Countries crumbled quickly – especially in the Netherlands, only annexed three years before. On 30 November 1813 William of Orange landed at Scheveningen. On 2 December he was proclaimed William I, Sovereign Prince of the Netherlands. By this time Prussian and Russian forces were operating in the Low Countries. Antwerp was one of the last bastions of Bonaparte's army, the garrison holding out against the allies for three weeks after the emperor had abdicated.

The restoration of Habsburg rule that some Belgians had looked for failed to materialize, as did the national independence proclaimed in the Brabant Revolution. The allied powers had come to the conclusion that a strong state was needed on France's northern border. Prussian territory was much extended in the Rhineland, with the acquisition of the old prince-bishoprics of Münster and Cologne and a slice of land made up of bits of Gelderland, Limburg and Liège. What remained of the Low Countries was to be ruled by William I: the Netherlands and Belgium as a united kingdom, Luxembourg as a personal fief in the new German Union. Luxembourg was raised to the status of Grand Duchy, so that William would be a royal highness whichever crown he was wearing. While the international peace congress at Vienna was still in progress, the final arrangements for the new United Kingdom of the Netherlands had not yet been reached. William I was to have been proclaimed king by the combined Great Powers (Austria, Britain, France, Prussia, Russia) at the conclusion of the congress. In March 1815 Bonaparte escaped from exile on Elba. Louis XVIII, the new king of the restored Bourbon dynasty, went into exile at Ghent. William proclaimed himself king at once, to forestall any attempt to reunite Belgium with France.

The allied forces started to mass around Brussels for a July offensive into France, but on 14 June Bonaparte himself invaded the Low Countries. After initial clashes – most spectacularly with the Prussians at Ligny on 16 June, when over 4000 died in the fighting and the town changed hands seven times in the course of the day – the French advanced on Wellington's quarters at Waterloo on 18 June. British, Dutch and Hanoverian forces faced them. The battlefield was broken by two farmhouses, around which there was long and furious fighting. In the summer twilight, after one of the bloodiest battles of an unprecedentedly bloody war, the arrival of the Prussian army finished Bonaparte's career.

THE UNITED KINGDOM OF THE NETHERLANDS, 1815–1830

William I ruled his new kingdom in accordance with a constitution drafted by Orangist monarchists. The kingdom had two official seats of government, The Hague and Brussels. The king could appoint and dismiss ministers at will, and take decisions without consulting them. Ministers were not responsible to the States General, but to the king. The States General was a largely advisory body, with even its budgetary oversight strictly limited. The lower house was elected by the provincial States; members of the upper house were appointed for life by the king. Liberal opinion, and even conservative constitutionalism, saw a constitutional legitimization of autocracy which both parts of the Low Countries had been spared in the *ancien régime*. The only justification was fear of renewed revolution.

One of the most culturally influential figures in the early nineteenth-century Netherlands was Willem Bilderdijk (1756–1831), already mentioned as a lawyer. He was a strange character, made stranger by having been a housebound invalid throughout his childhood and teenage years, and an opium-taker in later life. As an Orangist and convinced monarchist he went into exile in England when the Batavian Republic was proclaimed. There he set up house with a girl half his age he had been hired to tutor; the wife he had left behind in the Netherlands eventually divorced him, but he never remarried. In 1806 he returned to the Netherlands to serve the Napoleonic Kingdom of Holland, in part as King Louis's Dutch tutor. His loyalty to the Napoleonic monarchy was entirely opportunist: in 1813 he was an enthusiastic supporter of the new Orange monarchy. After 1817 he figured as the grand old man of Dutch letters, pontificating about moral decline in sharp and often flowing prose and verse. Despite the irregularities of his private life, his conservative Romanticism was an inspiration to Dutch anti-revolutionaries throughout the nineteenth century.

Bilderdijk's circle was receptive to the Réveil, or Revival, a Protestant reawakening which had begun in Switzerland around 1810. The emphases were on reconnecting with the ideas of the sixteenth-century reformers and on living Christianity to the full in the practical concerns of day-to-day life. In its aspect of practical Christianity the Réveil lay behind many charitable works, such as schools and hospitals. In its intellectual opposition to the ideas of the French Enlightenment and Revolution it laid the foundations of nineteenth-century Dutch conservatism. Comparable Catholic revival after 1815 was deliberately blocked by William I. Relaunched religious orders, the rebuilding of schools, hospitals and almshouses, even processions and pilgrimages were impeded by legal regulation and limitation. New state universities were founded in Ghent, in Liège and even in Leuven (where the Catholic university had been closed by the French, and was not re-established until 1839). Although Catholics were a substantial minority in the Netherlands, and an overwhelming majority in then more populous Belgium, William I was a determinedly Protestant monarch under the guise of neutrality.

Coal, Steam and Steel

Industrialization began before 1815 and continued after 1830 but key advances were made within that period. Partly this was due to the opportunities opened up by a united Netherlands in which old particularisms had lost their legal force. The French metric system, for instance, had been abolished in the euphoria of 1815, but was reintroduced in the United Kingdom of the Netherlands in 1821 as a conveniently uniform system of weights and measures. One of the most significant advances for the history of the Low Countries was in financial organization. In 1816 the Nederlandsche Bank was founded, its start-up capital underwritten by the formidable financial magnate Widow (Johanna) Borski. In 1822 William I founded the Société Générale to finance industrial development, and when the take-up of shares was slow he bought over a third of them himself. The Société Générale survives to this day as a major Belgian institution, the parent of a range of holding companies. Stocks and shares were an acceptable form of aristocratic income, and these major financial institutions gave an impetus to an unusually close integration of aristocratic fortunes into industrial development. Old-established aristocrats were not usually themselves factory-owners, but Belgium had a sort of gentlemanly industrial capitalism which strengthened inward investment.

At the union of 1815 Belgium had been allocated a share of the massive national debt the Netherlands had run up during the Napoleonic Wars. Despite the heavy taxes to pay off this share, industry began to flourish, and soon rivalled agriculture in its importance to the Belgian economy. Although Belgian agriculturalists would have liked some sort of tariff protection, Dutch commerce insisted on free trade, which also benefited Belgian industry. In the Netherlands, as in England, the old oligarchic capitalists remained more enamoured of financial and commercial services and overseas markets, disdaining domestic industries.

Lieven Bauwens is a hero of Belgian history, with streets and squares named after him. 'England refused to share its new technology' say old school textbooks (failing to mention that it was wartime). In 1796 Bauwens smuggled spinning machines to the Continent and set up factories first in Paris and later in Ghent. By 1805 he was running fully steam-powered cotton mills. In 1797 the Lancashire workman William Cockerill left England in search of a Continental capitalist who would fund him in building power looms. He ended up in Verviers in 1799. Bauwens and Cockerill made their fortunes from the demand for uniforms for Napoleon's armies. The Dutch textile sector was much slower to adopt new technology. The first mechanized textile factory was not founded until 1854 (the same year as the first in Luxembourg). Among the founders were the Stork brothers, giants in the industrial history of the Netherlands. Charles Stork (1822–1895) was also involved in setting up and running a major machine-tool workshop and the first Dutch cotton mill (1862), and was one of the first industrial employers in the Netherlands to fund health, pension, insurance and savings schemes for his workers, and maintain factory schools for their children. He built the 'garden city' of Lansink in Hengelo to provide sanitary dwellings for industrial workers.

Steam power relied on coal, and the early take-off of Belgian industry was in part due to the country having plentiful reserves, and the oldest coal mines on the Continent. Dutch hydraulics experts had their Belgian counterpart in the mining engineers of the Liège area, who had been improving their pumping techniques for generations as the mines got deeper. The demand for coal saw the more intensive exploitation of the coal fields around Liège, Charleroi and Mons. The Ardennes had long been a plentiful source of charcoal, but as industrialization progressed this became ever less useful. The first coke-powered blast furnace in the Low Countries was built at Seraing by William Cockerill's son John, in 1824, and by the 1830s he was running the world's largest integrated metallurgical and machine factory. Wallonian metallurgy and machine-building were revolutionized, and took a leading position in Europe. The

an attack on Brussels that was beaten off. The Liège volunteers commanded by Charles Rogier played an important part in the fighting, and volunteers from Luxembourg began to arrive in the capital shortly afterwards. There was no sense now of Brabant being one small nation federated with others: the *patrie* was regarded as the whole of the Southern Netherlands, united in opposition to Dutch despotism. A provisional government was set up, and on 4 October Belgian independence was proclaimed.

The provisional government convoked a National Congress to pass a constitution, and before it had even met decreed four essential liberties: freedom of education, of association, of the press and of religion. Meanwhile, fighting continued and by the end of October the Dutch army had been forced to withdraw from almost all of present-day Belgium, Luxembourg and Dutch Limburg. William's forces controlled only the citadel of Antwerp and the fortified cities of Luxembourg and Maastricht. The rest of the province of Luxembourg had embraced the revolution, the first in the duchy's history. From a neglected fief of the House of Orange, it became an integrated and influential part of Belgium, providing ministers for the government and generals for the army. Much of Dutch Limburg, ceded to the Republic by treaty in 1715 and 1794, was reincorporated into Belgium.

Late in 1830 the Great Powers intervened. Britain was not entirely unsympathetic to liberal revolution. France was all for it. Austria, Prussia and Russia were aghast. In November an international conference was convened in London. The Great Powers imposed a cease-fire on the belligerents while they determined their fate behind closed doors, and by the end of the year they were willing to recognize Belgian independence on certain conditions. Congress diplomacy failed to consider that the Belgians might refuse the conditions agreed by others, while William I refused to recognize Belgian independence on any terms. So matters were to rest until 1839.

On 3 February 1831 the National Congress voted on who should be offered the throne of the new kingdom. The most popular candidate was the duke of Nemours, younger son of King Louis-Philippe of France. The British put pressure on Nemours not to accept the Belgian throne, and in the end the new king of the Belgians was to be Queen Victoria's uncle, Leopold of Saxe-Coburg. While all this was going on, the National Congress had on 7 February approved the Belgian constitution. It provided for a parliamentary monarchy on the British model, with ministerial responsibility to a bicameral legislature. The lower chamber was directly elected, the upper chamber was partly elected, partly co-opted and partly hereditary. Only those who paid a certain amount of tax could vote, restricting the electorate to less than 2 per cent of the adult male population and ensuring the political hegemony of the bourgeoisie. The constitution further guaranteed the liberties proclaimed in the French revolutionary Declaration of the Rights of Man, plus the four liberties already proclaimed by the provisional government. The Belgian combination of British parliamentarianism with the French conception of rights was the model for nineteenth-century constitutional reform in several states within and beyond Europe. Leopold I was sworn in as monarch on 21 July 1831.

William I struck back at once. The Dutch army, again commanded by Prince William, invaded Belgium on 2 August. In a whirlwind campaign they occupied Turnhout and defeated the Belgians at Hasselt and Leuven, but French and British interventions forced a Dutch withdrawal. One Dutch fusilier, writing his memoirs of the campaign, speculated that victory had eluded them because 'We went into battle not, as in times past, with prayers, but with curses.'

In 1838 William I finally decided to recognize Belgian independence, and the Belgians were obliged to accept the terms set out by the Great Powers. The hardest to swallow was that half of Luxembourg and much of Limburg had to be returned to William I. The formalities were completed in 1839. The Scheldt was opened to Belgian shipping, but only at the cost of punitive tolls. These were bought off for a lump sum in 1863, after which Antwerp rapidly became a major port. Luxembourg had been treated as part of the United Kingdom of the Netherlands in 1815–30, despite its supposed independence and membership of the German Union. Now the part returned to William I received a confirmation of its independent status and a constitution of its own, as William had long ago promised. The dignitaries of the grand duchy petitioned for something on the Belgian model, but what they got was rather more Prussian.

William I abdicated in 1840. He was succeeded by his son, William II, who steered the same autocratic course in domestic politics. As Grand Duke of Luxembourg, William II took a harder line in finalizing (in 1842) the long negotiations over the status of the rump grand duchy within the German Customs Union, a matter William I had never found the time to concern himself with. The kingdoms of Belgium and the Netherlands and the grand duchy of Luxembourg became three distinctly separate political entities, albeit with two of them still ruled by the same monarch.

THE CONFESSIONAL DIVIDE, 1840–1878

After 1840, the three countries that now form the Benelux each went their own way, largely concentrating their political energies on their internal affairs. In 1847 a Belgian Liberal Party was formed, the first and for long the only nationwide political party in Belgium. The party machine, and the growth of middle-class prosperity, virtually guaranteed Liberal dominance of central government for decades to come. In 1848 Europe was shaken by a series of liberal-nationalist revolutions – in France, Germany, the Czech lands, Hungary, even (almost) in Luxembourg. Belgium remained quiet, although the potato blight of the mid 1840s, coupled in 1846 with a bad grain harvest, saw some local disturbances. The nation's peace was barely disturbed even by the infiltration of French revolutionary agitators, or by the presence in Brussels from 1845 to 1848 of an exiled German radical, registered with the police as Charles Marx. It was in Brussels that he and Friedrich Engels wrote the *Communist Manifesto*. When Louis Napoleon established his rule in France in the *coup* of 1851, Belgium became a refuge for the French opposition, as well as for some of those fleeing the failure of the Central European revolutions. Despite the threats of Napoleon III, Belgium's liberal press laws continued to provide scope for the publications of such dissidents.

In the crisis of 1848 William II sought to forestall the possibility of liberal revolution in the Netherlands by taking the initiative himself. Without consulting his ministers – and having no obligation to do so, as matters stood – he informed the speaker of the lower chamber that radical constitutional reforms would be acceptable to him. A committee was set up under the jurist Johan Rudolf Thorbecke (1798–1872), and in less than a month the new constitution was ready. The lower house of the States General was to be elected directly by secret ballot (on a qualified suffrage effectively limiting voters to the upper and middle classes). The upper house was to be elected by the provincial States rather than appointed by the crown. The crown was inviolable, and ministers were now responsible to the States General. Members of the States General could put questions to ministers without scheduling them in advance, and could initiate and amend legislation. The States General had become a modern parliament.

Thorbecke, the architect of the Dutch constitution, was a graduate of Amsterdam's Atheneum who had studied in Germany and imbibed the liberal-nationalist aspirations of German Romanticism. Obtaining a post at the new state university in Ghent in 1825, he was the first person to lecture in Dutch at a Belgian university, and had witnessed first-hand the growth of liberal opinion and the eruption of revolution. He became a member of the States General in 1840, and in 1844 was one of the backers of a fruitless proposal for constitutional reform. When a parliamentary constitution was to be drafted for the kingdom of the Netherlands, Thorbecke's intellectual attunement to the wellsprings of liberal nationalism and his long study of practicable reforms made him the perfect man for the job. At the end of the Second World War, a morale-boosting series of popular biographies of national heroes celebrated the 'cast-iron man' Thorbecke, 'scholar, jurist, statesman, historian, philosopher and writer', as the fifth great statesman of the nation, after William the Silent, Johan van Oldenbarnevelt, Johan de Witt and the stadholder William III.

Thorbecke's liberal government fell in 1853, in the face of massive Protestant agitation against the papal appointment of the first Catholic bishops in the Kingdom of the Netherlands. The leader of political and intellectual opposition to Thorbecke was Guillaume Groen van Prinsterer (1801–1876), a child of the Réveil and a proponent of royal power. He too was a historian, and archivist to the royal household. In his unremitting enmity to liberalism, Catholic emancipation and secular education Groen van Prinsterer shaped the political direction of the antirevolutionary interest. In response Catholic politicians gravitated to liberalism, as their best defence against a Protestant state.

In Luxembourg, a liberal parliamentary constitution granted in the aftermath of revolutionary rioting in 1848 was revoked in a bloodless *coup* in 1856. William III (1849–90) introduced a more autocratic constitution modelled on that of Prussia, slashing the electorate by almost two-thirds, reducing parliament to an advisory body, and restoring ministerial responsibility to the crown. This constitution remained in force until 1868, when parliamentary government was re-established. No such wholesale reversals threatened the liberal constitutional achievements in Belgium and the Netherlands.

In Belgium, the social nexus of political liberalism was closely associated with Masonic lodges, which in the course of the later eighteenth and early nineteenth centuries had been deeply affected by deist and anticlerical convictions. The lodges of Brussels were the forum where wealthy liberals agreed to fund the foundation of a 'free and secular' university in Brussels, the Université Libre which opened in 1834. As Continental Freemasonry became more and more atheistic so did

Liberalism. The values of Freemasonry were increasingly incompatible with Christianity. In 1837 the Belgian bishops issued a pastoral letter forbidding membership of Masonic lodges, despite the protest of the Belgian Grand Master that he was himself a devout Catholic. The division of public life into a Catholic camp (dominated by wealthy, conservative laymen) and a Liberal camp (dominated by wealthy, conservative Freemasons) began to take clear shape. The Liberal Party was to have plenty of church-going members, and the Catholic interest attracted conservatives with little interest in religion, but the clearest issue of political division was the relationship between Church and State, with education policy as the most important battleground.

The political co-operation of Catholics and Liberals in the early years of the Belgian state (1830–57) and of the Dutch constitutional monarchy (1848–78) was not solely due to strategic coalitions. In Belgium the founding fathers of Catholic political activism – as opposed to the salon medievalism of the Catholic aristocracy – were the lawyer Antoine Ducpétiaux (1804–1868) and the journalist Adolf Bartels (1802–1862). Both had opposed William I and suffered prosecution under his press laws. Both believed fervently in liberty and parliamentary rule. Catholic conservatives were sincerely attached to the constitutional liberties which enabled them to dominate local politics and organize a Catholic parliamentary opposition, but liberals accused them of wanting to put the clock back to the eighteenth century and of subjection to a foreign power (the papacy). Conversely, Catholic politicians insisted that political attempts to undermine the social influence of the Church breached the constitutional separation of Church and State, and the freedoms of education and association.

The collective Catholic participation in modern political life which characterized Belgium was quite different from the reactionary monarchism of French Catholicism, or the absence of a distinctively Catholic presence in the British parliamentary system. It was the Belgian model which inspired Catholic engagement in parliamentary politics in both the Netherlands and in Germany, where the Centre Party was to become the largest Catholic political party of the nineteenth century. Even in France a liberal Catholic such as Montalembert could see 'liberty as in Belgium' as the ideal.

A different style of Catholic politician came to the fore after 1848: internationalist, combative and highly critical of liberalism. Positions crystallized around attitudes to Italian Unification in the 1860s, and specifically to the survival of the Papal States. Freedom of opinion entitled Catholics to follow the teachings of the popes 'beyond the mountains' (*ultra montes*), and to support the struggle to maintain papal political power in central Italy. Young men from Catholic families in both Belgium and the Netherlands enlisted with the Papal Zouaves, the first modern brigade of international volunteers. For Ultramontanism, as for the Réveil, faith was a fundamental attitude to life, not a private conviction separate from political principles, business ethics, educational ideals, philanthropy and artistic taste. And Ultramontanes, like Anti-Revolutionaries, attacked the social consequences of liberal economics, offering mainly paternalistic and philanthropic remedies but preparing the ground for a more radical Christian Democracy. The series of Catholic Congresses organized in Mechelen in the 1860s put the keystone to a slowly constructed Catholic revival. This finalized the political division between Liberals (convinced that Catholics threatened the separation of Church and State), and Catholics (convinced that Liberals abused the power of the State to interfere in the life of the Church). The more hysterical on either side saw clericalist or Masonic conspiracies behind any political proposal – the more level-headed suspected such conspiracies only occasionally. Belgian Unionism, and the Dutch Liberal–Catholic cohabitation inaugurated under Thorbecke, were things of the past.

The Gothic revival was the artistic bridge between the Romantic medievalism of the 1810s and the confessionalized taste of the 1850s. The movement was lastingly institutionalized first in the Guild of St Thomas and St Luke, and later in the Sint-Lucas schools for decorative and applied arts. Bruges was one of the most important locations for the development of the new sensibility. Industrialization had passed the city by, leaving it a tiny provincial backwater physically little changed since the end of the fifteenth century, but much less busy than in the Middle Ages. The conservation of the cityscape was supplemented by renovation and new building in the Neo-Gothic style, to give the city a misleadingly uniform but visually captivating 'medieval' appearance.

The gravitation of Belgian Romanticism towards Catholicism can be seen in the novels of Hendrik Conscience (1812–1883), whose position in Flemish letters is comparable to that of Sir Walter Scott in Scotland, albeit without the same sort of international influence. An autodidact, Conscience had fought as a volunteer in the 1830 Revolution, when his blood thrilled at the battlecry of 'Liberty!'. In his historical novels, such as *The Lion of Flanders* (set in 1302), and *The Mayor of Liège* (about the murder of Pierre de La Ruelle), he identified the fight for freedom with the struggles of medieval artisans and seventeenth-century burghers, and contributed to a broadly liberal sense of Belgian national identity. This love of liberty remained with him throughout his life, but as he grew older he revised earlier work to excise expressions of youthful anticlericalism and to emphasize that the fullest liberty is to submit willingly to the divine will.

In the Netherlands the main theorist of Christian Art was Jozef Alberdingk Thijm, poet, businessman and intellectual figurehead of Catholic emancipation. His journal *De Dietsche Warande*, founded in 1855, brought together Flemings and Dutchmen with common interests in art and culture. It was Thijm who had lobbied for the restored archbishopric of 1853 to be in the Calvinist stronghold Utrecht, 'Willibrord's city', rather than in the more tolerant Amsterdam, as was first intended. Thijm's brother-in-law, P. J. H. Cuypers, was one of the greatest practitioners of the revival of Gothic and Northern-Renaissance styles. His long and busy career included a great deal of restoration work on medieval buildings – mostly churches and a few castles – and reached its summit with Amsterdam's Rijksmuseum (1885) and Central Station (1895). That a Catholic architect should be engaged for such prestigious secular projects was a sign of the growing social emancipation of the Catholic minority in the Netherlands.

The secularist answer to the Neo-Gothic was Neoclassicism, looking to pre-Christian Roman and Greek styles, and to the alleged rational, human and pagan inspiration of the art of the Italian Renaissance. While the aspiring artists and craftsmen of the Sint-Lucas schools were rubbing brasses and sketching ogees and rose-windows, their counterparts in the secular academies had nude drawing and lectures on symmetry and proportion. Patrons were found not in confraternities like the Guild of St Thomas but in the Masonic lodges.

That Brussels could be the capital of a new Europe was foretold by the crazed genius Antoine Wiertz (whose atelier is now a museum in Brussels), but for most of the nineteenth century Belgium was, in cultural terms, a suburb of Paris. Publishers made their living from pirating French best-sellers. At mid-century Brussels itself attracted many of the great French artists, usually fleeing scandal or persecution. Among those who sought temporary refuge were Victor Hugo, Alexandre Dumas and Charles Baudelaire (who vented his spleen against the city in *Pauvre Belgique!*). It was in a Brussels hotel in 1873 that Paul Verlaine fired two shots at his teenage lover, Arthur Rimbaud, and in Mons that he sat out his sentence for attempted murder. Namur now has a museum dedicated to the early Symbolist painter, etcher and engraver Félicien Rops, but in life he was much more highly thought of in Paris than at home, and Baudelaire reckoned him the one redeeming feature of his country.

In 1859, while living in lodgings in Brussels, the former colonial administrator Eduard Douwes Dekker (pen name Multatuli) wrote the novel *Max Havelaar, or the Coffee Auctions of the Dutch Trading Company*. Even after the colonial losses sustained in the Revolutionary Wars the Dutch had a far-flung overseas empire, and it grew considerably in the later nineteenth century. The jewel in the crown was Java, reoccupied in 1825 after a hard-fought war against native resistance. The Dutch slave trade had been abolished in 1818. The ownership of slaves was prohibited in the Netherlands East Indies in 1858 and in the Netherlands West Indies in 1863, but this was not the end of brutal exploitation. From 1830 until 1870 (in the case of coffee even longer) the Netherlands East Indies was subject to the Cultivation System: local elites were maintained in power in return for meeting quotas for agricultural produce, bought by the Dutch at fixed prices. The commoners who failed to meet the quotas could be cruelly punished, while those who succeeded received a pittance. *Max Havelaar* was published in 1860. Barring a few flashes of indignant satire it is one of the dreariest books ever written, but the humanitarian impact was far greater than the literary achievement. Dekker's novel sent shockwaves through the Netherlands and is still celebrated as a searing indictment of colonial oppression. It became a symbol for those seeking liberalization and humanitarian reform in the Dutch colonies, comparable in importance to *Uncle Tom's Cabin* (1852) for American abolitionists. For the next two decades Multatuli was the foremost 'freethinking' writer in Dutch, polemicizing against Christianity and the bourgeoisie. 'Max Havelaar' is now a brand name for 'ethical' produce from the Third World.

Liberal secularists assumed, as Spinoza's *Tractatus Theologo-politicus* had suggested, that with the legal guarantees of the *ancien régime* gone religion would wither as a public force. When it became apparent that a level playing field could even work to the advantage of the Churches, Belgian Liberals decided to change the rules of play. In 1879 they took measures to end subsidies to church schools, and to force state schools on a reluctant population at great expense. The ensuing 'school war' stimulated Catholic political organization. For almost 50 years Catholic politicians had rejected the formation of a nationwide party as foreign to their dedication to distinct local interests. In 1884 they united in the Catholic Party and swept to power in the general elections. From then onwards the Catholics (later the Christian Social Party) replaced the Liberals as the party of government. After 1915 they generally ruled in coalition with Socialists or Liberals, but they have had only a few brief spells entirely out of office.

In the Netherlands too, education policy was the catalyst for party formation and the breaking of Liberal hegemony. A new law in 1878 to improve conditions in primary schools imposed stringent quality requirements. There were subsidies to help state schools meet the targets but no financial support for church schools. Strict Calvinists and Catholics saw this as undermining free parental choice in education. The first nation-wide political party in the Netherlands, the Anti-Revolutionary Party led by Abraham Kuyper (1837–1920), was formed as a response. Many moderate Protestants had sought to embed non-denominational Bible study in the state curriculum. Kuyper, who succeeded Groen van Prinsterer as the leading figure in the anti-revolutionary movement in the early 1870s, had changed the terms of debate by insisting on independent Calvinist schools for Calvinist children. The fight for free schools also brought the Catholic parliamentarians, inspired by the priest-poet-politician H. J. A. M. Schaepman, into coalition with the Anti-Revolutionaries instead of with the Liberals. After 1901 it was very uncommon for either of these two 'confessional' parties not to be in government, although their weight in the governing coalition varied considerably. Smaller confessional parties also emerged, never as more than tiny minorities but occasionally exercising influence well beyond their numbers.

Kuyper's greatest triumph was in 1905, with the chartering of the Free University of Amsterdam. From then onwards, Dutch Calvinists could be educated according to openly Christian principles from nursery school to postgraduate level. The Dutch solution to the school war, adopted as a constitutional amendment in 1917, was that all schools meeting the quality requirements of the state inspectorate should receive funding on equal terms. Belgian secularists have always regarded such a possibility with horror, and have successfully fought (most vociferously in 1954–58) to maintain a two-tier funding system discriminating against confessional schools.

EMANCIPATORY MOVEMENTS, 1878–1914

By the middle of the nineteenth century the political principles that Liberals had fought to establish and defend were so widely accepted that

Liberalism as a distinct political creed was becoming redundant, while as a social and metaphysical doctrine its insufficiency was becoming more and more apparent. In the course of the later nineteenth century a variety of social and cultural movements contested Liberal dominance in ways that went beyond the cautious opposition of the earlier confessional conservatives.

At the end of the nineteenth century Belgium was the archetypal 'modern nation', in much the same way that the Netherlands was to be in the late twentieth century. In 1910 the French diplomat Henri Charriaut wrote of Belgium as a 'social laboratory' in which the crucial issues affecting the various great nations of Europe were all apparent and inspired 'a perpetual fever of reform' (*La Belgique moderne*, p. 1). In the same year a lengthier book, based on four years of research and entitled *Land & Labour: Lessons from Belgium*, was published in London. The author was Benjamin Seebohm Rowntree, a New Liberal intent on improving the life and dignity of working people by such means as temperance, social insurance, co-operative societies, smallholdings and allotments. All these were characteristic of Belgium, although Seebohm Rowntree did lament that Belgian temperance societies, 'only seek to check the consumption of spirits. They neither preach nor demand from their members abstinence from wine and beer.' He was particularly taken with the idea of cheap workers' season tickets to keep countryfolk working in industry from having to crowd into urban tenements. Nor was he the only English reformer captivated by the Belgian model. According to Catherine Webb, it was a Co-operative Women's Guild tour of Brussels and Ghent which brought back 'the seed for the future establishment of maternity centres in England'.

Land & Labour was not simply a declaration of the desirability of the Belgian model of social organization. Rowntree drew a negative lesson from the local character of poor relief. This was administered by committees whose members were appointed by the communal authorities. These committees for poor relief were permanent institutions, endowed with lands confiscated from the Church at the time of the French Revolution and drawing further funds from local taxes and charitable bequests. The local level of organization meant that the old and indigent in a poorly-endowed commune were far less likely to gain relief than those in comparable circumstances in a wealthier commune. Another problem was the readiness of most local committees, and the plethora of Catholic charities which continued to operate alongside them, to make small grants to help out those in temporary need. This could in effect subsidize employers unwilling to pay a living wage. The situation was comparable although not identical in the Netherlands, where the state would only intervene if all family ties and independent charities had failed to save a pauper from total destitution. Rowntree's solution, national insurance, led to him being hailed the 'Einstein of the welfare state'.

Trade Unions and Socialism

In the early days of industrialization a surprising number of employers sought to remain competitive not by mechanizing or reorganizing, but by driving down wages. Workers combined to demand higher pay, shorter hours and better conditions. Trade unions not only helped put weight behind these local and piecemeal demands, they also spearheaded the creation of a new working-class culture. The disappearance of traditional patterns of life and work, and of the networks of community and kinship that had sustained the moral universe of working people, resulted in the disintegration of families, criminality against the poor, casual violence and victimization, soaring numbers of prostitutes and widespread alcoholism. Trade unions, co-operatives, savings and insurance clubs, study groups and brass bands could all give a new sense of common purpose to alienated industrial workers.

Although trade unions flourished first among skilled workers, who suffered less of the grinding dehumanization of constant work at starvation wages, they came to be forums in which working people of all conditions could discuss and address their problems, and provide mutual support and encouragement. To give but one example, in 1865 members of the Fraternal Society of Weavers in Ghent set up a co-operative of the sort pioneered in Rochdale in 1844. By 1880, after a number of political disputes between members, this had developed into the explicitly Socialist institution Vooruit (Forwards), a co-operative bakery and pharmacy running a mutual health insurance scheme and a savings bank. It was also a cultural centre, providing honest entertainment and beer (but not spirits), and from 1884 it published its own daily newspaper. Churches and philanthropic employers backed schemes to restore dignity to working people, but trade unions and co-operatives did it most effectively, from the bottom up and from the inside out.

Trade unions made their appearance late in the Netherlands, and workers' combinations were technically illegal into the 1870s. In Belgium freedom of association allowed unions, but strikes were illegal until 1867. A

189

Socialist party called Le Peuple was founded in Brussels in 1860. In 1866 Le Peuple joined the International Workers Association, or First International (1864–77), and in 1868 hosted the Third International Workers Congress in Brussels. In 1877 provincial Socialist parties were founded for Brabant (based in Brussels) and for Flanders (based in Ghent).

Belgian Socialism was one of the influences on the Dutch tailor and union organizer Hendrik Gerhard (1829–1886). In 1869 Gerhard took the lead in setting up a Dutch section of the International in Amsterdam, under the name Nederlandsch Werklieden Verbond (Dutch Workers Union), more a general trade union than a political party. The first two Dutch trade unions had been founded in 1866, for the highly skilled trades of printing and diamond polishing. In 1868 an Association of the Companions of St Joseph was founded in Amsterdam, the beginnings of what was to become the Dutch Catholic trade union movement. In 1871 two more workers' organizations opposed to internationalism and socialism were founded: the left-liberal Algemeen Nederlandsch Werkliedenverbond (General Dutch Workers Union), and the more conservative and Protestant Vaderlandsche Werkmansvereeniging (Patriotic Workingmen's Association) 'for the furtherance of the interests of the working estate in accordance with God's word'. These four broad lines were to determine the confessional shape of the Dutch trade union movement, with the socialist and left-liberal unions largely dominant. A similar confessional structure developed in Belgium in tripartite Socialist-Christian-Liberal fashion, and in time trade unions declaredly founded on Christian principles rivalled and outstripped the Socialist unions in membership. In 1891 the various Christian associations of industrial and agricultural workers were brought together in the Belgische Volksbond or Ligue démocratique Belge.

Small-scale strikes and lock-outs were the rule, but there were a few major confrontations between the big unions and the state. The most famous of these were the series of strikes for the vote in Belgium (see below), and the 1903 railway strike in the Netherlands. This began among dockers in Amsterdam, but when the railwayman Dirk Vreeken was sacked for refusing to cross their picket lines the strike spread to the railways, and the whole industrial machinery of Amsterdam and its surroundings for miles around was brought to a standstill. Soldiers sent to break the strike had to walk because there were no trains running, and only arrived when it was all over. Within two days all the strikers' demands had been met, but a law was passed criminalizing any future strikes by public servants and railway employees.

The late nineteenth-century slump hit the working classes hard. Many bosses sought to safeguard their profit margins through lay-offs, wage-cuts and the neglect of safety standards. A number of unusually severe 'exemplary' sentences for thefts were well publicized and made the legal system seem simply a tool for keeping the destitute in their place. Great impetus was given to revolutionary agitation and to the political organization of the workers' movements. The nationwide organization of a Socialist party was achieved in the Netherlands in 1881, with the Social Democratic Union (Sociaal-Democratische Bond), and in Belgium in 1885, when various local parties were united in the Belgian Workers' Party (Parti des Ouvriers, Werkliedenpartij).

Revolutionary Marxism had become the main ideological underpinning of socialism, but in the course of the 1890s clear and binding choices were made in favour of democratic strategies – even then without renouncing a revolutionary goal. The chief immediate demand was that every adult man should have the vote within the existing parliamentary system. In the 1880s and 1890s the Belgian Workers' Party supported a series of political strikes and demonstrations in favour of universal manhood suffrage. These sometimes led to violent clashes, most bloody in 1886–87 and 1893. In 1893 manhood suffrage with some plural voting was conceded. Henceforth every man over the age of 25 could vote in parliamentary elections, but 'responsible' members of the electorate (landowners, employers, university graduates) could have up to three plural votes. Plural voting was eventually abolished in 1919.

The Dutch Socialists initially had less success in the struggle for the franchise, and were more reluctant to accept 'bourgeois' parliamentary strategies. The first socialist member of the lower house in the Netherlands was Ferdinand Domela Nieuwenhuis (1846–1919), a Lutheran preacher who in 1879 left his career in the Church for one in Socialist agitation and was elected member for Schoterland in 1888. In Belgium no Socialists were elected to the chamber of representatives until 1894, when 28 got in at once in the first general elections under manhood suffrage. In 1893 the Dutch Sociaal-Democratische Bond split over the issue of commitment to revolutionary agitation: Domela Nieuwenhuis foreswore parliamentary politics to embrace anarchism, but twelve splitters founded the Social Democratic Workers' Party (Sociaal Democratische Arbeiders Partij or SDAP) to fight the 1894 elections. Domela Nieuwenhuis continued to inspire an anarchist syndicalist movement, while the SDAP became the main party of the democratic left. Foremost among its leaders for the first 30 years of the party's existence was the Frisian poet and lawyer Pieter Jelles Troelstra (1860–1930). During the agrarian slump poachers and pie-stealers were among Troelstra's clients, and the justice meted out to them undermined whatever faith he had in Liberalism.

The Socialist parties of Belgium and the Netherlands were among those which began earliest and worked hardest to move from revolutionary to reformist socialism. Belgians and Dutchmen took a leading role in setting up the social democratic Second International of 1889–1947, the central office of which was first in Brussels and later in Amsterdam. They often met hostility and incomprehension from foreign revolutionary socialists and from Marxist intellectuals at home, especially after the Third International was founded in 1919 as a Soviet-led rival to the Second International. Emile Vandervelde (1866–1938), undisputed leader of the Belgian Workers' Party in the early twentieth century, came from a middle-class, left-liberal background and was a determined practitioner of reformist socialism. As chairman of the Second International from 1900 onwards he was a target for the anti-revisionist bile of 'orthodox' Marxists, including Lenin himself. Nevertheless, after the Belgian security services had infiltrated and broken up the syndicalist Parti Républicain Socialiste (1887–91), the Belgian Workers' Party remained the only party of the left until 1920, when the Belgian Communist Party was founded. The high-point of 'revisionism' came with the publication of *Zur Psychologie des Sozialismus* (1926) by Hendrik de Man, a member of the Frankfurt School who was soon to succeed Vandervelde as party leader. Dialectical materialism, class warfare, collectivization and the dictatorship of the proletariat were all abandoned, leaving only economic planning as the distinctive policy of the party.

In the Netherlands, Troelstra's political moderation and emphasis on supporting trade-union organization brought him into conflict with the editors of the Marxist journal *De Nieuwe Tijd* (1898–1927). The most vocal of these were Herman Gorter, a poet and a translator of Spinoza's *Ethica*, and Henriëtte Roland Holst, one of the leading Dutch proponents of revolutionary Marxism until a visit to the Soviet Union in 1921. Matters came to a head in the aftermath of the 1903 Railway Strike, when anarchist syndicalists and revolutionary socialists joined in calling for a general strike but Troelstra and the SDAP failed to back them. The SDAP split in 1909, with the hard-line Marxists expelled at the Deventer congress and forming a Sociaal Democratische Partij (later the Communistische Partij Holland). Even so Troelstra refused to form a governing coalition with the Liberals in 1913, unable to bring himself or his party to take part in what would of necessity be a bourgeois government.

Left Liberalism

While some Liberals considered Socialists beyond the pale, many were prepared to work with them. Like the New Liberals in Edwardian England, there were left-leaning Liberals in the Netherlands and Belgium who insisted that liberty, equality and fraternity were not best served by ignoring the constraints of class on individual choice. Young Liberals in the Netherlands, and Progressive Liberals in Belgium, sought various enabling measures that would provide working men with the means to take their place as citizens in a free and democratic society. Although such Liberals rejected class warfare, believing in a balancing of class interests, their ready alliances with the labour movement and their deep concern with the plight of the downtrodden contributed to the optimism of Socialists in Belgium and the Netherlands that capitalism could be reformed by democratic action. Liberal and Socialist thinkers also tended to share an emotive anticlericalism, giving them a common enemy even when they were uncertain of a common programme.

In Belgium a number of left-liberal publicists, partly based around the Institut Solvay (founded in Brussels in 1893), launched new ideas that were seized upon by intellectuals but had little immediate impact on the party leadership. The conservative, free-trade liberalism personified in Walthère Frère-Orban (Prime Minister 1867–70 and 1878–84) continued to dominate the party machine. In the twentieth century the Belgian Liberal Party was to become the mainstream party of the right while the Christian Democrats occupied the centre-left. In the Netherlands the Young Liberals exercised a more direct influence on the splintered Liberal 'family' (at odds over colonial governance, the franchise, and factory and social legislation). A series of Liberal ministeries in 1891–1901, particularly that under the left-liberal N. G. Pierson (1897–1901), was crucial in this respect. The issue of state compulsion, always sensitive in countries with strong liberal traditions, came to the fore in debates on public health policy, education and factory legislation. Together with electoral reform, these were the most urgent and divisive political issues of the nineteenth century. Cholera, typhus, smallpox and tuberculosis led to government intervention in the water supply, restrictions to freedom of movement, and compulsory vaccination; concerns over venereal diseases led to a controversial scheme for the state inspection of prostitutes. The progressives managed to build a Liberal consensus on all these issues, at least for long enough to see them into law.

Agriculture

The importation of cheap grain from North America caused a severe agricultural slump in Europe around 1880. One option for workers in a depression was moving to the places whose boom was causing the slump. Belgians, Dutchmen and Luxembourgers had their small share in this voluntary movement of peoples, principally to the USA, Canada, Argentina and Australia. For Protestant Dutchmen adaptation to WASP society was unproblematic. Or as a Dutch-American put it in 1913, 'Thrift, economy, cleanliness and other domestic qualities make the Dutch desirable citizens of our Republic.' There are still Dutch-speaking communities in the towns of Pella and Orange City in Iowa, and a large number of Luxembourg Americans in Cincinnati. Emigrants from industrial Wallonia gave Belgian names, including Charleroi, to factory towns in Pennsylvania. In the Netherlands a national committee was set up to channel and facilitate emigration to the Boer republics, with which there was a 'racial bond'. After the Boer War of 1899–1902 an association was called into being to maintain cultural links with the 'Dutch element' in southern Africa by subsidizing Dutch books and providing scholarships to Dutch universities.

But in comparison to many European countries, the Netherlands, Belgium and Luxembourg weathered the agricultural depression well, through rationalization, intensification, co-operative dairies, savings and insurance unions, state-sponsored education in new techniques, and an over-abundant use of the new chemical fertilizers. Far more than by efforts to instil temperance, Seebohm Rowntree was impressed by the agricultural achievements of industrial Belgium, and the mobility of labour facilitated by the densest light railway system in the world. Belgium, like most industrial countries, had to import certain foodstuffs to support its population (most notably American grain and Dutch dairy produce), but nevertheless the country was a net exporter of fruit, vegetables and refined beet sugar. In terms of agricultural yield per acre, and head of livestock per head of population, Belgium was ahead of the other countries for which figures were available – Great Britain, Germany, France and Denmark. Some of the figures would have been less clearly in Belgium's favour if Seebohm Rowntree had also considered the

Netherlands and Luxembourg, but this only reinforces the point that the Low Countries as a whole were at the forefront of what has been called the 'green revolution' of the late nineteenth century.

Social Christianity

In Belgium, the ubiquity of local co-operatives and mutual insurance societies was in large part a result of Social Catholicism. The Social Catholic movement had been growing piecemeal since the 1860s, but with the third Catholic Social Congress in Liège, in 1890, impetus was given to the formation of a *Ligue démocratique belge*. The Liège Christian Democrats, inspired by the radical priest Antoine Pottier and by the history professor Godefroid Kurth (Henri Pirenne's teacher), pressed for a minimum wage, compulsory social insurance, and worker representation in boardrooms. The Christian Social movement, like left-liberalism, wanted nothing to do with revolution or state ownership, but recognized the need for fraternal solidarity and state intervention to secure social justice in industrial society.

In 1891 Pope Leo XIII, who had previously been a papal diplomat in Belgium, expressed his support for the principles of Catholic social action in the encyclical *Rerum Novarum*. This gave great encouragement to those working for democracy and social reform, but did not end the dominance of wealthy, conservative laymen in Catholic politics. The priest-poet Schaepman, once the leading Catholic statesman in the Netherlands, spent his final years in political isolation because his party would not follow him in a social direction. The most active proponents of Catholic social action were generally priests – in the mill towns of the Twente, among the coalminers of Dutch Limburg, and in Flanders in the mill town Aalst. There the priest Adolf Daens and his brother Pieter, a printer and journalist, agitated for Catholic social action on the home turf of the paternalistic industrialist Charles Woeste, chairman of the Catholic Party and an opponent of Christian Democracy as detrimental to the due submissiveness of the lower orders. In 1893 the Daens brothers and others broke with the Catholic Party in order to give uncompromising expression to Christian Democracy in a Christene Volkspartij (Christian People's Party). After the Great War more room was found for Christian Democrats within the Catholic parties, and after the Second World War they dominated Catholic politics.

Under the leadership of Abraham Kuyper the broadly conservative Dutch Anti-Revolutionary interest was, similarly, gradually transformed into a political grouping which promoted social reform as the key to a godly society. Kuyper's leading idea was that Reformation was not a historical event, but an on-going Christian duty to combat compromises of principle. He saw Dutch politics as an 'antithesis' between parties based on Christian principles and those based on irreligious principles, intensely irritating the many practising Christians in liberal ranks. A minister of religion as well as a politician, theorist and journalist, Kuyper in 1886 led a break-away faction of strict Calvinists (Gereformeerden) from the Amsterdam congregation of the Dutch Reformed Church (Hervormden). In 1892 they merged with another Calvinist grouping which had arisen from an earlier schism in the national Church. The main protest of the exodus led by Kuyper was against the un-Presbyterian structure of synodal control and the prevalence of private judgement in doctrinal matters. Kuyper's Neocalvinism sought a return to the doctrines of Calvin's *Institutes* and the Synod of Dort, but in such a way as to attune their teachings to modern culture. He set out these principles in a stream of Dutch publications, and in the Stone Lectures delivered at Princeton in October 1898.

With the concept of 'sovereignty in one's own circle' Kuyper was the clearest theorist of 'pillarization', and under his guidance a strictly Calvinist pillar developed which had a relatively small core of adherents but inspired much broader Protestant feeling. The Anti-Revolutionary programme appealed to the mass of conservatively Protestant 'little people' largely ignored by Liberals and Socialists. Anti-Revolutionary social thinkers like A. S. Talma, minister in the 1908–13 coalition and the 'father of social security' in the Netherlands, sought to improve the lot of the 'little people', but were hampered from sweeping reforms by their commitments to the reconciliation of class differences and to the autonomy of the family and the community as against the state.

Feminism

The social and political inequalities addressed by Aletta Jacobs (1854–1929) were of a different order. In 1883 Jacobs tried to register as a candidate in the parliamentary elections in the Netherlands, but was refused. In 1879 she had already become the first woman in the country to qualify as a doctor of medicine, after the government had intervened to allow her to study at the University of Groningen. After graduating she had opened a clinic in Amsterdam where she provided free contraceptives to poor women. In response to the electoral fuss made by Dr

Jacobs and her supporters, the constitutional amendments of 1887 for the first time explicitly stated that women could neither vote nor stand in parliamentary elections.

Similar developments in women's education took place in Belgium in much the same period. Isala van Diest (1842–1916), the first Belgian woman to be a doctor of medicine, obtained her qualifications in Berne in 1877 but had to lobby until 1884 to be allowed to practice medicine in Belgium. Three young women did manage to enroll at the University of Brussels in 1880, after others had been refused entry in 1873 and 1878. This built on the developments in girls' secondary education championed by the Belgian pedagogue Isabelle Gatti de Garamond, publisher of the journal *Education de la femme*, and later founder of *Les Cahiers féministes* (1896–1905). It was in these years that girls' secondary education in Luxembourg was brought up to par with that of boys.

In 1894 Wilhelmina Drucker founded the Dutch Vereniging voor Vrouwenkiesrecht (Association for Women's Suffrage), of which Aletta Jacobs became president in 1903. The governments of the Netherlands and of Luxembourg bowed to pressure for votes for women in 1919. In Belgium, Liberals helped ultra-conservatives block all attempts to enfranchise women, whom they considered too readily swayed by priests. It was only in 1948, thanks to a bill introduced by a doyen of social Catholicism, senator Henri Carton de Wiart (1869–1951), that Belgian women were fully enfranchised.

Education and the suffrage were not the only concerns of feminists. One of the areas where bridges were built between feminism and the Christian Social movements was that of white slavery, prostitution and related public health issues. In her *Le Mouvement féministe* the Belgian Countess Marie de Villermont argued that Christian politicians were wrong to keep their distance from feminism: although many feminists were clearly involved with wrong-headed organizations and philosophies, they were addressing genuine social wrongs which must be righted.

Language Rights

Another sort of emancipatory struggle was that by which Dutch-speaking Belgians sought to have their language treated as the equal of French. A similar but more local movement in the Netherlands was to preserve and promote the Frisian language. This began in antiquarian circles in the 1820s and later in the century spread to agitation for language rights in school, church and law court. On an even smaller scale were the attempts to safeguard the linguistic rights of German speakers in Belgian Luxembourg. A leader of this movement was Godefroid Kurth, a Luxembourg-born professor at Liège who introduced modern methods of historical study there, as well as being an active Social Christian. The use of 'Flanders' to mean the Dutch-speaking parts of Belgium, rather than the old county of Flanders, dates from the nineteenth century, as does the notion of a single Flemish 'people'. The first stirrings of linguistic revival were apparent even in the late eighteenth century, but the movement really started under the United Kingdom of the Netherlands, when the numerical preponderance of Dutch speakers in the Low Countries as a whole gave greater standing to the Dutch language in Belgium (where it was called 'Flemish'). The first successes of political action came in the 1870s, with laws guaranteeing the use of Dutch in the law courts and the civil service. The introduction of universal manhood suffrage in 1894 gave a tremendous political boost to Dutch, as those who spoke no French now had some say in who governed them. In 1898 Dutch and French were given official parity as the two national languages, but the struggle to have effectively equal treatment for Dutch was to last into the 1970s. In the nineteenth century the Flemish movement was patriotically Belgian, seeing the development of the intellectual and cultural potential of Flanders as a strengthening of the Belgian state. This was to change somewhat during and after the Great War.

This was not an issue of Flemings against Wallonians (as it was to become after the Second World War), but largely of two sets of Flemish intellectuals with different linguistic allegiances. To a minor extent the dispute reflected a social divide between the Flemish upper and upper-middle classes, whose culture and education was almost exclusively French, and the lower and lower-middle classes who spoke mainly Flemish, but this is easily overstated. There were also wider sources of discontent. Flemish seasonal workers in barracks in the Hesbaye beet fields and in the industrial back-to-backs of Wallonia experienced some discrimination. Rowdy youths, whether in slums, taverns or universities, seized on linguistic differences as a pretext for violence much as their English equivalents seized on sports. Such episodes were well-publicized, but marginal to the fundamental democratic demand that the language spoken by the people should be the language of their laws and government.

A SECOND GOLDEN AGE

In the 1880s there were clear signs of a vigorous scientific, artistic and literary life in the Low Countries. There was a sense that the Netherlands was making up for lost time in its acceptance and development of new industrial methods, and that Belgium was reaping the rewards of its pioneering role in European industrialization. Even in Luxembourg, where railways still gave little competition to the old stage coaches, the steel industry was modernizing after 1872 and quickly carving a niche in the world economy.

Trade and services were still the dominant interests in the Dutch economy, and cheese, butter and tulips its most recognizable exports. As late as 1883, when Amsterdam held its first World Fair, it was decided that colonies and trade would be the theme. This would build on the sensation that the treasures of the Netherlands Indies had made at the Paris World Fair in 1878, while avoiding the potential for embarrassment in concentrating on manufactures. In 1887 the theme was food, and in 1895 hotels and travel. Well aware of their relative industrial backwardness, the Dutch government had suspended the Patent Law in 1869. A new law on patents did not come into force until 1912, and in the meantime Dutch entrepreneurs were free to adapt whatever technologies they could lay hands on. At the 1884 Union for the Protection of Industrial Property, meeting in Paris, the Dutch delegate was told to his face, 'You are a people of brigands.' But a combination of intellectual piracy and educational reforms paid off: from the 1880s the Dutch were again at the forefront of science and technology.

The old industries relied on steam-powered mechanization; the new industries were built around chemicals, petroleum and rubber. The first-wave coal and steel industrialization was still fundamental, and the discovery of new iron ore deposits in the southern tip of Belgium and Luxembourg, and of unsuspected coal deposits in Belgian and Dutch Limburg, gave it new impetus. At the same time there was a revolution in the retail trade, with shopping arcades, department stores and 'warehouse' retailers springing up in every city.

The Royal Dutch Petroleum Company was founded in 1890 to develop an oil field in Sumatra; in 1907 it entered a 60/40 partnership with its British rival, Shell, and it is now one of the largest business enterprises in the world. The Philips company, set up in 1891 to produce incandescent light bulbs, soon had a finger in every high-tech pie: radio, X-rays, televisions, sound systems, pharmaceuticals. Between 1900 and

1911 what had been a family-run shop set up in 1861 by Clemens and August Brenninkmeijer became the chain of C&A department stores across the Netherlands, and subsequently across Europe. These are just three of the most famous of the many modern enterprises begun in the Netherlands in this period.

In Belgium the Solvay brothers found investors for a company to make cheap soda for industrial purposes. A decade later they were among the leading chemical companies in Europe, making far more money from licences on the Solvay Process than from their own production. In 1867 the Delhaize brothers, one a professor of commercial engineering and one a veterinary surgeon, put into practice their theory that food could be retailed both more cheaply and more profitably if it was collected in a central warehouse and sold at a low profit margin. The Delhaize Group is now one of the world's wealthiest supermarket companies, trading in Europe, the USA and South-East Asia. One worldwide Belgian export is small arms. These are mainly produced by FN, founded as the Fabrique Nationale d'Armes de Guerre at Herstal in 1889. Before then the area had had a thriving cottage industry (with fifteenth-century roots) in handmade luxury hunting rifles, shotguns and pistols. The FN factories are an important contributor to the Belgian economy and their workers have been at the forefront of labour militancy.

Science and Technology

The notion of the period 1890–1930 – from Queen Wilhelmina's accession until the Great Depression – as a 'second golden age' was launched by Dutch historians of science. The main factor behind a string of scientific achievements is held to be changes to the school system, with new technical schools and polytechnics and a greater value placed on scientific education within the traditional academic system. The most obvious symbol of the success of these educational reforms is the clutch of eight early twentieth-century Nobel prize-winners from the Netherlands: in chemistry Jacobus van't Hoff for his work on the laws of chemical dynamics (1901) and Peter Debye for his research on molecular structure (1936); in physics the teacher–student partnership of Hendrik Lorentz and Pieter Zeeman for their work on the 'Zeeman effect' by which a strong magnetic field splits the spectrum of light (1902), Johannes van der Waals for an equation describing the physical behaviour of gases and liquids (1910), and Heike Kamerlingh Onnes for studies of the properties of matter at low temperatures (1913); in medicine Willem Einthoven for the invention of the electrocardiograph (1924) and Christiaan Eijkman (1929) for discovering a cure for beriberi – a disease first described in Jacob Bontius's *De Medecina Indicorum* (1642).

In Belgium a number of bodies promoted scientific research and education, most famously the Institut Solvay in Brussels. In terms of Nobel prizes Belgian scientists trailed somewhat, with only Jules Bordet being recognized for his work on the immune system (1919). The chemist Leo Baekeland (1863–1944), born and educated in Belgium, must be given a place among the main shapers of the twentieth-century world. He invented Bakelite (the first commercial plastic) and Velox paper (photographic paper that could be developed in artificial light), but although Belgians love to claim him as their own he was an American by the time he made his discoveries.

One after another, in the course of thirty years or less, a number of foreign inventions made their appearance in the Low Countries: the bicycle, the automobile, the aeroplane; the telegraph, telephone, radio and cinema. Eventually these were to transform the way people did business, but at first their main impact was on leisure. The tourist trade was among the beneficiaries. The healthiness of salt-water bathing and sea air were alleged from very early in the nineteenth century, but the boom years of the seaside resorts began in the 1880s. This was when towns along the North Sea coast with the appendix 'Bad' or 'aan Zee' took off, and buildings called Kursaal or Kurhaus appeared. It was also the last flowering of Spa as a fashionable watering-place. The railways opened up the seaside to day-trippers, and as workers gained weekends and holidays the beaches were democratized further. Bicycles and charabancs made tourism even more flexible, so that magazines, signposts and local clubs were set up to promote the attractions of the most obscure places. For those with money enough for a cruise, or wanting to emigrate in steerage, there were the ocean liners of companies like the Rotterdamsche Lloyd and Antwerp's Red Star Line. In the 1920s, the Netherlands' KLM and Belgium's Sabena were among the first European airlines to run long-distance international services, to Batavia (Jakarta) and to Leopoldville (Kinshasa), respectively.

The Press

The 1890s saw the beginnings of mass-circulation journalism, although the term has to be used somewhat lightly considering the small population of the Low Countries. The Lord Northcliffe of the Dutch press, at least in his own estimation, was H. C. M. Holdert, who bought *De Telegraaf* in 1900 and transformed it into an organ of the 'new' journalism, appealing to a much broader readership. The newspaper of the SDAP, *Het Volk*, began publication in the same year. One newspaper resolutely to resist the tendency to popular journalism was *De Standaard*, the organ of the ARP (edited by Abraham Kuyper himself from 1872 to 1922). It did not even carry theatre reviews, on principle. Strict Calvinists of a more conservative stripe than Kuyper's followers read *De Nederlander* (founded 1893). What is now the most prestigious daily in Dutch, *NRC-Handelsblad*, is the result of a postwar merger of two influential Liberal papers, the *Nieuwe Rotterdamsche Courant* and the *Algemeen Handelsblad*. Both had been founded before the mid-nineteenth century but changed considerably in the 'golden age' of journalism. The conservative *Amsterdamsche Courant* was founded as a weekly in 1672 and became a daily in 1847; it was sold to a new owner in 1882 and overhauled, losing its old political respectability in the process.

Of the Belgian papers which have survived to recent times, the Liberal *Het Laatste Nieuws* (1888) and *La Dernière Heure* (1906), the Socialist *Le Peuple* (1885) and *Vooruit* (1884, later *De Morgen*), and the Catholic *Het Volk* (1891) and *La Libre Belgique* (1915, initially as a clandestine publication) were all founded as mass-circulation dailies. The press in tiny Luxembourg would become just as multifaceted, with linguistic variation between French, German and Letzebürgesch as well as political variation between Christian, Liberal and Socialist interests, but the term 'mass circulation' no longer has any meaning on such a scale.

Literature

The impact of Emile Zola's naturalism reached a highwater mark in Belgium in 1880 through its championing by Camille Lemonnier, a francophone novelist of Flemish peasant life (as well as an essayist and art critic). Thereafter the literati turned away from 'the masses' in horror. The breakthrough of dandyish and symbolist alternatives to naturalism was heralded in 1881, when a group of young intellectuals founded the literary review *La Jeune Belgique*, identifying themselves with youth and novelty. The Symbolists Emile Verhaeren (a poet) and Maurice Maeterlinck (a playwright) were French-speaking Flemings who built up international reputations. A similar group in the Netherlands, which came to be called the *tachtigers* (eightiers, after the decade in which they worked), founded *De Nieuwe Gids* (The New Guide) in 1885, a title harking back to *De Gids* founded in 1837. The name expressed their desire to surpass the groundbreaking work of the past. They too adopted the aestheticist slogan 'Art for art's sake' and the view that art should be an original and personal expression of emotion. The most famous Dutch writer of the time, Louis Couperus, was not associated with the group but breathed the air of decadence. In the 1890s Dutch-speaking Flemings in the circle around the review *Van nu en straks* (Of Now and Later) drew their inspiration from both *La Jeune Belgique* and *De Nieuwe Gids*. There were dozens of tiny literary reviews available, but these three changed the terms of cultural debate.

This was also the era of the 'discovery' of Guido Gezelle, a West-Flemish priest and schoolmaster. He had been publishing increasingly self-expressive poetry in what is stereotyped as parochial obscurity since the 1850s, and he died in 1899. Shortly after his death a nephew, the novelist Stijn Streuvels, managed to get some of his work reprinted in Holland. Two of the arbiters of *tachtiger* taste, Albert Verwey and Willem Kloos, reviewed the collection with delight. Gezelle was suddenly the rage. He is still the best-known Flemish poet in Belgium and the Netherlands.

Such lyricism did not entirely displace naturalism. Zola continued to inspire some writers even as aesthetes turned their backs on him. The most famous example in the Netherlands is Herman Heijermans's play *Op Hoop van Zegen* – translated into English as *The Good Hope*, and recently adapted with the setting transposed to Hull. This denunciation of loss of life due to insurance fraud in the fishing business (with the key line 'fish is dearly paid') was first performed in Amsterdam in 1900, and met an enthusiastic reception across Europe and in New York. In Flanders, Cyriel Buysse's *Het gezin van Paemel* (1903) portrayed the break-up of a smallholding family under the various pressures of exploitation and oppression by landowners, urban bosses and the state.

Visual and Applied Arts

Far more than in literature, people working in the Low Countries broke new ground in the visual and applied arts. Among Symbolist painters the Dutchman Jan Toorop and the Belgian Fernand Khnopff were of international importance, and their dreamlike images can still unsettle.

Vincent Van Gogh failed as a Protestant evangelist in the rural Netherlands and the industrial slums of Belgium (the period that produced *The Potato Eaters*), and was kicked out of the Antwerp art academy for being unable to draw, but after his death he became one of the most famous painters in the world. An avant-garde artistic group called *Les Vingt* was formed in Belgium in 1883, Fernand Khnopff and James Ensor being among its founders. Ensor's best known works are *Christ's Entry into Brussels* (1889) and *The Baths at Ostend* (1890), both satirizing modern hypocrisy in grotesque crowd scenes that looked back to Bosch, but were not really appreciated until Surrealism had taken off.

In 1883 the Brussels Palace of Justice was completed, a monstrosity of nineteenth-century neoclassicist architecture and to Socialists the symbol of judicial brutality. It was begun in 1866 and was designed to give scope to Leopold II's megalomaniac desire to refashion the skyline of Brussels. In 1885 P. J. H. Cuypers's Rijksmuseum was inaugurated in Amsterdam, an eclectic stone encyclopaedia of medieval and Northern-Renaissance styles. The characteristically nineteenth-century neo-styles peaked with these monumental structures.

In the applied arts of the Belgian Sint-Lucas Schools (showcased at the Ghent World Exhibition of 1913) high Neo-Gothicism began to give way to Arts and Crafts and even, cautiously, to Art Nouveau. In abandoning the Neo-Gothic, the more conservative 'Delft School' in the Netherlands looked rather to older Romanesque and Byzantine models. Other designers and architects were intoxicated by the new possibilities held out by steel, glass and concrete. In Belgium Victor Horta and Henry Van de Velde started with the curving lines of Art Nouveau and moved to a geometrical Art Deco. In the Netherlands H. P. Berlage, who first came to wide attention with the 1903 Amsterdam Exchange, prefigured functionalism without entirely abandoning artistic flourishes. Beginning their work in the late nineteenth century, their careers peaked in the first half of the twentieth.

AROUND THE WORLD

The historian Eric Hobsbawm called the years 1875–1914 the 'Age of Empire'. In this period Europe reached the apogee of its global power. Even more so than other European nations, the Netherlands and Belgium took part on a scale out of all proportion to their size.

Luxembourgers had to be content with the Dutch colonial service before 1890, and thereafter with being 'reputed Belgians' by the manpower-hungry administration of the Congo.

As industrialized countries with limited imperial ambitions, Belgium and the Netherlands were both attractive sources of expertise for countries seeking to modernize, but reluctant to invite in major colonial powers or rivals. Independent states in South America, Africa, Asia and the Balkans employed Dutch and Belgian officials to oversee reforms of education, the police or the posts, and above all the construction of railways. President Kruger's concession to the Netherlands South African Railway for a line from Pretoria to Delagoa Bay (now Maputo) was one fruit of such concerns. In the same way, Turkey and Russia entrusted their rail links to the West – the Orient Express and the Nord Express – to the Compagnie Internationale des Wagons-Lits, founded in 1876 by the Belgian engineer Georges Nagelmaeckers and the American Civil War hero and carpet-bagger William d'Alton Mann. The Orient Express was made possible by the railway concession through the Balkans obtained in 1869 by the Belgian consul in Constantinople, Maurice von Hirsch, a fabulously wealthy philanthropist of Hungarian-Jewish origin who also promoted Jewish settlement in South America. A younger contemporary of Nagelmaeckers was the engineer and banker Edouard Empain, who financed the Paris metro and the tram systems of Moscow and Cairo. Empain also developed the luxurious Cairo suburb Heliopolis, and set up a mining company in the Congo. The tram systems of Teheran and Baghdad were built with a similar combination of French and Russian finance and Belgian engineering.

In the later nineteenth century China's 'self-strengthening' modernization offered opportunities for European engineers and bankers. In the 1890s the country's first industrial complex for steel production was built partly by the Cockerill firm. The Belgian consul general in Shanghai, Emile Francqui, greatly stimulated Belgian investment in China. In 1899 he brought in the concession for the 819-mile Peking–Hankow Railway, which went to a company set up by a former employee of Empain, Jean Jadot, who was also involved in building roads, railways, schools and hospitals in the Congo. Francqui's interests in China brought him into close association with the mining engineer Herbert Hoover (a future US president), with beneficial consequences for Belgium during and immediately after the First World War. There was Belgian involvement in the Shanghai tramways, the Kaiping coalmines and the electrification of Tianjin. In 1900 Belgium even acquired a 44-hectare treaty territory of its own in Tianjin, which was later to be the first foreign concession returned to direct Chinese rule. Unlike the Belgians, the Dutch in China eschewed the entrenched interests in the Treaty Ports and preferred to negotiate directly with local power-holders in the interior.

China also lured Belgian and Dutch missionaries of a new Catholic missionary congregation founded in Scheut (just outside Brussels) for the evangelization of Inner Mongolia. But there was considerable Dutch and Belgian participation in missions of many denominations all over the world. Best known in the English-speaking world are two Belgians who worked in what is now the United States: Pieter Jan De Smet, who preached to the Indians of the Rocky Mountains in the mid-nineteenth century, and Damiaan De Veuster ('Fr Damien'), who died a leper on the Hawaian island of Molokai in 1889.

Belgian efforts to make a mark in the world show a desire to catch up with other European countries. The Netherlands was one of the countries they were trying to gain on. In the century before 1913 direct Dutch rule spread from plantations and trading posts on the Moluccas and parts of Java to cover all of Sumatra, most of Borneo, the smaller Indonesian islands, and western New Guinea. This massive expansion of direct Dutch rule enabled the abandonment of the Cultivation System and the state monopoly on colonial trade, to be replaced with land taxes and other exactions. The spices and pepper of the seventeenth century had given way to sugar and coffee in the eighteenth. From the late nineteenth century prospectors were more interested in crude oil and rubber, which required a very different type of acquisition from the forced deliveries of the Cultivation System.

The new methods might have been more humane, but the colonies were still expected first and foremost to enrich the Netherlands. The national debt run up during the Napoleonic Wars was still being paid off, and financially the East Indies were considered 'the cork that keeps the country afloat'. From the 1870s Abraham Kuyper was attacking this view of colonialism, which in 1878 was condemned in Article 18 of the Anti-Revolutionary manifesto. When he formed his first cabinet in 1901, Kuyper accordingly made it a point of policy that the Netherlands East Indies would henceforth be ruled for the benefit of the native inhabitants.

In practice the ethical policy involved schooling an Indonesian elite in European science and administration, and promoting village democracy and social welfare. Kuyper's re-entry into politics in 1913 (having gone into the wilderness in 1909 after a party funding scandal) was an attempt to reinvigorate the ethical policy in the wake of the brutal conquest of Aceh in northern Sumatra. Although calls for independence were stifled as 'premature', measures for the advisory participation of natives in colonial government were more far-reaching than under any other regime in South-East Asia.

The Aceh War dragged on for many years. A much smaller military engagement took place in the West Indies. The arbitrary policies of the military dictator of Venezuela, General Cipriano Castro (1900–08), led to diplomatic embroilments with a number of European powers, particularly over his high-handed treatment of foreign investors. The Belgian debt, for instance, was repudiated in 1907. In 1908, when Castro broke off diplomatic relations with the Netherlands because of the sheltering of refugees from his regime in Curaçao, the Dutch destroyed the Venezuelan fleet and blockaded the ports. Castro's regime fell and General Gómez seized power (1908–35). After oil was discovered around 1914 Venezuela became one of the wealthiest countries in Latin America, and Gómez one of the richest men. The Netherlands was well placed to get its share, and Royal Dutch constructed installations on Curaçao and Aruba to refine Venezuelan crude oil.

A twisted caricature of ethical colonialism enabled Leopold II of Belgium (1865–1909) to obtain a large personal colony of his own. Most Belgians were indifferent, but a small circle of courtiers and financiers shared Leopold II's conviction that a modern European state needed colonies as a source of raw materials and as a market for manufactured goods. In 1877 H. M. Stanley completed his epic journey along the Congo River, and the *Association internationale africaine* was founded in Brussels to carry forward the exploration of Central Africa. The Berlin Conference of 1884–85 awarded the Congo basin to Leopold II as a personal fief. In 1889–90 an Anti-Slavery Convention met in Brussels, hosted by King Leopold. The upshot was an international treaty extending Leopold's sovereignty over the Congo Free State and empowering him to put down the Arab slave trade there. The king published the provision in his will bequeathing the Congo Free State to Belgium, and in return the Belgian parliament finally agreed to grant financial support to the king's pet project, which had so far relied on private investors. A loan of 25 million francs was voted for the purpose.

Once the Belgians had conquered Central Africa for their king, the commercial development of the region could begin. Leopold's Congo Free State was run simply as a profit business with the power of life and death (or mutilation) over the inhabitants. The royal rubber plantations introduced a variant of the Cultivation System, but with far crueller consequences for failures to meet quotas. Times had changed, however, and there was an international outcry at the proceedings of the Congo Free State Company. Not wanting to look bad, the king sent mixed messages by ordering that more humane ways be found to keep revenues up. Faced with the vagueness of standards of humanity and the hard figures of a bottom line, the administrators in Congo tended to carry on as they had done, and even to tighten the screws as rubber revenues fell.

The Congo agitation led by Roger Casement and Edmund Morel met some scepticism in Belgium, and more widely. British commercial rule in Rhodesia was hardly a model of humane exploitation but failed to draw the same scrutiny. There were reasonable suspicions that the British were out to discredit Leopold so they could get their hands on the mineral wealth of Katanga, in a replay of their recent take-overs of the Boer republics in South Africa. When it did become incontrovertibly clear that the Belgian war against the Arab slavers had led to the establishment of something far worse, there was no future for the Congo Free State. In 1908 the Belgian government annexed Congo, and installed its own version of ethical colonial government. Forced labour was stopped at once; the quotas for rubber deliveries were ended in 1912. Where the Congo Free State was a by-word for cruelty, the Belgian Congo became, by the lights of the time, a model colony. The housing projects, health programmes, public works and educational policy of the Belgian colonial administrators were among the most enlightened of any colonial power, but were imposed with a lack of sensitivity to local conditions and established customs which would have shocked Joseph II.

THE PEACE MOVEMENT

The violence of colonialism stood in stark contrast to late nineteenth-century optimism about peace and progress. War was confined to colonial conquests and police actions, and to the Balkan fringe of south-eastern Europe. Complacency about 'progress' was little shaken even by the British invasions of the Orange Free State and the South African Republic (Transvaal), which outraged Continental opinion. The Netherlands and Flanders, with the bond of a common language, were particularly disgusted. The unjustifiable invasions, the high mortality in the concentration camps, and the decision of the British rulers of

Transvaal to repudiate the old South African Republic's debts to Dutch investors all gave Britain the appearance of an imperial behemoth run amok.

Late nineteenth-century aspirations to prevent war, and when prevention failed to 'civilize' it, found their fullest expression in the International Peace Conferences held in The Hague in 1899 and 1907. The result of the conferences was the Hague Conventions, which extended the 1864 Geneva Convention, limited the use of indiscriminate weapons such as mustard gas and exploding shells, and set up an international court of arbitration, for the sessions of which Andrew Carnegie financed a 'palace of peace' which was opened in August 1913.

The head of the Dutch delegation at the Hague Conferences was Tobias Asser (1838–1913), a world authority on international law whose great-grandfather had drafted the Kingdom of Holland's Code of Commercial Law almost 100 years before. His contributions to the conferences led to him being awarded the 1911 Nobel Prize for Peace. In 1909 the Belgian delegate at the Hague Conferences, Auguste Beernaert, had jointly received the same honour with his French counterpart. The 1913 Peace Prize laureate, Henri-Marie Lafontaine, was another Belgian. Professor of international law at the progressive Université Nouvelle de Bruxelles since 1893, and a Socialist Senator since 1895, Lafontaine was president of the International Peace Bureau from 1907 until his death in 1943.

6

World Wars and World Peace, 1914–2002

THE GREAT WAR, 1914–1918

On 2 August 1914 the German army invaded Luxembourg. On the same day the Belgian government was presented with an ultimatum demanding the free passage of German troops. The German government insisted that these were not hostile acts, but necessary military manoeuvres. The Luxembourg government maintained a policy of 'strict neutrality', meaning it co-operated fully with the military forces of occupation but under formal protest of duress. A number of Luxembourgers abroad enlisted in the French Foreign Legion. The invasion of Belgium (which had rejected the ultimatum) began on 4 August. This infringement of Belgian neutrality, guaranteed by all the Great Powers, was the deciding issue that brought Britain into the war. This was much to the surprise of the Kaiser, whose advisors had thought the British unlikely to make war for a 'scrap of paper'. Despite desperately fierce fighting, the fortifications of Liège and Namur proved no match for German artillery. A zeppelin attack on the city of Liège was the first aerial bombardment in history.

The Germans had planned a lightning strike through the centre of Belgium to Paris. When they were delayed by the Belgians and halted at the Marne by the French they began a war of conquest in Belgium itself to secure their flanks. Antwerp fell after a fortnight of heavy bombardment during which the Fifth Belgian Division was reduced to trying to slow the German advance with bayonets fixed and unloaded rifles. The Belgian army withdrew westwards, finally retaining only a patch of territory beyond the river Yser, with the coastal plain before it flooded to stop the German advance. There they held the line until 1918, occasionally reinforced by intrepid volunteers who made it out of the occupied zone. Southwards of the Belgian front-line, the British and their Commonwealth allies manned the Ypres salient, which saw some of the bloodiest fighting of the war. Ypres was to be completely destroyed by German bombardment, but never fell into enemy hands. The war in Africa was more mobile, with the Belgian forces in Congo – including black African combat troops – engaging the Germans throughout the Great Lakes region.

During their initial advance German soldiers practised the policy of brutality which had already earned them the nickname 'Huns'. There were slaughters of civilians in Leuven, Dinant and elsewhere, and houses were deliberately set on fire. Often the sound of their own men firing was evidence enough for German officers that plain-clothes snipers were on the loose and reprisals against the civilian population followed at once. Allied propaganda made much of German beastliness but there was a hard basis of fact to the atrocity stories. After the deliberate destruction of lives and homes, one of the low-points of German *Kultur* was the burning of Leuven's university library, painstakingly rebuilt since its destruction by the French Revolutionaries.

Hundreds of thousands fled the deliberate violence of the invading Germans. Tens of thousands were soon living in refugee camps in the Netherlands, France and Great Britain, with thousands more in private lodgings. As early as October 1914 Leopold B. Hill of London brought out a Flemish–English phrasebook containing 'such words as are necessary for an every-day conversation'. This went from the standard polite phrases ('With your leave', 'May I trouble you?', 'I am much obliged'), through lines for renting a room, shopping and getting about, to such necessary items as 'Where are you hurt?', 'Now you must rest', 'Tomorrow you may walk for five minutes', and 'You will recover soon'. When Agatha Christie wanted a foreign detective for her first full-length novel (published 1919) the choice of a Belgian refugee was natural. The unofficial spokesman for the Belgians in England was Emile Cammaerts (1878–1953), not himself a refugee since he had been living in the country since 1908. In 1914 Elgar composed an orchestral accompaniment for readings of Cammaerts's poem 'Carillon', which was the concert-hall hit of the year. From 1933 to 1947 Cammaerts was to be professor of Belgian Studies at the University of London.

The provisioning of the unfortunates trapped within occupied Belgium fell to a National Aid and Food Committee. This was chaired by Emile Francqui, now director of the Société Générale, and as such one of the most powerful men in Belgian public life. Francqui worked closely with the US Food Administration, headed by his fellow China-hand Herbert Hoover. Hoover was also active in the Committee for the Relief of Belgium, and in projects for postwar reconstruction. Francqui himself was after the war a director of the Bank for International Reparation Payments.

A touchy subject throughout the war was Dutch neutrality. In the first days of the war the Dutch army was mobilized to man the border defences, and it remained in a state of readiness throughout the conflict. Both Germany and the Allies tended to think that the Dutch interpretation of neutrality favoured their enemies. A role similar to Cammaerts's as unofficial cultural ambassador was played for the Dutch by Pieter Geyl in London and by A. J. Barnouw at Columbia University in New York. Geyl in particular tried to put the Dutch case before the British public.

In the first days of the war the Belgian government was surprised and dismayed that the Dutch refused to allow the shipping of military *matériel* through the Scheldt, even for the defence of a fellow neutral from unprovoked aggression. As the war dragged on there was fear that Holland would function as a backdoor for German supplies. Accordingly the Allies blockaded the country, attempting to extract assurances from the Dutch government that they would not allow supplies through to Germany. The government was convinced that the Germans would take any such public commitment as a breach of neutrality. The Allies allowed imports to the Netherlands to resume only when a non-governmental organization headed by Dutch captains of industry, the Netherlands Overseas Trust Company, provided the assurances required. Even so, by the end of the war the Netherlands was suffering severe food shortages and rationing had been introduced.

Resistance in Belgium took the form of clandestine publications, intelligence gathering, and the smuggling of recruits and escaped prisoners of war out of the country, usually through Holland. The German reputation for inhumanity was given new life by the execution by firing squad of two intelligence gatherers in occupied Belgium, the British nurse Edith Cavell (1915) and the Belgian secret agent Gabrielle Petit (1916). Both were guilty under the laws of war, but the shooting of women was a gift to Allied propaganda. The comparable French execution (1917) of the original exotic dancer, Mata Hari – born in Leeuwarden as Margaretha Geertruida Zelle – seems not to have been taken so badly (perhaps because she was a less respectable individual) but it can still sometimes raise temperatures. A recent French history of the Benelux goes out of its way to explain that she was not even a very good dancer.

The pastoral letters of Désiré Joseph Mercier (1851–1926), Cardinal-Archbishop of Mechelen, and his public refusal to co-operate with the Germans, were an inspiration both in Belgium and abroad. His uncompromising resistance to foreign oppression was to be an enduring example to others: in 1937 Mgr. Paul Yu Pin, Vicar Apostolic of Nanjing, made a personal report to the papacy on the state of the Church in war-torn China. He took a few days before returning to his flock to make a pilgrimage to the tomb of 'the immortal Cardinal Mercier', 'a pastor of souls who, at a tragic time when his country was invaded and pillaged, raised his voice across the world to give the highest lesson in religion and patriotism'. Mercier's achievements went beyond his inspiring patriotism: before the war, when not yet a bishop, he founded an Institute of Philosophy at the University of Leuven which was at the forefront of the Scholastic revival; in the 1920s he gave an important impetus to ecumenism with the 'Malines conversations', a series of meetings held in Mechelen between unofficial representatives of the Anglican and Catholic Churches. Despite his worldwide fame on these grounds, Mercier is best remembered in Flanders with bitterness, due to his resolute opposition to Dutch as a medium of higher education.

The war saw a radicalization of the Flemish movement, both in occupied Belgium and among soldiers fighting on the Yser. The Germans in 1917 divided Belgium into separately administered Wallonian and Flemish territories, with capitals in Namur and Brussels respectively. They found a few Flemish nationalists willing to work with them to create a Flemish state dependent on Germany. Many of these flamingant 'activists', despised by most Flemings and in danger of prosecution for treason, went into exile after the War. Among Flemish troops on the Front there was grumbling at the second-class treatment they received from French-speaking officers and NCOs. The French-speaking Flemish poet and dramatist Maurice Maeterlinck, whose words were given undue weight by his status as a Nobel laureate, declared that the issue of the war was one of racial supremacy: saving the glories of Latin culture from the barbarism of the Germanic. Flamingants in the army were mortally offended by the notion that they should be thought to be fighting for the supremacy of Latin culture, and organized study groups among the soldiers to raise Flemish consciousness. By May 1918, fearing front-line mutinies in the face of the Ludendorff offensive, the Belgian government-in-exile in Le Havre set up a committee on the language issue, inviting leading figures of the 'Front Movement' to contribute. The crisis of the hour gave the little group of flamingant soldiers a brief moment in the spotlight, and a later feeling of betrayal when rapid results were not forthcoming.

The end of the war, and the example of Soviet Russia, breathed new life into revolutionary agitation. In November 1918 the Dutch Socialist leader P. J. Troelstra declared the Revolution and called upon the government to resign, but it became embarrassingly clear that he had misjudged the strength of his position. In some parts of the Netherlands volunteer Citizen Guards were formed for the protection of property and the maintenance of order but they had little in the way of spartakists to fight. November 1918 also saw the declaration of a Soviet Republic of Workers and Peasants in Luxembourg, after the Germans had left but before the 'liberating' French forces had arrived. Nobody took much notice at the time, but in January 1919 a more broadly based left-wing *coup* was launched. The French army intervened and to save the monarchy the Grand Duchess Maria-Adelheid abdicated in favour of her sister Charlotte.

At the end of the war Belgian foreign policy had two main aims: that the Germans contribute to postwar reconstruction with reparation payments and that Belgian security be more effectively ensured. As early as 1915 parts of the Belgian exile press had insisted that the failure of Great Power guarantees of neutrality required that Belgium be given more defensible borders. There were demands for the return of the Grand Duchy of Luxembourg and for those parts of the old Austrian Netherlands and prince-bishopric of Liège which had been ceded to the Prussians or the Dutch in 1715, 1794, 1815 and 1839. This annexationist agitation, particularly vigorous in the French-language press, severely strained Belgian relations with the Netherlands and Luxembourg, and even with some of the Allied Powers. In the event claims to parts of Luxembourg, Dutch Limburg and the southern shore of the Scheldt estuary were abandoned but the area around Eupen and Malmédy, a part of Germany which had once been in the prince-bishopric of Liège, was joined to Belgium. Here the German-speaking population of Belgium is concentrated, the tiny German community of present-day Belgian federalization (see page 3).

All the later Benelux countries were founding members of the League of Nations. Belgium and the Netherlands were also signatories of the 1922 'Nine Powers' Treaty of Washington which finalized the transfer of territory in the Far East. In the carve-up of the German colonies in Africa, Rwanda and Burundi came under Belgian adminis-tration by League of Nations mandate. Cardinal Mercier's lobbying to have King Albert appointed Guardian of the Holy Places (liberated from the Turks by the British in 1917) came to nothing.

THE CRISES OF PEACE, 1919–1939

Between the world wars, the Netherlands, Belgium and Luxembourg suffered from the effects of German hyperinflation in the early 1920s, and from the world slump of the 1930s. Particularly in Belgium, the loss of life and destruction of property meant a slow process of reconstruc-tion. The political ideologies of totalitarianism further contributed to a sense of gathering doom.

The collapse of the German currency in the aftermath of the Great War was a blow to the economies of Belgium, the Netherlands and Luxembourg, all to some extent dependent on exports and transit trade to Germany, and on the prospects of large reparation payments. The Franco-Belgian (re)occupation of the Ruhr, an industrial zone vital to the trade of the Low Countries, did little to help recovery. Luxembourg, with its political and economic dependency on Germany broken, sought economic alliance with France, but for diplomatic reasons the French referred them to Belgium. The result was a Belgium-Luxembourg customs union and the transfer of the Luxembourg railway concession (previously in German hands) to the Belgian railways.

The second half of the 1920s was a time of worldwide boom, in which Belgium, the Netherlands and Luxembourg all benefited. Britain replaced Germany as the foremost trading partner of the Netherlands. The consequent slump of 1929 affected the Low Countries as much as anywhere. The recession was prolonged by government reluctance to go off the Gold Standard. Britain did so in 1931, but having suffered from the impact of the German hyperinflation of the early 1920s the Low Countries clung to gold for years longer to maintain stable currencies: Belgium and Luxembourg until 1934, the Netherlands until 1935. The recession and its accompanying massive unemployment were met with revaluation, fiscal retrenchment and projects of public works.

A key demand of the Second International was the eight-hour day. With good reason it was argued that an eight-hour day would increase employment and improve labour productivity. Legislation to impose it was delayed not so much by doubts about the economic case as about the propriety of government intervention. More to take the wind out of Socialist sails than for any other reason, the eight-hour day was introduced in the Netherlands in 1919 and in Belgium in 1921 (after a partial measure in 1914). Most workers now had all of Sunday, Saturday afternoon and weekday evenings to themselves.

Popular Culture

There was a leisure revolution. The free time suddenly available to masses of people led to a golden age of mass entertainment, with cinema, radio, spectator sports, seaside day-trips and all its other facets. Highpoints for spectator sports were the 1920 Olympic Games, hosted in Antwerp, and those of 1928 in Amsterdam. The latter were the first (and so far only) Games to show-case korfball, a Dutch variant of basketball. Association Football had been imported from England by the leisured middle classes in the late 1870s. Immediately after the Great War, soccer was transformed from a middle-class enthusiasm to one of the most popular forms of mass entertainment. Predictably, the Dutch Football Association, founded in 1889, eventually split along confessional lines, with a Catholic 'Rooms Katholieke Federatie' (1925), a Socialist 'Nederlandsche Arbeiders Sport Bond' (1926), and a Protestant 'Christelijke Nederlandse Voetbal Bond' (1929) alongside the neutral 'Koninklijke Nederlandsche Voetbal Bond'. All were abolished by the invaders in 1940.

Other sports central to national identity are cycling in Belgium and skating in the Netherlands. Belgium was a charter member, along with the United States, France, Italy and Switzerland, of the Union Cycliste Internationale, set up in 1900. Wealthy Belgians were also among the early motor-racing enthusiasts, and in 1920 a racetrack was laid out at Francorchamps. The greatest sporting event in the Netherlands is the more democratic but highly infrequent Elfstedentocht, or Eleven Towns Tour, a skating marathon of over 100 miles going through the 11 municipal boroughs of Friesland. Naturally the race depends on the safety of the ice, and it has been held only 14 times since the first competition in 1909, most recently in 1997.

Spectator sports were no longer only for spectators: newspapers extended their sports coverage to increase their appeal to a mass market. Cinema news was similarly extended, and photojournalism made its appearance in the daily papers. The connection to wire services in the 1930s meant that mass-circulation newspapers were presenting the same news, often in the same words. The postwar literature professor Willem Asselbergs (a poet and journalist before the war) was to write in a 1951 literary history: 'The daily newspaper lost in pre-eminence as a vehicle of style what it gained in indispensability as an organ of information.' But culturally there were still clear differences: newspapers of different confessional hues reviewed plays, films and books in very different ways. Even radio stations had their pillarized allegiances.

The postwar efforts at reconstruction saw a boom in social housing, with the state providing funding and, in the Netherlands at least, co-ordinated planning for projects carried out by private builders. In some municipal housing projects modernist blocks of two or four-storey flats replaced the garden-suburb style of terraced crescents which housing co-operatives still favoured. Brussels, Rotterdam and Amsterdam South were the first cities in the Low Countries to resort to the sort of collective blocks which (often on an even bigger scale) were to become much more common in the 1950s and 1960s.

Intellectual life in the 1920s, and even more in the 1930s, was marked by political engagement with mass culture. One example is the 'red van' that toured the Netherlands, showing consciousness-raising films to audiences of workers. Politically and culturally, most of the signs of 'massification' were becoming clear before the end of the nineteenth century but made themselves felt in full force only during and after the Great War. Some of the most celebrated writers of the time crafted 'authentic' novels of rural life, along the lines of Stijn Streuvels's *The Flaxfield* (first published 1907; English translation 1989) and not a million miles from Cold Comfort Farm. The best writers, or so it seems now, were those who were critical of, or stood aside from, the mass movements of the time and the demand for authenticity.

Johan Huizinga, the great Dutch historian and philosopher of culture, from 1918 to 1938 published reflections both on modern mass organization and on the importance of play in human culture, as well as reading his own sense of cultural decline back into the Burgundian period in *The Waning of the Middle Ages*. Another critic of mass culture, from a Nietzschean rather than a humanist perspective, was the antifascist activist Menno ter Braak, who committed suicide on the day the Dutch army capitulated in 1940. Ter Braak found his fiercest literary opponent in the equally antifascist Catholic writer Anton van Duinkerken (the pen-name of Willem Asselbergs), who was later to be active in the cultural resistance to Nazism. In works such as his *Verdediging van Carnaval* (Defence of Carnival) Van Duinkerken extolled the festive 'togetherness' of popular culture without giving an inch to the totalitarian perversions of mass politics.

Among Belgian authors the detective novel found its master in the *liègeois* Georges Simenon, who wrote mainly in Paris. In Brussels the comic strip, one of the most characteristic forms of modern mass entertainment, reached new heights of artistic achievement in the Tintin stories of Hergé (Georges Remi). In Antwerp an advertising executive, writing under the pen-name Willem Elsschot, turned out jewels of brevity and wit about big-city misfits working in sales or advertising. His 1922 novella *Kaas* (about a shipping clerk turned unsuccessful cheese salesman) has recently appeared in English as *Cheese*.

Antwerp's big city standing was emphasized in these years by the first 'sky-scraper' in the Low Countries, a really rather modest edifice. The styles of building most characteristic of the years between the wars were late art nouveau, art deco and functionalism. In the Netherlands a movement around the review *De Stijl* (The Style), founded by the painter and designer Theo van Doesburg, sought to incorporate all the elements of art and design in a co-ordinated whole of straight lines, right angles and primary colours, all frills stripped away. The work of the painter Piet Mondrian (originally Pieter Mondriaan) and of the architect Gerrit Rietveld, both closely associated with *De Stijl*, was to have a strong impact on modernism in architecture and design.

This was the period in which Belgium brought forth René Magritte (1898–1967). Trained up in Symbolism, Magritte was gripped by Surrealism in the 1920s, and spent the best part of three years in Paris hanging out with André Breton and Paul Éluard. In 1930 he settled in Brussels and spent the rest of his life exploring variations on the themes he had made his own. His close contemporary Paul Delvaux (1897–1994) came to Surrealism later. His work is much more sombre than Magritte's playful paradoxes, filled with skeletons, out-of-place nudes and night-time railway platforms that convey a sense of loneliness, decay and despair.

The widespread idea that the world was losing stability and coherence was fed by the half-understanding reception in artistic circles of new models of psychology and anthropology, and of physicists' talk of relativity and quantum mechanics. The development of these last theories was stimulated by the scientific conferences organized in Brussels from 1911 onwards by the chemicals magnate Ernest Solvay

(1838–1922), himself an autodidact. The 1927 Solvay Conference brought together, among others, Max Planck, Marie Curie, Albert Einstein, Niels Bohr, Max Born, Erwin Schrödinger, Wolfgang Pauli and Werner Heisenberg. Another sphere in which science and culture overlapped was in the interest in social Darwinism. But the skin-crawlingly well-meaning Eugenetic Bureau funded by the Solvay Institute from 1922, or the Dutch Eugenetic Federation (1930) and Institute for Racial Biology (1933), never attained the prestige or influence of their models in Germany, Sweden and the United States.

Political Extremes

A series of laws enacted in the years 1917–19 considerably broadened the electorate in the Netherlands, Belgium and Luxembourg, and abolished plural voting. The only blot was that Belgian women did not yet have the full duties of citizenship laid upon them. Universal (manhood) suffrage strengthened the Socialist and Confessional parties at the expense of the Liberals. The Great War and the postwar economic disruptions gave many the impression that liberal capitalism had had its day. Prewar scandals – such as that in the Netherlands in 1909 when it was made public that Abraham Kuyper had put at least one contributor to party funds on the honours list – had already undermined confidence in party politics. The wartime effectiveness of businessmen in feeding their compatriots in both occupied Belgium and the blockaded Netherlands stimulated notions of technocracy. The 'age of the crowd' was also the 'age of the expert'. On top of all this there were in the 1930s various emergency measures that weakened parliamentary control in the interest of speedier government reactions to economic and political crises, and seemed to indicate that nineteenth-century parliamentary democracy was not the way of the future.

Alternatives to parliamentary democracy were not shy of coming forward. As times became more unsettled a number of revolutionary and totalitarian parties made their appeal to the masses, seldom with a united voice and never with tremendous success. The Dutch Communist Party was founded in 1918, as a continuation of the Marxist group expelled from the SDAP in 1909, and at its prewar electoral peak in the 1930s was getting close to 4 per cent of the national vote. The Belgian Communist Party was founded in 1920, as a splinter from the Belgian Labour Party, and obtained 6 per cent of the vote in the general elections of 1936. One of the leading Marxists of the Netherlands, and of

Netherlands India, was the railwayman Hendricus Sneevliet (1883–1942). In the early 1920s he was the foremost representative of the Third International in the Far East, the godfather of Indonesian Socialism and the only foreigner present at the foundation of the Chinese Communist Party. He returned to the Netherlands after falling out with his Chinese comrades. In 1929 he broke with the Communist Party to set up the Revolutionary Socialist Party (Revolutionaire Socialistische Partij), and in 1933 was elected to parliament while in prison. In 1932 a splinter of the SDAP set up the Independent Socialist Party (Onafhankelijke Socialistische Partij), which in 1935 united with the Revolutionary Socialist Party to form the Revolutionary Socialist Workers Party (Revolutionaire Socialistische Arbeiders Partij).

The far right was as frissiparous as the far left. The big man of Belgian fascism was Léon Degrelle, whose party was called Rex. It was formed in 1930 as a group within the Catholic Party calling itself Christus Rex, seeking to 'modernize' in a fascist direction. In 1935 it became a separate party, modelled on Mussolini's, and in the general elections of 1936 won 21 seats in the lower house and 12 in the senate. The 'Christus' was dropped when the party was condemned by the bishops, and it lost all but four seats in the 1939 elections. Another Belgian admirer of Mussolini was Joris van Severen, who in 1931 founded the tiny Verdinaso (an acronym for Union of Dutch-language National Solidarity). More significant was the Vlaamsch Nationaal Verbond, founded in 1933 as a common front for right-wing Flemish nationalists. In time it moved further to the right, effectively becoming a fascist-nationalist party in 1937 and the main party of collaboration in the first years of the war. The Flemish movement has understandably been tarred by the historical association of these tiny nationalist parties.

The first fascist party in the Netherlands was founded as early as 1922, as the Verbond van Actualisten (Union of Actualists). By 1925 it had collapsed into a number of splinter groups, but its weekly *De Vaderlander* had disseminated fascist thought among receptive minds. Such ideas spawned a series of fringe groups, one among many being the Zwart Front (Black Front) founded by Arnold Meijer in 1933. A less radical right-wing group was the Nationale Unie, an association of conservative intellectuals which moved further right in the early 1930s under the leadership of the Utrecht history professor F. C. Gerretson. In 1934 Gerretson (an advocate of homegrown Dutch fascism) resigned in disgust at the growing influence of Nazism. With Gerretson gone the Nationale Unie was torn apart by internal leadership struggles. The only really substantial fascist organization in the Netherlands was the NSB, standing for Nationaal Socialistische Beweging (National Socialist Movement). The NSB was founded in 1931 by two civil servants, A. A. Mussert (1894–1946) and Cornelis van Geelkerken (1901–1976). It was bank-rolled by the small number of Netherlands Indies members, and obtained almost 8 per cent of the vote in the 1935 provincial elections.

The numerous fascist and fascist-leaning organizations, constantly splintering and merging, each had its own 'leader' or 'strong man' unwilling to share the little pond with another big fish. The closest thing to a genuine strong man in Dutch political life was Hendrikus Colijn (1869–1944), a Calvinist of farming stock who made his career in the colonial armed forces and the Royal Dutch petroleum company before becoming leader of the Anti-Revolutionary Party in 1922. From 1933 to 1939 Colijn headed a shifting series of 'extraparliamentary' coalitions in which the ministers, appointed for 'expertise' rather than party affiliation, were responsible to parliament but not to a party line. He came to power on slogans promising forceful government, and gained support from conservative liberals as well as from the traditional anti-revolutionary grass roots. Among his earliest measures was a prohibition of civil servants and those in the armed forces and civil defence units being members of revolutionary organizations of the left or the right.

THE SECOND WORLD WAR, 1940–1945

The German invasion of Poland on 1 September 1939 was followed by eight months in which the future Benelux countries uneasily stuck to their obligations as armed neutrals. On 10 May 1940 the German army simultaneously invaded the Netherlands, Belgium and Luxembourg with no declaration of war. The Grand Duchess and her government fled Luxembourg on the day of the invasion. In the Netherlands, Queen Wilhelmina and her government escaped for England on 13 May. General Winkelman, left in over-all command of the Dutch forces, capitulated on 15 May after the aerial bombardment of Rotterdam, which was horrific by all preceding standards. It was to take a few days for the whole army to accept that the war was over and Middelburg shared Rotterdam's fate on 17 May. With the support of the rapidly retreating French and British armies the Belgians lasted until 28 May, with a final three-day battle on the Leie.

Occupation and Collaboration

Most of the Belgian government, and a fair number of parliamentarians, had left Belgium by 20 May and eventually ended up in England. As in the First World War, hundreds of thousands took to the roads, but this time there was nowhere to run: the Netherlands had already fallen and France was soon to follow. By September most of the refugees had been repatriated. The Belgian king and commander-in-chief, Leopold III, chose to remain with his troops and share their fate. He spent the next four years under very lenient house arrest in the royal palace at Laken before being deported as a hostage by the retreating Germans. This made a great difference to the experience of occupation in Belgium. With the head of state still in the country, the Belgian civilian administration remained in place under the oversight of the military forces of occupation. The Belgian courts and civil service could dispute, delay and reinterpret German orders in a way that was impossible in Luxembourg or the Netherlands. A Nazi administration was only imposed in July 1944, as part of the tightening-up after the Normandy landings.

Luxembourg was immediately declared a part of Germany under *Gauleiter* Gustaf Simon, although there was no formal act of annexation. 'Pure German' was decreed the official language, with both French and Letzebürgesch proscribed. Since Luxembourg was now considered part of Germany, German officials could be brought in to fill administrative posts as needed.

In the Netherlands a civilian regime under *Reichskommissar* Arthur Seyss-Inquart (1891–1946), an Austrian Nazi, was appointed within a fortnight of the capitulation. In 1940, unlike 1914, the German soldiers on the ground showed exemplary restraint in their treatment of civilians (although the new university library in Leuven, a memorial to American generosity, went up in flames just like its predecessor). For a few weeks it looked as though the occupation might be an unexpectedly civilized affair.

While most people were determined simply to keep out of trouble and hope for future liberty, the reality of life under German occupation often presented difficult choices. During and after the war the simple divisions of 'right and wrong' or 'black and white' were common for those who had clearly crossed or refused to cross a line. But many people made many small acts of both collaboration and resistance, and few had the stomach for committing their lives to a stand for or against the 'New Order'. Most petty collaboration and some more serious acts were motivated by opportunism and fear. There were other motivations, either ideological or simply well-meaning, which now seem both tragic and deeply perverse. It is, naturally, still a sensitive topic that can easily lead to heated debate or uncomfortable silence when broached.

Some sort of order had to be maintained during the occupation if the countries subjected were to survive to the end of the war and again prosper. This necessarily meant a degree of co-operation with the occupying forces. Furthermore, Belgian experience in the Great War had shown that the Germans would have no scruples about seizing industrial plant and workers and carrying them off into bondage if they got no co-operation on the spot. A systematic policy of choosing the 'lesser evil' was adopted by those left to keep things running in the absence of government – civil servants, policemen, bankers, captains of industry and church leaders. This meant entering the moral quagmire of balancing one evil against another, and deciding just how great an evil could still count as lesser.

One case among many is that of K. J. Frederiks, the Dutch Secretary General for Home Affairs. He considered stepping down but stayed on to prevent an NSBer being installed at the head of the domestic civil service, knowing that 'the principled will revile me'. Soon after the capitulation, a police chief, a civil servant and a professor set up the Nederlandse Unie, a body to organize non-fascist co-operation with the occupiers in the hope that the Germans would not give power to the NSB. It embodied the 'lesser evil' mentality and soon had over 400,000 members, but late in 1941 it was proscribed for its ideological hostility to Nazism.

For Leo Delwaide, mayor of Antwerp, the random arrest of Belgian Jews was the last straw. Unlike his counterpart in Brussels, he had agreed to the distribution of the yellow star through city offices, and he had allowed the Gestapo to call on the city police to help round up Jewish refugees. He drew the line (perhaps with some prodding from the civil service and the cardinal) at lending his police for the arbitrary detention of Belgian citizens. With surprising optimism towards the occupiers, Hendrik de Man disbanded the Belgian Labour Party with a declaration that its members should work constructively with the New Order in the hope that the National Socialists might clear the ground for a more truly Socialist future.

Less numerous but more deadly than those choosing the 'lesser evil' were those with positive enthusiasm for the New Order. The right-wing extremists of the interwar years were natural supporters. Many groups on the far right went a step beyond administrative, police and industrial collaboration, into political, ideological and armed support for Nazism. Even so, not all fascist organizations collaborated. Arnold Meijer's Zwart Front in 1940 renamed itself Nationaal Front, with the avowed aim of national independence, and while prepared for opportunist collaboration it was soon suppressed by the Nazis. Some of its members found their way into the NSB, some into the resistance. In Belgium, part of the Rexist youth wing took the line of resistance and formed the underground National Royalist Movement, which played an important part in the liberation of Antwerp in 1944.

Other fascist groupings were less averse to working with foreign invaders. The NSB leapt at the chance of obtaining real power in the Netherlands. A. A. Mussert was decreed 'leader of the Dutch people', but he was completely out of his depth and Seyss-Inquart entrusted him with no practical responsibility. The *Reichskommissar* reposed more trust in M. M. Rost van Tonningen, an NSBer who had long-standing links with the Austrian Nazis. Rost van Tonningen became secretary of the national bank and Secretary General for Economy and Finance, but he failed to dislodge Mussert as nominal leader. In Luxembourg, a tiny Volksdeutsche Bewegung was set up which quickly grew when membership became obligatory for those in positions of public trust. For the true brown in the annexed Grand Duchy, membership of the German NSDAP was an option.

The main body of the Belgian Rex movement, already fascist, took the final step to Nazism. In 1941 the SS lowered their height requirements and an *SS Sturmbrigade Wallonien* was recruited under the command of the Rexist leader Léon Degrelle. Flemish and Dutch SS auxiliary forces were already in existence. In 1943 Degrelle managed to get Walloons officially reclassified as a French-speaking Germanic racial group, giving them greater standing in the Nazi scheme of things. The Wehrmacht's auxiliary transport corps also recruited in the Low Countries, and home-guard and paramilitary units were raised which released German soldiers for combat duties. Armed collaboration was not always ideological. Although it was often inspired by fervent anti-Communism, due weight has to be given to unemployment (with the attendant risk of being called up for compulsory labour), a misplaced desire for adventure, and simple sadism.

Even comparatively moderate Flemish nationalists sought *rapprochement* with their Germanic brethren. Numerous Flemish nationalists had been flirting with fascism since the 1920s – foremost among them Joris van Severen, who was executed without trial during the retreat in May 1940. Many more of them saw Flemish autonomy as a potential silver lining in the dark clouds of war. As early as 1916 the ardent Pan-Germanic flamingant Jan Derk Domela Nieuwenhuis Nyegaard, a Dutch Protestant pastor of Scandinavian descent, had predicted the rise of a 'new William of Orange' who with mighty hand and iron rod would shepherd the Germanic peoples of Europe. The Führer turned out not to be quite what he had in mind, and during the Second World War he was imprisoned for publicly insulting officers of the German army.

Not all were as disillusioned in the New William of Orange that they got. In July 1940 Hitler instructed that the occupying forces in Belgium further the Flemish cause. The Vlaamsch Nationaal Verbond (VNV), the largest nationalist party and already pretty authoritarian in outlook, became the main collaborating organization in Flanders. As it became clear that the Nazis were unlikely to win the war the VNV cooled in its collaborationism and with full Nazification in 1944, the organization was put out to grass and the rival DeVlag (originally a cultural organization for Flemish–German friendship) became the official National Socialist party of the new *Reichsgau Flandern*. Degrelle's Rex was its counterpart in the *Reichsgau Wallonien*. From 1943 onwards, opportunist collaborators began to back-track and cover their rears, but the commitment of sincere fascists became all the more intense. Even during the retreat into Germany in the autumn of 1944 there were squabbles about who would be running the show after the ultimate victory. In the final winter of the war Degrelle was a sort of district governor over the parts of the Ardennes briefly reconquered by the Germans.

In the autumn of 1940 the occupiers ordered that all Jews register with the local authorities. The order was unconstitutional but was carried out without much complaint, with much greater efficiency in the Netherlands than in Belgium. This was the shining hour of the deliberate incompetence cultivated by so many Belgian functionaries, as only 42,000 Jews were registered, out of an unknown total of at least 60,000. Between a third and a half of the Jews in Belgium died, as against three-quarters in the Netherlands (a higher proportion even than in Germany).

In the spring of 1941 a Jewish Council was set up in Amsterdam, Jewish community leaders themselves being forced into the logic of the 'lesser evil'. In Belgium the same step was taken in the autumn. In the first half of 1942 confiscations of Jewish property began and Jews were ordered to wear an identifying yellow star in public. Under Seyss-Inquart the Netherlands had seen a creeping policy of isolating and brutalizing Jews; in Belgium the exclusions and confiscations of early 1942 were the first serious victimization most Jews experienced. One of the most significant exceptions was in April 1941, when members of a number of Flemish collaborationist organizations sought to demonstrate their enthusiasm for Nazism by organizing a pogrom of their own in Antwerp. A group of Jewish businessmen sued the Antwerp police for failing to intervene, and eventually won damages in the Belgian courts which the occupying authorities prohibited the city from paying.

Camps and Deportations

In May 1942 it was decreed that those who refused a summons to war work would be sent to concentration camps in Germany. It was no surprise that Jews were among the first to be called up for compulsory labour in the East. Deportations started in July 1942. Westerbork, the main transit camp in the Netherlands, had been set up in 1935 as a refugee camp for arriving German Jews. In Belgium the eighteenth-century Dossin barracks in Mechelen were used as a collection point. All sorts of people were sent to work camps and concentration camps for a range of reasons – over 600 forced labourers from Luxembourg were civil servants who had refused to join the *Volksdeutsche Bewegung* – but Jews, although a minority of deportees, were the largest group for whom 'work' was almost certain to mean death. Their children were also at risk; when challenged about the morality of their deportations Gestapo functionaries in the Low Countries sometimes pointed out that they did their best not to break up Jewish families.

In the summer of 1942 the occupying forces started calling up non-Jews for forced labour in Germany, freeing able-bodied Germans for military service. Those who went into hiding rather than do so may not seem especially heroic, but they were risking severe punishments to deny their labour to the Germans. These 'work-refusers' were by far the largest group to be helped by underground organizations.

Not only forced labourers faced transportation to Germany and beyond. With Hitler's surprise invasion of the Soviet Union in June 1941 the Gestapo began rounding up known and suspected Communists, sometimes including anti-Communist Russian refugees. These political prisoners, and members of the resistance, were initially sent to ordinary gaols or to camps in the occupied countries which were little cogs in the developing machinery of imprisonment, slavery and extermination: Amersfoort for the Netherlands, Breendonk for Belgium, Hunsruck for Luxembourg. Many ended up in labour camps or death camps in Germany and in occupied Poland. At Vught, in the Netherlands, there was a separate concentration camp for hostages: prominent individuals against whom nothing could be proved, held to be executed in retaliation for acts of armed resistance.

Resistance

The Germans were ruthless in suppressing open resistance, but numerous, often tiny, underground organizations sprang up to work against the occupiers. As one would expect, those active in them were a small minority of the population as a whole. Nevertheless, there were widespread but low-key demonstrations of loyalty to the prewar regime – in the Netherlands the wearing of carnations on Prince Bernhard's birthday, in Luxembourg the wearing of 'red lion' buttons on independence day, at the risk of being beaten up by pro-Nazi toughs.

In February 1941 Communist labour leaders in Amsterdam called for strikes in protest at the treatment of Jews, and the call was answered on a massive scale. This *Februaristaking* was virtually unique as a public show of solidarity with oppressed Jews in an occupied country, but it failed to make an impact on Nazi policy. In May 1941, the anniversary of the invasion, there was a wave of protest strikes in the Wallonian coalfields. Luxembourg saw a series of strikes and demonstrations when it was decreed in August 1942 that as Germans, they could be called up for service in the Wehrmacht. Protest strikes in the Netherlands in May 1943, triggered by orders that prisoners of war released in 1940 were to report for reinternment, were put down with great brutality.

Church leaders were unanimous in their view of Nazism as un-Christian, but largely preserved a cautious silence in public. The Dutch were again among the notable exceptions when it came to open denunciations. In Belgium no public stand was taken over the deportations (although the requisitioning of church bells was condemned), but Catholic charitable institutions unobtrusively played a crucial part in the networks helping those in hiding. Conversely, some Catholic priests gave propagandistic support to the war against Bolshevism, foremost among them Cyriel Verschaeve, a flamingant intellectual who retained enormous prestige despite being disowned by the bishops.

Even academic life had its moments of heroism. As early as

227

November 1940 R. P. Cleveringa, dean of the faculty of law in Leiden, protested publicly against the sacking of a Jewish colleague. He was arrested, the student body walked out, and the university was closed down until the end of the war. The liberal Université Libre in Brussels closed its doors in November 1941 to forestall interference in academic life. Monseigneur Van Waeyenberghe, rector of the Catholic University in Leuven, spent 18 months in prison rather than hand over the matriculation registers to the occupier. Among academic historians, two of the twentieth century's greatest biographers of Erasmus, Johan Huizinga (1872–1945) and Léon Halkin (1906–1998), were imprisoned by the Germans for their resistance activities.

In an atmosphere of terror and the danger of denunciation, personal friendships were central to the forming of networks of resistance. Anne Frank and her companions, for instance, were hidden by her father's business associates. The need for broad networks became apparent to Helena Kuipers-Rietberg, a Dutch housewife who was on the board of the Union of Reformed Women's Associations. At the end of 1942 she used her clergy and women's league connections to set up the Landelijke Organisatie (Nationwide Organization) to help those in hiding. By the end of the war the LO had about 15,000 members caring for between 200,000 and 300,000 people in hiding, and a small military wing in the Landelijke Knokploegen (Nationwide Heavies). Personal contacts continued to play a role in recruiting for such organizations: Henk Das, provincial leader of the LO in Utrecht, got involved in resistance work through an invitation from a friend in the Christian Korfball Association. Mrs Kuipers-Rietberg herself died in Ravensbrück concentration camp in 1944.

Many armed resistance groups were highly conservative, even reactionary. For the first year of the war the running was made by those motivated by old-fashioned ideals of Crown and Country, which in some cases were linked to a veneration of the constitution but often enough went with a deep disgust at the failures of interwar democracy. One of the first resistance groups in Belgium, the White Brigade (soon a generic name for such groups) was built by Liberal schoolmasters and youth groups in Antwerp. Phalanx in Belgium and the Ordedienst in the Netherlands consisted of old soldiers with an authoritarian frame of mind.

Organized left-wing resistance began in Belgium in the spring of 1941, when a liberal journalist, a communist doctor and a priest from Liège set up the Independence Front. It became a broad-based group,

228

much like the LO in the Netherlands, but was largely run by Communists after the German invasion of the Soviet Union. Also like the LO its main concern was not with armed resistance but it did have armed sections, called Patriotic Militias. There was a separate underground Communist Party, with a Belgian section of the international Communist intelligence network known as the Red Orchestra, and a Communist military wing, the Armed Partisans, which was the main rival to the dozens of tiny conservative groups gradually coalescing into the Secret Army.

The Independence Front was responsible for a unique achievement in occupied Europe. In 1943 50,000 counterfeit copies of *Le Soir*, identical in appearance to that published under German censorship, were printed for distribution on 5 November. The fake *Le Soir* included uncensored news and such items as the purported episode of a serialized novel, 'The Mystery of the Brown Chamber' by 'G. Stapo'. This stunt enabled far more people to read at least one uncensored newspaper than would otherwise have been possible. Another unique achievement had taken place half a year before. Late in the evening of 19 April 1943 three young men with a storm lantern and a pistol stopped the twentieth convoy taking Jews from Belgium to Auschwitz, near Boortmeerbeek, and managed to open one of the wagons. This was the only attempt to stop a deportation train.

One of the more mysterious disasters of the resistance was the unravelling of the Dutch networks set up in consultation with London. Captured radio operators sent back the messages the Germans requested, secure in the knowledge that in the absence of their secret security codes their transmissions would be ignored. Instead, the British ignored the lack of the security codes on which they had placed such emphasis in training. In a series of 'droppings' requested by the Germans over a period of months, 57 Dutch agents trained in England, 50 RAF crewmen and about 400 members of the Dutch resistance were arrested. This fiasco, known to the Germans as the *Englandspiel*, seriously undermined mutual trust within the Dutch resistance and government-in-exile, and between the Dutch and the British. There have even been speculations about treason in Whitehall, or that the British deliberately sold out the Dutch to distract the Germans from the planned landing in Normandy. The official history of the Secret Operations Executive pleads straightforward incompetence, and then blames the Dutch for being too literal-minded and trusting in authority.

The war continued in the colonies after May 1940. In the Battle of the

Java Sea on 27 and 28 February 1942 the Japanese destroyed the Dutch-British-Australian-American Combined Striking Force. The over-all commander, Rear Admiral Karel Doorman, went down with his flagship. Only four American destroyers got away. The Governor General of Indonesia capitulated to the Japanese on 9 March. More than 300,000 Dutch inhabitants of Indonesia were interned in prison camps, where about a tenth of them died. The Netherlands Antilles and Dutch Guyana (Surinam) remained under free Dutch rule for the duration of the war, and the Royal Dutch oil refineries in the West Indies contributed to the Allied cause. The Belgian Congo was virtually handed over to the British for the duration, despite the protests of some Belgian industrialists. Its copper, rubber, manganese and other natural resources were put at the disposal of the war effort. Uranium from the Congo was used in the first atomic bombs.

Liberation

A considerable difference in the experience of occupation was the timing of liberation. All of Belgium was liberated by November 1944, as well as the Netherlands south of the great rivers. On 4 September 1944, known as 'Dolle Dinsdag' (Mad Tuesday), a mistaken BBC report that the Allies had reached Breda led to panic among collaborators and their families, with up to 60,000 people fleeing the country and the clandestine press sardonically commenting on the new 'Drang nach Osten'. A week later the Allies crossed the Dutch border, but before the month was out the failure of the Arnhem offensive had condemned the northern provinces of the Netherlands to a further winter of occupation. During these harsh months, the 'Hunger Winter', there was little food or fuel available in the great conurbations of the western Netherlands and no means of transporting any. The Germans had looted the rolling stock and shut down the transport infrastructure of the country in retaliation for a railway strike. Over 20,000 people died of malnutrition, while those who could went begging through the countryside. Matters were made worse by the increased desperation of the Germans in their demands for forced labour and their retaliations against armed resistance. On 1 October 1944, after a resistance group attacked an officer's car, all the male inhabitants of the nearby village of Putten, numbering over 600, were rounded up. A few were shot on the spot, and the rest sent to concentration camps from which only a handful returned. The moral dilemma of committing acts of armed resistance in the knowledge

230

that civilians would be killed in retaliation is a theme of *De Aanslag* (The Assault), one of the early novels of the postwar writer Harry Mulisch.

The Grand Duchy of Luxembourg, and parts of the Belgian Ardennes, suffered the German counter-offensive of December 1944, known as the Battle of the Bulge. At tremendous cost the German advance was finally stopped by the Americans at Bastogne, in the Belgian province of Luxembourg.

The collaborators who fled the Netherlands on Mad Tuesday had good reason for nervousness: the liberation of Italy and France, and to a lesser extent of Belgium, had seen a confused and often over-enthusiastic 'repression' of 'bad elements'. In some cases Resistance Tribunals failed to observe due process, and there were instances of outright murder. Things quickly settled down and in all the soon-to-be-Benelux countries those accused of collaboration were interned and dealt with in legal fashion, a process which took years to complete. The optimists among them might use their time in prison to learn Spanish, as Franco's Spain or Perón's Argentina beckoned; the pessimists (it was joked) studied Russian. Justice being seen to be done was marred by some cases of unbalanced sentencing, with a few big fish getting off more lightly than small fry.

Seyss-Inquart was sentenced to death in the Nuremberg trials. Among the leaders of collaborationist movements, Mussert was executed in 1946. The historian H. J. Elias, head of the VNV in the last years of war, was also sentenced to death in 1946 but appealed for clemency, which was granted in 1951. Léon Degrelle (1906–1994) vanished and was sentenced to death *in absentia*. He later turned up in Spain, where he lived for the rest of his life, and a special 'Degrelle law' was passed to keep his death sentence from lapsing after ten years. The most recent to be in the news was a more minor figure. Dirk Hoogendam, a Dutch SS officer who went into hiding in Germany after the war, was only unearthed in 2001 and died in 2003 while awaiting trial.

AFTER THE WAR, 1945–2002

The years immediately after the war saw a spirit of reconstruction which hoped to break through the pillarized divisions of the 1930s to create organizations of foreward-looking patriots building a better future side by side. The governments of national unity saw Communists in the Belgian cabinet for the first time, and Socialists in the Dutch. The Communist Party reached the historic summit of its popularity and prestige in the late 1940s, with reaction to the 1948 *coup* in Czechoslovakia limiting its growth and the Soviet invasion of Hungary in 1956 sealing its decline. On the latter occasion an Amsterdam mob vandalized the eighteenth-century building where the Dutch Communist Party had its offices, one of the periodic outbursts of popular violence in the otherwise remarkably quiet political life of the nation.

In the Netherlands, socially minded members of the old parties together formed a new Partij van de Arbeid (Labour Party). But the confessional pillars still had fight in them, and within a few years the PvdA was just another Socialist party. The Belgian Labour Party made the oppposite name-change, being called back to life after the war as the Belgian Socialist Party, to emphasize that it was not just a party of the labour interest, but for all those wanting social reform. The deconfessional 'breakthrough' in the Netherlands was incomplete, but gained new momentum in the 1960s. In Belgium controversies about the future of the monarchy and the funding of secondary education forestalled any serious attempt at 'de-pillarization'.

The most pressing political problem facing Belgium at the end of the war was the return of the king. This issue was the main reason that the country went through nine governments in the years 1945–50. Leopold III had been deported by the Germans as a hostage in their retreat, but his failure to maintain a rigorous respect for the constitution during his earlier, largely nominal, captivity in Belgium raised doubts about his fitness to reign. In 1940 he had remained with his troops contrary to the advice of his ministers. After the capitulation he had sought a personal audience with Hitler to plead for clemency for his conquered people. In the course of the war members of his entourage had indulged in authoritarian pipe-dreams. But what was taken particularly badly was that during his captivity he had married his children's governess without ministerial authorization. Socialists and Communists saw the time as ripe for republicanism. More moderate minds were not enthusiastic about returning Leopold to the throne if an alternative could be found.

In 1944, with Leopold in German captivity, his younger brother Charles, who had spent the war in hiding, was elected regent by the joint chambers. In 1945 the king was liberated by the Americans near Salzburg, but his younger brother was already proving a more capable monarch. He did more than any one man to save the Belgian monarchy.

Charles remained regent while Leopold moved to Switzerland to await the outcome of the negotiations for his return. In March 1950 a referendum brought a slight majority in favour of the king, and a general election in June gave an overall majority in parliament to the Christian Democrats. Leopold returned to Belgium in July. Violent strikes and demonstrations, especially in the Liège area, precluded a peaceful restoration and seemed to bring the nation to the brink of civil war. In 1951 Leopold abdicated in favour of his 20-year-old son Baudouin (Boudewijn).

Reconstruction and Decolonization

A very different crisis of authority faced the Netherlands in the immediate postwar years, in Asia. Indonesia had been occupied first by the Japanese and then by the British and Australians. President Sukarno had proclaimed the independent Indonesian republic in August 1945. The British had no interest in fighting Indonesian nationalists and insisted the Dutch sort the situation out. A promising start was made, on paper, in setting up a loosely federated Indonesian commonwealth under the Dutch crown. The on-going resistance of Sukarno to federalization and repeated Communist attempts to seize power from him led the Dutch to launch a series of counter-insurgency campaigns, beginning in 1947. The commitment of manpower and money by an exhausted nation was phenomenal. Throughout the 1940s and 1950s Dutch politics was dominated by Catholic–Labour coalitions: neither party had any traditional enthusiasm for colonialism, but the conviction that surrender would show weakness, and that Indonesian raw materials would be needed for postwar reconstruction, steeled them to see the matter through. Jakarta was reoccupied and Sukarno captured, but UN and US intervention forced a Dutch climb-down. Wherever possible in Asia the Americans were backing anti-communist nationalists at the expense of European colonial powers. A series of secessionist wars of ethnic or religious colouring muddied the waters of Indonesian independence further. In the late 1950s, as Sukarno became more dictatorial and Dutch assets in Indonesia were nationalized, Europeans, Eurasians and Moluccans headed for the Netherlands. Moluccans and Eurasians added new colour to the kingdom, but were not warmly welcomed by the populace.

The commonwealth proposals which foundered on Indonesian nationalism met more success in the six Caribbean islands of Aruba, Bonaire, Curaçao, Saba, St Eustasius and St Maarten, and the mainland

233

colony of Surinam. In 1954 all were granted home rule under the Dutch crown, with local government in each and a collective States sitting in Curaçao. The Queen was represented by a Governor, but power resided in a council of ministers answerable to the States. Surinam soon went its own way, and became fully independent in 1975; the Netherlands Antilles are still under the Dutch crown.

The postwar years saw a determination to create a new Concert of Europe in which multilateral treaties would guarantee peace and promote prosperity. A remarkable number of international organizations sprang up. One of the first, and at least in its ideals a model for European integration, was the Benelux. Agreements in principle had already been made in London by the governments in exile, but the Benelux treaties were not drawn up until 1948, when a customs union was created. Further difficult negotiations followed, and in 1958 the Benelux became a full economic union. In the meantime the European Coal and Steel Community (1952), Euratom (1957) and the European Economic Community (1957) had to some extent made such a step redundant. Brussels and Luxembourg together host the major institutions – Parliament, Commission and Council – of the European Union, although at French insistence the European Parliament still holds some sessions in Strasbourg. The Benelux countries were three of the 12 to give up their national currencies in favour of the Euro on 1 January 2002.

In self-ironic imitation of the Benelux, a number of Danish, Dutch and Belgian artists, including the abstract expressionist Karel Appel, in 1948 founded a group called Cobra (from Copenhagen-Brussels-Amsterdam). The grouping was dedicated to challenging traditional artistic categories and Parisian hegemony in the art world by forming an experimentalist international. After exhibitions in Brussels, Amsterdam and Liège, Cobra disbanded.

Rather more seriously, all the Benelux countries abandoned their traditional commitments to neutrality to form permanent alliances with France and Great Britain in the 1948 Brussels Pact. All were founding members of NATO in 1949. The Benelux countries also supported the founding of the International Court of Justice in The Hague (1945) and the United Nations Organization (1949). Dutch and Belgian forces made a contribution to the UN's efforts in the Korean War. Important players in the new internationalism of the 1950s were the Dutch foreign minister J. W. Beyen and his Belgian counterpart Paul-Henri Spaak. Both played a crucial role in mediating the French–German compromises that enabled the conclusion of the Treaty of Rome (1957) which founded the

EEC, an initiative which was itself a result of recommendations by Beyen. The Belgian foreign minister Spaak had been first president of the General Assembly of the United Nations, and was to be secretary general of NATO from 1957 to 1961 (succeeded in the post by the Dutchman Dirk Stikker, 1961–64). Joseph Luns, who succeeded Beyen at the Dutch foreign office in 1956 and remained in place until 1971, took up something of their mantle, and was secretary general of NATO from 1971 to 1984. In the meantime, Belgium and the Netherlands being the most pro-Atlantic of the EEC nations, French withdrawal from NATO had seen AFCENT (Allied Forces Central Europe) moved to Brunssum in the Netherlands and SHAPE (Supreme Headquarters Allied Powers Europe) to just outside Brussels.

In more strictly national terms, the 1958 Brussels Expo is still an event of great symbolic significance. The Atomium (a massively scaled-up model of a molecule of steel), the Heysel exhibition halls, Brussels airport, and the automobile tunnels and underground tram system under the Brussels boulevards have remained as permanent reminders. Expo58 marked the return of prosperity and the end of the aftershocks of the war. It was the swan-song of Belgium as a unitary state and as a colonial power.

Representatives of the tiny Congolese middle class were flown to Belgium for the World Exhibition and saw first-hand how Europeans lived at home (at previous World Exhibitions less 'evolved' Central Africans were brought in to populate 'native villages' as part of the display). In 1959 strikes and demonstrations demanding independence were launched in the Belgian Congo, and Patrice Lumumba (1925–1961) was soon a recognized leader of the more radical agitators. The Belgian government called a conference on the future of the Congo early in 1960, proposing to phase in native political responsibility over a great many years, but could not allay Congolese demands for immediate independence. The independence of Rwanda and Burundi was to follow in 1962.

Paternalistic policies had given the Congo the most thorough system of primary schooling in Africa but next to no provision for further education or administrative or political careers for Africans. Lumumba, the first prime minister, was a former postal clerk who had most recently worked as a salesman for a brewery. He was certainly not lacking in sincerity, passion or intelligence, but he was hardly prepared for the job of heading a government. Belgian businessmen, administrators and soldiers were expected to stay on in the new republic to ease the transition to African rule. In the event, most Belgian civilians were evacuated as the Congo descended into a bloody multi-sided civil war over the post-colonial balance of power, stoked by old rivalries and by new Cold War alliances. The catalyst was the declaration of the independence of Katanga, the province richest in mineral resources. The country's first president, Joseph Kasavubu (1917–1969), dismissed his prime minister for calling in Soviet aid. Lumumba fled the capital but was captured and turned over to the Katangese secessionists. He was tortured and eventually killed, Belgian advisors disposing of his remains. UN peace-keepers were sent in to hold the country together. Moise Tshombe (1919–1969), leader of the attempted secession of Katanga, died in exile. President Kasavubu was set aside in the military *coup* that brought Mobutu Sese Seko (1930–1997) to power in 1965.

Welfare Reform

From the late 1940s to the mid-1970s a series of measures transformed welfare provision in the Netherlands, Belgium and Luxembourg. Universal old-age pensions, mandatory unemployment insurance, family allowance payments and a range of other entitlements were funded by employer/employee contributions. The trade unions reached the peak of their power, winning a range of benefits for their members. The Netherlands in 1976 adopted a law on disability benefit which is possibly the most generous ever. State-managed solidarity was also extended to those without social security contributions, creating locally and centrally funded institutions to provide universal basic coverage for those who otherwise slipped through the net. The insurance unions, hospitals, schools and trade unions which provide the institutional framework of the welfare system are the government's 'social partners'. Their historic roots lie in the confessional blocs of the late nineteenth and early twentieth centuries. The combination of increased government intervention in society and economy with the 'social partnership' of pillarized organizations led to something known as 'neocorporatism'. This has meant that the old confessional pillars retain much of their influence in public life, even while their doctrinal content has faded away. Individuals might belong to a Christian health insurance union, but send their children to secular schools (or vice versa) according to convenience and personal contacts. It is by no means unusual to find that the staff of nominally Christian institutions have no religious beliefs, but a vague notion that the Social Christian tradition offers a model of solidarity and activism which avoids the extremes of collectivization and liberal individualism. In Catholic and Calvinist institutions staff are recruited on professional qualifications and their opinions are their own affair as long as they refrain from openly attacking the beliefs of the institution. No such restriction seems to apply to those exercising religious ministry in the churches themselves.

As early as the 1920s the coalmines were recruiting in Poland. The postwar boom saw industrial workers recruited first in Italy, Portugal and Spain, later in Turkey and Morocco. The integration of Muslim immigrants into a 'pillarized' society has proved highly problematic, especially as being confessionally 'neutral' traditionally means opposing any overt religiosity.

The rising wages and guaranteed minimum incomes of the 1960s led to popular consumerism on the American model. Fridges, cars, televisions and other consumer durables were no longer reserved to the 'comfortably off', and popular entertainment became big business. In the Netherlands, the confessional pillars extended their presence into the world of television, with broadcasting slots shared out between the Liberal AVRO, the Socialist VARA, the Liberal-Reformed VPRO, the Catholic KRO, the Calvinist NCRV, the evangelical EO and the unaligned entertainment broadcaster TROS (as well as a vast number of smaller bodies). Only very recently have cable and satellite channels somewhat loosened the hold of the 'pillars' on television content in the Netherlands. In Belgium – in other respects still more obviously pillarized – there was a national broadcasting corporation, modelled on the BBC, now split into separate French and Dutch language bodies competing with a range of purely commercial channels.

Sexual Revolution

Equality of rights and entitlements between the sexes was one of the more significant demands to be put forward in the 1960s. In 1966 the women at FN in Herstal walked out demanding equal pay for equal work, to the surprise of trade union officials. From around 1970 female intellectuals began to protest injustices in education, pay, opportunities, family law, and the provision of public toilets, in an association called Dolle Mina (Mad Mina), the nickname of the Dutch suffragette Wilhelmina Drucker. They also demanded induced abortion as a right.

Attitudes to sexual and reproductive practices were changing as elsewhere in Europe, on the same sort of time-scale (effectively following the availability of antibiotics and the contraceptive pill). Induced abortion was legalized, practically on demand, in the Netherlands in 1983, in Belgium in 1990, after many years of the matter being left to the discretion of doctors. In Belgium this precipitated a constitutional crisis as the king refused to sign the bill against his conscience: he was declared temporarily incapable of carrying out his duties and the law was ratified by a one-day regency council. More recently the Netherlands and Belgium have both legalized 'mercy killing'. Laws against sodomy were repealed by the revolutionaries of the 1790s, but social acceptance of known homosexuals was another matter. The COC (Culture and Relaxation Centre) founded in the Netherlands in 1946, and the CCB (Cultural Centre of Belgium) founded in 1953, were 'homophile' bodies which encouraged participation in a homosexual subculture and called for greater social acceptance of public homosexuality. The COC was soon the largest such organization in the world. Holland (which in the 1730s had seen the largest co-ordinated police action against sodomites in pre-twentieth-century Europe) became famous for its tolerance of homosexuals. The first 'gay celebrity' of the Netherlands was the writer Gerard Reve, who has published charming volumes of inconsequential letters, but is more famous for his no-holds-barred literary explorations of homoeroticism, seduction and sadism. In both the Netherlands and Belgium it is currently possible for same-sex couples to have registry-office weddings.

The Flemish Movement

In Belgium the linguistic border was fixed by law in 1962. Thereafter a series of riotous demonstrations in the 1960s and 1970s brought down government after government. In February 1968 a government fell after student protests in Leuven that led to the splitting of the university – and its new library – into separate Flemish and French-language institutions. French-speaking historians sometimes like to suggest that Flemish nationalism is essentially a 'blood and soil' ideology, and that this accounts for the refusal to allow French-speaking students and professors to exercise their individual freedom to live and study in a Flemish town. The point carries weight, but the flamingant concern was less with individuals than with the long-term institutionalization of a large French-speaking presence. Wallonian politicians were coming to see some benefit in establishing institutional parity with the more numerous and increasingly vocal Flemings. In response to Flemish and Walloon demands for greater self-determination a series of constitutional changes were introduced from 1980 onwards. These culminated in the federal structure created in 1993, which devolved competences along the lines described in the introduction.

In recent years the key demand of mainstream Flemish nationalists is that social security and pensions also be regionalized, to stop what is caricatured as a flow of money from high-tech Flanders to post-industrial Wallonia. Resentment against the speakers of French is still apparent. It tends to be encouraged by the constant dredging up of nineteenth-century grievances and the ubiquitous myth that Flanders has suffered 1000 years of foreign oppression, rather than reflecting any experience of personal contact. The extreme forms of nationalism, embodied in the populist far-right Vlaams Blok, are republican and separatist but these demands are not played up in their election publicity, which concentrates on immigration and policing.

The late 1960s and early 1970s were a time of desperate constitutional tinkering. The Belgian constitution of 1831, which had been revised in 1893, 1920 and 1921, was revised again in 1967, 1968, 1969, four times in 1970 and twice more in 1971. In the Netherlands, which had a busier history of constitutional amendment, a commission was appointed in 1967 to study the issue of constitutional reform. It reported in 1971, and in 1972 the whole constitution was overhauled at one go.

Twilight of the Second Millennium

The 1970s were a moment of change in other respects as well. Major economic movements of inflation and unemployment aggravated the problems due to the decline of long-established industries. Quite apart from oil scarcity, the main source of income for mining towns and fishing villages simply disappeared. Ways of life which in some places went back for centuries collapsed. Luxembourg finally had it driven home that steel in itself was not enough to maintain an industrial lifestyle, and the government took measures to stimulate economic diversification. Although the last mine closed in 1981, the steel industry continues to work with imported ore. At the same time, it began to become clear how much long-term damage had resulted from the chemical and mineral products so prodigally exploited in and after the boom years. The economic and environmental crises coincided with the rise of a substantial drugs culture, constant political provocations from fringe groups and a wave of terrorist attacks: by various foreign nationalists seeking to shake European indifference to their causes, by leftist revolutionaries, and by suspected far-right gangsters. Active church-going, so recently the social norm, almost overnight came to be seen as an eccentricity. The public profile of Christianity reached its lowest point in 200 years.

In the Netherlands the number of unemployed more than doubled between 1975 and 1994; the number of pensioners rose from 925,000 in 1965 to over 2 million in 1990; and the number of those claiming invalidity benefit quadrupled from 175,000 in 1968 to 800,000 in 1990. The ratio of workers to those receiving welfare payments was one of the smallest in the world. The overburdening of the welfare state made politically imposed solidarity problematic. Retrenchment and reform were necessary, but consensus on whose entitlements should be reduced was difficult to reach. The 'Dutch miracle' of the 1990s was to reduce the burden of benefits without immediately unleashing massive pauperization or furious social protest, while maintaining the essentials of a welfare state and a flourishing economy. The key was public trust that the reforms were necessary and being carried out by the right people: the parties in power were those which had built the welfare system and derived most political benefit from being publicly associated with it. One of the most intractable problems now facing politicians is pension reform, since childlessness and opposition to immigration leave a shrinking pool of workers to pay for the growing class of pensioners.

Right-wing extremists, themselves experiencing a political resurgence, have blamed the social breakdown of the late twentieth century on the not so very numerous but (in inner cities) highly visible concentrations of 'guest workers' from Mediterranean lands and immigrants from former colonies. The ultra-nationalist Vlaams Blok was set up in Antwerp in 1979 to present a broad front of far-right candidates for the 1980 general election. In the Netherlands, the xenophobic Centrumpartij won its first seat in parliament in 1982. Vlaams Blok was dissolved in 2004 when convicted of incitement to racial hatred, but immediately regrouped under the name Vlaams Belang. The party has steadily increased its following, but the right-wingers of the Netherlands have repeated their forebears' inability to present a unified front. Something approaching right-wing populism only broke through into the Dutch mainstream after 2000, under the leadership of Pim Fortuyn – a flamboyant, charismatic and openly homosexual academic and entrepreneur. In the 2002 elections, in the run-up to which Fortuyn himself was shot dead by an animal-rights activist, his followers surged in popularity. They briefly became part of an unstable governing coalition with the conservative Liberals and the Christian Democrats, in the process losing all credibility as either conventional or alternative politicians.

On the international scene, ideals dear to the Dutch, Belgians and Luxembourgers – peaceful coexistence, harmonious consensus, autonomy in the private sphere – have proved difficult to export. This was underlined by the murder of ten Belgian paratroopers attached to UN peace-keeping forces in Rwanda in 1994, and the inability of the Dutchbat contingent of the UN forces in Bosnia to prevent the slaughter at Srebrenica in 1995. Localized violence is not the only obstacle to greater international co-operation in the field of human rights. A Belgian universal competency law for human rights violations – flagship Liberal legislation – was revised into toothlessness after American objections. It is perhaps still too early to lament with Thietmar of Merseburg that crimes can no longer be punished, but the effectiveness of the new International Criminal Court in The Hague remains to be seen.

Chronology of Major Events

BC

58–56	Caesar's conquest of Gaul.
53	Belgic Revolt.
22–12	Reorganizations of *Gallia Transalpina* leads to a separate *provincia Belgica* with distinct civilian, fiscal and military administrations.
13	Roman invasion of Germania (including Frisia).
12	Batavians supply Romans with auxiliary troops.

AD

9	Roman withdrawal from Germania (not including Frisia).
28	Frisian Revolt.
47	Frisians ally themselves with Rome.
69–70	Batavian Revolt.
c.80	Reorganization of Roman military frontier creates *provincia Germania Inferior*.
256	Frankish invasion.
258–74	Short-lived 'Gallic Empire' under Postumus and his successors.
297	Imperial unity restored under Diocletian's 'Tetrarchy'; administrative reforms split Belgic provinces into *Belgica Prima*, *Belgica Secunda*, *Germania Secunda*; make forest of the Ardennes an imperial possession.
314	First certain evidence of organized Christian communities in the Low Countries.
357	Area south of the Rhine delta ceded to Frankish federates.
406	'Great Invasion' of Germanic peoples.
c.455	End of Roman rule in the Low Countries.
481	Childeric, king of the Salian Franks, buried at Tournai.
c.500	Clovis, king of the Salian Franks, baptized.
c.500–c.600	Conversion of the Franks of the Low Countries to Christianity.

561	Low Countries south of the Rhine become the Frankish sub-kingdom Austrasia.
678–785	Conversion of the Frisians to Christianity.
714–719	Radbod, king of the Frisians, at war with the Franks.
717	See of Maastricht moved to Liège.
751	Pepin the Short, Austrasian nobleman, becomes first Carolingian king of the Franks.
754	Boniface martyred at Dokkum in Frisia.
800	Charlemagne crowned Emperor; rules much of Western Europe.
834–36	Repeated Viking raids destroy the prosperity of Dorestad.
843	Frankish kingdom divided into the Western Kingdom (France, including Flanders), the Eastern Kingdom (Germany) and the Middle Kingdom (the Low Countries, Lorraine, Burgundy, Provence and Northern Italy).
c.845	Viking settlement in the Rhine delta.
855	Middle Frankish Kingdom divided into Italy, Provence and Lotharingia.
864	Baldwin 'Iron Arm' becomes first count of Flanders.
869	Lotharingia incorporated into East Frankish Kingdom (Germany).
882–85	Viking rule in the Rhine delta.
891	Vikings defeated on the river Dijle, near Leuven.
c.916	Dirk becomes first count of 'West Frisia' (Holland).
954	Hungarian raiders reach the Low Countries.
963	Sigfrid, a count in the Ardennes, exchanges lands near Echternach for the castle of Lucilinburhuc (Luxembourg).
1096–99	Robert II, count of Flanders, and Godfrey of Bouillon, duke of Lotharingia, among the leaders of the First Crusade.
1127	Murder of Charles the Good, count of Flanders.
1170	Great Charter of Flanders, giving uniform legal codes to Arras, Bruges, Douai, Ghent, Lille, Saint-Omer and Ypres.
1188–99	Succession dispute in Luxembourg and Namur.
1190–91	Several rulers from the Low Countries die on the Third Crusade.
1198	Holy Roman Empire split between Welf and Hohenstaufen factions.
1203–10	Disputed succession in Holland.
1214	Battle of Bouvines: Philip Augustus of France reasserts his suzerainty over Flanders.
1224–25	'False Baldwin' in Flanders.
1231	Frederick II effectively recognizes independence of local rulers.
1236–38	First papal inquisitor in the Low Countries.
1246	Feast of Corpus Christi decreed in the diocese of Liège.

1247	William II, count of Holland, elected Holy Roman Emperor in opposition to Frederick II.
1278	First sailing of Italian galleys to Flanders.
1288	Battle of Worringen: Duke John of Brabant defeats his rivals for Limburg.
1296	Murder of Floris V, count of Holland and Zeeland.
1302	Battle of Kortrijk (or 'of the Golden Spurs'): Flemish guild militias and their allies defeat French knights.
1308	Henry VII of Luxembourg elected Holy Roman Emperor.
1312	Burning of the tower of St Martin's in Liège.
1323–28	Peasants' Revolt in Flanders.
1338	Edward III of England lands in Antwerp: Hundred Years War begins.
1345	House of Bavaria comes to power in Holland, Zeeland and Hainaut.
1346	Battle of Crécy: counts of Flanders and Luxembourg die.
1349–50	First outbreaks of plague in the Low Countries.
1355	Luxembourg becomes a duchy.
1356	Great Charter ('Joyous Entry') of Brabant.
1370	Destruction of Jewish community in Brabant.
1384	Flanders passes to Burgundian rule.
1421	St Elizabeth Flood around Dordrecht.
1426	University of Leuven opens.
1429	Namur passes to Burgundian rule.
1430	Brabant and Limburg pass to Burgundian rule.
1433	Jacqueline of Bavaria forced to abdicate: Holland, Zeeland and Hainaut pass to Burgundian rule.
1435	Boulogne and Picardy pass to Burgundian rule.
1443	Luxembourg passes to Burgundian rule.
1466	Philip the Good has 800 of the inhabitants of Dinant drowned in the Meuse for having hanged his son, Charles the Bold, in effigy.
1468	Wedding of Charles the Bold and Margaret of York. Charles the Bold's punitive expedition to Liège.
1469	Charles the Bold conquers Sundgau and Breisgau.
1473	Charles the Bold conquers Guelders. Edict of Thionville creates central institutions for all his lands.
1475	Charles the Bold conquers Lorraine and Bar.
1477	Death of Charles the Bold: Lorraine and Bar-sur-Seine, Guelders, Sundgau, Breisgau, Boulogne, Picardy and the Duchy of Burgundy lost to the House of Burgundy; Mary of Burgundy marries Maximilian of Habsburg.
c.1490	Antwerp replaces Bruges as commercial metropolis of Northern Europe.

1500	Future Charles V born.
1515	Prince Charles declared of age. Purchases lordship of Friesland.
1521	Tournai passes to Habsburg rule.
1523	First execution of Lutherans for their beliefs takes place in Brussels.
1528	Lordships of the bishops of Utrecht transferred to Habsburg rule.
1531	Administrative and legal reforms of Charles V.
1532	Witchcraft made a felony.
1535	Dutch Anabaptists seize power in Münster; persecution of Protestants and Anabaptists intensifies.
1540	Rebellion in Ghent.
1543	Guelders passes to Habsburg rule.
1555	Charles V retires; transfers rule to Philip II.
1559	New bishoprics established in the cities of the Low Countries; persecution of Protestants intensified.
1566	Iconoclastic Fury: churches vandalized; priests, monks and nuns murdered and maltreated.
1567	Duke of Alva arrives in the Low Countries; establishes the Council of Troubles (or 'Council of Blood') to suppress heresy and sedition.
1568	Beginning of the Dutch Revolt/Eighty Years War (to 1648).
1570	Mercator's *Theatrum Orbis Terrarum* published.
1572	Tenth Penny decreed; rebels seize Brielle and other towns in Holland and Zeeland.
1576	Pacification of Ghent seeks to establish *modus vivendi* between the loyal provinces and those under rebel control, and to expel foreign troops.
1579	Final breakdown of the Pacification of Ghent. Opposing Unions of Utrecht and of Arras formed.
1581	Union of Utrecht formally repudiates obedience to Philip II. Parma's reconquest of the Low Countries begins.
1584	William the Silent assassinated.
1585	Brussels and Antwerp return to royal rule. Amsterdam begins to replace Antwerp as the commercial metropolis of Northern Europe.
1585–91	Maurice of Nassau becomes stadholder in various provinces.
1590–97	Maurice of Nassau's campaigns secure the northern Netherlands for the United Provinces.
1598	Philip II bequeaths the Netherlands to Albert and Isabella, to revert to the king of Spain should either die childless.
1600	Battle of Nieuwpoort: Maurice of Nassau defeats royal forces but has to abandon his campaign in Flanders.
1602	Dutch East India Company formed.

1604	Ostend surrenders to the archdukes after a three-year siege.
1609	Beginning of Twelve Years Truce; United Provinces treated 'as though' sovereign.
1619	National Synod of Dort establishes strict Calvinism in Dutch Reformed Church. Johan van Oldenbarnevelt executed; Hugo Grotius imprisoned.
1621	Albert of Austria dies; the Netherlands revert to Philip IV of Spain. Twelve Years Truce lapses. Dutch West India Company formed.
1632	Crisis of Habsburg authority in the loyal provinces.
1635	France enters the war against the Habsburgs.
1640	Cornelius Jansen's *Augustinus* published.
1648	Treaty of Münster ends the Eighty Years War; sovereignty of Dutch Republic recognized. France still at war with the Spanish Monarchy.
1650	William II tries to seize power in the Republic; dies; 'First Stadholderless Period' begins (to 1672).
1652	First Anglo-Dutch War begins (to 1654).
1659	Treaty of the Pyrennees ends the Franco-Spanish War. French make territorial gains in the southern Low Countries.
1662	Dutch driven from Formosa.
1665	Second Anglo-Dutch War begins (to 1667).
1672	Third Anglo-Dutch War begins (to 1674); Louis XIV invades the Netherlands. Johan de Witt assassinated. William III proclaimed Stadholder.
1678	Treaty of Aix-la-Chapelle: Louis XIV gains further slices of the Habsburg Netherlands.
1688–91	William III invades the British Isles, displacing James II.
1695	Louis XIV bombards Brussels.
1700	Last Habsburg king of Spain dies; Louis XIV occupies the Habsburg Netherlands.
1702	William III dies; 'Second Stadholderless Period' begins (to 1747).
1703	War of the Spanish Succession (to 1713).
1715	Third Barrier Treaty.
1740	War of the Austrian Succession (to 1748).
1745	French invade Austrian Netherlands.
1747	French invade Republic; stadholderate restored, unified and made hereditary.
1751	Porcelain factory established at Tournai.
1759	Porcelain factory established at Weesp.
1773	Society of Jesus suppressed.
1780	Fourth Anglo-Dutch War begins (to 1784).
1781–87	Reforms of Joseph II.

1782	*Sara Burgerhart* published, first novel in Dutch.
1785	Patriot Revolution in the Dutch Republic (to 1787).
1788	Brabant Revolution in the Austrian Netherlands (to 1790).
1790	United States of Belgium proclaimed; Habsburg authority re-established.
1792	Beginning of French Revolutionary Wars. French invade Belgium.
1795	Belgium annexed to the French Republic; Batavian Republic proclaimed.
1798–99	Peasant revolts against French rule in Belgium and Luxembourg.
1803	Napoleonic Code promulgated.
1806	Louis Napoleon proclaimed King of Holland.
1810	The Kingdom of Holland annexed to Bonaparte's empire.
1811	Napoleonic Code comes into force in Holland.
1813	Napoleonic forces driven from most of the Low Countries.
1815	Proclamation of the United Kingdom of the Netherlands. Battle of Waterloo.
1818	Dutch slave trade abolished.
1825	Dutch control of Java re-established.
1830	Belgian Revolution; short war with the Netherlands.
1831	Belgian constitution ratified; short war with the Netherlands.
1835	Opening of the railway line Mechelen–Brussels, the first on the Continent.
1838	Treaty of London recognizes Belgian independence and guarantees neutrality.
1839	Luxembourg partitioned between Belgium and an independent Grand Duchy under William I of the Netherlands.
1840	William I abdicates.
1842	Luxembourg joins the *Zollverein* (German customs union).
1846	Founding of the Liberal Party in Belgium.
1848	Revolutionary rioting in Luxembourg. William II accepts parliamentary constitution and Liberal rule in the Netherlands.
1853	Restoration of Catholic hierarchy in the Netherlands; protests bring down Liberal government.
1856	Parliamentary government revoked in Grand Duchy of Luxembourg.
1858	Slavery abolished in Dutch East Indies.
1863	Slavery abolished in Dutch West Indies.
1866	Belgian Socialist organization Le Peuple affiliated to First International. First Dutch trade unions formed.
1867	Grand Duchy of Luxembourg withdrawn from German Union after Austro-Prussian War; parliamentary government restored.
1869	Dutch section of the First International founded.

1876	Opening of the North Sea Canal between Amsterdam and Ymuiden (begun in 1865).
1878	Foundation of the Anti-Revolutionary Party in the Netherlands.
1878–84	Intensification of 'School War' in Belgium and the Netherlands.
1881	Foundation of the Social Democratic Union in the Netherlands.
1884	Foundation of the Catholic Party in Belgium: Liberal hegemony broken.
1885	Foundation of the Belgian Labour Party. International Convention grants the Congo basin to Leopold II as the Congo Free State. Rijksmuseum opened in Amsterdam.
1891	Christian Democratic League founded in Belgium.
1897	Delft Conference of the International Co-Operative Alliance.
1898	Dutch and French languages given official parity in Belgium.
1899	First international peace conference at The Hague.
1903	Railway Strike in the Netherlands.
1905	Amsterdam Congress of the Second International.
1907	Second international peace conference at The Hague.
1908	Dutch destruction of Venezuelan fleet. Belgium annexes Congo Free State to end atrocious misgovernment.
1914	Belgium and Luxembourg invaded by the Germans; Dutch neutrality maintained.
1916	Foundation of Luxembourg Workers Union (Letzburger Arbechter-Verband).
1917	Universal manhood suffrage and proportional representation introduced in the Netherlands.
1918	End of the Great War. Dutch Communist Party founded.
1919	Female suffrage introduced in Luxembourg and the Netherlands; plural voting abolished in Belgium. Revolutionary agitation in Luxembourg and the Netherlands.
1920	Belgian Communist Party founded. Olympic Games held in Antwerp.
1921	Customs union of Belgium and Luxembourg.
1928	Olympic Games held in Amsterdam.
1932	Completion of the Zuider Zee 'enclosure' dike.
1934	Belgium and Luxembourg go off the gold standard.
1935	Monetary union of Belgium and Luxembourg. The Netherlands goes off the gold standard.
1940	Belgium, the Netherlands and Luxembourg invaded and occupied by the Germans (to 1945).
1942	Large-scale deportations of forced labourers and 'undesirables' begin.
1944	First agreements in principle for creation of Benelux. Liberation of most of Belgium and the southernmost parts of the Netherlands. German counter-offensive in the Ardennes.

1945	Liberation completed. International Court of Justice established in The Hague.
1947	Counter-insurgency campaign launched in Indonesia.
1948	First Benelux treaties. Belgian-French social security convention for cross-border workers. Belgian women fully enfranchised. Benelux countries, France and Britain sign Brussels Pact for mutual defence.
1949	Benelux countries are charter members of NATO and UNO. Independence of Indonesia.
1951	Leopold III abdicates after 'Royal Question' in Belgium.
1952	Benelux countries founder members of European Coal and Steel Community.
1953	Devastating floods in the Netherlands and coastal Flanders.
1957	Benelux countries founder members of Euratom and the E.E.C.
1958	Treaties for Benelux Economic Union ratified, to come into force 1960. World Expo in Brussels.
1960	Independence of Congo. Benelux Economic Union Treaties come into force.
1962	Independence of Rwanda and Burundi. Linguistic border fixed by law in Belgium. First Benelux agreements on cross-border co-operation in judicial and criminal matters.
1966	Public protests in Netherlands at Princess Beatrix's decision to marry a German.
1971	Eddy Merckx wins 54 races in one season.
1974	Luxembourg's Christian Social party out of office for the first time in over 50 years.
1975	Independence of Surinam.
1981	Last mine in Luxembourg closes.
1990	Constitutional crisis in Belgium when King Baudouin declines on grounds of conscience to ratify the legalization of induced abortion.
1992	Benelux countries signatories to Maastricht Treaty creating European Union.
1993	Regional devolution in Belgium. Belgian universal competency law on war crimes, crimes against humanity and genocide.
1995	Major floods in the Netherlands.
2000	Euthanasia legalized in the Netherlands.
2001	First same-sex civil weddings in the Netherlands.
2002	Benelux countries adopt Euro.

Select List of Dynasties and Rulers

MEDIEVAL COUNTS, DUKES AND PRINCE-BISHOPS

Counts of Flanders

864–79	Baldwin I, 'Iron Arm'
879–918	Baldwin II, 'the Bald'
918–65	Arnulf I, 'the Great' (with his son Baldwin III as co-ruler 958–62)
965–88	Arnulf II, 'the Younger'
988–1035	Baldwin IV 'the Bearded'
1035–67	Baldwin V, 'of Lille'
1067–70	Baldwin VI, 'of Mons' (personal union of Flanders and Hainaut, 1067–71)
1070–71	Arnulf III, 'the Unfortunate'
1071–93	Robert I, 'the Frisian'
1093–1111	Robert II, 'of Jerusalem'
1111–19	Baldwin VII, 'Hapkin'
1119–27	Charles the Good (son of Canute II of Denmark by Adela, daughter of Robert the Frisian)
1127–28	William Clito (great-grandson of Baldwin of Lille, and grandson of William I of England)
1128–68	Thierry of Alsace (grandson of Robert the Frisian, by Gertrude and Thierry II of Lorraine)
1168–91	Philip of Alsace
1191–94	Baldwin VIII (Baldwin V of Hainaut; ruled Flanders on behalf of his wife Margaret, daughter of Thierry of Alsace; stepped down in favour of his son at her death)
1194–1205	Baldwin IX, Emperor of Constantinople 1205–6 (personal union of the counties of Flanders and Hainaut)
1205–44	Joanna
1244–78	Margaret I

1278–1305 Guy of Dampierre (son of Margaret I and William of Dampierre)
1305–22 Robert (III) of Béthune
1322–46 Louis (I) of Nevers
1346–84 Louis (II) of Male
1384–1404 Philip the Bold (ruled Flanders on behalf of his wife, Margaret II)
1405 Margaret II
Union of Flanders with Burgundy. Margaret was succeeded by her son, John the Fearless of Burgundy.

Counts and Margraves of Namur

981–1011 Albert I
1013–18 Robert
1021–62 Albert II
1063–1102 Albert III
1102–39 Godfrey
1139–96 Henry the Blind (also count of Luxembourg, Longwy, Durbuy and Laroche)
1188–95 Baldwin V of Hainaut (Henry the Blind's designated heir; seized the county when Henry changed his will)
1195–1212 Philip I, margrave of Namur (in 1195 Namur became a marquisate)
1212–16 Yolanda (married Peter of Courtenay, Emperor of Constantinople)
1216–26 Philip II
1226–29 Henry II
1229–37 Margaret of Courtenay (the emperor Frederick II invested the power of margrave first in Ferrand of Portugal, count of Flanders, as her guardian 1229–32; then in Henry of Vianden, her husband, 1232–37)
1237–63 Baldwin of Courtenay, Emperor of Constantinople; sold the marquisate to Guy of Dampierre for £20,000
1263–98 Guy of Dampierre (also count of Flanders 1278–1305)
1298–1330 John of Dampierre (younger son of Guy of Dampierre by his second marriage)
1330–35 John II
1335–36 Guy II
1336–37 Philip III
1337–91 William I
1391–1418 William II
1418–29 John III
In 1421 John III sold his inheritance to Philip the Good, duke of Burgundy; upon his death Namur passed to Burgundian rule

Counts of Holland

c.916–39	Dirk I (also called Diederik, Theoderic, etc.)
939–88	Dirk II
988–93	Arnulf
993–1039	Dirk III
1039–49	Dirk IV
1049–61	Floris I
1061–91	Dirk V
1091–1121	Floris II, 'the Fat' (the first of his line to take the title 'Count of Holland')
1121–57	Dirk VI
1157–90	Floris III
1190–1203	Dirk VII
1203–13	succession disputed between Ada (daughter of Dirk VII) and William (his brother)
1213–22	William I
1222–34	Floris IV
1234–56	William II, King of the Romans 1247
1256–96	Floris V
1296–99	John I

John I was succeeded by his cousin, the Count of Hainaut, who united the two counties.

Counts of Hainaut

In 1051 Baldwin of Mons, soon to be count of Flanders, married Richildis, heiress of Hainaut, and ruled the county in his wife's right until 1070. They were succeeded by their son Arnulf, 1070–71, on whose death Flanders passed to his uncle and Hainaut to his brother.

1071–98	Baldwin II
1098–1120	Baldwin III
1120–71	Baldwin IV
1171–95	Baldwin V

Baldwin V of Hainaut ruled Namur on behalf of his uncle from 1188 and became Baldwin VIII of Flanders in 1191; on his death Flanders and Hainaut were united until the death of Margaret I in 1278 (see Counts of Flanders above) but Namur passed to a younger son. In Hainaut, Margaret was succeeded by her grandson, John of Avesnes, who also became count of Holland in 1299, uniting the counties of Hainaut and Holland.

Counts of Holland and Hainaut

1299–1304	John (II) (son of John of Avesnes by Aleidis, daughter of Floris IV)

1304–37	William III and I 'the Good'
1337–45	William IV and II
1345–54/6	Margaret (abdicated in Holland 1354 in favour of her son)
1354/6–58	William V and III (son of Emperor Louis IV by Margaret; deposed; d. 1389)
1358–89	regency of Albert (brother of William)
1389–1404	Albert
1404–17	William VI and IV
1417–33	Jacqueline (abdicated; d. 1436)

Union of Holland and Hainaut with Burgundy.

Counts and Dukes of Luxembourg

963–98	Sigfrid
998–1026	Henry I (also duke of Bavaria 1004–09 and 1017–26)
1026–47	Henry II (also duke of Bavaria 1042–47)
1047–59	Gilbert
1059–86	Conrad I
1086–96	Henry III
1096–1131	William
1131–36	Conrad II
1136–96	Henry IV (grandson of Conrad I; also count of Namur)
1196–1247	Ermesind
1247–81	Henry V, the Great (son of Ermesind and Walram III, duke of Limburg)
1281–88	Henry VI
1288–1310	Henry VII
1310–46	John the Blind (also king of Bohemia 1310–46)
1346–53	Charles (abdicated; also king of the Romans and king of Bohemia 1346–78)
1353–83	Wenceslas I (also duke of Brabant 1355–83; first ruler of Luxembourg to be styled duke of Luxembourg)
1383–1419	Wenceslas II. In 1415 Wenceslas pawned Luxembourg to his niece, Elizabeth of Görlitz, widow of Anthony of Burgundy, duke of Brabant. She remained acting duchess of Luxembourg until her death in 1443, when the duchy passed to Burgundian rule. Throughout this time hereditary title passed through another branch of the family.
1419–37	Sigismund (also king of Hungary 1387, king of the Romans 1410, king of Bohemia 1419. Sigismund's daughter Elizabeth married Albert of Austria.)
1437–39	Albert of Austria (in his wife's right; his daughter, Anne, married William of Saxony.)

1439–43   William of Saxony (in his wife's right; abdicated)
Union of Luxembourg with Burgundy.

Lord-Bishops of Utrecht

The see of Utrecht was established in 695 by St Willibrord. In the tenth century
a temporal lordship became attached to the see.

918–75	Baldric
976–90	Folcmar
990–95	Baldwin
995–1010	Ansfred
1010–26	Adelbold
1027–54	Bernold
1054–76	William
1076–99	Conrad
1100–12	Burchard
1114–27	Godebald
1128–39	Andrew of Cuyck
1139–50	Hartbert
1150–56	Herman of Horne
1156–78	Godfrey of Rhenen
1178–96	Baldwin of Holland
1196–97	Arnold of Isenburg (disputed election)
1196–97	Theoderic of Holland (disputed election)
1198–1212	Theoderic of Ahr
1212–15	Otto of Guelders
1216–27	Otto of Lippe
1227–33	Wilbrand of Oldenburg
1234–49	Otto of Holland
1249–50	Goswin of Randerath (disputed election)
1249–67	Henry of Vianden (disputed election)
1268–90	John of Nassau
1291–96	John of Sierck
1296–1301	William of Berthout
1301–17	Guy of Avesnes
1317–22	Frederick of Sierck
1322	Jacob of Oudshoorn
1322–40	John of Diest
1341–42	Nicholas of Caputino
1342–64	John of Arkel
1364–71	John of Virneburg
1371	Zweder of Oeterlo
1371–78	Arnold of Horne

1378–93	Floris of Wevelinkhoven
1393–1423	Frederik of Blankenheim
1423–55	Rudolph of Diepholt (disputed election)
1423–33	Zweder of Culemborg (disputed election)
1434–50	Walraven of Meurs (disputed election)
1455–56	Gijsbrecht of Brederode
1455–96	David of Burgundy
1496–1517	Frederik of Baden
1517–24	Philip of Burgundy
1524–28	Henry II of Bavaria (temporal lordship transferred to Charles V)

Prince-Bishops of Liège

The see of Liège was established in 706 by St Hubert, as the successor to the bishoprics of Tongeren and Maastricht. Under Notger, the bishops became lords of a principality within their wider ecclesiastical jurisdiction. In some cases dates of rule overlap by a year or two because an ailing or ageing bishop's successor might be appointed within his lifetime.

972–1008	Notger
1008–18	Balderik
1021–25	Walbodo
1025–27	Durand
1025–37	Reginard
1037–42	Nithard
1042–48	Wazo
1048–75	Theoduin
1075–91	Henry of Verdun
1091–1119	Otbert
1119–21	Frederik of Namur
1121–28	Adalbert of Leuven
1128–34	Alexander of Jülich (deposed)
1134–45	Adalbert of Chiny
1145–64	Henry of Leez
1165–67	Alexander of Oeren
1167–91	Rudolph of Zähringen
1191–92	Albert of Leuven (murdered)
1193–95	Simon of Limburg
1194–1200	Albert of Cuyck
1200–29	Hugh of Pierrepont
1229–38	John of Eppes
1238–39	William of Savoy
1240–46	Robert of Thourotte
1247–74	Henry of Guelders (deposed)

1274–81	John of Edingen
1282–91	John of Flanders
1291–96	*vacant*
1296–1301	Hugh of Châlons
1301–02	Adolph of Waldeck
1303–12	Thibaut of Bar
1313–44	Adolph de la Marck
1345–64	Engelbert de la Marck (translated to Cologne)
1364–78	John of Arkel
1378–89	Arnold of Horne
1389–1418	John of Bavaria (never ordained; resigned and married Elizabeth of Görlitz)
1418–19	John of Wallenrode
1419–56	John of Heinsberg (resigned)
1456–82	Louis of Bourbon
1482–84	*vacant*
1484–1505	John of Horne
1505–38	Everhard de la Marck
1538–45	Cornelius of Bergen op Zoom
1544–57	George of Austria
1557–65	Robert of Bergen op Zoom
1564–80	Gerard van Groesbeek
1581–1612	Ernest of Bavaria
1612–50	Ferdinand of Bavaria
1650–88	Maximilian-Henry of Bavaria
1688–94	Jean-Louis d'Elderen
1694–1723	Joseph-Clement of Bavaria
1724–43	Georges-Louis of Bergues
1744–63	John Theodore of Bavaria
1763–71	Charles d'Oultremont
1772–84	Franz Carl von Velbrück
1784–92	Caesar Constant van Hoensbroek
1792–94	François de Méan (French annexation; archbishop of Mechelen 1817–31)

Dukes of Brabant

In 1106 the duke of Lower Lorraine was deposed and the duchy was awarded to the counts of Leuven, who became dukes of Brabant

1106–28	Godfrey the Bearded (deposed, d. 1139)
1128–39	Walram II of Limburg
1139–42	Godfrey II
1142–90	Godfrey III
1190–1235	Henry I
1235–48	Henry II

1248–61	Henry III
1261–67	Henry IV
1267–94	John I, the Victorious (united the duchies of Brabant and Limburg in 1289)
1294–1312	John II
1312–55	John III
1355–1404	Joanna (her husband Wenceslas, duke of Luxemburg, ruled in her right until his death in 1383; Joanna abdicated in 1404 and died in 1406)
1404–06	regency of Margaret (sister of Joanna)
1406–15	Anthony
1415–27	John IV
1427–30	Philip of St Pol

Philip of St Pol was succeeded by his nephew, Philip the Good of Burgundy. Union of Brabant with Burgundy.

Counts and Dukes of Guelders

The earliest records of the dynasty are very unreliable, and names are given from the time of Otto I, who united Guelders, Zutphen, the Veluwe and the Bommelerwaard under his rule.

1184–1207	Otto I
1207–29	Gerard IV
1229–71	Otto II
1271–1318	Reinald I (went insane; declared incapable of rule in 1318; d. 1326)
1318–43	Reinald II, 'the Black' (styled Duke from 1339)
1343–61	Reinald III (deposed by his brother Edward in 1361)
1361–71	Edward
1371	Reinald III (restored; died shortly afterwards)
1371–79	Machteld (disputed succession; deposed by her nephew)
1371–1402	William I (disputed succession)
1402–24	Reinald IV
1423–65	Arnold of Egmond (resigned)
1465–71	Adolph of Berge (deposed by Charles the Bold)
1471–73	Arnold of Egmond (restored)
(1473–77	Charles the Bold, duke of Burgundy, conquers Guelders)
1477	Adolph of Egmond
1477–79	Catherine of Egmond (deposed)
(1479–92	Guelders under Burgundian rule)
1492–1538	Charles of Egmond
1538–43	William II

William II resigned the duchy to Charles V in 1543. Guelders became part of the Habsburg Netherlands.

BURGUNDY AND HABSBURG

From 1384 onwards the Valois dukes of Burgundy came to rule an increasing number of the counties and duchies of the Low Countries.

House of Valois

Dates are for rule as duke of Burgundy.

1363–1404	Philip the Bold (married Margaret, heiress of Flanders; ruled Flanders in her right from 1382)
1404–19	John the Fearless (also count of Flanders from 1405)
1419–67	Philip the Good (also count of Flanders; marquis of Namur from 1429, duke of Brabant and Limburg from 1430, count of Holland, Zeeland and Hainaut from 1433, duke of Luxembourg from 1443)
1467–77	Charles the Bold (also Flanders, Namur, Brabant, etc.)
1477–82	Mary of Burgundy (Flanders etc.; the Duchy of Burgundy itself was lost to France in 1477)

House of Habsburg (Spanish branch)

1482–1506	Philip the Fair (son of Mary of Burgundy and Emperor Maximilian I; married Joanna, heiress of Spain; king of Castile in his wife's right from 1504)
1506–55	Charles (king of Spain 1516–56; Emperor 1519–58; abdicated; d. 1559)
1555–98	Philip II of Spain
1598–1621	Albert and Isabella (Philip II bequeathed the Low Countries to his daughter Isabella as her dowry, to revert to the Spanish Monarchy should she or her husband die without issue, while the rest of his territories passed to Philip III of Spain)
1621–65	Philip IV of Spain (ceded independence to the United Provinces, 1648)
1665–1700	Charles II of Spain
(1703–13	War of the Spanish Succession)

House of Habsburg (Austrian branch)

1713–40	Charles VI
1740–80	Maria-Theresia
1780–90	Joseph II
1790–92	Leopold II
1792–97	Francis II

STADHOLDERS OF THE HOUSE OF ORANGE-NASSAU IN THE UNITED PROVINCES

From 1572 the stadholders played an important role in the administrative, military and diplomatic life of the United Provinces. Sovereign power resided with the representative assembly of each province. From 1584 to 1747 Holland and Zeeland on the one hand, and Friesland on the other, had different stadholders. Drenthe and Groningen sometimes shared a stadholder with Friesland, sometimes with the other provinces.

Holland and Zeeland

Utrecht, Overijssel and Gelderland generally (but not always) had the same stadholder as Holland and Zeeland. To a lesser extent the same was true of Drenthe and Groningen.

1572–84	William the Silent
1585–1625	Maurice (also Drenthe and Groningen from 1620)
1625–47	Frederick Henry (also Drenthe and Groningen from 1640)
1647–50	William II (also Drenthe and Groningen)
1650–72	*First Stadholderless Period*
1672–1702	William III (styled king of England from 1689; stadholder of Drenthe from 1696; last of the house in the direct line)
1702–47	*Second Stadholderless Period*
1747–51	William IV (see Willem Friso, below)
1751–95	William V (see below)

Friesland

1584–1620	Willem Lodewijk (also Drenthe from 1593, Groningen from 1595)
1620–32	Ernst Casimir (also Drenthe and Groningen from 1625)
1632–40	Hendrik Casimir (also Drenthe and Groningen)
1640–64	Willem Frederik (also Drenthe and Groningen from 1650)
1664–96	Hendrik Casimir (also Drenthe and Groningen)
1696–1711	Johan Willem Friso (also Groningen)
1711–51	Willem Friso (also Groningen from 1718, Gelderland and Drenthe from 1722, Holland, Zeeland and Utrecht from 1747 as William IV)

William IV was proclaimed hereditary Stadholder of the Republic in 1747 and was succeeded by his son, William V, in 1751. In 1795 the Batavian Republic was proclaimed. In 1806 Napoleon Bonaparte proclaimed his brother, Louis, king of Holland, but in 1810 the Kingdom of Holland was annexed to France. In 1813 the son of William V became Sovereign Prince of the Netherlands as William I, and he was proclaimed king of the United Netherlands in 1815.

KINGDOM OF THE NETHERLANDS

House of Orange-Nassau

1815–40	William I (abdicated; d. 1843)
1840–49	William II
1849–90	William III
1890–1948	Wilhelmina (in exile 1940–45; abdicated; d. 1962)
1948–80	Juliana (abdicated; d. 2003)
1980–	Beatrix

KINGDOM OF BELGIUM

House of Saxe-Coburg-Gotha

1831–65	Leopold I
1865–1909	Leopold II (also sovereign of the Congo Free State 1885–1908)
1909–34	Albert I
1934–51	Leopold III (prisoner 1940–45; in exile 1945–50; abdicated; d. 1982)
1951–93	Baudouin/Boudewijn
1993–	Albert II

GRAND DUCHY OF LUXEMBOURG

House of Nassau

At the break-up of the United Kingdom of the Netherlands in 1830, William I retained a large part of the Grand Duchy of Luxembourg. In 1890, at the death of William III without male issue, the Grand Duchy passed to Adolph of Nassau.

1890–1905	Adolph
1905–12	William IV
1912–19	Marie Adelaide (abdicated; d. 1924)
1919–64	Charlotte (in exile 1940–45; abdicated; d. 1985)
1964–2000	Jean (abdicated)
2000–	Henri

Selected Further Reading
in English

BOOKS TREATING MORE THAN ONE PERIOD

J. C. H. Blom and E. Lamberts (eds), *History of the Low Countries*, trans. James C. Kennedy (Oxford, 1999).

Britain and the Netherlands, a series of volumes containing papers delivered to the Anglo-Dutch Historical Conference.

Patricia Carson, *The Fair Face of Flanders* (Tielt, 1995).

Douwe Fokkema and Frans Grijzenhout (eds), *Dutch Culture in a European Perspective 5. Accounting for the Past: 1650–2000* (Basingstoke, 2004).

Jonathan Israel and Reinier Salverda (eds), *Dutch Jewry: Its History and Secular Culture (1500–2000)* (Leiden, New York and Cologne, 2002).

A. M. Lambert, *The Making of the Dutch Landscape* (London and New York, 1971).

Sheila D. Muller, *Dutch Art. An Encyclopedia* (New York, 1996).

James Newcomer, *The Grand Duchy of Luxembourg: The Evolution of Nationhood* (Lanham, MD, 1984).

R. W. Unger, *A History of Brewing in Holland 900–1900* (Leiden, 2001).

H. Van der Wee and E. Cauwenberghe (eds), *Productivity of Land and Agricultural Innovation in the Low Countries* (Leuven, 1978).

J. A. van Houtte, *An Economic History of the Low Countries, 800–1800* (London, 1977).

ROMAN TIMES

Julius Caesar, *Gallic War*, Books 1–2, 5–6 (English translations in Loeb Classical Library, Pengiun Classics, etc.).

Ton Derks, *Gods, Temples and Ritual Practices: The Transformation of Religious Ideas and Values in Roman Gaul* (Amsterdam Archaeological Studies 2, 1998).

John F. Drinkwater, *Roman Gaul: The Three Provinces* (London, 1998).

Tacitus, *Annals*, Book 4, chs 72–3; Book 11, chs 18–20; *Histories* Books 4–5 (English translations in Loeb Classical Library).

Edith Mary Wightman, *Roman Trier and the Treveri* (London, 1970).
Edith Mary Wightman, *Gallia Belgica* (London, 1985).
Greg Woolf, *Becoming Roman: The Origins of Provincial Civilization in Gaul* (Cambridge, 1998).

THE MIDDLE AGES

Patricia Carson, *James Van Artevelde: The Man from Ghent* (Ghent, 1980).
Geert H. M. Claassens and David F. Johnson (eds), *King Arthur in the Medieval Low Countries* (Leuven, 2000).
E. Colledge (ed.), *Reynard the Fox and Other Mediaeval Netherlands Secular Literature* (London, 1967).
Jean Froissart, *Chronicles*, ed. and trans. by John Jolliffe (London, 2001).
Galbert of Bruges, *The Murder of Charles the Good, Count of Flanders*, trans. and ed. James Bruce Ross (reissued Toronto, 1991).
F. L. Ganshof, *Feudalism* (reissued Toronto, 1996).
Hadewijch, *The Complete Works*, trans. by Columba Hart, with a preface by P. Mommaers (Mahwah, NJ, 1980).
Ellen Kittell and Mary Suydam (eds), *The Texture of Society: Medieval Women in the Southern Low Countries* (Basingstoke, 2004)
Henry Stephen Lucas, *The Low Countries and the Hundred Years' War, 1326–1347* (Philadelphia, 1976).
Jill Mann (ed. and trans.), *Ysengrimus* (Leiden, 1987).
David Nicholas, *The Metamorphosis of a Medieval City: Ghent in the Age of the Arteveldes, 1302–1390* (Lincoln and London, 1987).
David Nicholas, *Medieval Flanders* (London and New York, 1992).
Henri Pirenne, *Early Democracies in the Low Countries: Urban Society and Political Conflict in the Middle Ages and the Renaissance* (New York, 1963).
William of Rubruck, *The Mission of Friar William of Rubruck: His Journey to the Court of the Great Khan Möngke 1253–1255*, trans. by Peter Jackson, with introduction, notes and appendices by Peter Jackson and David Morgan (London, 1990).
Walter Simons, *Cities of Ladies: Beguine Communities in the Medieval Low Countries, 1200–1565* (Philadelphia, 2001).
R. C. Van Caenegem, *Law, History, the Low Countries and Europe* (London, 1994).
Adriaan Verhulst, *The Rise of Cities in North-West Europe* (Cambridge, 1999).

THE BURGUNDIAN PERIOD

C. A. J. Armstrong, *England, France and Burgundy in the Fifteenth Century* (London, 1983).
Peter Arnade, *Realms of Ritual: Burgundian Ceremony and Civic Life in Late Medieval Ghent* (New York, 1996).

Caroline Barron and Nigel Saul (eds), *England and the Low Countries in the Late Middle Ages* (Stroud, 1995).

Wim Blockmans and Walter Prevenier, *The Promised Lands: The Low Countries under Burgundian Rule, 1369–1530*, trans. by Elizabeth Fackelman, trans. revised and ed. by Edward Peters (Philadelphia, 1999).

Andrew Brown, *The Valois Dukes of Burgundy* (pamphlet; Oxford, 2001).

Dirk De Vos, *The Flemish Primitives* (Antwerp, 2002).

Johan Huizinga, *The Waning of the Middle Ages: A Study of the Forms of Life, Thought and Art in France and the Netherlands in the Fourteenth and Fifteenth Centuries*, trans. by F. Hopman (Penguin Books); alternatively as *The Autumn of the Middle Ages*, trans. by R.J. Payton and U. Mammitzsch (Chicago, 1996).

H. G. Koenigsberger, *Monarchies, States Generals and Parliaments: The Netherlands in the Fifteenth and Sixteenth Centuries* (Cambridge, 2001).

Thomas Kren and Scot McKendrik (eds), *Illuminating the Renaissance: The Triumph of Flemish Manuscript Painting in Europe* (Los Angeles, 2003)

Gerard Nijsten, *In the Shadow of Burgundy: The Court of Guelders in the Late Middle Ages*, trans. by Tanis Guest (Cambridge, 2004).

R. R. Post, *The Modern Devotion* (Leiden, 1968).

Walter Prevenier and Wim Blockmans, *The Burgundian Netherlands* (Cambridge, 1986).

Graeme Small, *George Chastelain and the Shaping of Valois Burgundy: Political and Historical Culture at Court in the Fifteenth Century* (Woodbridge, 1997).

P. Stabel, *Dwarfs among Giants: The Flemish Urban Network in the Late Middle Ages* (Leuven and Apeldoorn, 1997).

F. P. van Oostrom, *Court and Culture: Dutch Literature, 1350–1450*, trans. by Arnold Pomerans (Berkeley, Los Angeles and Oxford, 1992).

Richard Vaughan, *Valois Bugundy* (London, 1975), and other works by the same author.

Christine Weightman, *Margaret of York, Duchess of Burgundy, 1446–1503* (Stroud and New York, 1993).

THE EARLY MODERN PERIOD

Anonymous, *The Dutch Revolt: A Chronicle of the First Ten Years by an Anonymous Nun of 's-Hertogenbosch*, trans. and annot. by Paul Arblaster (Oxford, 2001).

M. S. Anderson, *The War of the Austrian Succession* (London, 1995).

Paul Arblaster, *Antwerp & the World: Richard Verstegan and the International Culture of Catholic Reformation* (Leuven, 2004).

C. D. Bangs, *Arminius: A Study in the Dutch Reformation* (Nashville, 1971).

A. E. Bell, *Christian Huygens and the Development of Science in the Seventeenth Century* (London, 1950).

C. R. Boxer, *The Dutch Seaborne Empire, 1600–1800* (London, 1990) and other works by the same author.

SELECTED FURTHER READING

E. Buijssen, *Between Fantasy and Reality: Seventeenth-Century Dutch Landscape Painting* (Baarn, 1993).
Charles Howard Carter, *The Secret Diplomacy of the Habsburgs* (New York and London, 1964).
Rudolf Dekker, *Childhood, Memory and Autobiography in Holland: From the Golden Age to Romanticism* (Basingstoke, 1999)
J. den Tex, *Oldenbarnevelt* (2 vols, Cambridge, 1973).
Jan de Vries, *The Dutch Rural Economy in the Golden Age* (New Haven, CT, 1974).
Henrietta Drake-Brockman, *Voyage to Disaster* (Nedlands, Australia 2000).
Alastair Duke, *Reformation and Revolt in the Low Countries* (London and New York, 2003)
Florike Egmond, *Underworlds: Organized Crime in the Netherlands, 1650–1800* (Cambridge, 1993).
Willem Frijhoff and Gordon Clark (eds), *Dutch Culture in a European Perspective, 1. 1650: Hard-Won Unity* (Basingstoke, 2004).
Pieter Geyl, *History of the Dutch-Speaking Peoples, 1555–1648* (reissued Phoenix Press, 2001).
M. P. Gutman, *War and Rural Life in the Early Modern Low Countries* (Princeton, 1980).
Craig Harline and Eddy Put, *A Bishop's Tale* (New Haven, CT, 2000), and other works by Craig Harline.
Jonathan I. Israel, *The Dutch Republic: Its Rise, Greatness and Fall, 1477–1806* (Oxford, 1995) and other works by the same author.
M. C. Jacob and W.Mijnhardt (eds), *The Dutch Republic in the Eighteenth Century* (Ithaca, NY, 1992).
W. E. Keeney, *Dutch Anabaptist Thought and Practice, 1539–1564* (Nieuwkoop, 1968).
Wim Klooster, *The Dutch in the Americas* (Providence, RI, 1997).
J. Lucassen, *Dutch Long Distance Trade Migration, 1600–1900* (Amsterdam, 1991).
J. Lucassen and C. A. Davids (eds), *A Miracle Mirrored: The Dutch Republic in European Perspective* (Cambridge and New York, 1995).
Philip Mansel, *Prince of Europe: The Life of Charles-Joseph de Ligne (1735–1814)* (London, 2003).
Walter S. Melion, *Shaping the Netherlandish Canon: Karel van Mander's 'Schilder-Boeck'* (Chicago, 1991).
Gerhard Oestreich, *Neostoicism and the Early Modern State* (Cambridge, 1982).
Geoffrey Parker, *The Army of Flanders and the Spanish Road, 1567–1659: The Logistics of Victory and Defeat in the Low Countries' Wars* (Cambridge, 1990).
Geoffrey Parker, *The Dutch Revolt*, Revised edition (London, 1985) and other works by the same author.
R. Po-Chia Hsia and Henk van Nierop (eds), *Calvinism and Religious Toleration in the Dutch Golden Age* (Cambridge and New York, 2002).
Johannes Menne Postma, *The Dutch in the Atlantic Slave Trade, 1600–1815* (Cambridge, 1990).
J. L. Price, *Dutch Society, 1588–1713* (New York, 2000).

264

Herbert H. Rowen, *The Princes of Orange* (Cambridge, 1988).

Simon Schama, *The Embarrassment of Riches: An Interpretation of Dutch Culture in the Golden Age* (New York, 1987).

P. Sonnino, *Louis XIV and the Origins of the Dutch War* (Cambridge, 1988).

R. A. Stradling, *The Armada of Flanders: Spanish Maritime Policy and European War, 1568–1668* (Cambridge, 1992).

W. Ph. te Brake, *Regents and Rebels* (Cambridge, MA, 1989).

Werner Thomas and Luc Duerloo (eds), *Albert & Isabella, 1598–1621: Essays* (Turnhout, 1998).

J. D. Tracy, *Holland under Habsburg Rule, 1506–1566: The Formation of a Body Politic* (Berkeley, CA, 1990) and other works by the same author.

Herman van der Wee, *The Rise of the Antwerp Market* (3 vols, The Hague, 1963).

A. Th. van Deursen, *Plain Lives in a Golden Age*, trans. by M. Ultee (Cambridge, 1991).

Martin van Gelderen, *The Political Thought of the Dutch Revolt, 1555–1590* (Cambridge, 1992).

Henk F. K. Van Nierop, *The Nobility of Holland: From Knights to Regents, 1500–1650* (Cambridge, 1993).

C. D. van Strien, *British Travellers in Holland during the Stuart Period* (Leiden, 1993).

J. L. van Zanden, *The Rise and Decline of Holland's Economy* (Manchester, 1993).

G. K. Waite, *David Joris and Dutch Anabaptism, 1524–1543* (Ontario, 1990).

CONTEMPORARY HISTORY

Anonymous, *Belgium. The Official Account of What Happened 1939–1940* (London, 1941).

Jan Bank and Maartine van Buuren (eds), *Dutch Culture in a European Perspective 3. 1900: The Age of Bourgeois Culture* (Basingstoke, 2004).

A. J. Barnouw, *Holland Under Queen Wilhelmina* (New York, 1923) and other works by the same author.

Marina Boudart, Michel Boudart and René Bryssinck, *Modern Belgium* (Palo Alto, CA, 1990).

Martin Conway, *Collaboration in Belgium. Léon Degrelle and the Rexist Movement, 1940–1944* (New Haven and London, 1993).

W. P. Coolhaas and G. J. Schutte, *Critical Survey of Studies on Dutch Colonial History* (The Hague, 1980).

Léon Degrelle, *Campaign in Russia* (Bristol, 1985).

M. R. L. Foot, *SOE in the Low Countries* (London, 2001).

Anne Frank, *The Diary of a Young Girl*, ed. by Otto H. Frank and Mirjam Pressler, trans. by Susan Massotty (London, 1997).

Christopher Hibbert, *Arnhem* (London, 2003).

Robin L. Hogg, *Structural Rigidities and Policy Inertia in Inter-War Belgium* (Brussels, 1986).

John Horne and Alan Kramer, *German Atrocities, 1914: A History of Denial* (New Haven, CT, 2001).

Joost Kloek and Wijnand Mijnhardt (eds), *Dutch Culture in a European Perspective 2. 1800: Blueprints for a National Community* (Basingstoke, 2004).

E. H. Kossmann, *The Low Countries, 1780–1940* (Oxford, 1978).

C. Lis, *Social Change and the Labouring Poor: Antwerp 1770–1860* (New Haven, CT, 1986).

J. Mokyr, *Industrialization in the Low Countries 1795–1850* (New Haven, CT, 1976).

E. D. Morel, *King Leopold's Rule in Africa* (London, 1904) and other works by the same author.

Janet L. Polasky, *Revolution in Brussels, 1787–1793* (New Hampshire, 1987).

Simon Schama, *Patriots and Liberators: Revolution in the Netherlands 1780–1813* (London, 1977).

Kees Schuyt and Ed Taverne (eds), *Dutch Culture in a European Perspective 4. 1950: Prosperity and Welfare* (Basingstoke, 2004).

B. Seebohm Rowntree, *Land & Labour: Lessons from Belgium* (London, 1910).

William Z. Shetter, *The Netherlands in Perspective: The Dutch Way of Organizing a Society and its Setting* (Utrecht, 2002).

H. M. Stanley, *The Congo* (2 vols, London, 1885–86).

Arnold J. Toynbee, *The German Terror in Belgium* (London, 1917).

Vincent Viaene, *Belgium and the Holy See from Gregory XVI to Pius IX (1831–1859). Catholic Revival, Society and Politics in 19th-century Europe* (Brussels, 2001).

W. H. James Weale, *Belgium, Aix-la-Chapelle and Cologne: An Entirely New Guide Book for Travellers* (London, 1859).

Gordon L. Weil, *The Benelux Nations: The Politics of Small-Country Democracies* (New York and London, 1970).

Index

Aachen (Aix-la-Chapelle), 34, 35
   Treaty of (1668), 157, 160, 246
   Treaty of (1748), 164
Aalst, town in East Flanders, 50, 195
Aardenburg, Roman site in West
   Flanders, 20
abbeys, *see* religious houses and
   orders
Abjuration, Act of (1581), 126–7
abortion, induced, legalized, 237–8
Aceh, region of Indonesia, 207
Acre, city in Middle East, 48, 68–9
Ada (d. 1206), Scottish princess,
   82–3
Ada, heiress of Holland (*c.*1203), 70,
   252
Adalbert, saint, (d. 740), 39
Adam de la Halle (d. 1288), medieval
   playwright, 87
Adams, William, 17th-century
   navigator, 135
Adamson, John, 16th-century
   mercenary leader, 123
Adela, daughter of Robert the Frisian,
   queen to Canute II of
   Denmark, 51, 250
Adelbold, bishop of Utrecht
   (1010–26), 40, 254
Adolph of Waldeck, bishop of Liège
   (1301–2), 85, 256
Adrian of Utrecht, later Pope Adrian
   VI (1522–3), 109, 113, 119
Aduard, Cistercian abbey, 63
Aduatuci, Belgic tribe, 12–3
Aerssen, Cornelis van (1637–88),
   159
Aetius (d. 454), Roman general, 25–6
Affligem, Benedictine monastery in
   Brabant, 45
Africa, 13, 26, 48, 102, 132, 136–7,
   171, 194, 205, 207–9, 211,
   215, 235–6

Agricola, Rudolph, 15th-century
   humanist, 109
agriculture, 7, 8, 10–11, 24–5, 42–3,
   53, 59–62, 90, 157, 164, 169,
   177, 194–5
Agrippa, Heinrich Cornelius
   (1486–1535), occultist, 146
Aix-la-Chapelle, *see* Aachen
Alan of Lille (d. 1203), philosopher
   and theologian, 66, 75
Alberdingk Thijm, Jozef (1820–89),
   writer, 185
Alberic, 8th-century bishop of
   Utrecht, 32
Albert I, Holy Roman Emperor
   (1298–1308), 85
Albert I, king of the Belgians
   (1909–34), 210–11, 215, 260
Albert of Bavaria, count of Holland
   and Hainaut (1389–1404), 96,
   253
Albert of Cuyck, bishop of Liège
   (1194–1200), 69, 255
Albert of Leuven, bishop of Liège
   (1191–2), 69, 255
Albert (1559–1621), archduke of
   Austria, 128
   see also Albert and Isabella
Albert and Isabella, 'the Archdukes',
   co-sovereigns of the Habsburg
   Netherlands (1598–1621),
   129–31, 141–3, 151, 154,
   245–6, 258
Albertus Magnus (*c.*1200–80),
   philosopher and theologian, 75
alchemy, 146
Alcuin (*c.*735–804), English monk,
   32
Aldgisl, 7th-century Frisian king, 31
Alexander III, king of Scotland
   (1249–86), 82
Alexander the Great, 87, 100

Alfonso (d. 1284), English prince, 82
Alfred the Great, king of Wessex
    (871–99), 36
Alkmaar, town in Holland, 84, 173
All Saints' Flood (1 November
    1570), 122
Alliance of Nivelles (1308), 92
Almere, 62
    see also Flevo, Zuider Zee,
    IJsselmeer
almsgiving, see poor relief
almshouses, 176
altarpieces, 104–5, 112
alum, 58, 102, 111
Alva, Don Fernando Alvarez de
    Toledo (1507–82), duke of,
    121–5, 245
Amandus (d. c.675), apostle of
    Flanders, 28–9
Ambiorix, ancient Belgic tribal
    leader, 13, 19
Amboina (Ambon), Indonesian
    island, 135
Ambrose (c.339–97), bishop of
    Milan, 24
Americas, 112, 120, 132, 134–7,
    151–2, 159, 167–9, 186, 194,
    207, 230, 247
Amersfoort, 112, 227
Amstel, lord of, see Gijsbrecht
Amstel, river and district in Holland,
    62, 114, 166
Amsterdam, 5, 62, 94, 106, 111,
    114–19, 133–4, 138, 140,
    145–50, 155–6, 163–4, 173,
    178, 185, 190, 192, 196, 203,
    225, 227, 232, 234, 245, 248
Amsterdam South (urban
    development project), 217
Atheneum Illustre (1632), 148,
    181
Central Station (1895), 185
Free University (1905), 187
Olympics (1928), 216
Produce Exchange (1903), 204
Rijksmuseum (1885), 185, 204,
    248
Schouwburg, 150
World Fair (1883), 199

Anabaptism, Anabaptists, 115–17
Anglo-Dutch Wars:
    First (1652–4), 156–7
    Second (1664–7), 157
    Third (1672–4), 160
    Fourth (1780–4), 167–8
    annexationist agitation (1918–20),
    214
Anselm of Liège, 11th-century
    chronicler, 46
Ansfrid, count of Huy, later bishop of
    Utrecht (995–1010), 39–40
Anthony of Burgundy, duke of
    Brabant (1406–15), 97, 253,
    257
Anthony of Egypt (d. 356), hermit,
    24
Anti-Revolutionary interest (later
    Party), 175, 182, 184, 187,
    195–6, 206–7, 221
Anti-Slavery Convention (Brussels,
    1889–90), 207
anticlericalism, 4, 182–3, 193
Antioch, city in the Middle East, 24,
    48, 68
Antwerp, town in Belgium, 8, 32, 57,
    64–5, 89, 91–4, 103, 106,
    110–12, 114–15, 117–18, 120,
    125, 126, 128, 131, 132–4,
    137, 138, 141–4, 150–1, 152,
    154, 155, 158, 168, 178, 180,
    201, 210, 218, 223, 224, 226,
    228, 240, 244
    citadel, 125, 174, 179
    Olympics (1920), 216, 248
    St Michael's abbey, 64–5
Antwerp, marquisate, 50, 54–5
Apeldoorn, town in Gelderland, 161
Appel, Karel (1921–), Dutch artist,
    234
Aquitaine, Frankish subkingdom, 27
Arabs, Saracens, 42, 47, 75, 207
Aragon, Spanish subkingdom, 109,
    112
Archangel, town in Russia, 134
architects, architecture, 9, 24, 33, 59,
    104, 107, 143, 176, 184–5,
    204, 217–18

Arctic, 134
Ardennes, forest and region, 2, 9, 11, 20, 23–4, 71, 122, 177, 225, 231, 242, 243, 248
Aremberg, Jean de Ligne (1525–68), count of, 121
Argentina, 194, 231
Arians, 23, 26
aristocracy, 10–11, 18, 25–9, 34–5, 39, 48, 51, 54, 87, 90, 92–3, 115, 120–1, 123, 126–7, 164–5, 176, 183
Aristotle, ancient Greek philosopher, 75–6, 148–9
Arles, Council of (314), 21
Arlon, town in Belgian Luxembourg, 14, 56, 93
Arminians, Arminianism, 139–41, 147, 148
Arminius, Jacobus (1560–1609), Dutch theologian, 139
Arnhem, town in Gelderland, 54, 230
Arnold of Egmond, duke of Guelders (1423–65 and 1471–3), 99, 257
Arnold of Isenburg, would-be bishop of Utrecht (1196–7), 69, 254
Arnolfini, 15th-century Italian banking family, 105
Arnulf, king of the East Franks (887–99), 37
Arnulf I, count of Flanders (918–65), 39, 250
Arras, 27, 28, 66, 87, 243
art, artists, 33, 39, 45, 65, 81, 94, 100, 104–5, 110, 112, 120–1, 143–5, 151, 159, 184–6, 199, 202–4, 218, 234
Art Deco, 204, 218
Art Nouveau, 204, 218
Artevelde, Jacob van (1290–1345), rebel leader in Flanders, 91
Artevelde, Philip van (1340–82), rebel leader in Flanders, 95
Arthur, legendary British king, 87, 103
artisans, craftsmen, 28, 30, 57–8,

85–6, 88–9, 103, 104, 107, 108, 133, 143, 169, 185
Artois, 59, 61, 100, 125
Aruba, Caribbean island, 207, 233
Asia, 25, 47–8, 68, 102, 111, 200, 205, 207, 233
Asselbergs, see Duinkerken
Asser, Mozes Salomon (1754–1826), expert on commercial law, 173
Asser, Tobias (1838–1913), expert on international law, 209
Association Football, 216
Athanasius (d. 373), bishop of Alexandria, 23–4
atheism, 113, 137, 147, 149, 182–3
atrocities, 13, 15, 17, 86, 89, 93, 98, 100, 124–5, 153–4, 207–8, 211, 225–7, 230–1, 236, 241, 244
Attila the Hun, 25
Auber, Daniel François Esprit (1782–1871), operatic composer, 178
Augustine (354–430), bishop of Hippo, 24, 45, 64, 158
Augustinians, 75, 114, 142, 158
Augustus, Gaius Julius Caesar Octavianus (63 BC–AD 14), Roman emperor, 14–15, 16
Aurich (now in Germany), 53
Ausonius, Decimus Magnus (d. 395), Roman poet, 24
Australia, 135, 194, 230, 233
Austrasia, Frankish subkingdom, 27–9, 31, 243
Austria, 125, 160, 162–5, 169, 170, 174, 179, 224
Austrian Netherlands, 162–72
autocracy, 165, 168–9, 175, 178–80, 182
automobile, 201, 216, 235
Auxerre, 97

Baduhenna, Grove of, 15
Baekeland, Leo (1863–1944), Belgian-American inventor, 201
Baghdad, 205

Bahía, 136
Bakelandt, Lodewijk (d. 1803),
    bandit, 172
Baldric, bishop of Utrecht (918–75),
    38, 254
Baldwin, king of Jerusalem
    (1100–18), 47–8
Baldwin Iron Arm, count of Flanders
    (864–79), 36, 243, 250
Baldwin II, count of Flanders
    (879–918), 36, 50, 250
Baldwin V, count of Flanders
    (1035–67), 50–1, 250
Baldwin VII, count of Flanders
    (1111–119), 44, 250
Baldwin IX, count of Flanders
    (1194–1205), Latin emperor of
    Constantinople (1204–5),
    70–72, 80, 250
Baldwin II, count of Hainaut
    (1071–98), 48, 252
Baldwin the Brave, count of Hainaut
    (1171–95), and of Flanders
    (1191–4), 68, 69, 70, 250, 252
Balliol, John de, king of Scots
    (1292–6), 83
Baltic area, 48, 61, 62, 111, 133, 134,
    151, 163, 165, 167
banditry, 43–4, 123–4, 164, 172
banks, banking, 3, 102, 130, 133,
    142, 150, 176, 189, 194, 205,
    212, 224
Bar, 68, 82, 100
Bar-sur-Seine, 97
Barentsz, Willem (d. 1597), Dutch
    explorer, 134
Barnouw, A.J., 20th-century Dutch
    author, 77, 212
Barrier Treaties, 162–3, 164
Bartels, Adolf (1802–62), Belgian
    journalist and politician, 183
Batavia (Jakarta), 135, 201, 233
Batavian Legion, 170–1
    see also Patriot Movement
Batavian Republic (1795–1806),
    171–3, 175
Batavians, ancient Germanic people,
    14, 16–22, 25, 242
Batavian Revolt, 16–18, 145

Baudelaire, Charles (1821–67),
    French poet, 185–6
Baudouin, king of the Belgians
    (1951–93), 233, 238, 249, 260
Bauwens, Lieven (1769–1822),
    industrial spy, 177
Bavaria, 69, 162–3
Bavarian dynasty in Holland and
    Hainaut, 91–2, 96, 98, 244,
    253
Bavarian dynasty in Liège, 153, 256
Bavay, town (Roman Bagacum), 14
Bavo (d. c.653), patron saint of
    Ghent, 29
Bayard, magic horse, 67
Beaker People, prehistoric culture, 9
Beatrice of Nazareth, nun, 77
Beatrijs, Middle Dutch poem, 77
beef, 20, 60, 133
beer, ale, brewing, 58, 60, 61, 101,
    132, 135, 163, 188–9, 235
Beernaert, Auguste (1829–1912),
    politician, 209
Begga (d. 693), abbess of Andenne,
    29
Beggars (insurgents during early
    stages of the Dutch Revolt),
    120–4
Beghards, 76
Beguines, 76–8, 138
belfries, 59
Belgae, 10–13, 17–18
Belgian Revolution (1830), 178–9
Belgica, province of the Roman
    Empire, 14–15, 23, 25, 242
Belgische Volksbond, see Ligue
    démocratique belge
Belgium, United States of (1790),
    170
Belgium-Luxembourg customs union,
    215
Benelux, 7, 221, 234, 249
Bengal, 135
Beowulf, Old English poem, 30
Berchmans, Jan (1599–1622), Jesuit,
    143
Berg, German county, 55, 81
Berg, Henry (1573–1638), count of,
    152–3

Bergen op Zoom, town in North
    Brabant, 153, 164
Berlage, Hendrik Petrus
    (1856–1934), Dutch architect,
    204
Berlin Conference (1884–5), 207
Bernard (1090–1153), abbot of
    Clairvaux, 63–4
Bernlef, 9th-century bard, 32
Bernold, bishop of Utrecht
    (1027–54), 40, 254
Bertin, 7th-century missionary, 28
Beyen, J. W. (1897–1976), Dutch
    foreign minister, 234–5
Bible, biblical translations and texts,
    32, 33, 65–6, 79, 87, 115, 117,
    118, 137, 145, 148–50, 187
Biblia Regia, 110
bicycles, 201, 216
Bilderdijk, Willem (1756–1831),
    Dutch lawyer and poet, 173,
    175
Bitburg, town in Luxembourg, 93
Black Death, *see* pestilence
Blaeu, Joan (1596–1673), son of
    following, 147
Blaeu, Willem Jansz. (1571–1638),
    maker and dealer in globes and
    maps, 146
Blenheim, Battle of (1704), 162–3
Bloemhof, Premonstratensian abbey,
    64, 75
Bockelson, Jan (1510–36), 'John of
    Leyden', 116
Boendale, Jan van (1279–c.1350),
    poet, 89, 91
Boer republics, 194, 208–9
Boer War, 208–9
Boerhaave, Herman (1668–1738),
    professor of medicine, 147
Bokkerijders, 164
Bolland, Jean (1596–1665), first
    editor of the *Acta Sanctorum*,
    151
Bollandists, 151
Bolshevism, *see* Revolutionary
    Socialism
Bonaire, Caribbean island, 233

Bonaparte, Napoleon (1769–1821),
    French commander, 173–5,
    247, 259
Boniface VIII, pope (1294–1303), 85
Boniface (680–754), Anglo-Saxon
    missionary on the Continent,
    32, 243
Bonn, town in the German
    Rhineland, 19, 160
Bontius, Jacob (1592–1631), 147,
    201
books, 32, 33, 65–6, 67, 87, 98, 100,
    105–7, 108, 109, 110, 112,
    114–15, 118, 119, 121, 129,
    141, 143, 149–51, 194, 211,
    217, 261–6
Bordet, Jules (1870–1961), Belgian
    bacteriologist, 201
Borgloon, town in Limburg, 55
Borneo, 206
Borselen, Frank van (1395–1470),
    knight of the Golden Fleece,
    99
Bosch, Hieronymus (c.1450–1516),
    painter, 112, 144, 204
Boudewijn, *see* Baudouin
Boulogne, 22, 23, 244
Bourbon family, 161, 162–3, 174,
    178
Bouvines, Battle of (1214), 71–2,
    243
Brabant, duchy, 7, 37, 45, 52, 54–5,
    59, 64, 69–70, 79, 81–2, 88,
    89, 92–4, 96–7, 100, 112, 115,
    126–8, 141, 152, 169, 172,
    179, 244, 247, 256–7
    province, 8, 190
Brabant Revolution (1788–90),
    169–70, 247
brass, 58
brass bands, 189
Brazil, 136, 148
Breda, town in North Brabant, 151,
    154, 169, 230
    taking of (1590), 128
    Siege of (1624–5), 151
    Atheneum (1646), 148
    Treaty of (1667), 157

Breisgau, 100, 244
Brethren of the Common Life, 107
brewing, *see* beer
Brielle, town in South Holland, 122, 245
Britain, 8, 17, 22–3, 36, 102, 154, 160, 161–2, 163, 165, 167, 168, 170, 171–2, 174, 179–80, 183, 194, 208–11, 215, 221, 229, 230, 234
  see also England, Scotland, Wales
Brueghel, family of painters: Peter the elder (*c*.1525–69), Peter the younger (1564–1638), Jan (1568–1625), 144
  Massacre of the Innocents, 121
Bruges, town in Flanders, 5, 52, 57, 59, 64, 66, 74, 75, 85–6, 88, 91, 93, 100, 102–4, 105, 106, 111, 134, 139, 142, 146, 154, 157, 184
  Bruges Matins (1302), 86
Bruno (*c*.925–65), archbishop of Cologne and duke of Lotharingia, 38, 39
Brunssum, town in Dutch Limburg, 235
Brussels, 59, 79, 92, 94, 97, 114, 115, 126, 128, 146, 153, 158, 165, 169, 172, 174, 175, 178–9, 181, 182, 185, 186, 188, 190, 192, 193, 201, 204, 207, 213, 217, 218, 223, 234, 235
  Atomium (1958), 235
  bombardment of (1695), 161–2
  cathedral, 94
  Grand'Place, 162
  Manneken Pis, 162
  Palace of Justice (1883), 204
  Town Hall, 59, 162
  University, 182, 197, 228
  World Fair (1958), 235
Brussels Capital Region, 3
Brussels Pact (1948), 234
builders, *see* architecture
Bulgaria, 71, 102
Bulge, Battle of the (1944), 231
bullion, 11, 30, 111, 120, 135

Burchard of Avesnes (*c*.1175–1244), 71, 80
Burgundy, 27, 28, 35, 63, 95–7, 99–100, 101, 108, 112, 161
burials, 9, 26, 30, 32, 33, 39, 70, 84, 92, 169
Burundi, 215, 235, 239
butter, 102, 132, 199
Buysse, Cyriel (1859–1932), author, 203

C&A department stores, 199–200
cabbala, Jewish mysticism, 146
Cairo, 205
Calais, 98
Calvin, Jean (1509–64), French reformer, 117, 196
Calvinism, Calvinists, 117–18, 120–1, 125, 126, 129, 137, 138–41, 144, 148, 149, 150, 158, 159, 185, 187, 196, 202, 237, 246
Cambrai, town now in France, 23, 38, 52, 57, 83, 99
  bishopric, 28, 40, 42, 43, 52, 99, 100, 105, 119
Cammaerts, Emile (1878–1953), Belgian writer, 211
Canada, 194
canals, 8, 15, 16, 133, 135, 141–2, 151, 153, 157, 165, 248
Cananefates, Germanic tribe in the Low Countries, 14, 17, 19
Canary Islands, 111
canons regular and secular, 44–5, 54, 63–5, 69, 74, 85, 99, 107, 125
Canossa, 45
Canute I, king of Denmark and England (1019–35), 50
Canute II, king of Denmark (1080–6), 51
Cape Colony, 136–7, 171
capital, 58, 94, 133, 169, 176–7, 193, 200, 205–6, 219
capitulation, 221
Carausius, M. Aurelius Maesaeus, Roman ruler (286–93), 22–3

Caribbean, 136, 137, 171, 186, 207, 230, 233–4
Carnegie, Andrew (1835–1919), American industrialist, 209
carnival, 2, 218
Carthage, 24
Carton de Wiart, Henri (1869–1951), Belgian Christian Democrat, 197
Casement, Roger (1864–1916), Anglo-Irish diplomat, 208
Cassel, town now in France (Roman Castellum Menapiorum), 14, 20
Castile, 109, 112
Castro, Cipriano (1858–1924), Venezuelan dictator, 207
Catalonia, 154
Cathars, 73
Catholic Church, Catholics, 1, 2–3, 4, 21–95 passim, 107, 114, 119–20, 121, 124, 125, 129, 130, 131, 133, 137, 138, 141–3, 148, 150–1, 153, 155, 158, 161, 173, 176, 178, 182–7, 188, 190, 195, 202, 206, 213, 216, 217, 220, 227, 236–7
Catholic political parties, 186–7, 195, 220, 233
Cats, Jacob (1577–1660), Dutch poet and jurist, 150, 156, 157
Catuvolcus (d. 53 BC), ancient Belgic tribal leader, 13
Cavell, Edith (1865–1915), Red Cross nurse and British spy, 212
Caxton, William (c.1422–91), first English printer, 67, 106–7
Ceylon, 135
Chambers of Rhetoric, 105–6, 150
Champagne, region in France, 58, 102
Charlemagne, Holy Roman Emperor (800–14), 31–5, 36, 38, 48, 67, 173, 243
Charleroi, town in Hainaut, 177
Charleroi, town in Pennsylvania, 194

Charles, count of Flanders, regent of Belgium (1944–51), 232–3
Charles Alexander of Lorraine (1712–80), 164, 166
Charles of Egmond, duke of Guelders (1492–1538), 112, 257
Charles the Bald, king of the West Franks (843–77), 35, 36
Charles the Bold, duke of Burgundy (1467–77), 100–1, 103–4, 106, 108, 244, 257, 258
Charles the Fat, king of the East Franks (881–7), 37
Charles the Good, count of Flanders (1119–27), 51–2, 243, 250
Charles I, king of Great Britain (1625–49), 155, 156
Charles II, king of Great Britain (1651–85), 155, 160
Charles II, king of Spain (1665–1700), 162, 258
Charles V, Holy Roman Emperor (1519–56), 96, 109, 110, 112–13, 114, 115, 118, 120, 122, 245, 255, 257, 258
Charles VI, Holy Roman Emperor (1711–40), 163, 258
Charles VI, king of France (1380–1422), 97
Charles VII, king of France (1429–61), 106
Charlotte, grand duchess of Luxembourg (1919–64), 214, 221, 260
Charriaut, Henri, 20th-century French diplomat, 188
Chastellain, Georges (c.1405–75), diplomat and chronicler, 106
Châtillon, Jacques de (d. 1302), French nobleman, 85–6
Chaucer, Geoffrey (c.1340–1400), English poet, 53
Chauci, ancient Germanic tribe, 16
cheese, 133, 194, 199, 218
chemicals, chemistry, 58, 146, 194, 199, 200, 201, 239
Chièvres, William of Croy (1458–1521), lord of, 109

Childeric (d. 481), war leader of the Salian Franks, 26, 242

China, 134, 135, 205–6, 213 see also porcelain

Chlodovech, see Clovis

Chlothar I, king of the Franks (d. 561), 27

cholera, 193

Christian Democracy, 184, 190, 195–6, 233, 240

Christianity, passim

Chrétien de Troyes (d. c.1183), French poet, 66

Churchill, John (1650–1722), duke of Marlborough, 161, 162–3

Cingetorix, ancient Belgic tribal leader, 13

Cistercians, 63, 67, 68

citizenry, citizenship, 17, 21, 56–7, 59, 81, 85–90, 100, 107, 124, 128, 133, 138, 141, 170, 178, 185, 193, 219, 223

Classicus, conspirator against Roman rule, 17–18

Claudius Labeo, commander of auxiliary cavalry, 18

Claudius, Roman emperor (41–54), 16

Clemens non Papa (c.1510–c.1556), composer, 105

Clement 'VII', antipope (1378–94), 95

Cleveringa, R. P. (1894–1980), 228

Cleves, German principality, 54, 55, 81, 118

cloth, see textiles

Clovis, king of the Salian Franks (481–511), 26–7, 34

co-operatives, 188, 189, 194, 195, 217, 248

Co-operative Women's Guild, 188

coal, coalmining, 102, 177, 195, 199, 205, 227, 234, 237, 239

CoBrA, artistic group (1948), 234

COC, homophile group (1946), 238

Cockerill, William (1759–1832), English engineer and industrialist, 177

Cockerill firm, 177, 205

cod, 132, 133

coffee, 135, 186, 206

coins and currency, 11, 19, 25, 30, 42, 72, 97, 115, 215, 234

coke, 177

Colijn, Hendrikus (1869–1944), Dutch prime minister, 221

Cologne, 14, 17, 22, 28, 38, 39, 42, 55, 64, 65, 73, 75, 79, 81, 143, 153–4, 160, 174

colour, 4, 58–9, 105, 145, 218

Columbanus (543–615), Irish missionary, 28

commerce, trade, 5, 9, 30, 35–6, 37, 49, 51, 54, 56–9, 62, 79, 91, 101–3, 106, 111, 115, 120, 131, 132–7, 141–2, 144–5, 151–2, 157, 163, 167–8, 173, 177, 186, 199–201, 206, 207–8, 215

Communists, 2, 181, 192, 219–20, 226, 227, 228–9, 232, 233, 248

Compagnie Internationale des Wagons-Lits, 205

concordat (1801), 173

confession (sacrament), 66, 74–5, 77

Congo, 205, 207–8, 211, 230, 235–6, 248, 249

Congress of Vienna (1814–15), 174

Conrad I, king of the Germans (911–18), 38

Conrad II, Holy Roman Emperor (1027–39), 40

Conrad IV, Holy Roman Emperor (1250–54), 72

Conrad the Red (d. 955), duke of Lotharingia, 38

Conscience, Hendrik (1812–83), Flemish author, 184–5

conservatism, 175–6, 183, 188, 193, 195–6, 220, 221, 228, 229, 240

Constantine, Roman emperor (307–37), 21, 23, 24

Constantinople (now Istanbul), 23, 24, 47, 71, 205, 250, 251

Constantius Chlorus, Roman emperor (305–6), 22–3

Constantius II, Roman emperor
(337–61), 23
constitution, constitutionalism, 175,
183, 225, 228
Belgium, 179–80, 232, 238, 239
Luxembourg, 180, 182
the Netherlands, 171, 173, 175,
181–2, 187, 197, 239
see also Joyous Entry, Union of
Utrecht
convents, see religious houses and
orders
Corbulo, Gnaeus Domitius, 1st-
century Roman general, 16
Cornwall, 58, 102
Corpus Christi, Feast of, 78
Council of Troubles (1568), 121
Counter-Remonstrants, see Gomarists
Couperus, Louis (1863–1923), Dutch
author, 203
courts of law, judiciary, 11, 14, 16,
49, 57, 61, 72, 73, 101,
113–15, 116, 119, 129, 150,
168, 169, 172–4, 198, 204,
209, 222, 226, 234, 241
courts, courtiers, courtliness, 3, 23–4,
32, 34, 39, 40, 56, 66–7, 68,
70, 81, 82, 83, 92, 103–4, 106,
109, 129, 142, 144, 146, 152,
154, 161, 207
craft guilds, 28, 79, 88–90, 108, 126,
162, 169, 170
see also artisans
craftsmen, see artisans
Crécy, Battle of (1346), 91, 244
credit, 47, 111, 133, 142, 152, 167,
169, 207
criminal gangs, see banditry
Cromwell, Oliver (1599–1658),
English general and politician,
148, 156–7
Crusades, crusaders, 46–8, 52, 68, 70,
71, 74, 81, 87, 95, 97, 243
Crutched Friars (Brothers of the
Cross), 74
Cultivation System, 186, 206
Curaçao, Caribbean island, 136, 207,
233, 234

Cuypers, Petrus J. H. (1827–1921),
Dutch architect, 185, 204
cycling, see bicycles

Daendels, Herman (1762–1818),
Dutch Patriot, 170–1
Daens, Adolf (1839–1907), priest-
politician, 195
Dagobert I, Frankish king (d. 639),
28–9
daily press, see newspapers
Damien, name in religion of Jozef De
Veuster (1840–89), 206
Damme, town in Flanders, 64–5, 71,
86, 102, 103
Dante Alighieri (1265–1321), Italian
poet, 5, 76, 92
David of Burgundy, bishop of
Utrecht (1455–96), 99, 255
de Bakker, Jan (d. 1525), Lutheran
martyr, 114
de Coninck, Pieter (d. c.1332),
weaver, 86
de Gaulle, Charles (1890–1970),
French general and politician,
1
De Hoogh, Pieter (1629–84), painter,
145
de Labadie, Jean (1610–74), French
sectarian, 159
de Lichte, Jan, 18th-century bandit
leader, 164
de Man, Hendrik (1885–1953),
Socialist politician, 192, 223
de Ruyter, Michiel Adriaanszoon
(1607–76), Dutch admiral,
160
De Smet, Pieter Jan (1801–73),
Dutch missionary, 206
De Stijl, 20th-century artistic group,
218
De Veuster, see Damien
de Witt, Johan, (1625–72), Dutch
statesman, 157, 160, 182
Debye, Peter (1884–1966), Dutch
physicist, 200
Degrelle, Léon (1906–94), Belgian
fascist, 220, 224, 225, 231

Deken, Agatha (1741–1804), Dutch author, 166
del Rio, Martin (1551–1608), Jesuit, 118–19
Delaware, river, 136
Delft, town in Holland, 127, 132, 248
Delft School, 20th-century artistic group, 204
Delftware, 132
Deltaworks, flood-prevention project, 6
Delvaux, Paul (1897–1994), Belgian painter, 218
Delwaide, Leo, acting mayor of Antwerp 1940–44, 223
Demerara, region of Guyana, 136
Dender, river, 50
Dendermonde, town in Flanders, 50
Denmark, Danes, 30, 32, 36, 37, 50, 52, 62, 102, 114, 133, 134, 155, 194
Descartes, René (1596–1650), French philosopher, 5, 149
Deshima, island off Nagasaki, 135
design, 143, 184, 204, 218
Deventer, town in Overijssel, 32, 40, 54, 62, 69, 85, 106, 107, 116, 128, 148, 192
Dhuoda, Frankish noblewoman, 33–4
Diemen, Anthony van (1593–1645), Dutch admiral, 135
Diest, Isala van (1842–1916), MD, 197
Dijon, town in Burgundy, 97
dikes, dams, flood barriers, 5–6, 59, 60, 62, 63, 122–3, 124
Dinant, town in Namur, 57, 211, 244
Diocletian, Roman emperor (284–305), 21, 22–3, 25, 242
Dirk I, count of Holland (c.916–39), 37, 39, 243, 252
Dirk II, count of Holland (939–88), 39, 252
Dirk III, count of Holland (993–1039), 40, 46, 252
Dirk IV, count of Holland (1039–49), 40, 252
Dirk VII, count of Holland (1190–1203), 69, 70, 252

Dodoens, Rembert (1517–85), botanist, 110, 135, 146
Doesburg, Theo van (1883–1931), 218
Dokkum, town in Friesland, 32
Dolle Mina, feminist group, 237
dolmens, 9
Dominicans (Order of Preachers), 74–5, 85, 142, 158
Donatius, 6th-century bishop of Tongeren, 27
Doorman, Karel (1889–1942), Dutch naval officer, 230
Dordrecht, town in Holland, 83, 85, 90, 102, 132, 141, 150
Dorestad, early-medieval town in the Rhine delta, 35, 36, 37, 57, 62
Battle of (689), 31
Douai, town now in France, 66, 85, 94, 148
Douwes Dekker, Eduard, see Multatuli
Downs, Battle of the (1639), 154, 157
Drenthe, province of the Netherlands, 8, 9, 19, 163, 164, 259
Drucker, Wilhelmina (1847–1925), feminist, 197, 237
druids, 11, 17, 21
Drusus Major, Nero Claudius (38–9 BC), Roman general, 15
Ducpétiaux, Antoine (1804–68), Belgian politician, 183
Dufay, Guillaume (c.1400–74), Flemish composer, 105
Duinkerken, Anton van, pen-name of Willem Asselbergs (1903–68), 217
Dumas, Alexandre (1802–70), senior, French playwright, 185
Dumouriez, Charles (1739–1823), French general, 170
dunes, 5, 63, 90, 133
Dunes, Cistercian abbey, 63
Dunkirk, town now in France, 127, 130, 142, 152, 160
Dutch East India Company, see VOC
Dutch Guyana, see Surinam

Dutch language, 1, 3, 7, 26–7, 55,
    66–7, 77, 86, 114, 117, 134,
    149, 166, 173, 182, 194,
    197–8, 213–14, 237, 238–9
Dutch Reformed Church, 118,
    135–41 passim, 156, 196, 246
    see also Calvinism
Dutch Revolt (1568–1648), 121–31,
    151–5
Dyck, Anthony van (1599–1641),
    painter, 144
dyeing, dyers, dyestuffs, 58, 59, 60,
    105, 111, 112

East Anglia, 61, 76, 103
East Indies, 134–6, 137, 171, 186,
    206–7
    see also Indonesia
Eburones, ancient Belgic tribe, 12–13
Echternach, town in Luxembourg, 20,
    31, 56, 93, 243
education, 3, 7, 13, 32, 35, 39, 45–6,
    65–6, 75, 106, 109, 129, 142,
    147–8, 165, 169, 176, 177,
    182, 184, 186–7, 194, 196–7,
    198, 200, 205, 206, 213,
    227–8, 235, 236
Edward the Confessor, king of
    England (1042–66), 50
Edward I, king of England
    (1272–1307), 48, 82, 83
Edward III, king of England
    (1327–77), 90–91, 92
Edward IV, king of England
    (1461–70, 1471–83), 101
Egbert of Trier, archbishop of Trier
    (977–93), 39, 40
Egmond, place in Holland, 39, 83
Egmont, Lamoral (1522–68), count
    of, 120, 121
Egypt, 20, 24, 44, 172
Eijkman, Christiaan (1858–1930),
    Dutch bacteriologist, 201
Einthoven, Willem (1860–1927),
    Dutch physiologist, 201
Elbe, river, 8, 16
electoral franchise, 171, 180, 182,
    191, 193, 196–7, 219

Eleonora (d. 1298), English princess,
    82
Elfstedentocht, skating marathon, 216
Elftrude (d. 929), English princess,
    36
Elgar, Edward (1857–1934), English
    composer, 211
Eliezer ben Joel ha-Levi
    (1140–1225), rabbi, 79
Eligius (c.590–660), Frankish
    missionary bishop, 28–9
Elizabeth I, queen of England
    (1559–1603), 122, 127
Elizabeth of Görlitz, duchess of
    Luxembourg (1416–43), 98,
    253
Elizabeth of Vermandois (d. 1183),
    countess of Flanders, 66
Elizabeth (d. 1316), English princess,
    83
Elsschot, Willem, pen-name of
    Alfons Jozef De Ridder
    (1882–1960), 218
Elzevier, family of publishers, 147
emblems (illustrated literary genre),
    143, 150
Emma (d. 1052), queen of England,
    50
Emo, 13th-century abbot of
    Bloemhof, 75
Empain, Eduard (1852–1929),
    engineer and entrepreneur, 205
Ems, river, 14, 16, 53
endorsement, 111
England, English, 6, 7, 9, 30–1, 32,
    35, 48, 50–1, 59, 67, 70–1, 74,
    81–5, 90–98, 102, 111,
    114–15, 118, 120–30, 134–6,
    148, 155–7, 159–61, 166, 167,
    171, 175, 177, 188, 211, 216,
    221–2, 229
English Channel, 12, 156
engravers, 112, 144, 186
Enkhuizen, town in Holland, 63, 94,
    111, 134
Enlightenment, 148, 149, 164–6
Ensor, James (1860–1949), Belgian
    painter, 204

Erasmus, Desiderius (1466–1536),
Dutch humanist, 109–10, 113,
119, 149, 228
Erembald family, 51–2
Ermesind, countess of Luxembourg
(1199–1247), 56, 68, 70–1, 80,
253
Ernest (1553–95), archduke of
Austria, 128
Esch-sur-Alzette, town in
Luxembourg, 178
Essen, Joannes van (d. 1523),
Lutheran martyr, 114
Estates General of the Seventeen
Provinces, 100, 108, 122,
124–6, 153
Ethical Policy, 206–7
Eucharist, 33, 78, 94, 125, 138, 153
Eugene (1663–1736), prince of
Savoy, Habsburg general, 162
eugenetics, 219
Eupen, town now in Belgium, 214
Euro, currency, 234
European institutions, treaties,
unification, 2, 7, 185, 234–5
Eva, 13th-century recluse, 78
Evelyn, John (1620–1706), English
diarist, 145
Eyck, Jan van (d. 1441), painter,
104–5

famine, 42, 90, 181
Far East, 112, 135–6, 205–6, 215,
220
Farnese, see Parma
Fascism, 220–1, 223–5
February strike (1941), 227
feminism, 159, 196–7, 237
Ferdinand of Aragon, king of Spain
(1479–1504), 109
Ferdinand of Bavaria, prince-bishop
of Liège (1612–40), 153–4
Ferdinand (1609–41), Cardinal-
Infante, 153
Ferrand of Portugal, count of
Flanders in his wife's right
(1212–44), 71–2
fertilizer, 60, 194

festivals, 2, 34, 40, 74, 78, 87, 93,
104, 145, 151, 169, 172, 218,
227
finance, 3, 11, 19, 25, 30, 42, 47, 72,
97, 102, 111, 115, 130, 133,
142, 150, 152, 167, 169, 176,
189, 194, 205, 207, 212, 215,
224, 234
Finn, Frisian king, 30
fish, fisheries, 5, 6, 20, 53, 58, 60,
62, 101, 112, 132–3, 134, 203,
239
Flanders, county, 5, 7, 29, 36–7,
43–5, 49–52, 54, 57–60, 62,
63, 68, 70–3, 80, 85–6, 90–1,
93, 95, 97, 100, 101, 102, 112,
117, 126–8, 130, 142, 157,
160, 162, 164, 170, 172, 190
region of Belgium, 3, 198, 208, 213,
225, 238–9
flax, 60, 61, 217
Flemish movement, 198, 213–14,
224–5, 238–9
Fleurus, Battle of (1690), 161
Flevoland, province, 4, 6
Flevo, lake, 14, 15
see also Almere, Zuider Zee,
IJsselmeer
flooding, floods, 5–6, 18, 62, 90,
122–3, 124, 210–11
Floreffe, Premonstratensian abbey, 64
Floris III, count of Holland
(1157–90), 68, 71, 252
Floris V, count of Holland
(1256–96), 63, 82–5, 87, 244,
252
flyboat, 134
FN (Fabrique Nationale d'Armes de
Guerre), 200, 237
Formosa (Taiwan), 135–6
fortifications, 11, 12, 15, 17, 20, 22,
40, 42–4, 55–7, 72, 82, 84, 99,
123–5, 135, 137, 154, 162,
163, 168, 171, 174, 179, 210
Fortuyn, Pim (1948–2002), Dutch
demagogue, 240
France, Frenchmen, 1, 4, 6, 8, 9,
34–6, 40, 41, 43, 45, 47, 48,

50, 56, 66, 67, 70–2, 73–6, 79, 80–3, 85–6, 91, 95, 96–7, 99, 101, 102, 105, 111, 112, 117, 121, 123, 125, 128, 129, 130, 141, 153–5, 157, 160–4, 165, 167–75, 176, 179, 180, 181, 183, 185–6, 188, 194, 205, 209, 210–15, 216, 221–2, 231, 234, 235

Franche Comté, region now in France, 127, 161

Francis of Assisi (1182–1226), religious leader, 73–4, 87

Francis (1554–84), duke of Anjou, 126

Franciscans, 74, 75–6, 85, 113, 142 see also friars

Francorchamps, motor racing track, 216

Francqui, Emile (1863–1935), Belgian financier, 205, 212

Franeker, town in Friesland, 30, 123 university, 147

François-Henri de Luxembourg-Montmorency, (1628–95), 161

Frank, Anne (1929–45), teenage diarist, 228, 265

Franks, Germanic people, 22–3, 25–38, 42, 48, 57, 67

Fraternal Society of Weavers (Ghent), 189

fraternities, 33, 142, 169

Frederick I (Barbarossa), Holy Roman Emperor (1155–90), 67–8, 69,

Frederick II, Holy Roman Emperor (1212–50), 71–3

Frederick III, Holy Roman Emperor (1452–93), 100, 108

Frederick Henry (1584–1647), prince of Orange, 152–3, 154–5

Frederik of Blankenheim, bishop of Utrecht (1393–1423), 99

Freemasonry, 146, 182–3

French language, 1–4, 7, 86, 87, 106–7, 111, 114, 159, 160, 185, 197–8, 202, 213, 224, 237, 238–9

Frère-Orban, Walthère, Belgian Prime Minister (1867–70, 1878–84), 193

friars, 74–5, 142

Friesland, Frisians, 2, 4, 5, 14–16, 17, 19, 20, 25, 26, 29–33, 36, 37, 40, 42, 48, 52–3, 60, 63, 64, 75, 82, 89, 92, 112, 116, 117, 119, 121–3, 124, 126, 128, 156, 159, 160, 162, 163, 164, 216

Frisian language, 1, 27, 197–8

Frisiavones, Germanic tribe in the Low Countries, 14, 19

Froissart, Jean (c.1338–c.1404), chronicler, 91, 106, 262

Functionalism, 20th-century artistic movement, 204, 218

Galba, Servius Sulpicius, Roman emperor (68–9), 16

Galbert of Bruges, 12th-century chronicler, 52, 66, 262

gangsters, see banditry

Ganshof, F. L., 20th-century historian, 41, 262

Gatti de Gamond, Isabelle (1839–1905), feminist educationalist, 197

Geelkerken, Cornelis van (1901–76), Dutch fascist, 221

Gelderland, Guelders, 52, 53, 54, 55, 62, 69, 81, 89, 93, 100, 108–9, 112, 126, 127, 128, 130, 141, 160–1, 163, 164, 172, 174, 244, 245, 257, 259

Geneva, 117

Geneva Convention (1864), 209

Gerard Groote (1340–84), preacher, 107

Gerard, Balthasar (1557–84), killer of William of Orange, 127

Gerhard, Hendrik (1829–86), Dutch labour organizer, 190

Gerlach, 11th-century hermit, 44

German language, 1, 3, 7, 56, 66, 114, 198, 202, 214

Germany, Germans, 1, 2, 4, 9, 10, 13, 15–18, 24–6, 32, 34–5, 38–9, 46, 47, 48, 53–5, 58, 59, 62, 69, 71, 74, 76, 93, 101, 102, 106, 110, 111, 114, 116–17, 118, 119, 121, 123, 125, 129, 143, 151, 153, 159, 160, 165–6, 181, 183, 194, 210–15, 221–32, 234
Germanic provinces of the Roman Empire, 19, 22, 23, 25
German Union, 174, 180
Gerretson, F. C. (1884–1958), Dutch fascist leader, 220
Gertrude (626–59), abbess of Nivelles, 29
Gerulf, 9th-century Frisian count, 37
Geyl, Pieter (1887–1966), Dutch historian, 7, 212, 264
Gezelle, Guido (1830–99), Flemish poet, 203
Ghent, 36, 57, 58, 66, 74, 85, 88, 89, 91, 93, 95, 99, 108, 109, 117, 124, 126, 142, 158, 165, 174, 177, 188, 189, 190, 243, 245
Pacification of, 124–5, 245
St Bavo's, 29, 104
University, 176, 182
World Fair (1913), 204
Ghibbeline, see Hohenstaufen
Gijsbrecht (1235–1303), lord of Amstel, 62, 83–4
Gilbert of Ghent (d. 1095), 51
Gilbert of Tournai (d. c.1280), 76
Gilles Binchois (d. 1460), 105
gin, 101, 163
Gisela, illegitimate daughter of Lothar II, 37
Godfrey 'Sea–king', Viking leader, 37
Godfrey of Bouillon (c.1060–1100), crusader, 47–8, 243
Godfrey of Fontaines, 13th-century philosopher, 76
Godfrey of Rhenen, bishop of Utrecht (1156–78), 68, 254
Goes, Hugo van der, 15th-century painter, 105

Golden Fleece, order of knighthood, 97, 121
Gomarus, Franciscus (1563–1641), Reformed theologian, 139
Gomarists, 139–40
Gombert, Nicolaas (c.1490–c.1556), 105
Goméz, Juan Vincente, Venezuelan dictator (1908–35), 207
Gorm, Danish king (d. c.958), 37
Gorter, Herman (1864–1927), Dutch writer, 192
Gothic revival, 184–5, 204
Gouda, town in Holland, 59, 119, 132, 168
grain, 20, 59, 61, 90, 111, 122, 133, 164, 165, 181, 194
Granvelle, Antoine Perrenot, cardinal of (1517–86), 120
Gregory of Utrecht (c.707–c.775), 32
Gregory VII, pope (1073–85), 45
Grimestone, Edward, 17th-century translator, 83
Grimoald (d. 714), 29, 39
Groen van Prinsterer, Guillaume (1801–76), Dutch statesman, 182, 187
Groenendael, 78
Groningen, province, 4, 119, 121, 123, 126, 128, 162, 163, 164, 259
town, 53, 57, 77, 99, 109, 123, 128
university, 147, 196
Grotius, Hugo (1583–1645), Dutch jurist, 140–1, 147
Guelders, county (later duchy), see Gelderland
Guelph, see Welf
Gueux, see Beggars
Guido of Anderlecht (d. 1012), 47
Guild of St Thomas and St Luke, 184, 185
guilds, see craft guilds, fraternities, militia guilds
guillotine, 172
Guy of Dampierre, count of Flanders (1278–1305), 80–1, 83, 85–6, 88, 251

Guy of Avesnes, bishop of Utrecht (1301–17), 85
Guyana, 136
see also Surinam
gypsies, 138

Haarlem, 124, 132, 138, 144, 145, 165, 178
Habsburgs, 100, 108, 112, 121, 129–30, 141, 146, 151–4, 157, 161, 162–3, 168–72
Hadewijch (early 13th-century), 77–8, 262
Haemstede, Adriaan van (c.1525–62), Dutch Reformed martyrologist, 117–18
The Hague, 92, 104, 112, 114, 115, 126, 131, 137, 146, 156, 160, 168, 175
  Treaty of (1795), 171
  Conferences, 209
  International Court of Justice, 234
  International Criminal Court, 241
Hainaut, 7, 8, 50, 54, 55–6, 59, 61, 68, 79, 80, 85, 92, 93, 96, 97–8, 100, 117, 125, 160, 162, 244
Hals, Frans (1580–1666), painter, 145
Hamburg, 35, 59
Hanseatic League, 62
Harald, 9th-century Viking leader, 36, 37
Harald Hardrada, king of Norway (1045–66), 51
Harderwijk, town in Gelderland, 148
health, 3, 77, 169, 176, 177, 189, 193–4, 197, 201, 205, 208, 236
Heelu, Jan van, 13th-century poet, 82
Heijermans, Herman (1864–1924), Dutch playwright, 203
Heiligerlee, Battle of (1568), 121
Helder, Den, place in North Holland, 172
Hellevoetsluis, 171
Helmont, Frans Mercurius van (1618–99), alchemist, 146

Helmont, Jan Baptist van (1577–1644), alchemist, 146
Hemmema, Rienck, 16th-century Frisian farmer, 122–3
Henric van Veldeke (c.1150–1210), poet, 66–7
Henry I, Saxon king of Germans (919–36), 38
Henry I, king of France (1031–60), 50
Henry I, duke of Brabant (1190–1235), 69–70
Henry II, Holy Roman Emperor (1002–24), 40
Henry II, king of England (1154–89), 51
Henry III, duke of Brabant (1248–61), 79
Henry IV, Holy Roman Emperor (1054–1106), 45–6
Henry IV, 'the Blind', count of Luxembourg (1136–96), 56, 68, 70, 251, 253
Henry V, Holy Roman Emperor (1106–25), 46
Henry V, king of England (1413–22), 97
Henry V, count of Luxembourg (1247–81), 80, 253
Henry VI, Holy Roman Emperor (1190–7), 68–9, 71
Henry VI, count of Luxembourg (1281–8), 81, 253
Henry VII, count of Luxembourg (1288–1310), 92, 244, 253
Henry Bate of Mechelen (1246–c.1310), 13th-century philosopher, 76
Henry of Bavaria, bishop of Utrecht (1524–8), 112, 255
Henry of Ghent (d. 1293) philosopher and theologian, 76
Henry of Thuringia, Holy Roman Emperor (1246–7), 72
Henry the Lion (1129–95), duke of Saxony and Bavaria, 69

heresy, 23–4, 73, 76, 107, 113–20, 140, 147, 158
Hergé, pen-name of Georges Remi (1907–83), artist, 218
hermits, 24, 27, 28, 34, 39, 44–5, 47, 72, 78
herring, 36, 101, 102, 132–3, 136, 152
Herstal, place near Liège, 34, 200, 237
's-Hertogenbosch, 82, 92, 121, 137, 152, 153
Herzogenrath, town now in Germany, 55
Hesbaye, region of Belgium, 8, 198
Heyn, Piet (1577–1629), naval commander, 152
Hildegard, 10th-century countess of Holland, 39
Hirsch, Maurice von (1831–96), philanthropist, 205
Hoff, Jacobus van't (1852–1911), physical chemist, 200
Hoffmann, Melchior (c.1500–c.1543), German Anabaptist, 116
Holdert, H. C. M. (1870–1944), 202
Holland, 2, 4, 5, 6, 7, 37, 39, 52, 53–4, 59, 60, 62, 63, 69, 70, 82–5, 89–90, 92, 93, 96, 97, 98–9, 100, 111, 116, 122, 126, 128, 131, 132–4, 138–40, 151, 154, 155–6, 157, 158, 160, 164, 168, 171, 238
  Court of, 114–16, 150
  Kingdom of (1806–10), 173, 175
Hooft, Pieter Cornelisz (1581–1647), magistrate and man of letters, 149–50
Hoorn, town in Holland, 63, 111
Hoover, Herbert (1874–1964), American politician, 205, 211
Horta, Victor (1861–1947), Belgian architect, 204
hospitals, see health
housing, 5, 10, 20, 43, 53, 107, 124, 133, 135, 145, 176, 208, 211, 217

Hubert (d. 727), first bishop of Liège, 39, 255
Hudson, Henry (c.1565–1611), navigator, 136
Hugo, Victor (1802–85), French author, 185
Huizinga, Johan (1872–1945), Dutch historian, 217, 228, 263
Hundred Years War, 91, 97
Hungary, Hungarians, 38–9, 42, 47, 92, 102, 170, 181, 205, 232
Huns, 25, 211
Huy, town near Liège, 27, 57, 74
Huygens, Christiaan (1629–95), scientist, 147
Huygens, Constantijn (1596–1687), statesman and poet, 150
hygiene, see health

Iconoclastic Fury, 120–1
IJssel, river, 15, 33, 40, 54, 62, 111, 128
IJsselmeer, 8
  see also Flevo, Almere, Zuider Zee
imperialism, 206–8, 215, 233–4, 235–6
Indonesia, 206–7, 220, 230, 233
  see also East Indies
industrialization, 176–8, 188–90, 194, 199–200, 205, 223–4, 237, 239
Indutiomarus, ancient Belgic tribal leader, 13
Inner Mongolia, 206
Innocent II, pope (1130–43), 64
inquisition, inquisitors, 73–4, 77–8, 110, 120, 243
Institut Solvay, 193, 201, 219
Institute for Racial Biology, 219
insurance, 3, 111, 133, 168, 177, 188, 189, 194, 195, 203, 236
intellectual property, 144, 185, 199
International Exhibitions, see World Fairs
International Peace Bureau, 209
International Workers Association, 190, 192

internationalism, 183, 190, 192, 209, 215, 220

internment, 226–7, 230, 231

investiture controversy, 45–6

Iona, 28

Ireland, 28, 102, 154, 161, 162

Irish missionaries, 28, 32, 33

iron, 9, 11, 178, 199

   see also steel

Isaac, Heinrich (*c*.1450–1517), composer, 105

Isaac son of Eliyahu Chasan of Oxford, 14th-century copyist, 79

Isabella, queen of Spain (1479–1504), 109

Isabella, Infanta of Spain, *see* Albert and Isabella

Isabella of Luxembourg, countess of Namur (1263–98), 80–1

Islam, 4, 237

   see also Arabs, Indonesia, North Africa, Turks

Italy, 13, 14, 20, 24, 25, 26, 33, 34, 35, 39, 47, 58, 68, 69, 72, 73, 92, 102, 105, 109, 112, 121, 123, 129, 134, 153, 154, 163, 184, 216, 231, 237

Jacoba, *see* Jacqueline

Jacobs, Aletta (1854–1929), feminist, 196–7

Jacobsen, Jan (d. 1622), Dunkirk sea captain, 152

Jacqmin, Charles (1761–99), resistance leader, 172

Jacqueline, duchess of Bavaria, countess of Holland, Zeeland and Hainaut (1417–33), 98–9, 253

Jadot, Jean (1862–1932), entrepreneur, 205

Jakarta, *see* Batavia

James II (1633–1701), king of Great Britain, 161, 246

Jansenism, 158, 159

Jansen(ius), Cornelius (1585–1638), Dutch theologian, 158

Japan, Japanese, 135, 230, 233

Java, 135, 186, 206

   see also East Indies, Indonesia

Java Sea, Battle of the (1942), 230

Jemappes, Battle of (1792), 170

Jerusalem, 44, 47–8, 68, 87

Jesuits, 118, 135, 142–3, 148, 150–1, 154, 158, 159, 165

Jews, 18, 21, 23, 78–9, 93–4, 138, 147, 148–9, 165, 173, 205, 223, 225–6, 227, 228, 229, 244

Joan, countess of Flanders (1205–44), 71–2, 80, 250

Joanna and Wenceslas, joint rulers of Brabant (1355–83/1404), 93, 97, 257

Joanna, 'the Mad', queen of Castile (1504–9), 109, 112, 258

John I, king of England (1199–1216), 71

John I, 'the Victorious', duke of Brabant (1267–94), and of Limburg (1289–94), 81–2, 244, 256

John II, duke of Brabant (1294–1312), 79, 81, 257

John I, count of Holland (1296–9), 83, 84, 85, 252

John II, count of Holland, *see* John (II) of Avesnes

John III, duke of Brabant (1312–55), 91, 93, 257

John III, marquis of Namur (1418–29), 97, 251

John IV of Brabant (1415–27), 97, 98

John of Austria (1547–78), Spanish commander and governor general of the Netherlands, 125

John of Avesnes, father of the following, 80

John (II) of Avesnes, count of Hainaut (1278–1304), and of Holland (1299–1304), 80, 85, 252

John of Bavaria (1372–1425),
bishop-elect of Liège
1389–1418, later consort of
Elizabeth of Görlitz, 98, 104,
256
John of Dampierre, marquis of
Namur (1298–1330), 81, 251
John of Heinsberg, prince-bishop of
Liège (1419–56), 99, 256
John the Fearless, duke of Burgundy
(1404–19), 97, 98, 251
John II, 'the Good', king of France
(1319–64), 96
Jordaens, Jacob (1593–1678),
Flemish painter, 144
Joseph II, Holy Roman Emperor
(1780–90), 168–70
Josquin des Prez (1440–1521),
composer, 105
journalism, see newspapers
jousts, see tournaments
Joyous Entry, 93, 129, 168, 169, 244
Judith, 9th-century countess of
Flanders, 36
Juliana of Liège (1192–1258),
visionary, 78
Julius Caesar (100–44 BC), Roman
politician and general, 10–14
Julius Civilis, conspirator against
Roman rule, 16–19, 145
Julius Sabinus, conspirator against
Roman rule, 18
Julius Tutor, conspirator against
Roman rule, 17
Jülich, German principality, 55, 81

Kampen, town in Overijssel, 54, 62,
116
Kamperduin, Battle of (1797), 171
Kant, Immanuel (1724–1804),
German philosopher, 166
Karel ende Elegast, medieval
romance, 67
Kasavubu, Joseph (1917–69),
president of Zaire, 236
Katanga, region of Congo, 208, 236
Kempen, region of Belgium, 8, 59,
172
Kennemerland, district in Holland, 84

Khnopff, Fernand (1858–1921),
203–4
Kiev, 35
Klaarkamp, Cistercian abbey, 63
KLM, Dutch national airline, 201
Kloos, Willem (1859–1938), Dutch
poet, 203
knighthood, knights, 43, 44, 48,
49–50, 51, 52, 56, 62, 71, 81,
82, 86, 97, 103, 121, 219
Koerbagh, Adriaan (d. 1669), atheist,
147
Korean War, 234
korfball, 216, 228
Kortrijk, Battle of (1302), 86, 184,
244
Kruger, Paul (1825–1904), president
of Transvaal, 205
Kurth, Godefroid (1847–1916),
Belgian historian, 195, 198
Kuyper, Abraham (1837–1920),
Dutch statesman, 187, 195–6,
202, 206–7, 219

La Ruelle, Pierre de (d. 1637), mayor
of Liège, 154, 184
La Tène, ancient culture, 10–11, 15
Labadists, 17th-century sect, 159
lace, 157
Lactantius, Lucius Caecilius
Firmianus, 3rd–4th-century
Christian writer, 24
Lafontaine, Henri-Marie
(1854–1943), 209
Lambert (c.636–c.700), bishop of
Maastricht, 39
land reclamation, 5–6, 43, 59, 63
languages, see Dutch, French,
Frisian, German
Lansink, 177
Lassus, Orlandus (c.1532–94),
composer, 105
Lateran, Fourth Council of (1215), 74
Lauwer, creek, 53
laws, 44, 46, 47, 49, 51, 62, 65, 66,
72, 73, 79, 88, 94, 99, 101,
113, 115, 118, 120, 129, 138,
147, 148, 169, 171, 172,

173–4, 181, 183, 187, 190, 194, 198, 199, 219, 231, 236, 237–8, 241
League of Nations, 214–15
Lech, Battle on the (955), 38
Ledenberg, Gilles van, secretary of Utrecht States 1588–1618, 140
Leeuwarden, town in Friesland, 30, 123, 132, 212
Leeuwenhoek, Antonie van (1632–1723), microscopist, 147
Lefèvre, Raoul, 15th-century writer, 107
Leicester, Robert Dudley (c.1532–88), earl of, 127–8
Leiden, town in Holland, 124, 132, 143, 145
  university, 124, 128, 129, 138–9, 146–7, 228
Leipzig, Battle of (1813), 174
leisure, 87–8, 165, 169, 172, 201, 216–17
Lek, river, 16, 54
Lemonnier, Camille (1844–1913), novelist, 202
Leo III, pope (795–816), 34
Leo XIII, pope (1878–1903), 195
Leopold I, king of the Belgians (1831–65), 179–80, 260
Leopold II, Holy Roman Emperor (1790–2), 170, 258
Leopold II, king of the Belgians (1865–1909), 204, 207–8, 248, 260
Leopold III, king of the Belgians (1934–51), 222, 232–3, 249, 260
Leopoldville (Kinshasa), 201
Lessius, Leonardus (1554–1623), Jesuit moralist, 142
Leuven, county, 54–5
  town, 37, 79, 92, 94, 153, 172, 180, 211
  town hall, 59
  university, 106, 109, 113, 114, 118, 128–9, 146, 148, 158, 176, 211, 213, 222, 228, 238, 244

Liberalism, Liberals, 2–3, 4, 175, 178, 179, 181–7, 190, 192, 193–4, 196, 197, 202, 219, 221, 228, 237, 240, 241
Liberation, 224, 230–1, 248–9
Lier, town near Antwerp, 128
Ligne, Charles Joseph (1735–1814), prince of, 164–5, 170
Ligny, Battle of (1815), 174
Ligue démocratique belge, 190, 195
Liège, (prince-)bishopric, 7, 39–40, 42, 45–6, 50, 52, 55, 69, 73, 85, 88, 92, 93, 99, 113, 119, 120, 162, 170, 174, 214
  town 8, 34, 44, 56, 57, 58, 64, 65, 75, 89, 98, 100, 108, 152, 153–4, 177, 179, 195, 210, 233, 234
  university, 176, 198
Lille, town now in France, 66, 243
Limburg, duchy, 52, 55, 81, 96–7, 100, 125
  province, 2, 8, 10, 13, 44, 141, 164, 172, 174, 179, 180, 195, 199, 214
linen, 60, 132, 163
Linschoten, Jan Huygen van (1563–1611), explorer, 134
Lipsius, Justus (1547–1606), philosopher, 128–9, 144
Lisbon, 131
literature, 13, 18, 24, 29, 30, 32, 66–7, 77–8, 86–8, 105–6, 109–10, 149–51, 159, 165–6, 175, 181, 184–5, 186, 192, 197, 201–3, 213, 217–18, 229, 230–1, 238
Lobith, village in Gelderland, 37
Loevestein castle, state prison, 141, 155
London, 82, 161, 188, 211, 212, 229, 234
  Conference of (1830), 179
  university, 7, 211
Loo, palace, 161
Loon, county, 52, 55, 66, 98
Loos, Cornelis, 16th-century theologian, 119

Lorentz, Hendrik Antoon (1853–1928), Dutch physicist, 200
Lorraine, principality, now in France, 8, 35, 100, 101, 121, 243, 244
Lothar I, Holy Roman Emperor (840–55), 35, 36
Lothar II, Holy Roman Emperor (1131–7), 64
Lothar II, king of Lotharingia (855–69), 35, 37
Lothar of Hochstaden, would-be bishop of Liège, 69
Lotharingia (Lower), 35–8, 40, 43, 47–8, 52, 54–5, 69–70, 75, 100
Louis I, Holy Roman Emperor (814–40), 35
Louis I, 'of Nevers', count of Flanders (1322–46), 91
Louis II, 'the German', Holy Roman Emperor (855–75), 35
Louis II, 'of Male', count of Flanders (1346–84), 91, 93, 95
Louis II, count of Loon (1195–1218), 70
Louis IV, 'of Bavaria', Holy Roman Emperor (1314–47), 91, 92
Louis VII, king of France (1137–80), 73
Louis IX, king of France (1226–70), 48
Louis XI, king of France (1461–83), 106, 108
Louis XIV, king of France (1643–1715), 148, 157, 160, 161–2
Louis XV, king of France (1715–74), 163
Louis XVIII, king of France (1814–24), 174
Louis-Philippe, king of the French (1830–48), 178, 179
Louis Bonaparte, king of Holland (1806–10), 173, 175
Louis of Bourbon, bishop of Liège (1456–82), 99, 100
Louis of Orleans (1372–1407), dauphin of France, 97

Louis (1538–74), count of Nassau-Dillenburg, 124
Ludger, 8th-century Frisian missionary, 32–3
Lumumba, Patrice (1925–61), 235–6
Luns, Joseph (1911–2002), Dutch politician, 235
Lutgart of Tongeren (1182–1246), visionary, 77
Luther, Martin (1483–1546), German reformer, 113, 114
Lutheranism, Lutherans, 65, 114–15, 129, 138, 139, 142, 159, 191, 245
Luxembourg, county, later duchy, 7, 52, 56, 68, 70, 81, 92, 93, 98, 100, 120, 125–6, 162, 170, 171, 172, 243, 244, 247
  grand duchy, 1–2, 3, 7, 9, 24, 174, 177, 178, 179–80, 181, 182, 194–5, 197, 199, 202, 210, 214–15, 219, 221, 222, 224, 226, 227, 231, 236, 239, 247, 248, 249
  town, 93, 171, 178, 234
Lyons (Roman Lugdunum), 14

Maarland, village on the island of Voorne in Zeeland, 86
Maas (Meuse), river, 8, 9, 16, 25, 27, 35, 37, 39, 54, 56, 57, 68, 124, 151, 152, 153, 154, 163, 244
Maastricht, 14, 39, 40, 57, 153, 154, 164, 171, 179, 243, 255
Madrid, 113, 120, 153
Maerlant, Jacob van (1235–94), poet, 86–7, 89
Maeterlinck, Maurice (1862–1949), playwright, 202–3, 213
magic, 67, 118–19, 146
Magritte, René (1898–1967), Belgian artist, 218
Mainz, 25, 171
Malacca, 135
Malmédy, 214
Malplaquet, Battle of (1709), 163
Mander, Carel van (1544–1606), artist and art historian, 144, 145

Mansfeld, Peter Ernest (1517–1604), count of, 126
Margaret of Alsace, countess of Flanders (1191–4), 70, 250
Margaret of Austria (1480–1530), duchess of Savoy, 109
Margaret of Constantinople, countess of Flanders and Hainaut (1244–78), 71, 80, 250, 252
Margaret of Hainaut, countess of Holland and Hainaut (1345–54/6), 91, 92, 253
Margaret of Male, countess of Flanders (1384–1405), 95, 96, 97, 251
Margaret of Parma (1522–86), regent of the Netherlands (1564–7), 120
Margaret of York (d. 1503), duchess of Burgundy, 103–4, 107, 244
Margaret Porete (d. 1310), mystical writer, 78
Margaret (d. 1318), English princess, 81–2
Margaret, 'the Maid of Norway' (1283–90), 82
Maria-Adelheid (Marie Adelaide), grand duchess of Luxembourg (1912–19), 214, 260
Maria-Theresia, Empress (1740–80), 163–6, 258
Mariëngaarde, Premonstratensian abbey, 64
Mark, German principality, 55
Marne, river, 10
Marne, Battle of the (1914), 210
marriage, marriage alliances, weddings, 26, 36, 37, 46, 51, 53, 56, 68, 70–2, 80–3, 90–1, 96–9, 103, 104, 108, 109, 113–14, 169, 173, 175, 232, 238
Martin (d. 397), bishop of Tours, 24, 28, 89
Martyrs, Book of, see van Haemstede
Marx, Karl (1818–83), revolutionary theorist, 181
Mary, duchess of Burgundy (1477–82), 100, 108, 244, 258

Mass, see Eucharist
mass culture, 216–18
Massys, Quentin (d. 1530), painter, 112
Mata Hari, assumed name of Margaretha Zelle (1876–1917), dancer and spy, 212–3
mathematics, 45, 111, 146, 147
Matilda, queen of England (1066–83), 50
Matilda, queen of England (1141–53), 51
Matthias (1557–1619), archduke of Austria (later Holy Roman Emperor, 1612–19), 125, 128
Matthys, Jan (d. 1534), Anabaptist leader, 116
Maurice of Nassau, prince of Orange (1619–25), 128, 130, 140, 151–2
Maximianus, Marcus Aurelius Valerius, co-emperor of Diocletian (286–305), 22
Maximilian of Austria, Holy Roman Emperor (1493–1519), 100, 108–9, 111, 244, 258
Mechelen, lordship, 100, 128
town, 83, 93, 101, 124, 125, 128, 142, 146, 178, 184, 213, 226, 247
Medemblik, castle, 82
Mediterranean area, 23, 25, 111, 151, 157, 240
Meijer, Arnold (1905–65), fascist leader, 220, 224
Memling, Hans (c.1430–94), painter, 105
Menapians, ancient Belgic tribe, 12, 14, 18, 20, 22
Menasseh ben Israël (1604–57), rabbinic scholar, 148
Mennonites, 117, 133, 138, 150
Mercator, Gerald (1512–94), cartographer, 110, 245
merchants, 10, 21, 23, 30, 35–6, 40, 51, 53, 57–9, 73, 79, 85, 91, 102–3, 111, 126, 131, 133–5, 137, 142, 163, 168

Mercier, Désiré Joseph (1851–1926),
    cardinal-archbishop of
    Mechelen, 213, 215
Merian, Maria Sibylla (1647–1717),
    painter, 159
metallurgy, 28, 58, 102, 111, 177–8,
    199, 205
metric system, 173, 176
Metsys, see Massys
Meuse, see Maas
Middelburg, 57, 102, 103, 122, 132,
    137, 150, 159, 221
Milan, 35, 121
militia guilds, citizen militias, 81, 86,
    88, 90, 104, 108, 121, 128,
    164, 167–8, 169, 170, 178,
    214, 228, 229
mining, 111, 177, 195, 205, 237, 239
ministerials, 43, 62, 66
Mithras, 21
Mobutu Sese Seko (1930–97), 236
Mocha, Red Sea port, 135
modernism, 217, 218
Molucca, Moluccans, 135, 206, 233
    see also East Indies, Indonesia
Mondrian, Piet (Pieter Mondriaan,
    1872–1944), Dutch artist, 218
money, see banks, coins, credit,
    finance
monks, monasteries, 24, 27, 28–9,
    31–2, 33, 34, 36, 37, 39, 44,
    45, 46, 50, 53, 55, 63–5, 67,
    75, 77–8, 87, 89, 90, 92, 107,
    109, 113, 114, 116, 120, 121,
    142, 153, 164
    see also religious houses
Mons, 177, 185
Morel, Edmund (1873–1924), 208,
    265
Moretus, Jan (1543–1610), printer-
    publisher, 110
Morini, ancient Belgic tribe, 12, 14
Moscow, 174, 205
Muiden, castle, 84, 150
Mulisch, Harry, 20th-century
    novelist, 231
Multatuli, pen-name of Eduard
    Douwes Dekker (1820–87),
    Dutch writer, 186

multilateralism, 155, 162, 174,
    179–80, 234
Mundy, Peter (c.1596–c.1667), 145
Muscovy, see Russia
music, musicians, 3, 33, 45, 100,
    104–5, 178, 189
Mussert, A.A. (1894–1946), fascist
    leader, 221, 224, 231
Mussolini, Benito (1883–1945),
    fascist dictator, 220
Münster, 33, 116–17, 155, 157, 160,
    174
Münzer, Thomas (c.1490–1525),
    radical reformer, 116

Naarden, 84, 124
Nagelmaeckers, Georges
    (1845–1905), Belgian financier
    205
Namur, county (later marquisate), 52,
    56, 64, 68, 71, 80–1, 86, 93,
    96, 97, 100, 125
    town, 9, 14, 57, 125, 163, 185,
    210, 213
Nancy, 101
Naples, 154, 178
Napoleon III, 181
Napoleonic Code (1803), 173
Napoleonic Wars, 172–3, 174–5, 176,
    206
Nationaal Socialistische Beweging
    (NSB), 221, 223, 224
national debt, 130, 176, 206, 207,
    209
NATO, 234–5
Navigation Act (1651), 156
Nazism, 218, 220, 222–7
Neanderthals, 9
Neerwinden, Battle of (1693), 161
Neerwinden, Battle of (1793), 170
Neocalvinism, 196
Neoclassicism, 185
Nervians, ancient Belgic tribe, 12, 13,
    14, 18, 26
Netherlands South African Railway,
    205
neutrality, 122, 154, 167, 168, 210,
    212, 214, 221, 234

New Amsterdam, 136
new bishoprics, 119–20
New Netherland, 136, 160
New York, 136, 203, 212
newspapers, 3, 138, 189, 192, 201–2, 216–17, 229
Nieuwenhuis, Ferdinand Domela (1846–1919), Socialist leader, 191
Nieuwpoort, 142, 153, 160, 191
 Battle of (1600), 130, 245
Nijmegen, 14, 19, 20, 37, 40, 57, 68, 85, 121, 168
 Treaty of (1678), 161
Nivelles, 28, 29, 37
 Alliance of (1308), 92
Nobel prizes, 200–1, 209, 213
nobility, see aristocracy
Noot, Henri van der (1731–1827), 169–70
Norbert of Xanten (c.1080–1134), monastic reformer, 63–5
Norbertines, see Premonstratensians
North Africa, 13, 26, 48, 102, 237
North Sea, 5, 6, 8, 9, 14, 35, 52, 53, 76, 100, 134, 171, 201, 248
Norway, 51, 82, 102, 142
Nothomb, Jean-Baptiste (1805–81), 178
Nova Zembla, 134
Novgorod, 58
numerology, 146, 149

Obrecht, Jacob (c.1450–1505), composer, 105
Ockeghem, Jean (c.1421–c.1497), composer, 105
oil, 20, 60, 102, 199, 206, 207, 230, 239
Old Catholics, 158
Old Rhine, 10, 12, 14, 16, 17, 18, 21, 22, 26, 37
Oldenbarnevelt, Johan van (1547–1619), statesman, 140, 150, 182, 246
Olennius, 1st-century Roman commander, 15
Omer (Audomarus), bishop of Thérouanne (d. c.670), 28

Orangists, 167–8, 175
Oratorians, 142
Order of the Golden Fleece, see Golden Fleece
organized crime, see banditry
Orient Express, 205
orphans, 44, 71, 98, 137, 173
Ortelius, Abraham (1527–98), cartographer, 110
Ostend, 130, 142, 152, 157, 168, 204, 246
Otbert, bishop of Liège (1091–1119), 46, 47, 255
Otto I, Holy Roman Emperor (962–73), 34, 38–9
Otto I, count of Guelders (1184–1207), 69, 257
Otto IV, Holy Roman Emperor (1198–1218), 69–72
Otto of Lippe, bishop of Utrecht (1216–27), 72, 254
Oudenaarde, Battle of (1708), 163
 Battle of (1790), 170
Oudenburg, Roman site in West Flanders, 20
Oudewater, 118
Overijssel, 26, 33, 40, 54, 62, 85, 99, 128, 160–1, 164, 259
Oversticht, see Overijssel

paganism, 11, 14, 17, 18, 21, 23, 26, 27, 28, 29, 31, 39, 48, 110, 185
painters, paintings, see arts
Paris, 1, 8, 27, 50, 66, 71, 78, 97, 147, 170, 177, 178, 185–6, 199, 205, 210, 218, 234
 university, 75, 76, 115, 117
 universal exposition (1878), 199
Parma, Alessandro Farnese (1545–92), prince (later duke) of, 125–8, 245
Partij van de Arbeid (PvdA), 232
Paston, John, the younger, 103–4
Patriot movement, 167–8, 169, 170
Paulinus, bishop of Trier (d. 358), 23
peace movement, 43–4, 66, 74, 117, 124, 130, 147, 153, 155, 174, 208–9, 214, 234–5, 241

peasants, 42–3, 44, 47, 59–60, 61, 81,
  82, 86, 90, 116, 122–3, 136,
  144, 153, 157, 170, 172, 202,
  203, 204, 214, 217, 244, 247
Peking-Hankow Railway, 205
pensionary, 89
Pepin of Herstal (d. 714), mayor of
  the palace to the kings of
  Austrasia, 29, 31, 39
Pepin of Landen (c.580–640), mayor
  of the palace to the kings of
  Austrasia, 29
Pepin the Short, king of Franks
  (751–68), 31, 32, 34, 243
pepper, 102, 135, 136, 206
Peter the Hermit (d. 1115), preacher
  of the crusade, 47
Petilius Cerialis, 1st-century Roman
  general, 18
Petit, Gabrielle (1893–1916), 212
Philip I, 'the Fair', duke of Burgundy
  (1482–1506) and king of
  Castile (1504–6), 108–9, 112
Philip I, marquis of Namur
  (1195–1212), 68
Philip II, 'Augustus', king of France
  (1180–1223), 68, 70, 71, 72,
  80
Philip II, king of Spain (1556–98),
  110, 113, 120, 121, 125, 126,
  128, 129
Philip III, king of Spain (1598–1621),
  129, 131, 151
Philip IV, king of Spain (1621–65),
  151, 153
Philip IV, 'the Fair', king of France
  (1285–1314), 85, 86, 88
Philip VI, 'of Valois', king of France
  (1328–50), 91
Philip of Alsace, count of Flanders
  (1167–91), 66, 68, 70
Philip of St Pol, duke of Brabant
  (1427–30), 97
Philip of Swabia, Holy Roman
  Emperor (1198–1208), 69–70
Philip the Bold, duke of Burgundy
  (1363–1404), 95–7
Philip the Good, duke of Burgundy

  (1419–67), 97–100, 104, 106
Philip William, prince of Orange
  (1554–1618), 129
Philippa of Hainaut (d. 1369), 90–1
Philippe de Commynes (1447–1511),
  106
Philips company, 199
physics, 66, 200
Picardy, 61, 117
Pichegru, Charles (1761–1804),
  French general, 171
Pierson, N. G. (1839–1909), Dutch
  Prime Minister (1897–1901),
  193
Pietism, 158–9
pillarization, 2–3, 196, 217, 231–2,
  236, 237
piracy, pirates, 16, 122, 134
Pirenne, Henri (1862–1935), Belgian
  historian, 57, 195, 262
plague, 90, 91, 93, 139, 157, 244
Plantin Office, publishing house
  (1550–1876), 110, 144, 147
Plantin, Christopher (c.1520–89),
  Antwerp publisher, 110
Poitiers, Battle of (1356), 96
Poland, 59, 165, 221, 227, 237
polders, 5–6, 59–60, 63
poor relief, 33–4, 115, 188–9
porcelain, 132, 166, 246
Portugal, 94, 111, 120, 129, 134–7,
  151, 237
Postumus, M. Cassianus Latinius,
  Roman general, 22, 242
potato, 165, 181, 204
Pottier, Antoine (1849–1923), radical
  priest, 195
predestination, 139, 141, 158
Premonstratensians (Norbertines), 64,
  75, 116
printing, see books
prints, 112, 144, 186
prison camps (Amersfoort,
  Breendonk, Hunsruck, Vught),
  208, 226–7, 230
privateers, 122, 130, 134, 136, 152
prostitutes, 148, 189, 194, 197
Protestantism, 1, 2, 4, 107, 113–18,

123, 137, 141, 144, 148, 153, 156, 168, 175–6, 182, 187, 190, 194, 196, 204, 216, 225, 245
Provence, 11, 14, 35, 243
Prussia, 59, 162, 163, 165, 166, 168, 174, 175, 179, 182, 214, 247
Psalms, 32, 33, 34, 67
public health, *see* health
Putten, village in Gelderland, 230

Radbod, Frisian king (679–719), 31, 243
radio, 3, 199, 201, 216, 217, 229
Railway Strike (1903), 190, 192, 248
railways, 3, 8, 178, 190, 192, 194, 199, 201, 205, 215, 218, 220, 230, 247, 248
Ramillies, Battle of (1706), 163
Rampjaar (Year of Disaster) 1672, 160
Ravyah, 79
Red Star Line, 201
refugees, 50, 61, 93, 116, 121, 133, 136, 139, 141, 143, 145, 148, 150, 170, 207, 211, 222, 223, 226
regents, 126–7, 140, 145, 151, 154, 155, 160, 163, 164, 165, 167, 168, 170
religious houses and orders, 28–29, 31–3, 39, 42, 50, 55, 63–5, 75, 87, 90, 92, 107, 109, 116, 120, 154, 164
Rembrandt Harmensz van Rijn (1606–69), artist, 145
Remi, Belgic tribe, 11
Remigius (c.438–c.533), bishop of Rheims, 27
Remonstrants, 139–41, 158
reparations, 212, 214, 215
representative assemblies, estates, parliaments, 64, 92–3, 100, 108, 111, 112, 122–6, 130, 131, 135, 139, 140, 141, 142, 149, 153, 154, 155, 156, 160, 162, 168, 169, 170, 171, 175,

179–82, 183, 187, 191, 196–7, 207, 219–22, 233, 234, 240, 247, 259
republicanism, 126, 156, 167, 232, 239
Resistance, 212, 218, 222, 224, 226–7, 228–9, 230, 231
retail trade, 199–200
Reve, Gerard, 20th-century Dutch writer, 238
Réveil, 175–6, 182, 184
Revolution: American (1776), 167
   Batavian (1785), 171, 247
   Brabant (1788), 169–70, 174, 247
   French (1789), 34, 170, 176, 180, 188, 211, 238, 247
   French (1830), 178
   Belgian (1830), 178–80, 182, 184, 247
   French (1848), 181
   Central European (1848), 181
   Bolshevik (1917), 214
Revolutionary Socialism, 191, 192, 214, 219–20, 240, 248
Rex, Belgian fascist party, 220, 224, 225
Reynard the Fox, 67, 262
Rheims, 11, 14, 21, 23, 26, 27, 42, 46, 69
Rhine, 1, 2, 4, 6, 8, 9, 10, 12, 14–26, 35, 37, 40, 53, 54, 57, 62, 76, 81, 151, 153, 171, 242, 243
Rhineland, 4, 9, 61, 63, 65, 81, 102, 107, 111, 116, 151, 171
Richard I, king of England (1157–99), 68, 70
Richelieu, Armand Jean du Plessis, cardinal and duke (1585–1642), 153, 154
Riebeek, Jan van (1619–77), Dutch colonizer, 136
Rietveld, Gerrit (1888–1964), architect, 218
Rijswijk, Treaty of (1697), 162
Rimbaud, Arthur (1854–91), French poet, 185
roads, 6, 8, 20, 22, 25, 49, 55, 81, 165, 205

Robert I, 'the Frisian', count of
  Flanders (1071–93), 51, 66, 250
Robert II, count of Flanders
  (1093–1111), 47, 51, 243, 250
Robert III, 'of Béthune', count of
  Flanders (1305–22), 81, 86,
  251
Robert le Petit, alias le Bougre, 13th-
  century inquisitor, 73
Robles, Don Caspar de, governor of
  Friesland (1572–6), 123
Rocroi, Battle of (1643), 154
Rodange, Michel (1827–76),
  Luxembourgeois writer, 67
Roermond, 37, 54, 153, 154
Rogier, Charles (1800–85), 179
Roland Holst, Henriëtte (1869–1952),
  192
Romanticism, 149, 175, 181, 184
Rome, 1, 11–19, 21, 23, 24, 31, 33,
  34, 35, 39, 47, 64, 65, 69, 71,
  92, 95, 113, 118, 242
  Treaty of (1957), 234
Rops, Félicien (1833–98), artist, 186
Roric, Viking leader, 36, 37
Rosicrucian order, 146, 149
Rossum, Maarten van (1478–1555),
  military commander, 112
Rost van Tonningen, M. M.
  (1894–1945), 224
Rosweyde, Heribert (d. 1629), Jesuit,
  150
Rotterdam, 6, 8, 132, 135, 140, 145,
  147, 178, 217, 221
Rotterdamsche Lloyd, 201
Royal Dutch Petroleum Company,
  199, 207, 221, 230
Royal Question, 232–3, 249
rubber, 199, 206, 208, 230
Rubens, Peter Paul (1577–1640),
  143, 144, 145
Rudolph of Zähringen, bishop of
  Liège (1167–91), 55, 68, 74,
  255
Ruhr, 215
Ruotger, see Bruno of Cologne
Rupert of Deutz (c.1075–1130),
  monk, 65

Rur, river, 55
Russia, 35, 102, 134, 165, 167, 172,
  174, 179, 205, 214, 226, 231
Ruysbroeck, Jan van (1293–1381),
  mystical writer, 78
Rwanda, 215, 235, 241, 249

Saba, Caribbean island, 233
Sabena, Belgian national airline, 201
Sabis, Battle of (57 BC), 12
Sacrament of Holy Miracle, 94
sacraments, 64, 137
  see confession, Eucharist,
  marriage
St Elizabeth Flood (19 November
  1421), 90
St Eustasius, Caribbean island, 233
St Martin, Caribbean island, 136, 233
Saint-Omer, town now in France, 66
salt, 11, 20, 60, 101, 102, 136
Sambre, river, 8, 56, 68
Saxons, Saxony, 8, 20, 22, 25, 26, 27,
  29, 30, 32–3, 34, 38, 42
Scandinavia, 33, 35–6, 37, 62, 225
Schaepman, Hermanus J. A. M.
  (1844–1903), statesman and
  writer, 187, 195
Scheldt, 6, 8, 9, 12, 25, 35, 36, 37,
  50, 52, 53, 57, 64, 102, 131,
  151, 154, 157, 171, 180, 212,
  214
Schenkenschans, fort, 154
Scherpenheuvel, basilica, 143
Scheut Missions, 206
Scheveningen, 174
Schiermonnikoog, island, 63
Schimmelpenninck, Rutger Jan
  (1761–1825), politician,
  173
schools, see education
Schuurman, Anna Maria van
  (1607–78), early feminist, 159
Scotland, Scots, 28, 82–3, 103, 123,
  125, 129, 130, 148, 161, 162,
  168, 184
secularism, 2, 4, 182–3, 185, 186,
  187

Seebohm Rowntree, Benjamin (1871–1954), social reformer, 188, 194, 265
Selle, *see* Sabis
seminaries, 169
Seraing, 177
serfdom, 43, 51, 57, 61
Servatius (d. 384), bishop of Tongeren, 23, 67
Severen, Joris van (1894–1940), Flemish fascist, 220, 225
Seville, 131, 151
Seyss-Inquart, Arthur (1891–1946), Nazi, 222, 224, 226, 231
Shanghai, 205
shipping, 24, 62, 102, 122, 130, 131, 132–5, 136, 152, 156, 163, 167, 178, 180, 212
Sicily, 75, 154
siege warfare, 12, 13, 101, 122, 124, 130, 137, 151, 246
Siger of Brabant (*c*.1240–*c*.1284), philosopher, 76
Sigismund of Luxembourg, Holy Roman Emperor (1410–37), 97, 98
silk, 35, 58, 102, 103, 135, 141
silver, 24, 30, 103, 111, 120, 122, 135, 152, 225
silver fleets, 152
Simenon, Georges (1903–89), crime writer, 218
Simon of Limburg, would-be bishop of Liège (1193–95), 69, 255
Simon of Tournai, 13th-century master of Paris, 66
Simon, Gustaf (1900–45), Gauleiter of Luxembourg, 222
Simons, Menno (1496–1561), Anabaptist leader, 117
Sint-Lucas schools, 184, 185, 204,
Sint-Truiden, town, 79
skating, 216
slave trade, slavery, 12, 25, 42–3, 132, 137, 186, 197, 207, 208, 227, 247
Sluis, 102
   Battle of, 91

slump, 90, 120, 191–2, 194, 215
smallpox, 156, 193
Sneevliet, Hendricus (1883–1942), socialist activist, 220
Snyders, Frans (1579–1657), painter, 144
Sociaal-Democratische Arbeiderspartij (SDAP), 191
Sociaal-Democratische Bond, 191
Social Christianity, 195–7, 198, 236
social Darwinism, 219
social partnership, 236
Socialism, 2, 187, 189–92, 193, 196, 202, 204, 209, 214, 215–16, 219–20, 223, 232, 237, 247
Société Générale, 176, 212
Society of Jesus, *see* Jesuits
Soignes, forest, 153, 172
Solvay Conference (1927), 219
Solvay, Ernest (1838–1922), industrial chemist, 218
Somme, 9, 37, 50
Sound, 155
South Africa, 171, 205, 208, 209
Spa, town, 201
Spaak, Paul-Henri (1899–1972), statesman, 234, 235
Spain, Spaniards, 20, 26, 75, 91, 94, 102, 103, 109, 111, 112, 113, 121, 122, 123, 124, 125, 129, 130, 134, 152, 153, 155, 160, 162, 163, 165, 231, 237
spectator sports, 216
spices, 58, 102, 111, 120, 134, 135, 206
Spiegel historiael, 87
Spinola, Ambrogio (1567–1630), military commander, 130, 151, 152
Spinoza, Baruch (1632–77), philosopher, 149, 159, 186, 192
Srebrenica, 241
Sri Lanka, 135
SS, 224, 231
stadholderate, 126, 128, 140, 152, 155–6, 157, 160, 162, 163–4, 168, 259
Stamford Bridge, Battle of (1066), 51

Stanley, Henry Morton, adopted
name of John Rowlands
(1841–1904), explorer, 207,
265
Statenvertaling, 149
States, see representative assemblies
statues and carvings, 13, 33, 64, 77,
120, 143, 162
Stavoren, town, 62, 63, 82
steam power, 177, 199
steamships, 135, 178
steel, 199, 204, 205, 234, 235, 239,
249
Steenkerque, Battle of (1693), 161
Stephen, king of England (1135–54),
51
Stevin, Simon, (1548–1620),
mathematician and military
engineer, 146
stockbreeding, 15, 53, 60, 61, 122,
133, 153, 194
Stoicism, 128–9
Stork, Charles (1822–95),
industrialist, 177
Strasbourg, 116, 234
Streuvels, Stijn, pen name of Frank
Lateur (1871–1969), writer,
203, 217
strikes, 189, 190, 191, 192, 227, 230,
233, 235, 248
study groups, 137, 159, 189, 213
Stuyvesant, Peter (1592–1672),
colonial administrator, 136
sugar, 102, 111, 112, 135, 136, 194,
206
Sukarno, Achmed (1901–70), first
president of Indonesia, 233
Sumatra, 199, 206, 207
Sundgau, 100, 244
Surinam, 136, 159, 230, 234
Sutton Hoo hoard, 30
Sweden, 102, 155, 160, 219
Switzerland, 2, 34, 76, 109, 115, 117,
121, 175, 216, 233
Symbolism, 218
synagogue, 79, 149, 158
syndic, 89
Synod of Dort, 141, 156, 196, 246
Syrians, 23

Tacitus, Publius Cornelius
(c.56–c.120), Roman historian,
13, 16, 18, 19, 38, 129, 145,
261
Talma, A. S. (1864–1916), politician,
196
Tanchelm (d. 1115), preacher, 64,
65
Tasman, Abel (1603–59), navigator,
135
taxation, 16, 19, 92, 122
technocracy, 219
Teheran, 205
television, 3, 199, 237
temperance, 188, 194
Temple, Sir William (1628–99),
diplomat, 137
Teniers, David, the younger
(1610–90), painter, 144
Tenth Penny, 122, 125, 245
ter Braak, Menno (1902–40),
essayist, 217
Ter Doest, Cistercian abbey, 63
terpen (artificial mounds), 5
terrorism, 239–40
Tervuren, 153, 166
Texel, 171
textiles, 11, 24, 58–9, 60, 88, 90, 91,
102, 103, 105, 111, 112, 117,
120, 132, 163, 177
Theoderic of Ahr, bishop of Utrecht
(1198–1212), 69, 254
Theoderic, would-be bishop of
Utrecht (1196–7), 69, 254
Theodore of Celles (d. 1236),
religious founder, 74
Theoduin, bishop of Liège
(1048–75), 57, 255
Thierry of Alsace, count of Flanders
(1128–68), 52, 250
Thietmar of Merseburg (969–1019),
chronicler, 40, 241
Thionville, 93, 178
Edict of (1473), 101, 244
Third International Workers Congress
(1868), 190
Thérouanne, town, 14, 28, 43
Thomas Aquinas (c.1225–74),

philosopher and theologian, 75, 76, 78, 79, 81
Thomas of Cantimpré (1201–71), 75, 77
Thomas van Herentals (d. 1530), Franciscan, 113
Thomas à Kempis (c.1380–1471), ascetical writer, 107
Thorbecke, Johan Rudolf (1798–1872), politician, 181, 182, 184
Thysius, Antonius (1603–65), calvinist theologian, 138–9
Tianjin, 205, 206
Tiel, 37, 40, 54
Tienen, 20, 21, 79, 153
tiles, 20, 132
toleration, 142, 158, 168, 264
tolls, 8, 40, 42, 49, 55, 62, 68, 72, 147, 163, 180
Tongeren, 13, 14, 20, 27, 28, 39
Toorop, Jan (1858–1928), painter, 203
Torhout, 35
torture, 119, 169, 171, 172
Tostig (d. 1066), English nobleman, 50
totalitarianism, 215, 219
tourism, 201
Tournai, 14, 23, 26, 27, 28, 42, 43, 52, 57, 59, 64, 66, 71, 99, 105, 112, 119, 163, 166, 245, 246
tournaments, 80, 82, 103, 104
towns, 14, 19, 20, 21, 22, 23, 24, 49, 56–7, 59–60, 66, 71, 85–90, 92, 98, 104–6, 108, 113–14, 115, 116, 120, 124, 126, 129, 138, 141, 142, 147, 150, 168, 169, 188
trade, see commerce
trade unions, 3, 189, 190, 236, 237, 247
transit camps, 226
Trazegnies, village in Hainaut, 80
Trent, Council of (1545–63), 119
Treveri, Belgic tribe, 11, 13
Trier, 11, 14, 20, 21, 23–4, 25, 27, 35, 37, 39, 100, 119, 120, 153

Troelstra, Pieter Jelles (1860–1930), politician, 192, 214
Tromp, Maarten (1598–1653), Dutch admiral, 154, 156, 157
Tshombe, Moise (1919–69), Katangese secessionist, 236
Tungrians, ancient Belgic tribe, 14, 18, 20, 23
Turkey, Turks, 47, 48, 97, 111, 113, 170, 205, 237
Turnhout, Battle of (1789), 170
Twelve Years Truce, 131, 141, 151, 246

Ultramontanism, 184
unemployment, 215, 224, 236, 239, 240
Union Cycliste Internationale, 216
Union of Arras (1579), 125, 127, 245
Union of Utrecht (1579), 126, 127, 138, 140, 141, 155–6, 245
United Kingdom of the Netherlands (1815–30), 175–8, 180, 198, 247, 260
United Nations Organization (1949), 233, 234, 235, 236, 241, 249
United States, 8, 167, 168, 169, 186, 194, 200, 201, 206, 216, 219, 222, 230, 231, 232, 233, 237, 241
universities, 3, 7, 75, 106, 107, 109, 114, 124, 147–8, 176, 182, 187, 194, 196–7, 198, 209, 211, 212, 213, 222, 227–8, 238, 244
Urban II, pope (1088–99), 47, 66
Urban VI, pope (1378–89), 95, 96
Utrecht, 14, 30, 31, 32, 39, 40, 42, 52, 54, 57, 64, 65, 67, 68, 69, 72, 83, 84, 85, 88, 89, 93, 100, 103, 106, 107, 108, 112, 119, 125, 127, 128, 140, 148, 158, 160, 161, 164, 167, 185, 228
cathedal tower (1382), 107
Treaty of (1713), 162
Union of (1579), 126, 127, 138, 140, 141, 155-6, 245
University of, 148, 220
Utrecht Psalter, 33

Vaenius (Van Veen), Otto
(1556–1629), artist, 143
Valenciennes, 56, 57, 74, 91, 92, 100,
121
Valentinian I, Roman emperor
(364–75), 24
Valentinian III, Roman emperor
(425–55), 25–6
Van de Velde, Henry (1863–1957),
architect, 204
Van Gogh, Vincent (1853–90),
painter, 145, 204
Vandervelde, Emile (1866–1938),
socialist leader, 192
Vedastus (d. 539), bishop of Arras,
27
Veleda, 1st-century Germanic
prophetess, 18
Velsen, 15
Velsen, Gerard van, 13th-century
conspirator against Floris V,
83–4
Veluwe, region of the Netherlands, 8,
54, 161, 257
Venezuela, 136, 207, 248
Venlo, 54, 153, 154
Verbond van Actualisten, 220
Verdinaso, 220
Verhaeren, Emile (1855–1916),
writer, 202–3
Verlaine, Paul (1844–96), French
poet, 185
Vermeer, Johannes (1632–75),
painter, 145
Verschaeve, Cyriel (1874–1949),
Flamingant, 227
Verstegan, Richard (c.1548–1640),
writer, 150
Verviers, 177
Verwey, Albert (1865–1937), poet,
203
Vesalius, Andreas (1514–64),
anatomist, 110
Vespasian, Roman emperor (69–79),
16–18
Visscher, Anna (1583–1651) and
Maria Tesselschade
(1594–1649), poets, 150

Vitellius, Aulus, would-be Roman
emperor, 16–17
Vlaams Blok, 239, 240
Vlaamsch Nationaal Verbond (VNV),
220, 225, 231
Vlie, river, 84
VOC, 135–7, 147
Voes, Hendrik (d. 1523), Lutheran
martyr, 114
Voetius, Gijsbrecht (1589–1676),
theologian, 148, 159
Volksdeutsche Bewegung, 224, 226
Vonck, Jean-François (1743–92),
revolutionary, 169–70
Vondel, Joost van den (1587–1679),
prince of poets, 149–50
Vooruit (Forwards), co-operative,
189
Vranckx, Sebastian (1573–1647),
painter, 144

Waal, river, 16, 37, 54,
Waals, Johannes van der
(1837–1923), physicist, 200
Walbodo, bishop of Liège (1021–5),
40, 255
Walcheren, island, 137
Wallonia, region of Belgium, 3, 8,
58, 100, 125, 177, 194, 198,
213, 224, 225, 227, 238, 239
Walter of Bruges (d. 1307),
philosopher, 76
Warns, Battle of (1345), 92
Waterland, district in Holland, 84
Waterloo, Battle of (1815), 174–5,
247
Wazo, bishop of Liège (1042–8), 46,
255
weavers, 58, 61, 86, 88, 89, 91, 132,
170, 189
Webb, Catherine (1859–1947), social
reformer, 188
Weesp, 166, 246
Welf, 69–72, 243
welfare, 188–9, 206–7, 236, 240
see also poor relief
Weser, river, 8, 15

West India Company, 136, 151, 152, 246
West Indies, 134, 136, 137, 159, 186, 207, 230, 247
Weston, Richard, 17th-century writer on agriculture, 61
Westrozebeke, Battle of (1382), 95
Weyden, Rogier van der (d. 1464), painter, 105
whaling, 132
Wier, Johan (1515–88), 118
Wiertz, Antoine (1806–65), painter and writer, 185
Wijnaldum, 30
Wilfrid of Hexham (634–709), bishop of the Northumbrians, 31
Wilhelmina of Prussia (1751–1820), consort of stadholder William V, 168
Wilhelmina, queen of the Netherlands (1890–1948), 200, 221, 260
Willaert, Adriaan (d. 1562), composer, 105
William Clito, count of Flanders (1127–8), 52, 250
William I, king of England (1066–87), 50–1, 52, 250
William I, count of Holland (1213–22), 70–2, 252
William I, prince of Orange (1544–84), 121, 127, 128, 129, 163, 245, 259
William I, king of the Netherlands (1815–40), 174, 175–6, 178, 179, 180, 183, 247, 260
William II of Holland, Holy Roman Emperor (1247–56), 63, 72, 75, 82, 244, 252
William II, duke of Guelders (1538–43), 112, 257
William II, prince of Orange (1647–50), 155–6, 246, 259
William II, king of the Netherlands (1840–9), 178, 180, 181, 247, 260

William III, prince of Orange (1650–1702), 156, 160–2, 246, 259
William III, king of the Netherlands (1849–90), 182, 260
William III of Holland and I of Hainaut (1304–37), 91
William IV, prince of Orange (1711–51), 162, 164, 259
William IV of Holland and II of Hainaut (1337–45), 92
William V, prince of Orange (1751–1806), 164, 168, 171, 259
William VI of Holland and IV of Hainaut (1404–17), 98
William of Dampierre, consort of Margaret, countess of Flanders, 80, 251
William of Moerbeke (c.1215–86), translator, 75
William of Saxony, titular duke of Luxembourg (1439–43), 98, 253
William of Ypres, 12th-century mercenary, 51, 52
Willibrord (658–739), Northumbrian missionary, 31–2, 185, 254
Winchester, 58
windmills, 4, 5, 6, 42
wine, 20, 21, 27, 78, 81, 102, 111, 188
Winfrid, see Boniface
witchcraft, 118–19, 245
Woerden, 83, 114, 139–40
Woeste, Charles (1837–1922), politician, 195
Wolff, Christian (1679–1754), German philosopher, 166
Wolff, Elizabeth (1738–1804), novelist, 166
World Fairs, 199, 204, 235
Worringen, Battle of (1288), 81, 82, 244
Wulfram, Frankish missionary to the Frisians, 31

Xanten, town, 17, 20, 63

Ypres, 8, 59, 66, 74, 85, 91, 93, 115,
      142, 160, 163, 243
   Siege of (1383), 95
   in Great War, 211
Yser, river, 210, 213

Zeeland, 5, 6, 10, 52, 53, 83, 84, 85,
      86, 90, 91, 92, 93, 96, 97, 98,
      99, 100, 101, 103, 122, 124,
      126, 128, 130, 131, 134, 153,
      155, 156, 157, 160, 164, 244,
      245, 258, 259
Zeeman, Pieter (1865–1943),
      physicist, 200
Zelle, Margaretha Geertruida, see
      Mata Hari

Zola, Emile (1840–1902), 202,
      203
Zoniën, see Soignes
Zouaves, 184
Zoutleeuw, 79
Zuider Zee, 6, 14, 53, 62–3, 82,
      116
   see also Flevo, Almere,
      IJsselmeer
Zutphen, county, 54, 257
   town, 54, 62, 124, 128
Zwart Front, 220, 224
Zwentibold, duke (or king) of
      Lotharingia (d. 900), 37
Zwin, 102
Zwolle, 62, 106, 107, 116